WESTERN POLITICAL THEORY

PART 3
NINETEENTH AND TWENTIETH CENTURIES

HARCOURT   BRACE   JOVANOVICH,   INC.

New York   •   Chicago   •   San Francisco   •   Atlanta

WESTERN POLITICAL THEORY

PART 3

NINETEENTH AND TWENTIETH CENTURIES

LEE CAMERON McDONALD

Pomona College

ISBN: 0-15-595299-4

Library of Congress Catalog Card Number: 68–19235

Printed in the United States of America

Acknowledgments

APPLETON-CENTURY-CROFTS—for excerpts from *The Statesman's Book of John of Salisbury,*
translated by John Dickinson. Copyright by Alfred A. Knopf, Inc., 1927. Copyright,
1955, by Lindsay Rogers. Reprinted by permission of Appleton-Century-Crofts, Division
of Meredith Corporation.

BARNES & NOBLE, INC.—for excerpts from Thomas Aquinas, *De regimine principum* in
Selected Political Writings, tr. by J. G. Dawson; ed. by A. P. D'Entreves, 1959.

BENZIGER BROTHERS, INC.—for excerpts from Thomas Aquinas, *Summa Theologica,* English Dominican tr., copyright 1947 by Benziger Brothers, Inc.

BASIL BLACKWELL & MOTT LTD.—for excerpts from Thomas Aquinas, *De regimine principum* in *Selected Political Writings,* tr. by J. G. Dawson; ed. by A. P. D'Entreves,
1959. For excerpts from Dante, *The Divine Comedy,* tr. by Geoffrey L. Bickersteth,
1965.

THE BOBBS-MERRILL COMPANY, INC.—for excerpts from David Hume: *Political Essays,*
edited by Charles W. Hendel, copyright © 1953, by The Liberal Arts Press, Inc., reprinted by permission of the Liberal Arts Press Division of The Bobbs-Merrill Company, Inc.

BURNS & OATES LTD.—for excerpts from Thomas Aquinas, *Summa Theologica,* English
Dominican tr., 1947.

CAMBRIDGE UNIVERSITY PRESS—for excerpts from Robert Tucker, *Philosophy and Myth in
Karl Marx,* 1961.

CLARENDON PRESS, OXFORD—for excerpts from *The Dialogues of Plato,* 4th ed., tr. by
Benjamin Jowett, 1953, by permission of the Clarendon Press, Oxford. For excerpts
from Plato, *The Republic,* tr. by F. M. Cornford, 1945, by permission of the Clarendon

Press, Oxford. For excerpts from *Nicomachean Ethics* in *The Works of Aristotle,* tr. and ed. by W. D. Ross, Vol. 9, 1925, by permission of the Clarendon Press, Oxford. For excerpts from Aristotle, *Politics,* tr. by Ernest Barker, 1958, by permission of the Clarendon Press, Oxford.

J. M. DENT & SONS LTD.—for excerpts from Plato, *Parmenides, Thaeitetos, Sophist, Statesman,* tr. by John Warrington, Everyman's Library Edition, 1961. For excerpts from Thomas Aquinas, *Selected Writings,* ed. by M. C. D'Arcy, Everyman's Library Edition, 1950, © revisions J. M. Dent & Sons Ltd. 1964. For excerpts from Thomas Hobbes, *Leviathan,* ed. by A. D. Lindsay, Everyman's Library Edition, 1950. For excerpts from John Locke, *Second Treatise* in *Two Treatises of Civil Government,* ed. by William S. Carpenter, Everyman's Library Edition, 1924.

E. P. DUTTON & Co., INC.—for excerpts from Plato, *Parmenides, Thaeitetos, Sophist, Statesman,* tr. by John Warrington, Everyman's Library Edition, 1961. For excerpts from Thomas Aquinas, *Selected Writings,* ed. by M. C. D'Arcy, Everyman's Library Edition, 1950. For excerpts from *Leviathan* by Thomas Hobbes. Introduction by A. D. Lindsay, Everyman's Library Edition. Reprinted by permission of E. P. Dutton & Co., Inc. For excerpts from John Locke, *Second Treatise* in *Two Treatises of Civil Government,* ed. by William S. Carpenter, Everyman's Library Edition, 1924.

HAFNER PUBLISHING COMPANY—for excerpts from Baron de Montesquieu, *The Spirit of the Laws,* tr. by Thomas Nugent; ed. by Franz Neumann, 1949. For excerpts from Jean-Jacques Rousseau, *The Social Contract,* tr. by G. D. H. Cole; rev. and ed. by Charles Frankel, 1947.

HARVARD UNIVERSITY PRESS—for excerpts reprinted by permission of the publishers from R. M. Gummere, translator, Seneca, *Epistulae Morales,* Cambridge, Mass.: Harvard University Press, 1953. For excerpts reprinted by permission of the publishers from W. A. Oldfather, translator, Epictetus, *Discourses,* Cambridge, Mass.: Harvard University Press, 1926. For excerpts from Dante, *The Divine Comedy,* tr. by Geoffrey L. Bickersteth, 1965.

INDIANA UNIVERSITY PRESS—for excerpts from *The Histories of Polybius,* tr. by E. S. Shuckburgh; Introduction by F. W. Walbank, 1962.

ALFRED A. KNOPF, INC.—for excerpts from Albert Camus, *The Rebel,* tr. by Anthony Bower, Random House, Vintage Books, 1956.

LUTTERWORTH PRESS—for excerpts from *Reformation Writings of Martin Luther,* tr. by Bertram Lee Woolf, 1952.

OXFORD UNIVERSITY PRESS—for excerpts from *Il Principe,* by Niccolo Machiavelli, translated by Luigi Ricci, revised by E. R. P. Vincent and published by Oxford University Press, 1906. Reprinted in *The Prince and The Discourses,* Random House, Modern Library, 1940.

RANDOM HOUSE, INC.—for excerpts from *Basic Writings* of *Saint Augustine,* ed. by Whitney J. Oates, 1948.

GEORGE B. SABINE—for excerpts from Cicero, *De republica* in *On the Commonwealth,* tr. by George H. Sabine and Stanley B. Smith, Bobbs-Merrill, n. d.

SCM PRESS LTD.—for excerpts from John Calvin, *Institutes of the Christian Religion,* I & II, tr. by Ford Lewis Battles; ed. by John T. McNeill, Library of Christian Classics, 1960.

THE UNIVERSITY OF CHICAGO PRESS—for excerpts from Karl Jaspers, *The Future of Mankind,* by permission of The University of Chicago Press. Copyright © 1961 by The University of Chicago. All rights reserved.

THE WESTMINSTER PRESS—for excerpts from *Institutes of the Christian Religion,* I and II, Library of Christian Classics, Vols. XX and XXI, edited by John T. McNeill and translated by Ford Lewis Battles. The Westminster Press. Copyright © 1960, W. L. Jenkins. Used by permission.

JOHN WILEY & SONS, INC.—for excerpts from David Easton, *A Systems Analysis of Political Life,* 1965.

To Claire

PREFACE

A book is what it is. Cut its pages properly and, inescapably, its virtues and vices are spread before all who can read and care to read. This makes the writing of prefaces a precarious enterprise, whether they are meant to serve as enticements or diversions. Should you therefore be overcome with curiosity about Plato, by all means proceed at once to page 5, where begins a well-meant chapter on that estimable sage. With or without prefatory preparation, you will find that if the chapter works you will want to read further—not just in McDonald, though that would be nice, but in Plato, which is even nicer.

This book, which examines the contributions of major Western political thinkers from ancient Greece to the present, includes a revision of my *Western Political Theory: The Modern Age,* which analyzed political thinkers from the seventeenth to the twentieth centuries. The present volume is thus a big book of commentary born in an age of small paperbacks and anthologies. In this sense, it is unconventional—influenced perhaps by the political philosophers in its pages who have questioned convention.

Some skeptics will wonder what can justify the attempt to compress more than two thousand years of political thinking into a few hundred pages. Their skepticism should be respected, for such sanity as the world knows is much in tempered skepticism's debt. In my 1962 preface I suggested that my aim was not to save the world or to make money (though, if the truth be known, I was opposed to neither aim), but rather to fulfill a "long-felt need in the author to write a book." That need having so long ago been met, I must find another justification for this second book. A second book, I am happy to report, is easier to write than a first book and provides even more pleasure in the writing. But it takes longer, because a second book is a less reliable excuse for avoiding service on committees. One way or another a decade of my life has spanned the writing of this book. Though I have tried to make the experience appear painful, I have in fact learned much of worth, much that I treasure, in writing this book. If others learn something in reading it, I shall be doubly grateful.

In the 1962 preface I most soberly thanked

a good many friends and scholars for manifold aid and comfort. Most of them should be thanked again for this volume. But instead I will merely mention a few others who have been generous with their expertise for the sake of this volume: Herbert Deane, Josiah Gould, Harry V. Jaffa, Harvey C. Mansfield, Jr., Leonard Munter, Frederick Sontag, and Theodore Waldman. Typists Mrs. Gladys Burton and Mrs. Shirley Martin each deserve special kudos. Thanks are due also to Pomona College and the Danforth Foundation for leave time and an Award, respectively, which made possible two periods of sustained research and writing in Cambridge, Massachusetts, and Claremont, California.

My youngest son—who at four months of age was induced to accept full responsibility for all errors of fact or interpretation in the 1962 book—is still my youngest son, but he is now six years old and a standout in first-grade research techniques. He stoutly refuses to shoulder additional burdens. I have no choice but to take the blame myself for the defects in what follows.

L. C. M.

Claremont, California

A NOTE ON THE PAPERBOUND EDITION

This volume is part of a variant printing, not a new or revised edition, of *Western Political Theory: From the Origins to the Present*. Some users of that book have requested a three-volume version that would enable them to fit the text into the particular patterns of their teaching and scheduling. To meet that request, the publishers have prepared this printing, consisting of three separate volumes that exactly reproduce the text of the one-volume version of *Western Political Theory: From the Origins to the Present*. Part One, now subtitled *Ancient and Medieval,* contains Chapters 1 through 7 of the original text; Part Two, *From Machiavelli to Burke,* contains Chapters 8 through 17; and Part Three, *Nineteenth and Twentieth Centuries,* contains Chapters 18 through 28. Since the variant printing is intended as a convenience to instructors and students, some of whom have had occasion to use the one-volume version, the original pagination, index, and list of selected readings are retained in the new printing. The difference between the one-volume and three-volume versions of the book is a difference only in form.

CONTENTS

21

MARX, *488*

Life, 488. Historical Materialism and the Dialectic, 491. Alienation, 493. The Theory of Objective Development, 495. The Theory of Surplus Value, 498. Accumulation, Immiserization, Revolution, 499. Communism and the Classless Society, 501. Conclusion: Ideology and Ideals in Social Change, 503.

22

NIETZSCHE, *505*

Life, 505. Nietzsche as Philosopher, 507. The Dionysian Myth, 509. Eternal Recurrence and Superman, 510. Nietzsche as Critic, 511. Good and Evil, Good and Bad, 513. Will-to-Power, 515. Conclusion, 516.

23

THE TWENTIETH CENTURY, *518*

Who Is Important? 518. Totalitarianism, 519. Liberalism in the Twentieth Century, 524. Existentialism, 533. A Note on Eastern and Western Political Thought, 540. Conclusion, 541.

24

LENIN, *542*

Life, 542. Lenin as Philosopher, 544. Party and Revolution, 546. Imperialism, 549. The State and the Dictatorship of the Proletariat, 551. Conclusion, 553.

25

DEWEY, *555*

Life, 555. Subject and Object, 557. Facts and Values, 558. Past and Present, 560. Individual and Society, 561. Community, 562. Social Planning, 564. Conclusion, 565.

WESTERN POLITICAL THEORY

PART 3
NINETEENTH AND TWENTIETH CENTURIES

18

THE NINETEENTH CENTURY

A century can be a mental image as well as a span of years. If we wish to be metaphorical, we can think of the nineteenth century as the parent of the twentieth century; and the fact that, each in our own way, we *are* the twentieth century makes the nineteenth century the parent of our own most cherished ideologies. Seen in this way, the nineteenth century begins not in 1801 but in 1789, with the French Revolution, or possibly in 1815, with the Congress of Vienna. From our viewpoint, which may still be too close for good focus, the essence of nineteenth-century thought would seem to center around process, growth, and evolution. The eighteenth century was also progressive but in what now seems an abstract and mechanical way. (The eighteenth century is our grandparent, respected but distant and outmoded.) Men were concerned in the eighteenth century with choosing the most rational method by which to order society and the world. In the nineteenth century society and the world seemed to be charging blindly forward by natural impulse and scholars were bent on finding the key to growth. The geometrical mode of thinking had been replaced by the biological.

A sense of hard but rewarding destiny flavors the work of Hegel, who discovered process as a philosophical concern. Growth as a nonrational, subconscious pattern was part of Darwin's biological thinking and ultimately of Freud's psychological thinking. The simple atomistic individualism of early liberal thought was done for. In relation to this new emphasis Bentham must be regarded as basically an eighteenth-century figure, neat and tidy and rather static. But his vigorous influence on nineteenth-century English politics warrants that he be given a separate chapter (Chapter 19) as a nineteenth-century figure. Hegel (Chapter 20) is without question a nineteenth-century thinker, as are his inverted disciple Marx (Chapter 21) and most members of the socialist movement. In the name of the individual, Nietzsche (Chapter 22) revolted against everything the nineteenth century stood for and in so doing delighted paradox-lovers by affirming a good part of what the nineteenth century stood for.

Of these four men, more later. First we must sketch a backdrop for their solos—a crude backdrop, no doubt, with some oversimplified issues and a few one-dimensional bit-players, but what more can be done for a century so ripe with contention and so alive with change?

Thanks in part to Hegel, with the nineteenth century we enter the age of ideology, the age of "isms," so in what more appropriate way can we organize this chapter than around the symbols "liberalism," "conservatism," and "socialism," which serve as background and foreground to Bentham, Hegel, and Marx, respectively?

LIBERALISM

One has only to recall the distance we have traversed from Locke to Harrington to Montesquieu to Godwin to be struck by how complicated liberalism as a movement was. Its central tenet was, apparently, that the free individual, the liberated individual, is the proper goal of social policy. "Free" had meaning not in some obscure metaphysical sense but rather in the more practical sense of being unbound by traditional hierarchical authority. Individuals were empowered to seek private ends that, it was more or less assumed, were at least somewhat inhibited by a rational propensity toward decent behavior in man as man. Optimism was a recurring ingredient in liberalism. Yet, except for a few figures like Condorcet and Godwin, almost everywhere it was a qualified optimism, for, as we have noted, the need for mechanical devices to control "liberated" men was frequently stressed. The legislature in Locke and the legislator in Bentham were not without quite restrictive responsibilities.

English Utilitarianism

The mechanical practicalism implicit in the English empiricist tradition came to full flower in the utilitarianism of Jeremy Bentham (1748–1832) and his immediate followers. Without trespassing on Chapter 19, we can say at this point that the essence of Bentham's system was his "felicific calculus," whereby the legislator could calculate the worth of any legislative proposal by examining the more or less quantifiable pleasures and pains of the mass of the citizens, each citizen counting for one and no more than one. Bentham's basic assumptions were that (1) through the index of pleasure and pain, is and ought can be united (what is most pleasurable to man is what is best for him); (2) social reform, "improvement," is necessary to maximize pleasure and can be achieved only by the elimination of "fictions," superstition, and mystique (typified, for example, by natural law) and the rationalization of laws, penal systems, and social programs; (3) the only legitimate end of government is "the greatest good of the greatest number."

James Mill

Although the influence was reciprocal, Bentham inspired no man more fully than he did James Mill (1773–1836). This stern Scots journalist, the archetype of the ex-Calvinist, carried the utilitarian gospel to the world and with the aid of skillful agitators like Francis Place helped create a climate favorable to the English Reform Bill of 1832. After Mill wrote *The History of India* (1817), which lifted him out of poverty, he was able to turn to more fundamental issues, namely the principles of associationist psychology expounded in his *Analysis of the Phenomena of the Human Mind* (1829). Valiantly as he tried, it can hardly be said that he succeeded in bridging the gap between the realm of simple sensations of pleasure and pain and the world of ideas. Nevertheless, he provided a base of sorts for utilitarian ethics and politics. This base Bentham himself hardly needed, but he did need Mill to change him from an aristocratic to a democratic reformer.

James Mill's political thought is most clearly revealed in the article on *Government* that he wrote for the *Encyclopaedia Britannica* in 1820. More explicitly than in Bentham's writings, this article reveals the middle-class bias of utilitarianism. Government exists to protect and extend individual interests (that is, pleasures) the foremost of which is the enjoyment of property. Distrusting Montequieu's system of checks and balances to keep rulers on the straight and narrow, Mill places his faith in a system of perfect representation. The suffrage must be universal but the flavor of legislation would come from one class:

There can be no doubt that the middle rank, which gives to science, to art, and to legislation itself, their most distinguished ornaments, the chief source of all that has exalted and refined human nature, is that portion of the community of which, if the basis of Representation were ever so far extended, the opinion would ultimately decide. Of the people beneath them a vast majority would be sure to be guided by their advice and example.[1]

On the one hand, Mill's approach was deductive, which no doubt made it possible for him to plump for a radically egalitarian politics without seeing the possible implications of this for his equally deductive bourgeois economic theories. On the other hand, there was at the time not much more evidence supporting Mill's opponents, men like Macaulay, who argued that the extension of the suffrage would inevitably lead to the destruction of property rights.

John Stuart Mill

James Mill's son, John Stuart Mill (1806–73), possessed a far more subtle mind than his father. Despite, or possibly because of, the "forced draft" education imposed by his father, a ruthlessly rigorous regime that denied him every pleasure of childhood, John Stuart saw progressively more clearly the weaknesses of utilitarianism as a doctrine. But his liberation from his father came too late to permit his natural genius to break through into the new philosophy of which he was capable. Having organized a "Utilitarian Society" at age sixteen, he called himself a utilitarian to the end.

Young Mill's strengths and weaknesses are well illustrated in his famous On Liberty (1859). In this essay he defends freedom of thought, action, and association with rhetoric

so felicitous that readers are still moved by it today. "If all mankind minus one were of one opinion, and only one person were of the contrary opinion, mankind would be no more justified in silencing that one person than he, if he had the power, would be justified in silencing mankind."[2] Any suppression of speech implies the infallibility of the suppressor, a futile possibility, as Mill showed with ample historical evidence; it overlooks the needed truth that is buried in every erroneous statement; and it denies to individuals the opportunity to test truth by the challenge of error, a challenge without which once-truthful propositions dry up and become "dead dogma, not a living truth."

Despite its eloquent libertarian appeal, On Liberty is marked by the uncertainties of Mill's position. Still an egalitarian, he was nevertheless bothered by the psychological "tyranny of the majority"—a term borrowed from De Tocqueville—which can fetter the development of unique individuals. His criterion of good social policy was still determined by the essentially negative utilitarian proposition that "the sole end for which mankind are warranted, individually or collectively, in interfering with the liberty of action of any of their number, is self protection. . . . the only purpose for which power can be rightfully exercised over any member of a civilized community against his will is to prevent harm to others."[3] Yet throughout he revealed an implicit faith in a positive concept of evolving truth against which good and bad social policy is presumably measured. (Since Mill had read Hegel—with, as he said, "a kind of sickening feeling"—it is possible that his concept of truth born of clashing opposites was influenced by Hegel.)

He was still tied to the utilitarian standard of pleasure and pain but spoke now of "utility in the largest sense, grounded on the permanent interests of a man as a progressive

[1] *Government*, in E. A. Burtt, ed., *The English Philosophers from Bacon to Mill* (New York: Random House, Modern Library, 1939), p. 888.

[2] *On Liberty*, in *Utilitarianism, Liberty, and Representative Government* (New York: Dutton, Everyman, 1951), p. 104.

[3] Note the exemption of those not in "civilized communities," in which category Mill explicitly placed children and members of "barbarian nations."

being." This interpretation took all the precision out of the old standard. In fact, there was not much left of Bentham's simple, almost physiological, units of pleasure and pain when Mill said in *Utilitarianism,* "It is better to be a human being dissatisfied than a pig satisfied; better to be Socrates dissatisfied than a fool satisfied."[4]

Mill's outstanding economics textbook, *The Principles of Political Economy* (1848), dominated its field for half a century but became less laissez faire in orientation with each of many succeeding editions until Mill was finally admitting, as against the old "iron-law-of-wages" theory, that trade unions could raise real wages. Like his father, John Stuart was interested in schemes of representation and in *Representative Government* (1861) he put upon the Hare system of proportional representation an impossibly heavy burden of reform, hoping not only that it could give minority parties a voice in government but that it could thereby stimulate rationality and individuality in the body politic —even though, ironically, Mill did not trust individuals with a secret ballot. He did trust women, however, as "superior in moral goodness"—especially Mrs. Taylor, who became his wife after a twenty-year courtship—and worked hard for woman suffrage, both during his four years in Parliament and by writing *The Subjection of Women* (1869).

Mill's greatest intellectual effort was probably the *System of Logic* (1843), noted especially for its four methods of experimental inquiry. The last section, "On the Logic of the Moral Sciences," is of special interest to us here. It deals with a subject that still fascinates us today—the methodology of the social sciences. Much influenced by Comte's sociology,[5] Mill considered and rejected as inappropriate to social studies the loose empiricism of the "chemical or experimental" method and the unreal generalizing of the "geometrical or abstract" method, for which he singled out Bentham himself as an example. The special sociological method he suggested was the "physical or concrete deductive" method, by which general propositions common to "large classes of observed facts" were to be obtained. The complexity of social data required, felt Mill, use of both direct and "inverse" deductive operations. Sometimes one could deduce generalizations by reasoning and then confirm them by observation. Sometimes one must begin with conclusions obtained "provisionally from specific experience" and afterward connected "with the principles of human nature by *a priori* reasonings."[6] The latter technique was particularly appropriate to historical data.

The "principles of human nature" referred to above were in essence the "laws of mind" that Mill assumed were largely demonstrated by associationist psychology. He hoped to bridge the gap between this psychology and large-scale sociological generalizations with a new science of character formation called "ethology," which would study the causes and effects of successive "states of mind" in their sociological context. By thinking of character as the effect of habitual will he evaded the old pleasure-pain axis. Recognizing that such a science could not be as exact as physics, he nevertheless hoped it might be as exact as meteorology.

Mill's hopes were, of course, unfulfilled and his methodology would not be of much practical use today. The important point, however, is that in the *Logic* "science" conceived on a close analogy to physical science was being applied to man in his social setting in a new and more rigorous way, yet without the disregard for historical insights characteristic of earlier utilitarianism.

Mill was very much a "man in the mid-

[4] *Utilitarianism,* in *Utilitarianism, Liberty, and Representative Government,* p. 12. See also Mill's *Essays on Politics and Culture,* Gertrude Himmelfarb, ed. (Garden City, N. Y.: Doubleday, Anchor, 1963).

[5] See p. 444, below. Mill, in his own *Auguste Comte and Positivism,* 3rd ed. (London: Turner, 1882), calls Comte as great as Descartes or Leibnitz, although Mill had criticized some of Comte's canons of proof and was also, of course, highly critical of his repressive social views.

[6] *System of Logics,* Bk. VI, Ch. 9, sec. 1, 8th ed. (London: Longmans, Green, 1925), p. 585. Book VI has recently been published as *The Logic of the Moral Sciences,* Henry Magid, ed. (Indianapolis: Bobbs-Merrill, 1965).

dle," placed in a state of tension by virtue of the sympathetic insights of his quick and open mind, which could see the worth in competing trends: democracy versus aristocracy; laissez faire versus welfare state; the autonomous individual versus the value of social cohesion; a nonmoral social science—called, ironically, "moral science"—versus humane reformism. As Hobhouse wrote, "in his single person he spans the interval between the old and the new liberalism."[7]

Austin

Another utilitarian with a quite different kind of influence was John Austin (1790–1859). London neighbor of Bentham and James Mill, Austin was appointed by their intervention to the chair of jurisprudence at the new University College, London. Though he failed as a lecturer, he succeeded in founding a new school of legal theory. Mainly through *The Province of Jurisprudence Determined* (1832) and to some extent *Lectures on Jurisprudence* (1863) he became the spokesman of "analytical jurisprudence." He was fearful of universal suffrage and more conservative than Bentham. But he must be discussed under the general heading of liberalism because his strong utilitarian beliefs, which complemented if they did not determine his theory of law, were directed at the same traditionalist targets battered by Bentham: natural law, social myths, nonrational legal custom, and metaphysics generally. He believed that the good of society was merely the aggregate of individual interests. He believed in education, free trade, limited government, and Locke's empiricism. He disparaged attempts to erect a good of the whole that would transcend all private values.[8]

Austin's jurisprudential mission owed much to Hobbes's theory of sovereignty and was dedicated to clearness, precision, and concreteness. He concerned himself with "positive" law in the full sense of the word—the exposition of law as it is, not confused with considerations of what it ought to be. "The science of jurisprudence . . . is concerned with positive laws, or with laws strictly so called, as considered without regard to their goodness or badness."[9] Law is, very simply, the command of the sovereign. And who is the sovereign? ". . . if a determinate human superior, not in a habit of obedience to a like superior, receive habitual obedience from the bulk of a given society, that determinate superior is sovereign in that society." And what of ancient law? ". . . (borrowing the language of Hobbes) 'the legislator is he, not by whose authority the law was first made, but by whose authority it continues to be a law.' "

Austin added fuel to the reformist fires of Bentham's legal criticisms by his claim that law properly conceived must be clear, determinate, and positive; but the very strength of his logic restricted his theoretical impact. To overcome loose social fictions, legal obscurantism, and the dead hand of the past, he sought to erect a hard logical structure, eschewing moralism and delineating law as only a means to an end, while holding in abeyance consideration of the ends of society. He, like Hobbes, clearly distinguished between the legal and the moral.[10] To this extent his efforts were toward a wholly formalistic theory of law, that is, a *science* of law.

But he also wanted a science of *law* and not mere power, a theory of authority and not mere force. He was unwilling to make sovereign anyone who could grab power momentarily. To make this clear he was forced to enter the empirical realm through his

---

[7] L. T. Hobhouse, *Liberalism* (New York: Holt, Rinehart and Winston, 1911), p. 107. See Joseph Hamburger, *Intellectuals in Politics: John Stuart Mill and the Philosophical Radicals* (New Haven: Yale Univ. Press, 1965).

[8] Utilitarians did not believe, he said, that "the lover should kiss his mistress with an eye to the common weal." For the dry Austin, an unexpected burst of humor. Quoted in John Bowle, *Politics and Opinion in the Nineteenth Century* (New York: Oxford Univ. Press, 1954), p. 73.

[9] *Lectures on Jurisprudence,* Lec. 5, in W. Jethro Brown, ed., *The Austinian Theory of Law* (London: Murray, 1906), p. 35.

[10] For the implications of this distinction see the exchange between Huntington Cairns and Stuart M. Brown, Jr., in Carl J. Friedrich, ed., *Community* (New York: Liberal Arts Press, 1959), Chs. 2–3; and see H. L. A. Hart, *The Concept of Law* (London: Oxford Univ. Press, 1963).

definition of sovereignty. The sovereign is one who receives *"habitual* obedience from the *bulk* of a given society." Once the habits of the masses are involved we are faced with an empirical sociological determination of no mean proportions. Bentham preferred to talk about the pleasure-pain calculations of individuals and legislator rather than the habits of large masses. This definition would have made it much easier to build a logical system, although the resulting system would have been further removed than Austin's from social reality.

English utilitarianism, though subject to many mutations, was still doing at the end of the nineteenth century what it was doing at the beginning: trying to reform fellow Englishmen by telling them to be logical, a difficult if not impossible task in any age and place, but a liberalizing task notwithstanding.

Continental Liberalism

We frequently read that liberalism in England was concrete—grounded in tangible electoral, parliamentary, and judicial practices—whereas French liberalism was abstract —inflated by revolutionary rhetoric never brought to earth. But the Charter of the Bourbon restoration in 1814 moved sharply away from revolutionary ideology and instead of expounding the Rights of Man itemized a few rights of Frenchmen. High property qualifications prevented it from being a democratic instrument so far as representation was concerned, but it did grant religious liberty, freedom of speech, equality before the law, and, above all, the inviolability of property—for although it was granted by Louis XVIII, this was a bourgeois charter. The old aristocracy had been decimated by the French Revolution. Its spokesmen were, as we shall see, the very reactionary writers such as De Maistre and De Bonald, who were more officeholders than landowners. The bourgeoisie, by contrast, were strong, having won over the peasant proprietors, but their economic wealth came from commerce and finance rather than manufacturing. Hence the clash, as someone

has noted, was between aristocrats without land and capitalists without factories and the pressing task of liberal theory was to mediate between the two.

Royer-Collard

Among those who tried to mediate were the badly named Doctrinaires, so few in number that "they could all find room on a sofa" but with considerable influence. Their leader was Pierre Paul Royer-Collard (1763–1845),[11] the philosopher of the Charter; another prominent member was the historian François Guizot, who ultimately became Premier. To the left of these two was the novelist Benjamin Constant, organizer of the Liberal Party in 1817. Unlike the moderate Doctrinaires, he regarded the Charter as but a stepping stone to something better and often attacked the men who supported it.

Despite a tentative move toward practicalism, we find in Royer-Collard's theory of sovereignty a recurrence of the visionary faith in words that has so plagued France. Royer-Collard tried to elaborate a conception of sovereignty that, because it was divorced from individual interests, could not be attached to any concrete political institutions. Yet, haunted by the memory of the Terror, he also insisted on the safeguards of a system of separation of powers. He distinguished between two types of interest in society: liberty, especially of speech, press, and judicial process, which he associated with the popular —actually, the bourgeois—Chamber of Deputies; and stability, which was maintained by the power of the elite group of Peers.

Royer-Collard saw more clearly than most liberals that government must necessarily reflect the social structure around it and this was his major theoretical strength. Yet at the same time he tended to exagger-

[11] Royer-Collard's political thought is almost wholly contained in his speeches, many of which are collected in A. G. P. Brugière de Barante, *Vie politique de M. Royer-Collard*, 2 vols. (Paris: Didier, 1861). The best exposition of his thought in English is Harold J. Laski, *Authority in the Modern State* (New Haven: Yale Univ. Press, 1919), Ch. 4.

ate the causal force of written constitutions, making almost a fetish of the Charter. Moreover, if government must accurately reflect the realities of society, it seems a bit disproportionate to give monarchy and the nobility roughly two thirds of the political power, as his system did. The bourgeoisie were possibly short-changed but even more so were the masses, whom he regarded as both politically inexperienced and corruptible. His hope that a deep affection for the constitution would rise up out of the masses was therefore quite unrealistic. Later in life, Royer-Collard's idea of sovereignty in reason began to take on a more explicitly middle-class coloration. Invoking Aristotle's idea of reason as a mean, he made the median position of the middle class in society an argument for the rationality of its having a disproportionate share of power.[12]

Constant

Benjamin Constant (1767–1830) was as antidemocratic as Royer-Collard or Guizot, but the tool he used as a check on popular sovereignty was an eighteenth-century conception of natural rights that the historicism of the Doctrinaires had destroyed. In this sense, Constant was a throwback to an earlier period. But in another sense, he was ahead of the Doctrinaires. In his use of the word "sovereignty" he brought the term back to earth from the abstract "sovereignty in reason" as used by Royer-Collard:

one must not build upon an abstract idea in the illusion that it can increase the sum of individual liberty. . . . there is a part of human life which necessarily remains individual and independent, and has the right to stand outside all social control. Where the independent life of the individ-

ual begins, the jurisdiction of the sovereign ends. Rousseau failed to see this elementary truth.[13]

Constant also saw more clearly than most of his contemporaries the importance of a party system as a prerequisite for effective cabinet government—an insight De Ruggiero interestingly attributes to Constant's Protestant background—and possessed in general a realistic grasp of the subtleties involved in making a parliamentary machine run. Equipped with this realism, he could see the futility of the recurring quest for a new *polis.* In the most famous of his essays, "Ancient and Modern Liberty" (*c.* 1818), he contrasts the Greek *polis,* which can control everything but is in turn controlled by the freemen who participate in it, with the modern state, in which, because of its size and complexity, this kind of participation is impossible. In such a society, liberty has meaning only in the negative sense of freedom *from* state interference. This was Constant's answer to Rousseau and, as well, an assertion of middle-class independence.

De Tocqueville

It is a mark of the difference between the two countries that one of the best known of the French liberals of this period, Alexis de Tocqueville (1805–59), is called a conservative by citizens of the America he studied so engagingly in *Democracy in America* (1835). That a "conservative liberal" is not really a contradiction in terms need not invalidate the contrast between a France uncertain of its future and the lively frontier egalitarianism that so impressed De Tocqueville in the United States. The great virtue of De Tocqueville as a thinker is that, though an aristocrat, he could appraise the virtues and faults of democracy with cool detachment. Without rebelling against his class, he could, unlike the other French liberals, rise above class feeling. He traveled in America and wrote about it with one eye on France. This helps

---

[12] Guizot, a more prolific political writer and also more the expedient politician, was close to Royer-Collard in most respects. He also stressed the value of middle-class moderation as against the dangerous "power of the word Democracy." A touch of cynicism is apparent in such phrases as, "All are in turn democrats as against those above them, aristocrats as against those below" (*Democracy in France,* trans. anon. [New York: Appleton-Century-Crofts, 1849] pp. 11, 25).

[13] *Cours de politique constitutionelle (Constitutional Politics,* 1839), p. 64. Quoted in Guido de Ruggiero, *History of European Liberalism,* trans. by R. G. Collingwood (Boston: Beacon Press, 1959), p. 161.

to explain the almost deductive quality of his comments. The theme of *Democracy in America,* insinuating itself between pungent comments on associations, religion, lawyers, and popular manners, is that equality is dangerous but may nevertheless be a price worth paying for liberty. The danger is tyranny, the new and subtle tyranny of the majority: ". . . the majority possesses a power which is physical and moral at the same time; it acts upon the will as well as upon the actions of men, and it represses not only all content, but all controversy."[14]

But De Tocqueville also recognized that the centralizing tendencies of modern industry and the machine mentality arising from the division of labor, rather than merely pernicious doctrines, were causal roots of what he thought was a growing egalitarian conformity. Moreover, he was open-minded enough to see, in the words of one of his chapter titles, the "causes which mitigate the tyranny of the majority in the United States." In the restless, competitive, fluid side of American life he found an alternative to the compartmentalization of French society, the "great number of watertight compartments, small, self-contained units, each of which watched vigilantly over its own interests and took no part in the life of the community at large."[15] This tendency of French life was what had enabled the Revolution to be so swift and sweeping, yet even when De Tocqueville wrote it had not been eliminated, nor, indeed, has it been wholly eliminated even today. His hopes for keeping equality libertarian were no doubt based too heavily on a parallel hope that political equality need not necessarily lead to social equality; but whatever the basis of his hopes and fears, De Tocqueville had a more clear-eyed perception of the irreversibility of the revolutionary forces than any of the reactionaries or most of the liberals of his day. He "dispelled a

nightmare by showing that the democratic idea, far from being a revolutionary aberration, stood upon the highway of French history."[16] Had middle-class theorists been as flexible as De Tocqueville and held less tightly to their class positions, possibly the middle class itself would have been better able to surmount the jab from the Right in the Revolution of 1830 and the jolt from the Left in the Revolution of 1848. Even though they saw the relationship of social structure to politics more clearly than did the English utilitarians, historically speaking, the French liberals could never lead the nineteenth-century parade.

Von Gneist

If the French liberals were not conspicuous successes, how much less so were the German liberals. Liberalism in Germany reflected the divided nation and the antiquated feudal system within which the theorists wrote. The typical liberal concern for rights took on a legal, if not a legalistic, bent. But in trying to make individual rights into an objective reality immune from practical politics, the theorists succeeded mainly in making them abstract. Rudolph von Gneist (1816–95), leader of mid-century German liberals, aimed in his theory of *Der Rechtstaat* (the legal state) to define a sphere of popular freedom in such a way that it would not weaken the force of unified monarchical authority. He thought he found an answer in administration; the result was a highly circumscribed bureaucratic liberalism.[17]

Von Treitschke

A more fundamental attack on the problem was to follow the lead of Hegel and redefine the concept of freedom. Heinrich von Treitschke (1834–96) in *Freedom* (1861), a reply to Mill's *On Liberty,* offered the classic exposition of the German alternative to

---

[14] *Democracy in America*, Ch. 14, trans. by Henry Reeve (New York: Oxford Univ. Press, Oxford World's Classics, 1946), p. 192.

[15] *The Old Regime and the French Revolution* (1856), trans. by Stuart Gilbert (Garden City, N. Y.: Doubleday, Anchor, 1955), p. 77.

[16] De Ruggiero, p. 191.

[17] See *Vier Abhandlungen über das constitutionelle Prinzip* (1864), discussed in Leonard Krieger, *The German Idea of Freedom* (Boston: Beacon Press, 1957), pp. 356–58.

English liberalism. He supported freedom, but of a somewhat different brand from Mill's. "Whoever sees the state as only a means for the ends of the citizens must logically demand . . . freedom from the state not freedom in the state."[18] Only the latter would suit Treitschke. By English standards this was half-hearted liberalism at best. In their preoccupation with law many German scholars in the latter half of the nineteenth century—typified by C. F. von Gerber, Paul Laband, and Georg Jellinek—showed a similar fascination with an abstract "will of the state"; only now as "analytical jurisprudence" it was a will divorced from moral values as well as from the power of a flesh-and-blood monarch. Suspended in this no-man's-land between power and morality, legality itself became a kind of self-justifying and dangerously elusive entity, either powerless morality or amoral power, depending on factors the scholars did not care to discuss. At least the analytic-positivist jurisprudence of Austin gave the sovereign human form and deferred to a realm of social morality beyond the law, which might hold him accountable. Theories tend, however, to become more abstract as the possibility of free choice between the practical political alternatives associated with those theories declines. In this respect Germany was an ideal locale for abstract theory.

Mazzini

In Italy, too, the divided character of the once proud nation affected the political theory of liberalism and the lack of a strong middle class made republicanism futile. This situation spawned the sometimes pathetic, always romantic idealism of that diverse group of nationalist agitators called the *risorgimento* (resurrection). The best-known member was Joseph Mazzini (1805–72), whose cosmopolitanism came from the fact that he was forced to spend most of his life outside the country he was trying to save. Somewhat in the fashion of Rousseau, Mazzini was impressed by a natural goodness in man that drives him toward cooperation and community, an in-

clination to be at one with something greater than the self. Mazzini's brand of liberalism was several steps removed from atomistic individualism. His major book was not on the Rights of Man, but on the *Duties of Man* (1840–43). The message was liberal to the extent that Mazzini insisted on a criterion of meaningful duty as being self-imposed duty, which in turn required a democratic environment.

There is much of Rousseau in this doctrine, but Mazzini's great contribution is that he applied his criterion of self-imposed duty not only to the state but to all associations and he welcomed a plurality of associations within the state as Rousseau had not. At least on the theoretical level, Mazzini was therefore much more than a mere nationalist. But the possibilities of this theory of free associations were, unfortunately, unrealized. A neo-Hegelian nationalism hung over Mazzini's attempt to make the state a very special association, the one that was common to all men, while at the same time he somewhat fuzzily tried to set apart from both state and lesser associations an inviolable realm of individual freedom.

Social Darwinism

"Social Darwinism" is a handy label for a school of antipolitical theorists who flourished spectacularly in the second half of the nineteenth century. By means of rather clumsy analogies they were able to seize upon Charles Darwin's theories of biological evolution and, stressing terms like "natural selection" and "survival of the fittest," to transfer this authority to the much older theory of laissez faire. Their theory was liberal in that it would free the individual from governmental restraints, but perhaps not so liberal in respect to the socio-economic restraints from which it did not free the individual.

Spencer

As Polanyi labored to demonstrate,[19] the

---

[18] Quoted in Krieger, p. 367.

[19] Karl Polanyi, *The Great Transformation* (Boston: Beacon Press, 1957).

free-market doctrines of the economic liberals were implemented only by carefully organized planning, as nonspontaneous as any planning; but they nevertheless insisted that the free market was in some sense prior to government, that it was "natural," and that governmental economic policy could do little more than get in the way. "The policy of laissez faire as applied to the workers was a policy of negation, derived from a philosophy of complacency compounded with antipathy to the unsuccessful. It received its harshest justification at the hands of the last of the bourgeois liberals, Herbert Spencer."[20] The harshness of Herbert Spencer (1820–1903) was, however, coated with a generous layer of historicist optimism:

Pervading all nature we may see at work a stern discipline which is a little cruel that it may be very kind. That state of universal warfare maintained throughout the lower creation, to the great perplexity of many worthy people, is at bottom the most merciful provision which the circumstances admit of. . . . By the aid of . . . purifying process, as well as by the fighting so universal in the pairing season, all vitiation of the race through the multiplication of its inferior samples is prevented, and the maintenance of a constitution completely adapted to surrounding conditions, and therefore most productive of happiness is assured.[21]

Spencer at least had the virtue of greater consistency than most liberals. He could and did point with some alarm to state interventions his lax liberal brethren had let slip by: enforced vaccination, rural drainage, coal-mine safety regulations, laws preventing the exploitation of boy chimney sweeps, and many other horrendous measures. There were, of course, some exceptions to Spencer's proscription on state meddling. He approved laws restraining the blowing of locomotive whis-

tles (Spencer suffered from insomnia) and the making of boned corsets for women (they deformed the female figure).

All this makes it appear that Spencer approved of no coercion whatsoever; but he was, of course, not this hopeless. As Wolin has suggested,[22] the liberals were forced to face the reality of society; but by making it a separable, natural backdrop to an evil government, they were better able to condemn the latter while ignoring the former. Hence, "freedom" meant freedom from government, not escape from all coercion. Man "must have a master; but the master may be Nature or may be a fellow man. When he is under the impersonal coercion of Nature, we say that he is free; and when he is under the personal coercion of some one above him, we call him . . . a slave, a serf, or a vassal."[23] It is curious, but in passages like this we find it possible to put this extreme opponent of state power and enemy of metaphysics alongside the most idealistic, antiliberal German statist: in one case the individual is free—and helpless—before Nature, in the other, before the state.

The naturalism expressed in this passage was by no means casual.[24] The revival of Spencer by today's right-wing publicists has only added to the obscurity into which his nonpolitical writings have fallen, but he thought of himself as a synthesizer of all human thought. His scheme for the *Synthetic Philosophy* was, in conception, as ambitious as Comte's. As part of the plan he wrote *First Principles* (1862), *Principles of Biology* (1864–67), *Principles of Psychology* (1872), *Principles of Sociology* (1876), and *Principles of Ethics* (1896). In ethics Spencer

20 J. Salwyn Schapiro, *Liberalism and the Challenge of Fascism* (New York: McGraw-Hill, 1949), p. 105.

21 Herbert Spencer, *Social Statics,* abridged and rev. ed. (New York: Appleton-Century-Crofts, 1892), pp. 149-50. This book was originally published in 1851, eight years before Charles Darwin's *The Origin of the Species.* It was Spencer, not Darwin, who coined the phrase, "survival of the fittest." Social Darwinists *used* Darwin, but their ideas were not generated by him.

22 Sheldon Wolin, *Politics and Vision* (Boston: Little, Brown, 1960), Ch. 9.

23 Spencer, *Essays, Scientific, Political, and Speculative,* Vol. III (New York: Appleton-Century-Crofts, 1896), p. 450.

24 The chapter titles of *Man Versus the State* (Caldwell, Idaho: Caxton Printers, 1954) suggest the content: "The New Toryism," "The Sins of Legislators," "Over-Legislation," and so on. The London unemployed Spencer explains very simply: "They are simply the good-for-nothings, who in one way or another live on the good-for-something."

belonged to the utilitarians, sharing their faith in an ultimate happiness divorced from transcendental values and sharing their inability to see society as an organic whole. But now a theory of historical evolution was grafted on and loosely drawn scientific laws were invoked in behalf of political conclusions. For example, the Lamarckian theory of the inheritance of acquired characteristics was used to explain why the better society of the future would be populated with the competitive English types Spencer so admired—a non-Darwinian theory, incidentally.

Thanks in a small measure to Comte, from whom he continually tried to distinguish himself, Spencer moved steadily from a social biology toward a social physics; but it remained a pseudoscience of society nevertheless.

The fundamental confusion which he never surmounts is due to the fact that a priori conceptions of individual rights with which he starts do not and cannot accord with the organic and evolutionary conception of the State which he attains through the use of natural science. . . . Spencer's logic is really bare and mechanical. It is a matter of constant antitheses which are too clear-cut to correspond to life.[25]

By this means Spencer could with the utmost certainty announce that society was evolving beyond war and that war would soon disappear from the earth.

Evolution was indeed Spencer's God. But "His God has betrayed him. We have evolved beyond Spencer."[26]

Sumner

Spencer's American disciple William Graham Sumner (1840–1910) was both less pretentious and more realistic than his English counterpart. Without attempting a *Synthetic Philosophy,* he focused an unsenti-

mental eye on what he took to be the fine fruits of unregulated struggle. Yet no more than in Spencer could his lucid, commonsense prose conceal the confused philosophy of history that lurked behind every premise. The struggle that was so natural and so productive referred in the end not to military, moral, or power struggles at large but to a very special kind of economic struggle that required "liberty under law" to insure "peace for the laborer and security for the capitalist." The cooperative emotions required to build that kind of liberty under law were left unexplored, because the results of such inquiry would have contradicted the basic Social Darwinist dogma that "Competition . . . is a law of nature. Nature is entirely neutral; she submits to him who most energetically and resolutely assails her. She grants her rewards to the fittest."[27] Another, deeper, contradiction is embedded in this passage. Nature is entirely neutral. Yet "she"—neutral, though not, please note, a neuter—seems invariably to abandon her neutrality when it comes to handing out prizes. For the "fittest" —a term with unmistakable moral connotations in both Spencer and Sumner—always win.

Social Darwinism is important because so many people have believed in it, both before and after it was given that label. From Lord Brougham to Carnegie to Goldwater, economically successful men have copied or created similar theories to justify their success. The whole nineteenth century, a century of industrial upsurge and progressive cosmology, was a stimulus to such theories. The apex was certainly the Victorian era, toward the caricature of which we all look at times with nostalgia; for there life was real, the struggle was heroic—but the good always won.

[25] Ernest Barker, *Political Thought in England, 1848 to 1914,* 2nd ed., rev. (London: Oxford Univ. Press, 1947), p. 71.

[26] Crane Brinton, *English Political Thought in the Nineteenth Century* (Cambridge, Mass.: Harvard Univ. Press, 1949), p. 227.

[27] "The Challenge of Facts," in A. G. Keller and M. R. Davie, eds., *The Essays of William Graham Sumner,* Vol. II (New Haven: Yale Univ. Press, 1934), p. 95. Sumner, it should be pointed out, was no apologist for American "robber barons." He opposed the protective tariff and the Spanish-American War even at the risk of losing his Yale professorship.

CONSERVATISM

To conserve something is easier than to liberate something, so the term "conservatism" is not one that imposes rigorous definitional limits. Under its broad canopy we may and will group such diverse figures as the reactionary-technocratic-positivistic Comte, the half-liberal Green, and the romantic elitist Carlyle. If anything holds them together it is the assertion of social tradition as a value superior to privately determined individual rights—and even to this statement must no doubt be added, to fit Carlyle's case: "by ordinary individuals." At bottom, a social good prior to and greater than individual goods was what liberals could not assert. Though in many ways flourishing in the nineteenth century, the liberals had a more difficult time ignoring the factor of social tradition and the organic wholeness of political orders after the disruption of the French Revolution than they had had before. By the same token, conservatism as a whole in the nineteenth century was deeply marked by memories of the Revolution. The early and most intense reactors turned their reaction into a name for the group to which they belonged.

The Reaction

Edmund Burke was the best-known exponent of these antirevolutionary feelings; but his own temperament, as we have seen, and the stable constitutional pattern of his nation, restrained him from the extremism that characterized France then as it does today. The explosive mixture of Revolutionary egalitarianism, Bourbon absolutism, and Napoleonic militarism created a poor climate for the constitutional moderates of France. Although they, too, lived with the memory of Revolutionary excesses, a man like De Maistre seems better to fit the dark mood of the times.

De Maistre

A nobleman and civic official who was Sardinian ambassador to Russia from 1803 to 1815, Joseph de Maistre (1776–1847) was a fanatic absolutist and ecclesiast. He did not simply disapprove of unorthodoxy and democracy. He loathed, despised, and raged against them. He dismissed the argument for popular suffrage by noting that children and lunatics may be represented in court by persons they have not chosen and, since the people are "a perpetual child, a perpetual lunatic," why not let another speak for them?[28] To give power to the people, De Maistre felt, was to unmuzzle a tiger. Absolutism was essential for the simple reason that society would fall apart without it.

Perhaps De Maistre's greatest significance is his role as a negative critic of liberalism and some of its easy claims, especially in its quest for a secular freedom. His criticism, however, at best tended to be extreme. Locke, Voltaire, and Rousseau alike were ridiculed for envisioning a mythical state where there are so many "wills loose in the world" that anarchy followed by slavery is inevitable. The idea of the social contract is a foolish abstraction. Popular sovereignty is an altogether empty concept that merely bemuses the liberals. The rash of legislation with which revolutionaries always indulge themselves can only weaken the body politic, for authority is best accepted *in toto* and not chopped up into nothing by an attempt to put everything into legal terminology.

De Maistre's negative attack did nevertheless stem from a rich theological base. Like St. Augustine, he felt that government was made necessary by original sin. The most that one can do with sinful, emotional, unreasoning, prejudiced man is to pound him over the head with the correct prejudices until he behaves himself sufficiently to maintain social order—until, in effect, he does the right thing for the wrong reason. This is why the Roman Church is the model for all government: man must be ruled by mystery, and the supreme authority of the Pope is the highest mystery. *"Infallibility* in the spiritual

[28] *Considérations sur la France* (1796), Ch. 4. Quoted in Roger Soltau, *French Political Thought in the Nineteenth Century* (New Haven: Yale Univ. Press, 1931), p. 21.

order and *sovereignty* in the temporal order are perfectly synonymous words."[29] But mystery alone is not enough. Another essential cement of the social fabric is the restraint of terror produced by the executioner (*bourreau*), whose mission is painted in ghastly hues in the dialogues *Soirées de St. Petersburg* (1822), all the more ghastly because of the proper pride De Maistre gives the executioner after he has expertly and professionally tortured a hapless soul.[30]

Such bizarre strains aside, De Maistre is probably most original in relating his ideas on authority to the process of language formation. Somewhat in the manner of Vico,[31] he regarded the creation of language as a mysterious, mythical process that is destroyed as soon as it becomes self-conscious. Like primitive religion (indeed, like all religion) language is simply *there,* its origins shrouded in mystery, yet inseparable from even the most rational activity of the human mind. The absolute identity of thought and language, in which De Maistre believed, imprisons man in the culture that produces language without possibility of escape, for moral conscience itself is subsequent to language. Perhaps, then, De Maistre was being consistent and not merely chauvinistic in finding a cause for unity in the spread of French as the international language.

De Maistre, finally, treated the problem of war with poetic, sardonic, morbid insight. He saw war as a universal expression of blood lust, collective guilt, and ritual sacrifice peculiar to the human animal. His discussion of sacrifice is ingenious. An essential part of society's need to live, he felt, was the process—called "reversibility of merits"—whereby the innocent are made to atone for the sins of the guilty. (De Maistre is not clear on the matter of where Louis XVI stood in this exchange!)

De Maistre made the dark side of the human psyche the characteristic side and the necessity of its control by mysterious and unquestioned political authority became for him virtually self-evident. Twentieth-century conservatives have surpassed De Maistre in logic, but none has surpassed him in the power of expression, and for a defender of mystery the power of expression becomes in a practical way all-important. A less, or possibly more, charitable way of assessing this talent was Lamartine's comment on De Maistre that the man was superior to the writer and the writer was superior to the thinker.[32]

De Bonald

De Maistre's contemporary Louis de Bonald (1753-1840)[33] likewise saw religion as the only firm basis for social organization and shared De Maistre's nostalgia for the feudal past. De Bonald was fascinated by triads; he molded his whole thought to fit a triangular pattern. The basic triad was cause, means, effect. The cause of society was God, its means absolute sovereignty, and its effect man himself, who was, needless to say, utterly a social creature. Society itself, thus, was the ultimate authority, because man was made by and for society, or by and for God, which amounted to very much the same thing. Analogous triads existed for religion: God, priests, believers; for politics: king, nobility, people; and for the family: father, mother, children.

De Bonald indulged in a more elaborate empirical study than De Maistre to prove that man is shaped by society but he did not have De Maistre's sense of historical develop-

---

[29] *Du Pape*, Ch. I, sec. I (Paris: Garnier, n.d.), p. 21. See also De Maistre's *On God and Society,* trans. by L. M. Porter, in Elisha Greifer, ed. (Chicago: Regnery, 1959).

[30] *Soirées de St. Petersburg*, Disc. I, Vol. I (Lyon: Vitte, 1924), pp. 31–35.

[31] See Elio Gianturco, *Joseph De Maistre and Giambattista Vico* (Washington, D.C.: privately published, 1937). This book includes an excellent bibliography on De Maistre.

[32] Cited by Jules d'Ottange, Preface to *Du Pape*, p. 5. Much of De Maistre has recently been made available in English in Jack Lively, ed., *The Works of Joseph de Maistre* (New York: Macmillan, 1965).

[33] Exiled during the Revolution, De Bonald was minister of instruction in 1808, a deputy in 1815, a peer in 1823. He refused to take the oath of allegiance to Louis Philippe. His chief works were *De la législation primitive* (1802) and *Recherches philosophiques sur les premiers objets des connaissances morales* (1818).

ment and was not much concerned to explain how it is that men rebel *against* the society that controls them, though he granted that this, like rebellion against God, was part of man's grim fate. Speaking of the French Revolution he said, "a people who, in their desire for written laws, have lost their customs, impose on themselves the hard necessity of writing everything, even their customs."[34] De Bonald took Rousseau's general will and, by denying that all individuals harbored it, turned it into a rationale for simple monarchy. But at least he took pains to distinguish between absolute power, which he defended, and arbitrary power, which he did not.

In general, De Bonald's more static position enabled him to cling to the present with a tenacity even greater than De Maistre's, and the authority of language as the symbol of man's inability to remake his society was even more important to him. Yet in a curious lapse he attacked the contractualists at one point by postulating the inevitable development of a future society somewhat comparable to the old governmentless state of nature that was the heart of his enemies' doctrine.

Fichte

Germany, still essentially an agrarian nation at the beginning of the century and politically but a collection of feudal principalities, had early begun to develop a self-conscious national philosophy with strong romantic elements. Romanticism in Germany had a profound influence on conservative thought at this time, as did French romanticism later in the century. Von Herder, the eighteenth-century "champion of intuition against analysis, of faith against the intellect, of history against science,"[35] was the movement's mentor and the scientific rationalism of the *Aufklärung* was its target. Its leaders opposed the search for universal laws and gloried in subjective relativism. Herder had been

[34] *Législation primitive* (Paris: Le Cere, 1857), title page.
[35] H. S. Reiss, in the Introduction to his edition of *The Political Thought of the German Romantics, 1793–1815* (Oxford: Blackwell, 1955), p. 2.

largely apolitical but fear of the anarchy that, the romantics felt, accompanied the analytic thought of the Enlightenment (the French Revolution was, of course, the great example) led them to stress a religion and a community safe from analysis. The stress on subjective individuality on the one hand and the sanctity of the community on the other suggests an inner tension in romanticism that is not illusory. The romantics did in fact tend to exempt only the man of genius from the heavy hand of duty.

The poet Johann Friedrich von Schiller, who gave Hegel his beginning tenet—*"Die Weltgeschichte ist das Weltgericht"* ("World history is world justice")—and the reformer Wilhelm von Humboldt were more individualistic than the romantics and favored less state interference. But they too criticized reason as the key to enlightenment. The unsavory features of later German nationalism are often traced back to Johann Gottlieb Fichte (1762–1814), first rector of the University of Berlin. Fichte began his career as a rationalist and never abandoned rationalist categories—his self-designation as the inheritor of Kant's mantle led to a repudiation by Kant himself—but he became increasingly divorced from this tradition in fact and is generally considered in the camp of German romantics. In practical politics he moved from Jacobinism to conservative nationalism.

Fichte incorporated some liberal symbols, such as contract and freedom of thought, in his political theory but his devotion to communal unity seemed to contradict their typical meaning. He rejected separation of powers on the grounds that the state's will must be single and free of the taint of private interests. The three ascending stages of civil contract, as Fichte saw it, were property, which was self-oriented; protection, which involved mutual security; and association, in which all men agree to a rule of law made and administered by a single fixed will to which they all subordinate themselves. The subordination was to be more than merely external; it also included a subjective feeling of trust. The state thus created was endowed with a mystical quality. It was, as he said, "not merely a *compositum* but a *totum*. In the organic body every part continuously preserves the whole and by preserving it the part itself is preserved; the citizen's relation to the state is precisely the same."[36]

In *Der Geschlossene Handelstaat* (*The Closed Commercial State,* 1800) Fichte describes his ideal of a state fully self-supporting and economically independent. The entire economy is controlled by the state, all individuals are assigned their work, a rigid hierarchy of classes is established, foreign trade is abolished, and war is sanctioned if necessary to establish "natural" frontiers. The only right available to the citizen is the right of emigration. Perhaps the most famous work of Fichte is *Addresses to the German Nation* (1808), made up of inflamed appeals to German nationalism. Obviously stirred by Napoleon's defeat of Prussia, Fichte points to the need to bring together the high culture of German life with the power that can make it effective in the world. This great mission requires economic self-sufficiency, proper pride in nationhood, and the devotion and sacrifices of individuals to the state.[37]

Hegel followed Fichte at the University of Berlin and shared many of his nationalistic sentiments and to some extent his mode of exposition. Hegel can be called part of the Reaction but he fits into no categories neatly because as a man of genius he transcended the old to invent new categories. For that reason he deserves a chapter to himself (Chapter 20). What Hegel gave to the nineteenth century was a sense of the dynamic movement of history. What the Reaction as a whole gave to the nineteenth century was a conception of man as a dependent, nonself-directing member of a predetermined social group. The conception would be ignored or rejected by the liberals but would return again in different form with the socialists.

Positivism

Positivism, as Frankel points out,[38] is a double-barrelled word. It suggests first of all a matter-of-fact orientation—concern for what is rather than what ought to be, distrust of metaphysics, support for science. In this sense, it is not so much conservative as scientifically neutral on those questions on which conservative and radical emotions are spent.

The term is also identified with certain specific attempts to systematize social knowledge by the use of methodologies akin to those of the natural sciences, the most famous if not the first of which is Comte's "Positive Philosophy." John Stuart Mill, as we have seen, made an exploratory effort in the same direction in his *System of Logic.* He was an economic liberal and a political reformer. Spencer likewise contributed to what he called positive philosophy. He was an economic liberal and a political conservative. The disparity in the social views of these three men is enough to suggest that positivism itself does not necessarily fit under the general heading of "conservatism." But whether or not he was conservative, positivist Comte was indubitably antiliberal. He was directly influenced by De Maistre (as well as by utopian socialism). We shall discuss Comte under the heading of conservatism, therefore, because he fits into this category not well but better than into any other.

Comte

A one-time secretary to the utopian socialist Saint-Simon, Auguste Comte (1798–1857) was a troubled and impoverished tutor of mathematics. He published a six-volume *Cours de philosophie positive* from 1830 to 1842 and a four-volume *Système de politique positive* from 1851 to 1854.[39] Both works were

---

[36] *Grundlage des Naturrechts* (*Foundations of Natural Law,* 1797), in Reiss, pp. 44–73. The passage quoted occurs on p. 73. See the editor's commentary in the Introduction, pp. 11–22.

[37] See the Thirteenth Address, in Reiss, pp. 102–18.

[38] Charles Frankel, "Positivism," in Virgilius Ferm, ed., *A History of Philosophical Systems* (New York: Philosophical Library, 1950). See also Walter M. Simon, *European Positivism in the Nineteenth Century* (Ithaca: Cornell Univ. Press, 1963).

[39] See Comte, *A General View of Positivism,* trans. by J. H. Bridges (Stanford, Cal.: Academic Reprints, n.d.). This represents the first volume of the 1848 edition of the *Système,* which has been widely reprinted.

marked by an unbelievable intellectual arrogance. Comte refused to read any of his contemporaries' writings because he knew, a priori, they were unworthy of him. Though not a qualified scientist he undertook in the *Cours de philosophie* to cover the frontiers of knowledge in all the natural sciences. His arrogance was not, however, a substitute for work. He worked and wrote with a fearful zeal and made life even harder for himself by arbitrary self-imposed rules, such as writing seven chapters of seven sections of seven sentences with no repetition of words in consecutive sentences—all this to improve, he said, his style. Thus he did not exempt even himself from what Mill called his "frenzy for regulation."

For all its massive bulk, the Comtean system can be summarized rather briefly. History, he said, falls into three distinct stages: the theological, the metaphysical, and the positive. The first stage, progressing from primitive polytheism to monotheism, lasted until the end of the Middle Ages. As man shed the superstition of supernatural religion, he began to put his faith in impersonal gods, in metaphysical abstractions such as "nature" or "natural rights," and in fictions such as "social contract" or "sovereignty of the people." The eighteenth century was the apex of the metaphysical stage, a necessary step in the progressive unfolding of history, but still laden with errors. By the nineteenth century the positive stage was ready to be born and Comte generously offered himself as midwife. It may be an index of Comte's egocentricity that two of the three stages of human history were telescoped into the last two of twenty or thirty centuries.

The positive stage is the stage of science. Theology and metaphysics are now set aside in order to look at the positive facts of society, the world as it is. Using the understanding that is gained from this look, mankind, through the agency of certain men, will be able logically to induce "invariable laws of phenomena," which may then be manipulated in order to establish a reign of perfect harmony on earth. The basic tool for this reconstruction of society is, of course, science but

all sciences, it seems, are not equal (nor are all men, as it turned out). Comte arranged the sciences in a hierarchical order from the simplest and most basic, mathematics, at the bottom, to the most complex at the top. Here was the queen of them all, "sociology"— Comte invented the term after "social physics" proved inadequate—perched atop the pyramid, giving imperious orders. There can be no doubt that Comte earned his title, the Father of Sociology.

The technocracy Comte describes in his *Système de politique positive* as appropriate to the positivistic age is a magic mixture of De Maistre's reactionary theocracy and Saint-Simon's or Fourier's gadget-filled socialist utopia. The temptation to make fun of it is almost irresistible. A committee of three bankers will handle industry, commerce, and agriculture, respectively. In the elaborately constructed thirteen-month Positivist Calendar there will be special days for honoring "the higher dignity of the banking element." There will also be a Festival of the Proletarian at which great inventors will be fêted. Education of the young until age fourteen will be entirely in the hands of women, whom Comte regarded as superior to men in morality and "social feeling." A rigorous educational regime will be imposed on everyone until age twenty-one. An Occidental Committee is charged with the responsibility of spreading the Positivistic gospel slowly but surely around the world. In what Comte thought a perfectly reasonable scheme of representation, the committee will be made up of eight Frenchmen, seven Englishmen, six Germans, five Italians, and four Spaniards. The committee meetings will always be in Paris. Outside, the green Positivist flag will fly, with "Order and Progress" on one (the "male") side, and "Live for Others" on the other (the "female") side. This flag must be distinguished from that used for religious services, which is adorned with the image of a woman thirty years old, holding her son in her arms.

Having taken the old religion away from positivistic man, Comte felt obliged to give him a new religion, Catholicism without

Christianity, as it is frequently called. The Religion of Humanity had hymns, meditations on great men, a trained positivist priesthood, and even a trinity: the Great Being (humanity), the Grand Fetich (earth), and the Grand Medium (space). "Love . . . is our principle; Order our basis, and Progress our end."

The details of Comte's political-social-religious dream world could be spelled out interminably. But rather than look at details we must look at what is important in his overall effort to reorganize society. Part of what is important in Comte is, of course, simply the typical nineteenth-century traits that he, like many others, represented: hopefulness and confidence in the progressive character of historical evolution, fascination with industry and technology and the possibilities of extensive social regulation, and faith in science. But the most important part of Comte is what he did not share with many, a recognition of the problem of separating "heart and intellect" and of the role society plays in such a separation. The theological stage of history had failed because it was unintelligent. The metaphysical stage of history had failed because it was only intelligent: it had failed to produce a social system that did justice to the affective side of man and his need for the warmth of belonging. In a graphic metaphor, Comte said that, as in the old fable a man died when he saw his own ghost, each age passed away when it saw the ghost of itself in the succeeding age.[40] The failure of the French Revolution to provide orderly emotional substance behind the individualistic abstractions it espoused led directly, Comte felt, to the anarchic dénouement of that particular drama, a drama very much on Comte's mind. The elaborate artificiality of Comte's Religion of Humanity is apt to lead us away from the fact that his insights

into the social necessity of some kind of religion were often penetrating. As Comte put it, "the principal religious difficulty is to secure that the external shall regulate the internal without affecting its spontaneity," a problem of special difficulty when "the intelligence is in insurrection against the heart." But eventually, positivist science gives back, as Caird puts it, what it has seemed to take away, namely a basis for religious belief. John Stuart Mill approved of the taking away but was dismayed by what was put back. "Others may laugh, but we could rather weep at this melancholy decadence of a great intellect."[41] Mill was not complaining merely of the quaint excesses of the Religion of Humanity but of the presumptuous way Comte was trying to make over man: "Like the extreme Calvinists, he requires that all believers shall be saints, and damns them (after his own fashion) if they are not."

In his peculiar way, despite his frightening solutions, Comte had an insight into the deficiencies of his own society: the abstract, impersonal, mechanical quality of life in the new industrial age; the loss of traditional faith, which called for some kind of substitute; and the exaggeration of economic values at the expense of the affective.

Idealism

The term "idealist" has two quite distinct meanings. In its popular sense it refers to anyone who is altruistic, who thinks well of his fellow man, who is hopeful and charged with good will. In the technical philosophical sense it refers to one who believes that ideas and the ideational rather than matter, spirit, or something else, are the substance of ultimate reality. Although these generalizations should not be taken too seriously, it may be said, on the one hand, that the popular idealist tends to be nonconservative as a matter of temperament, simply because he is willing to venture forth to make improvements in an imperfect world and, possibly, to let others have free rein in their attempts at improve-

---

[40] Quoted in Edward Caird, *The Social Philosophy and Religion of Comte* (New York: Macmillan, 1885), p. 18. This is a first-rate sympathetic interpretation of Comte from Caird's neo-Hegelian point of view. See also Hans Barth, *The Idea of Order*, trans. by Ernest W. Hankamer and William M. Newell (New York: Humanities Press, 1960), Ch. 5.

[41] Mill, *Auguste Comte and Positivism*, p. 199.

ment. On the other hand, insofar as his views affect politics at all, the philosophical idealist tends to be conservative to the extent that he regards the realm of ultimate truth in ideas as accessible only to the few rather than to the many. Most philosophical idealists seem to find themselves in this position. Plato, paradoxically, was conservative to the point of being utopian. Kant, with his individualism, did, it is true, bring a new liberal spirit into idealism. But Hegel, though his "spirit" absorbed "idea" and his conservatism was of a uniquely dynamic variety, must be counted both an idealist and a conservative.

Green

The so-called Oxford Idealists, neo-Hegelians all, displayed the incipient tendencies toward conservatism that one might expect. But practical English individualism kept creeping in, sometimes in disguise, to divert and even thwart authoritarian conclusions. Thomas Hill Green (1836–82), the dominant figure in the group,[42] was the most liberal; or, one might better say, he rejected the old liberalism in such a way as to help create a new liberalism. Green was an idealist in both of the preceding senses and as a hard-working elected member of the Oxford City Council and School Board, a temperance leader, and a philosophy professor, he knew political thought and action from many angles.

Liberty was, in a way, Green's fundamental concern; but this was not liberty in the old liberal sense of absence of restraint, or negative liberty. His concept of liberty is positive—not freedom *from* but freedom *for*—and is part of a long tradition:

freedom is in some sense the goal of moral endeavor . . . there is some will in a man with which many or most of his voluntary actions do not accord, a higher self that is not satisfied by the objects which yet he deliberately pursues.

Some such notion is common to those different theories about freedom which in the rough we have ascribed severally to the Stoics, St. Paul, Kant, and Hegel. . . . So far as the proposition means anything it would seem to represent Kant's notion . . . of there being two wills or selves in a man, the "pure" will or ego and the "empirical" will or ego, the pure will being independent of a man's actual desires and directed to the fulfillment of a universal law of which it is itself the giver.[43]

The problem in Green and the Oxford Idealists stems not so much from this Kantian view of selfhood as from the attempt to identify this "higher self" with the purposes of the state. The state is at one point called a "society of societies" but it is not the simple existential phenomenon the utilitarians took it to be. "It is a mistake to think of the State as an aggregation of individuals under a sovereign." It is a moral entity, somehow identical with the "true selves" of all. It "secures and extends the exercise of powers which men, influenced in dealing with each other by an idea of common good, had recognized in each other as being capable of direction to that common good. . . . It is not a state unless it does so." As against the legalistic utilitarians, Green goes to great lengths to illustrate the degree to which we all depend upon some conception of the common good to maintain social life itself. His existential and experiential evidence on behalf of this contention was perhaps Green's strongest feature.

One of the latter-day members of the movement said of the Oxford group: "[They] went for their philosophical inspiration to some very undemocratic sources, to Plato and to Hegel, as well as to Kant and the seventeenth century Puritans; but their purpose in so doing was to carry out better and more thoroughly what the Utilitarians had begun."[44] Such a statement tends to minimize the sharp differences that in fact separated the idealists from the utilitarians. For one thing,

[42] Others were F. H. Bradley, Bernard Bosanquet, D. G. Ritchie, and Edward Caird. Their influence continued into the twentieth century through such figures as A. D. Lindsay, the Master of Balliol College. See Lindsay, *The Modern Democratic State* (New York: Oxford Univ. Press, 1947).

[43] *Lectures on the Principles of Political Obligation*, sec. 19 (London: Longmans, Green, 1941), pp. 18–19.

[44] A. D. Lindsay, in the Introduction to *Lectures on Political Obligation*, p. ix.

Green was not much interested in the mechanics of democracy, systems of representation and the like. The *Lectures on Political Obligation* were addressed to questions that were more ethical than legal or political, in the narrow sense of those words. His thought was democratic only in the sense that its premise was also a democratic premise, namely—in the words of one of Green's chapter titles—"Will, not force, is the basis of the state."[45] While most utilitarians regarded rights as the expression of individual self-interest, Green saw rights as but one aspect of the necessity for all moral acts to be directed toward a common good. Rights, thus, inhere in individuals only insofar as those individuals are members of a society that recognizes such rights. Society (or, rather, the state) is the determiner of the good, instead of the individual, as was the case in both contractualist and utilitarian thought.

Green is not, however, it must be hastily added, as authoritarian as this might make it appear. ". . . if we regard the state as the sustainer and harmonizer of social relations it would follow that the individual can have no right against the state; that its law must be to him of absolute authority. But in fact as actual states at best fulfill but partially their ideal function, we cannot apply this rule to practice." There follows what is, perhaps necessarily, a somewhat cloudy discussion of when the individual can resist the dictates of his state, from which Green concludes that the individual has no rights against the state "founded on any right to do as he likes. Whatever counter-rights he has must be founded on a relation to the social well-being, and that a relation of which his fellow citizens are aware. He must be able to point to some public interest, *generally recognized as such* [our italics], which is involved in the exercise of the power claimed by him as a right." Although Green read and admired John Stuart Mill, there is a world of difference between Green's reliance upon what is generally accepted and Mill's one man who is justified in standing alone against the whole world.

The problem of rights takes us to the central problem in Green, one we have already hinted at—the problem of the relationship between state and society, or, what is almost the same thing, between the state as power and the state as moral consensus. On the one hand, Green speaks in this fashion: "To ask why I am to submit to the power of the state is to ask why I am to allow my life to be regulated by that complex of institutions without which I literally should not have a life to call my own." The state here appears to be the natural force of the social whole from which we can never escape and to which we owe everything. Government is but a minor part of this complex. On the other hand, the state seems also to be a specific institution, a part and not the whole. It is the "sustainer and harmonizer of social relations," a function that "actual states at best fulfill but partially." In this context the state is finite and partial. It is creature not creator. It is not the source of moral standards but is to be judged by moral standards arising elsewhere, from society at large or, perhaps, from T. H. Green at large:

the state, or the sovereign as a characteristic institution of the state, does not create rights, but gives fuller reality to rights already existing. It secures and extends the exercise of powers, which men, influenced in dealing with each other by an idea of common good, had recognized in each other as being capable of direction to that common good. . . . It is not a state unless it does so.[46]

Contemplating this confusion between state and society, Hobhouse, who regarded himself as a spokesman for post-utilitarian liberalism, says, "it is only misleading to identify the entire [social] fabric with a state organization which is only one of its necessary components. . . . By playing between these two meanings, we get the worst

---

[45] *Lectures on Political Obligation*, p. 121. See the discussion in Barker, *Political Thought in England*, pp. 30–31. Subsequent quotations are from this edition.

[46] *Ibid.*, sec. 133, p. 138.

of both worlds.".[47] Hobhouse finds many other inconsistencies: for example, in one place Green regards rights as "made by recognition"; in another place, rights "remain rights though any particular state or all states refuse to recognize them." But Hobhouse does more than merely point out discrepancies. He launches a devastating attack on the fundamental tenets of the whole school, namely that true individual freedom lies in conformity with our "real will"; that our "real will" is identical with the "general will"; and that the "general will" is embodied in the state. All of this, finds Hobhouse, rests upon metaphor rather than evidence, sentiment rather than logic.

Hobhouse, we must confess, seems to win his argument; but on pragmatic grounds he is opening the door to more state regulation than the older liberals would have liked and, on nonpragmatic grounds, the net effect of Green's doctrines is precisely the same. Though his specific economic ideas are strictly middle-class, Green sees the function of the state as a moral one: to improve the character of its individual members. In the simplest terms it can be said that he helped to justify the positive state by metaphysical arguments, while men like John Stuart Mill and Hobhouse were accepting the positive state without abandoning as decisively the tenets of early liberalism. It should not be surprising that political idealism, as it was refined and extended, moved in both conservative and liberal directions: conservative in men like Bosanquet in England and, to the far right, Gentile in Italy; liberal in men like Croce in Italy, Barker in England, and Hocking in the United States.

Political idealism corrected the error of those liberals who failed to take the independent moral worth of society seriously and made the individual unrealistically autonomous. In so doing, idealism, like virtually all movements of thought, overcorrected and made

possible authoritarian extension.[48] But no system is perfect and, despite his inconsistencies, we can hardly help but be grateful for the good will that animated everything Green wrote.

Elitism

If idealism is only tenuously related to conservatism, how much more so is elitism, by which we mean any view that assigns the capacity to govern to a specially selected group or type of individual. If we wish to play with labels, we could call Burke a conservative, half-liberal elitist, Comte a reactionary-radical elitist, and Marx a radical-socialist elitist. Perhaps the purest kind of elitism is that which looks longingly to "great men," almost irrespective of ideology. Nietzsche, as we shall see in Chapter 22, is a writer in this category.

Carlyle

Another such writer is Thomas Carlyle (1795–1881) and we shall pay him brief attention here. He cannot be called typical of nineteenth-century elitists, since the genre is without common markings, but he could probably have happened only in the nineteenth century. Carlyle had no system. System is probably impossible for one who believes that history is nothing but the biography of great men. A simple conception of history, you say, and it is: ". . . no time need have gone to ruin, could it have found a man great enough, a man wise and good enough."[49] But, though simple, not without mystery. "History is the essence of innumerable Biographies. But if one Biography, nay, our

---

[47] Leonard T. Hobhouse, *The Metaphysical Theory of the State: A Criticism* (London: Allen & Unwin, 1918), p. 82. Hobhouse at this point is actually attacking Bosanquet but the point is valid against Green as well.

[48] Perhaps Green's clearest and most conspicuous departures from Hegel's conservatism were his erection of universal brotherhood as a political goal and his vigorous attacks on war as a solution to international tensions. Moreover, as John R. Rodman has argued, in his attack upon "privilege," "Green stood squarely in the mainstream of the Radical tradition" (Introduction to his edition of *The Political Theory of T. H. Green* [New York: Appleton-Century-Crofts, 1964], p. 9).

[49] *Heroes, Hero-Worship, and the Heroic in History* (1841), Lec. 1 (New York: Burt, n.d.), p. 15.

own Biography, study and recapitulate it as we may, remains in so many points unintelligible to us, how much more must these million, the very facts of which, to say nothing of the purport of them, we know not, and cannot know!"[50] In the dazzling stylistic pyrotechnics of Carlyle's essays one finds doubt and faith, compassion and cruelty. He is wholly subjective and egocentric, a former Calvinist infected by German romanticism, building little cofferdams against the democratic tides.

Carlyle detested the industrial revolution and what it did to men:

I will venture to believe that in no time, since the beginnings of Society, was the lot of these same dumb millions of toilers so entirely unbearable as it is even in the days now passing over us. It is not to die, or even to die of hunger, that makes a man wretched; many men have died; all men must die,—the last exit of us all is in a Fire-Chariot of Pain. But it is to live miserable we know not why; to work sore and yet gain nothing; to be heart-worn, weary, yet isolated, unrelated, girt-in with a cold universal Laissez-faire; it is to die slowly all our life long, imprisoned in a deaf, dead, Infinite Injustice, as in the accursed iron belly of a Phalaris' Bull! This is and remains forever intolerable to all men whom God has made. Do we wonder at French Revolutions, Chartisms, Revolts of Three Days?[51]

Yet Carlyle had no reforms in mind to correct the evils of industrialism other than paternal reliance on great men, in this case the "Captains of Industry," who, "if Industry is ever to be led, are virtually Captains of the World! If there be no nobleness in them, there will never be an Aristocracy more." By the same token, utilitarian slogans about liberty were nothing as against the need for men who could keep the ignorant masses from destroying themselves.

You do not allow a palpable madman to leap over precipices; you violate his liberty, you that

are wise. . . . Every stupid, every cowardly and foolish man is but a less palpable madman: his true liberty were that a wiser man, any and every wiser man, could, by brass collars, or in whatever milder or sharper way, lay hold of him when he was going wrong, and order and compel him to go a little righter.[52]

Democracy is only an option when men despair of finding heroes who can lead them. That the casting of a vote in a polling booth constitutes a significant act of self-leadership is a nonsensical and superstitious fiction of "our National Palaver." That all men are in some sense equal is nothing less than ridiculous.

As he grew older, Carlyle seemed less and less charitable toward the working man; but at all periods he seemed to think that the need to worship great men was psychologically necessary as well as socially useful: ". . . if worship even of a star had some meaning in it, how much more might that of a hero! Worship of a hero is transcendent admiration of a great man. I say great men are still admirable; I say there is, at bottom, nothing else admirable."[53] Little wonder that, given Carlyle's latent Calvinism, the duty of obedience to superiors becomes a prime virtue and the style of leadership of the hero over the masses becomes comparable to that of a drill sergeant handling raw recruits. Fluctuating between humanitarian concern for the victims of laissez faire and castigation of their idleness, between praise of great men and blame of the mere "talkers" in Parliament, Carlyle offered few solutions to "the condition of England." To call him a feudal socialist is misleading. But the term is, perhaps, appropriate to his admirer, Ruskin.

Ruskin

John Ruskin (1819–1900) was not a socialist in our meaning of the term. The label "feudal socialism"[54] is a testament to the

---

[50] *On History* (1830), in *Critical and Miscellaneous Essays,* new ed. (New York: Appleton-Century-Crofts, 1871), p. 220.

[51] *Past and Present* (1843), Bk. III, Ch. 13, in *Works* (London: Chapman & Hall, n.d.), Vol. X, pp. 210–11.

[52] *Ibid.,* p. 212.

[53] *Heroes, Hero-Worship, and the Heroic in History,* p. 13.

[54] Also applied to William Morris (1834–96), the eccentric poet, Oxonian, and furniture manufacturer who

power of the socialist symbol in the late nine-teenth century and also to the power of the in-dividualistic assumptions against which social-ism fought. Any alternative to the competi-tive-individualistic society that produced and was produced by the machine tended to be shunted into the socialist camp, since there the anti-individualists seemed to have their headquarters. Ruskin—artist, art critic, Ox-ford professor, and supporter of a fantastic variety of good causes—has been a much neglected figure in the history of political thought. His call for the reorganization of a decadent society in the interests of creating the necessary preconditions for great art has a disorderly pungency about it that is still compelling. The materialism, the blindness to economic misery, and the cheap standards he saw everywhere around him evoked a pas-sionate appeal for a cooperative rather than a competitive society, one that sanctified honest craftsmanship rather than tawdry success.

Ruskin criticized classical economics for its disregard of man's "social affections," for treating him like a "covetous machine." To stimulate a sense of craftsmanship in all men he would pay good and bad workmen identi-cal wages, on the analogy of physicians' uni-form fees, so that the motives for doing better work would be intrinsic to the job and not tainted by mercenary feelings. And he would establish government workshops and factories that would turn out model creations of every necessity and art at model prices. This would hold aloft a standard of excellence for private enterprise and enable every man to know the experience of buying "bread that was bread, ale that was ale, and work that was work."[55]

Ruskin scarcely considered the bureau-cratic implications of his proposals, although a deep-seated paternalism rode along with the sometimes progressive, sometimes regres-sive notions. He blamed the system for un-employment but he blamed the unemployed even more. He would have had the govern-ment give work to the unemployed but with-hold wages until the worker "has come to a sounder mind respecting the laws of unem-ployment." Like Plato he made rulership a restricted profession and equated democracy with anarchy. A brilliant but erratic man, al-most the equal of Carlyle in literary powers, Ruskin—with the help of Morris—inspired the subsequent Guild Socialist movement. In his desire to make every man an artist he would have treated men as children; yet his vision of a society dominated at every level by a soothing blend of cooperative affection and pure artistic value is as much an indict-ment of the twentieth-century machine age as it was of the society of its own day.

Racism

The elitism of certain nineteenth-century racists is different in kind from the elitism we have been discussing. Its significance is more historical than intrinsic. Today we look at these writings to find the roots of Nazi and Fascist race theories. But we can regard them also as one manifestation of the concern for biology as a key to history peculiar to the Darwinian age. Their content is less reward-ing.

The two best-known racists of the later nineteenth century were Count Arthur Joseph de Gobineau (1816–82), a Frenchman claim-ing German blood, and Houston Stewart Chamberlain (1855–1926), an Englishman claiming German blood.[56] De Gobineau res-

---

helped organize the Socialist League in 1884. Like Ruskin, he was dedicated to the elimination of the "eyeless vulgarity" of Victorian culture but, as revealed in his fictional utopia, *News From Nowhere* (1890), he was more willing to entertain thoughts of revolution.

[55] *Unto This Last* (1860), in *The Seven Lamps of Architecture, Sesame and Lilies, Unto This Last* (Boston: Estes, n.d.), p. 144.

[56] See De Gobineau, *Essai sur l'inégalité des races humaines* (1853–55), trans. by A. Collins as *The In-equality of Human Races* (London: Heinemann, 1915); Chamberlain, *Die Grundlagen des neunzehnten Jahr-hunderts,* 2nd ed., trans. by J. Lees as *The Foundations of the Nineteenth Century* (London: Lane, 1912). An important disciple of De Gobineau in France was Hip-polyte Taine (1828–93), who attacked the "metaphysical concepts" of general will, social contract, and consent of the governed, stressed in the manner of Hegel and Treitschke the naturalness of conflict and the "positive fact of force," and sought a return to the "organic rules of society," namely (1) rule by aristocracy, (2) regional-ism combined with naturalism, and (3) heightened race

urrected and polished up the label "Aryan" to designate those people he thought biologically superior, the Persians in Asia and the Teutons in Europe. Europeans in general (except for the "somewhat inferior" Jews) were superior to the Chinese, and the Chinese were superior to the Negroes. De Gobineau's training in poetry led him to the "scientific" conclusion that the process of polluting Aryan blood with that of inferior races had better stop or we would all be in trouble. Chamberlain likewise thought that the Teutons were responsible for everything good in philosophy, politics, economics, science, culture, and lager beer. The most Teutonic people of all, the Germans, were, it follows, a "master race," a concept defended by reference to the indisputable fact that there are many, many different breeds of dogs, and some can bark louder than others.

SOCIALISM

Liberalism established the authority of the individual, against which the conservatives reasserted the authority of the community. Socialism in the nineteenth century was groping toward the establishment of the authority of the class. But this culmination in the work of Marx was preceded by a wide variety of non-Marxian socialisms. Perhaps the best known are the works of the utopian socialists, of whom we may look briefly at three—Saint-Simon, Owen, and Fourier.

Utopian Socialism

Every age seems to produce its utopias. From Plato to More to Orwell men have been fascinated by tales of what might be but is not. A utopia (literally, "no place") may be optimistic or pessimistic. Today's utopias, called "science fiction," run toward

the pessimistic. In the nineteenth century they were generously optimistic.

Saint-Simon

The colorful character of Count Claude Henri de Rouvroy de Saint-Simon (1760–1825) has perhaps spread an undeserved veneer of glamor over all subsequent utopians. Defiant, egoistical, and impulsive, he dashed off to fight—and fight well—in the American Revolution and afterwards headed for Mexico to try to persuade the viceroy to build something like the Panama Canal. Back in France he renounced his title and supported the Revolution but nevertheless wound up in jail. There came his great vision: Charlemagne appeared to him in a dream and commissioned him to become a great philosopher. He spent the rest of his life and his fortune trying—unsuccessfully. In poverty, he attempted suicide in 1823 but the shot was not fatal and he lingered on for two more years.

Saint-Simon left behind a mountain of writings demonstrating that the workers (*les industriels*) produced the most of what was valuable but received the least by way of reward. He proposed that the whole society be organized as a factory with each man rewarded solely on the basis of his work. The politics of this transformation Saint-Simon left wholly unexplored; and though he left behind a dedicated band of disciples, they were not much help on the point.[57]

Owen

Of considerably greater influence were Robert Owen (1771–1858) and Fourier. Owen's is the story of a successful businessman who became a radical reformer. Rising from a draper's apprenticeship to become a prosperous Manchester cotton manufacturer, he decided to attempt an experiment when he took over what was supposed to be a

consciousness. See also the American, Madison Grant, *The Passing of the Great Race* (New York: Scribner's, 1916).

[57] See Frank E. Manuel, *The New World of Henri de Saint-Simon* (Cambridge, Mass: Harvard Univ. Press, 1956). Saint-Simon's influence is, in part, the subject of Manuel's *The Prophets of Paris* (Cambridge, Mass.: Harvard Univ. Press, 1962).

model factory at New Lanark, Scotland. This factory had been blessed with schools for children, which they attended *after* their eleven-and-a-half-hour working day (in twelve years only fourteen children had died from overwork). The town saw large families crowded into one room, garbage piling up in the streets, pubs galore, and every Saturday night a wild, despairing debauch. Owen cleaned up the place. He introduced sanitation, nursery schools, and good cheap whiskey combined with fines for drunkenness. By the time he came to America to set up his New Harmony, Indiana, experiment, he was so famous he was asked to address Congress. The Indiana experiment, incidentally, cursed with a democratic constitution, gave Owen all kinds of trouble. But with or without trouble, Owen became a symbol of encouragement to popular education, workers' cooperatives, and labor unions.

Philosophically, Owen began as a Benthamite. But one major deviation put him on a distant shore: he rejected self-interest as the basis of happiness. Furthermore, man is, he felt, a product of his environment and society can therefore transform self-interest into altruism:

there is no fixed standard, in any part of the world, of a good or a bad man; both terms have ever been the creation of the prejudices and imaginations of the human mind, according to the education it has received. . . . Men are made to be what they are, by their organization, and the external circumstances which act upon and influence it. None are or can be bad by nature; their education is always the business or work of society and not of the individual.[58]

Owen does recognize inherited, "constitutional" factors, but he does not seriously examine the interaction between inheritance and environment, nor does he wrestle with the philosophic problem of how a completely determined man can transform the environment that makes him what he is. Owen simply *assumes* that the essential nature of man is altruistic, using rather conventional English notions of altruism.

If one were to eliminate, therefore, such encumbrances as property, family, and orthodox religion, the spontaneous urge for human solidarity would burst forth:

The individuality of man, unavoidable by his nature, which is, now, through ignorance, a cause of so much disunion of the human race, will become the cause of the more intimate union, and of the increase of pleasure and enjoyment. Contrasts of feelings and opinions which have been, hitherto, causes of anger, hatred and repulsion, will become sources of attraction, as being the most easy and direct mode to acquire an extended knowledge of our nature and of the laws which govern it.[59]

The shallowness of Owen's thinking is apparent. Good and bad are wholly relative and dependent upon peculiarities of environment. Change certain nineteenth-century environmental conventions and the true laws of man's good nature will be revealed. The two propositions can hardly be made compatible.

Owen's deepest faith was in industrial efficiency and his great antagonist was the "pandemonium" of a society constructed around and hence perpetuating egocentric economics. As long as society was based on such economic assumptions, all the "political devices" attained by the liberals—equal representation, extensions of the suffrage, and so forth—were worthless. Almost by default, therefore, Owen reduced political problems to unimportance and was blind to the totalitarian possibilities of his ideal society. Without such "political devices" for self-protection the individual was wholly absorbed in the social unit. Owen's ideal society was held together by a rigid class structure based wholly on age. He loved children—they were so malleable. Children were the trainees. The middle-aged did the work, the old governed, and the oldest handled foreign affairs. (His

[58] Robert Owen, *The Book of the New Moral World* (London: Effiingham Wilson, 1836), pp. 74-75. His other major work is *A New View of Society* (1813). See Margaret Cole, *Robert Owen of New Lanark* (New York: Oxford Univ. Press, 1953), and Arthur L. Morton, *The Life and Ideas of Robert Owen* (New York: Monthly Review Press, 1963).

[59] *Ibid.*, pp. 90-91.

ideal-sized unit was, of course, the town, not the nation.)

What about conflict within the community? There would not be any, since altruists do not have conflicts. Government would be, therefore, merely the administration of things rather than the rule of men—in anticipation of the Marxist utopia. The general will would reign supreme. But even Rousseau had wrestled with the problem of controlling the particular will. Owen simply ignored such problems. He could not imagine the possibility of an individual wanting to leave an Owenite association.

Owen was a practical as well as a theoretical failure. The working class had already found cause for some hope in political participation, in achieving the liberal reforms Owen scorned. Actually he had a distaste for hard political conflict. A genteel and benevolent paternalist, he thought he could persuade wealthy men to see the light and that would be enough. He had a falling out with one of his lieutenants in 1834 when he accused the man of stirring up class hatred in articles calling for a general strike. Owen approved of the general strike but somewhat inconsistently thought agitation for it should be carried on in a spirit of complete magnanimity, "merely by an overwhelming moral influence, which influence individuals and nations will speedily perceive the uselessness and folly of attempting to resist."[60] Workers were not interested, however, in harmony for its own sake. They hated the bosses and wanted to get out of them what they could. Hence, ironically, Marx was to call Owen a "class collaborator."

Fourier

Charles Fourier (1772–1837) was a slightly insane traveling salesman who, with amazing perseverance and enthusiasm, wrote mounds of repetitious prose in hotel rooms all over Europe. On the surface, he seems to be the opposite of Owen. Owen was a radical en-

vironmentalist; Fourier was a radical non-environmentalist. Human nature was not malleable; it was fixed, static; human passions have been the same in all periods of history. This would seem to provide a solid base for conservatism. But Fourier argued that these fixed passions are good as well as fixed and that existing social organization has frustrated and perverted them. Hence, by changing the social organization, man's natural goodness would be liberated. In practical results, then, Fourier is very close to Owen. One changes man, the other liberates the real man.

Like Bentham, Fourier had a mania for classification and worked out a catalogue of the twelve basic human passions. He, like Owen, attacked the competitive chaos of the new capitalistic society but he admired its efficiency and productivity. Like the French reactionaries, he stressed the value of solidarity within small communities, to which he gave the name phalanxes (*phalanstères*). His descriptions of life in the phalanxes were incredibly detailed—we shall charitably omit his similarly detailed descriptions of life on other planets—with heavy emphasis on the centralized kitchen that turned out the fabulous meals that Fourier, a bachelor, probably never enjoyed in reality. Given free play, the twelve passions of man (the five senses; the four "group passions" of friendship, love, family feeling, and ambition; and the three "distributive passions" for planning, change, and unity) will automatically combine into the one supreme passion of love for others. When people come together in phalanxes of from four hundred to two thousand, share a great central building, and work at the tasks they most enjoy (mainly agricultural), everyone is happy. Even the dirty work of garbage collection and slaughtering gets done voluntarily because, as we all know, this is what children most love to do.

Reflecting the capitalist mentality Fourier thought he was expunging, the economics of the phalanx is that of a joint stock company. All invest in the enterprise and the profits are split five twelfths to labor, four twelfths to capital, and three twelfths to talent. The gov-

[60] Quoted in G. D. H. Cole, *Robert Owen* (London: Benn, 1925), p. 216.

ernment was more democratic than in Owen's associations, since officers were elected, but with everyone so full of joy, little government was needed. Movement between phalanxes was possible without hindrance, as was movement between jobs within phalanxes. If Owen erred on the side of too little movement, surely Fourier erred on the side of too much movement. Harmony would become anarchy.

Yet despite what seems extreme impracticality Fourierism was tried in France and worked with some success;[61] some forty Fourierist phalanxes were established in the United States. The most famous was Brook Farm in Massachusetts (the subject of Hawthorne's novel *The Blithedale Romance*), which had been established earlier by George Ripley but was converted to the Fourier gospel through the efforts of Albert Brisbane in 1844. The New England transcendentalists —Emerson, Thoreau, Alcott, Hawthorne— looked on approvingly. All the Owenite and Fourierist experiments failed eventually but the spirit of new life in America was an encouraging atmosphere for such ventures and it was great fun while it lasted.[62]

Anarchism

Proudhon

Pierre-Joseph Proudhon (1809–65) is hard to classify, but he was probably the first man to call himself an *anarchist,* that is, one opposed to all organized government, so we shall accept the designation.[63] An impoverished printer's compositor who read everything he set and seemed to forget none of it, he criticized Owen and Fourier for inad-

vertently substituting a new despotism for an old. He drove sharply to the root of their defect, their assumption of inherent human goodness. Somewhat in the terms of traditional religion—though he was strongly anti-clerical—Proudhon saw man as characterized rather by an inner struggle between good and evil and responsible for his own condition as much as conditions are responsible for him. Man's passions are not all evil, but they need to be contained.

It follows that real advance is always spiritual advance. On these grounds Proudhon unsparingly and even-handedly attacked *both* capitalism and socialism, being one of the few political theorists in the nineteenth century who did. His first well-known book was *Qu'est-ce que la Propriété? (What Is Property?* 1840). The answer to the question made him notorious: "Property is theft." Property is "the mother of tyranny," the "negation of equality." Not property but labor is the basis of production and under capitalism labor is denied its rightful reward. He was proud of his answer and proud of his notoriety but it made him appear more radical than he actually was. He did, it is true, reject the whole political and religious structure of his day as a tool of economic interests and in this came very close to Marx. And he had the radical's disdain for "solutions." "I build no system. I ask an end to privilege, the abolition of slavery, equality of rights, and the reign of law. Justice, nothing else; that is the alpha and omega of my argument: to others I leave the business of governing the world."[64] Yet like Saint-Simon and Comte he hoped for a science of politics and he was fascinated by the possibility of Lockean contract applied at the nongovernmental level. In order to diminish the power of the central government, he wanted to see a network of contracts between producers for specific purposes, creating "a world of spontaneous self-governing producers."

The aim of Proudhon's scheme was also radical in its simplicity. He sought the pro-

---

[61] See industrialist Jean Godin's description of his "familistère" in *Social Solutions,* trans. by Marie Howland (New York: Lovell, 1886).

[62] Not that Fourierism was the last display of sentimental utopianism in America. Edward Bellamy's charming utopian romance *Looking Backward* (1887) touched off in the late eighties and nineties a wave of "Nationalist Clubs" devoted to Bellamy's technocratic anticapitalist principles.

[63] The classification of Proudhon continues to be a problem. Schapiro regards him as a "herald of fascism" (*Liberalism and the Challenge of Fascism,* Ch. 14).

[64] *What Is Property?* trans. by Benjamin R. Tucker (New York: Humboldt, 1876), p. 14

motion of human dignity conceived in the light of his own stolid peasant virtues, his somewhat puritanical humanism. Though more pessimistic than Owen and Fourier, he felt that by exercising his own personal responsibility man could conceivably reorganize society. He called himself a theorist of poverty, a defender of the poorer classes. What is generally regarded as his major work was *Système des contradictions économiques ou la philosophie de la misère. (The Philosophy of Poverty,* 1846),[65] which led to Marx's brilliant refutation, *The Poverty of Philosophy.* Marx called Proudhon "utopian" because he did not recognize the necessity for a large-scale, class-based revolution, the same criticism Marx made of Owen and Fourier. But Proudhon called Owen and Fourier utopian on quite different grounds, namely, their acceptance of the idea of ultimate harmony, a coming age when moral struggle would cease. On these grounds, as we shall see, Marx, too, is utopian. Alone among the four, Proudhon does not share the progressive eschatology characteristic of the nineteenth century.

Bakunin and Kropotkin

More consistently anarchistic were two exiles from the Russian nobility, Michael Bakunin (1814–76) and Prince Peter Kropotkin (1842–1921). Bakunin exercised greater influence by his activity in organizing and guiding revolutionary secret societies throughout Europe than he did by his disorderly writings,[66] though he felt that he had established the scientific validity of his theories. Private property, religion, and all political authority, he felt, were institutions appropriate for the containment of passions and fears in man's lower stages of development; but evolution had now brought man to a new stage in which coercion could be

replaced by enlightened persuasion once the demoralizing hold of the entrenched power-wielders was broken. Kropotkin traced historically the cooperative as distinguished from the competitive traits of men and concluded that mutual aid rather than conflict explains the survival of human groups. The law of the state was made necessary only after society was divided into hostile classes by pernicious economic doctrines. Like Ruskin, Fourier, and various other nineteenth-century thinkers, he envisioned a future society of free association, where men would work for the joy of creativity and share the fruits of their labor in the spirit of brotherhood. The hopeful background provided by such ideas as these is not, as we shall see, irrelevant to the supposedly more hard-headed Marxist socialism.

The Varieties of Socialism

The nineteenth century was the gestation period for a new approach to political and economic organization called socialism, a name that first appeared in an Owenite magazine. The mosaic of its many youthful varieties is a colorful sight, one that we can scarcely begin to reproduce here. The seemingly unrelenting march of industrialism across Europe brought forth in its wake reactionary feudal socialists like Ruskin and Morris, slightly mad blueprinters of the future like Fourier, and unclassifiable geniuses like Proudhon. The list of utopian fiction the age produced is quite remarkable: Étienne Cabet's *Voyage to Icaria* (1839), Lord Lytton's *The Coming Race* (1870), W. H. Mallock's *The New Republic* (1877), Edward Bellamy's *Looking Backward* (1887), Theodor Hertzka's *Freeland* (1890), William Morris' *News from Nowhere* (1890), and Eugene Richter's *Pictures of the Socialistic Future* (1893).

Socialist organizations were being founded, merged, dissolved, and founded again in bewildering profusion. From the Chartist uprising in 1848, England's milder version of the revolutions occurring all over Europe that year, until sometime in 1854 a group of dedicated "Christian Socialists" met in London

---

[65] Perhaps Proudhon's best work was *De la justice* (1861), in four volumes.

[66] The Russian nationalist Theodore Herzen relates how Bakunin and Proudhon fell to arguing about Hegel one night and in the best bohemian tradition continued arguing until the next morning, neither man changing his physical or intellectual position.

for weekly Bible reading and discussion of social problems. Their leader was the distinguished theologian F. D. Maurice, and a member was Charles Kingsley, the cleric and novelist, whose novels of social protest, *Alton Locke* (1850) and *Yeast* (1851), were widely read. Before the abortive Chartist march of workers on Parliament (April 10, 1848), Kingsley and John Ludlow, a Fourierist, had stayed up all night writing placards calling for justice. The group sponsored a Workingmen's College in London, which Maurice headed until 1872.

In 1879 the American Henry George published *Progress and Poverty,* a discerning attack upon the wage-fund theory of economics in particular and landlordism in general. His less discerning solution of the single tax on land nevertheless evoked tremendous response at home and abroad, and Henry George Schools of Social Science were founded that still survive in the 1960s. George made five trips to England, impressing such men as George Bernard Shaw, William Morris, and the Marxist Henry Hyndman. In Germany Ferdinand Lassalle and August Bebel, in France Fernand Pelloutier, in England the Fabian Society[67] in their quite different ways labored for the triumph of the working class. Trade unionism, syndicalism, anarchism, Fabianism, guild socialism, Marxian socialism, and other isms more numerous than we care to remember bear witness to a new society struggling both to understand and to correct itself.

Ideas need organizations to make them socially effective, although the best ideas are not always, of course, matched with the best organizations. The political strength of socialism, especially Marxian socialism, was certainly increased by its connection with workers' organizations that in greater or lesser degree reflected the new society born of industrialism. Yet, parodixically, it was the old liberal ideas of individual freedom that sparked the socialist protest and gave it much of its moral content at the very time it was speaking for a class to which old-fashioned liberal individualism was becoming irrelevant.

CONCLUSION

The nineteenth century is perhaps as close to the present as we can get and still talk intelligibly about such broad schools of thought as liberalism, conservatism, and socialism—even though we shall continue to try with twentieth-century materials. Part of the difficulty is that vision blurs when objects are too close to us. But the difficulty is compounded by the fact that traditions theretofore relatively stable were dramatically overturned in the nineteenth century. A tradition of logic was overturned by Hegel; a tradition of speculation was overturned by Marx; a tradition of morals was overturned by Nietzsche. The century was also revolutionary in its application of theory to practice. It was a tremendous change to move in one century from the heyday of the small private entrepreneur struggling to be free of feudal restrictions to the day of the mass, class-based party struggling against the large capitalists. The sweep of this change can be seen by comparing the work of Bentham, whom we examine next, with the work of Marx, whom we shall examine later.

---

[67] Founded by George Bernard Shaw, Sidney and Beatrice Webb, and Graham Wallas, and later joined by H. G. Wells, Ramsey MacDonald, Keir Hardie, and G. D. H. Cole. The faith of Fabianism was a faith in facts: rigorous factual analysis of specific social conditions "without fear or favor" would open the way to reform. The faith prompted some brilliant essays. See George Bernard Shaw, *Essays in Fabian Socialism* (Edinburgh: Clark, 1932); *Fabian Tracts,* Nos. 1–181 (London: The Fabian Society, 1884–1916); and *Fabian Essays* (London: The Fabian Society, 1931). A new edition of the *Fabian Essays,* edited by John Rodman, will be published in 1968.

19

BENTHAM

To make Jeremy Bentham a nineteenth-century great rather than an eighteenth-century near-great takes a bit of justifying. His utilitarian descendant John Stuart Mill, who was indubitably a nineteenth-century figure and had as well a richer, more sensitive intellect, might better seem to deserve this chapter. But Bentham can be regarded as great not for what he was but for what he did. An eighteenth-century *philosophe* in mentality, he was a necessary bridge between that frame of mind and nineteenth-century democratic reforms. He spoke with an eighteenth-century distaste for medieval superstition and could scarcely have understood the warm reverence for a sense of community that animated the feudal socialists of later nineteenth-century England. Yet he also represented a practical, calculating, counting kind of logic that was both typically English and typically middle class. The political fruit of this logic was the extension of the suffrage—one man, one vote—symbolized by the Reform Bill of 1832, which was being born as Bentham died. Jeremy Bentham was an eighteenth-century man, yes; but by being democratized, he carried the whole liberal tradition with him into the more democratic nineteenth century.

LIFE

Jeremy Bentham, the eldest son of a modestly successful London attorney, was a remarkably precocious child, writing Latin at five and reading Voltaire at six. The small, weak, and excessively sensitive boy had a miserable time when he was sent to the Westminster School in 1755 and was not much happier when at the age of twelve he entered Queen's College, Oxford. He early wrote, it is said, more easily in French than in English; this may have some significance in explaining his attraction to the French utilitarians.

After receiving his B.A. in 1763 he began to study law at Lincoln's Inn, mainly to please his father. He also returned to Oxford to hear Blackstone's popular lectures on the British Constitution and noted that they were full of fallacies and illogical doctrines. This iconoclastic reaction became a public indictment with the publication of Bentham's *Fragment on Government* (1776). Bentham went to the bar as a "bear to the stake" and, to the despair of his father, his career as a barrister was brief and utterly unsuccessful.

In retreat from the world of affairs, Bentham turned with relief and joy to speculation and reform. But for some time it was only a speculative kind of reform. Bentham preferred to inform the powers that be rather than to challenge them directly. Although critical of the self-evidence of natural-law propositions, Bentham took for granted another kind of self-evidence, inasmuch as he fully expected that those in power, having been shown the correctness of a course of action, would naturally follow it. Bentham's reading during these years, the early seventies, indicates the tradition of which he was a part: Locke, Montesquieu, the Italian Beccaria's work on prison reform, Helvetius' *De l'esprit,* Hume's *Treatise of Human Nature* (1739 and 1740), and Barrington's *Observations on the Statutes* (1766), which helped focus Bentham's attention on the specifics of legal reform. If one can grant the distinction, Bentham was first and foremost a legal reformer rather than a political reformer, although political reform eventually came to hold his attention. His study convinced him that English law was irrational, cruel, cluttered, and burdened with historical irrelevancies from which only lawyers benefited. English law was "a mere jungle of unintelligible distinctions, contradictions, and cumbrous methods through which no man could find his way without the guidance of the initiated, and in which a long purse and unscrupulous trickery gave the advantage over the poor to the rich and to the knave over the honest man."[1]

From all this emerged Bentham's "fundamental axiom," the keystone of his whole outlook: "The greatest happiness of the greatest number . . . is the measure of right and wrong."[2] The phrase itself Bentham attributes to Beccaria, although it actually originated with Hutcheson. The conception is not, at any rate, novel. What Bentham did with it is what counts.

The *Fragment,* published anonymously, did not stay anonymous. It brought Bentham a modicum of fame, enough at least for him to make the acquaintance of the sometime premier Lord Shelburne. This led in turn to contacts with other important people, including one who came to be a chief interpreter and disciple, the Swiss Étienne Dumont.

In 1787 Bentham's *Defense of Usury* was published. The book was an application of Adam Smith's economic principles in a way Smith himself had not condoned; but Bentham respectfully appended a letter to Smith at the end of the book. Two years later came Bentham's greatest work, *An Introduction to the Principles of Morals and Legislation,* which was originally to be but the first part of a massive system. The inability to finish schemes once begun was a special Bentham trait. He was continually being aroused by new ideas that led him away from old projects. The result of this penchant was that most of his writings had to be assembled for publication by his disciples if they were to be assembled at all. Fortunately, Bentham had a flair for attracting disciples.

If Bentham was a philosophic reformer rather than either a philosopher or a politician, he was also a powerful critic. His incisive criticisms of everything from Pitt's Poor Law Bill to French colonialism were acute and disinterested, and often effective. But his fascination with an immense variety of inventions and schemes of reform was largely divorced from considerations of political strategy. Bentham was incapable of being a true party man. Metropolitan police reform, a new type of interest-bearing note, a "frigidarium" for preserving foods, and, above all, his model prison, the Panopticon, consumed his attention. The Panopticon, which supposedly required the most in the way of prisoner industry and the least in the way of supervisory time, drained from Bentham much money and energy before the

[1] Sir Leslie Stephen, *The English Utilitarians* (London: Duckworth, 1900), Vol. 1, p. 278.

[2] Preface to *Fragment,* in John Bowring, ed., *Works* (Edinburgh: Tait, 1838–42), Vol. 1, p. 227. All quotations from Bentham in this chapter are taken from this edition, hereinafter referred to as *Works.*

final frustration of having it rejected by the government.

In 1802 Dumont published *Traités de législation de M. Jeremie Bentham,* a collection of translated and original French pieces that, thanks to Dumont's editing, gave a more straightforward picture of Bentham's thought than the master himself could have put together.

Some time before 1809 (according to Bentham himself) and after the failure of the Panopticon, Bentham awoke to the fact that mere assertion of the best course did not lead governors to adopt it. At this point he began to move in the direction of egalitarian democracy. It was James Mill—who had met Bentham in 1808—who really converted Bentham to political radicalism. Moreover, as Halévy put it, Bentham gave Mill a doctrine and Mill gave Bentham a school. Francis Place, the tailor turned practical politician, also helped turn utilitarianism into a popular political movement. With Bentham's funds the group began in 1824 to publish an organ, the *Westminster Review,* edited by John Bowring, which turned out to be a first step toward the Reform Bill of 1832. The year before, young John Stuart Mill had organized a group devoted to discussing morals and politics and called it the Utilitarian Society.

Bentham's work with codes of law was remarkable for its extent. For ten years he worked on his *Rationale of Evidence.* James Mill published part of it as *An Introductory View of the Rationale of Evidence* (1812) and John Stuart Mill edited a five-volume version in 1827. The *Constitutional Code* came in 1830, two years before Bentham's death. The *Plan of Parliamentary Reform* had appeared in 1818. This work drew the attention of scholars and officials in Spain, Portugal, Tripoli, and Greece, as well as such diverse figures as John Quincy Adams, then the American ambassador to Britain, Aaron Burr, who was cooking up nefarious schemes for Mexico, and Simon Bolivar. In 1811 Bentham wrote to President James Madison proposing a Pannomion, or code of laws, for the United States.[3]

In *The Book of Fallacies* (1824) he ridiculed all sorts of old and irrational customs as well as those who were "alive to possible imaginable evils, dead to actual ones, eagle-eyed to future contingent evils, blind and insensible to all existing ones."

To the end, as Stephen points out, Bentham remained something of a child. Untouched by tragedy or profound love, he was aloof from the realities of practical politics or bitter struggles of any kind. He was an amiable and crotchety bachelor who lived simply, loved gardening and cats and mice—a juxtaposition that, as Stephen put it, "suggests problems as to the greatest happiness of the greatest number"—followed a rigid daily work and walk schedule, and had no use at all for poetry. Yet his amazing intellectual vigor compensated for his shallowness and preserved an example, in Stephen's words, "of the power which belongs to the man of one idea."[4]

THE CRITIQUE OF BLACKSTONE

The first and possibly the most fundamental task Bentham performed was the negative one of undercutting the easy assumptions of conservative brands of eighteenth-century natural law. This he did most effectively in *A Fragment on Government.* The audacity of Bentham's attack on Blackstone, it must be confessed, accounts for no small part of the *Fragment*'s appeal, even today. Bentham cited on the title page a statement from Montesquieu's *L'esprit des lois* to the ef-

---

[3] Bentham delighted in making up new names: the frigidarium, the Panopticon, a Chrestomathic school. To him we owe such terms as "codify," "international," "maximize," and "minimize."

[4] Stephen, pp. 231 and 234. An edition of *The Book of Fallacies* titled *A Handbook of Political Fallacies* has been edited by H. A. Larrabee (New York: Harper & Row, 1962).

fect that nothing retards the progress of knowledge as much as a bad work by a celebrated author because, once having been instructed by it, one must then begin to undeceive oneself. With the greatest energy and enthusiasm Bentham chose to undeceive the reader about the great Blackstone. Fortunately, Bentham in 1776 was not yet afflicted by the prolix style that marred his later work.

But as the preface shows, this is not simply a work of negative criticism, for Bentham is sharing from the outset his great discovery for the reformation of the moral world and the challenge of applying this discovery: ". . . with so little method and precision have the consequences of this fundamental axiom, *It is the greatest happiness of the greatest number that is the measure of right and wrong,* been as yet developed." On this premise, with but a modest show of reluctance, Bentham is brought to point out "some of what appeared to me the capital blemishes of that work [Blackstone's *Commentaries*], particularly this grand and fundamental one, the antipathy to reformation; or rather, indeed, of laying open and exposing the universal inaccuracy and confusion which seemed to my apprehension to pervade the whole." But, of course, it is not merely Blackstone that Bentham is after but what Blackstone represents—the English law in all its constraining, stagnating mumbo-jumbo—for example, *"Equity,* that capricious and incomprehensible mistress of our fortunes, whose features neither our Author, nor perhaps anyone is well able to delineate." And the "tyranny of judge-made law" which was about as bad in Bentham's eyes as the tyranny of "priest-made religion."[5]

In the *Fragment* Bentham frankly aspires to be a "censor" rather than an "expositor," that is, to be a teacher of the art and science of legislation rather than one who merely explains what is. He finds Beccaria the "father of censorial jurisprudence." He admires Montesquieu as the author of a work "of a mixed

5 *Codification Present,* in *Works,* Vol. 5, p. 92.

kind." But before Montesquieu "all was unmixed barbarism." Bentham's objection to Blackstone includes the charge that he is a censor in disguise. He pretends merely to explain the law as it is but actually goes out of his way to justify it.

Two major prongs of Bentham's attack are against contract theory and the separation of powers. He is boring from within the liberal tradition, so to speak, and in the name of common sense knocking the props from under what other liberals had thought the natural products of reason. With telling accuracy Bentham points out how Blackstone in one place uses "society" as a synonym for "government" and in another makes it compatible with the state of nature. In one place it is an original contract in society that produces the state. In another place there seems to be no such thing as an original contract.

Bentham wished to replace contractual assumptions with utilitarian principles. Promises of past subjects to past kings, and vice versa, or even contemporary agreements between kings and subjects provide in themselves no adequate criteria of good government. Only utility can do that, the utility "which alone depends not upon any higher reason, but which is itself the sole and all-sufficient reason for every point of practice whatsoever." In simplest form, Bentham's argument aimed to show that the original contract, however conceived, must have rested on utility and, if so, there were no logical grounds by which utility in the present could be superseded by an out-of-date contract.

In addition to directing assaults upon Blackstone's naive contractualism, Bentham waged war against his simple faith in England's "mixed constitution" and the classical conception of government it implied. The classical typologies were primarily useful to Blackstone, said Bentham, so that "he may save himself the expense of thinking." This typology, you may recall, consisted of (1) government of one, monarchy, whose cardinal virtue was power; (2) government of the few, aristocracy, whose virtue was wisdom; and (3) government of the many, democracy, whose virtue was goodness. Each had its corrupt forms: tyranny, oligarchy, "and then," notes Bentham, "a sort of government fit to break one's teeth, called an *Ochlocracy.*" Blackstone thought the magic of the English Constitution was that it combined the best of each form in its mixed system. Bentham noted that this was shown solely by demonstration, not by empirical evidence, and that the same logical argument could be used to prove that England combined the worst of the three corrupt forms. Along the way Bentham showed how empty of content was the idea of supposedly classical democracy, the government of "all over all," since anything short of this impossible and anarchic extension would by definition be aristocracy or oligarchy.

Bentham's examination of Blackstone's classical conception of democracy suggests two things. First, Bentham was bent on rejecting all theories that were defended mainly on the grounds of traditional sanctity. At least he wished to subject all such time-honored views to the corrosive test of utility. Second, he was not yet a democrat. The dissection of the classical conception of democracy implied no substitution of a modern conception. Bentham's picture of pure democracy comes close to Tom Paine's, whose *Common Sense* was inflaming the American revolutionaries in the same year of 1776. But Bentham was showing the concept to be irrelevant, while Paine was showing it to be the ideal for a good society. Conservatives like Blackstone and Burke, however, were identifying government and society. Bentham was thus neither a conservative nor a revolutionary democrat.[6] The utilitarians and the Tories were together in rejecting the Whig contract theory. This union of utilitarianism and conservatism was, as we have seen, uniquely personified in Hume. Hume had made Blackstone more defensive and had made Bentham's work that much easier.

Bentham had the honesty to acknowledge Hume's contribution and, even more generously, to grant that contract theory may not always have been bad: "With respect to this, and other fictions, there was once a time, perhaps, when they had their use. . . . But the season of *Fiction* is now over."

Bentham was not much more respectful to other forms of natural-law reasoning. Certain practices men universally acceded to, which, because they were so widely accepted, had no need of proof:

In theory they were assumed for axioms: and in practice they were observed as rules. If, on any occasion, it was thought proper to make a show of proving them, it was rather for form's sake than for anything else. . . . On such an occasion the commonplace retinue of phrases was at hand; *Justice, Right Reason* required it, the *Law of Nature* commanded it, and so forth; all which are but so many ways of intimating that a man is firmly persuaded of the truth of this or that moral proposition, though he either thinks he *need not,* or finds he *can't,* tell *why.*[7]

People wish to be governed by the principle of utility, that is, by the standard of their own happiness, but simply do not yet understand that this is so. Their faith in obedience to the king results from his governing in their interests and not vice versa. Bentham punctures the theory of general obedience by showing that it is impossible to rule out altogether the extraordinary situation when obedience to the letter of the law is disastrous; by this means he brings the reader back again and again to the consideration of utility. Promises, in short, are not and should not be self-enforcing. They are kept for a reason. Subjects should obey kings only "so long as the probable mischiefs of obedience are less than the probable mischiefs of resistance" and the duty to obey is synonymous with the interest in obeying.[8] There are overtones of contemporary pragmatism in Bentham's attempt to reduce disputes over the legitimacy of legislation to

---

[6] See Elie Halévy, *The Growth of Philosophic Radicalism,* trans. by Mary Morris (Boston: Beacon Press, 1955), pp. 129–30. Compare John Plamenatz, *The English Utilitarians* (Oxford: Clarendon Press, 1958).

[7] *Fragment,* p. 269.

[8] In the original, the phrase is italicized. "Mischiefs" is one of the vital, but undefined, terms in Bentham's lexicon.

questions of "conjecture concerning so many future contingent matters of fact," in which evidence—almost by itself—seems to play the deciding role. "Men, let them but once clearly understand one another, will not be long ere they agree."

Bentham's touching faith in the social harmony that springs from a common understanding of future consequences has radical implications; but at this stage Bentham cannot be said to have given defenders of rebellion even a foothold from which to transform utility into practical political radicalism. By what sign shall it be known that the mischiefs of rebellion are less than the mischiefs of submission? In general, "it is impossible to find an answer." A particular person must count on "his own internal persuasion of a balance of *utility* on the side of resistance." But without a common sign of such a point, the supreme governor's field of authority "must unavoidably, I think, *unless where limited by express convention*, be allowed to be *indefinite.*" The supremacy of the existing English constitution seems to have crept back into Bentham's theory under a rule different from but no less intractable than that of natural law. Moreover, although Bentham expressly denies that he intends to stifle reform, his semantic realism plays into the hands of governors. The word "duty," for example, "if applied to persons spoken of as supreme governors, is evidently applied to them in a sense which is figurative and improper."

In the *Fragment* Bentham had not yet formulated an ideal theory of government; indeed, he was hardly interested in forms of government. Like Hume, from whom he had gained so much, he felt that the quality of the laws meant much more than their source and, in hard reality, that the habit of obedience may mean more than any logic. The invitation to rebellion that Paine's conception of natural rights gave to the Americans had no place in Bentham's conception of utility at this time. Hence he supported the king against Wilkes and opposed the American rebels. Later, making friends with the Whigs—the Crown had declined to pay

Bentham a sum he claimed—he seemed to deviate from his earlier position to the extent of praising the separation of powers in the English Constitution (*On the Influence of Time and Place in Matters of Legislation and Indirect Legislation*, 1782). Still later, he returned to a more rigorous, if somewhat different, line and attempted to have these passages suppressed.

UTILITY AND LEGISLATION

The *Fragment* was a masterful critique. *An Introduction to the Principles of Morals and Legislation* (1789) was a constructive effort, less successful but more important than the *Fragment*. The nature of Bentham's interest is shown by the fact that *Morals and Legislation* was meant to be merely the preliminary statement of principles upon which was to be built a penal code. His temperament is shown in his failure to complete the project. Here Bentham attempted to spell out the principles of utilitarianism—the word is actually James Mill's. The opening words of the work are so succinct, they reveal so forcefully Bentham's strengths and biases, that they are worth quoting at some length:

Nature has placed mankind under the governance of two sovereign masters, *pain* and *pleasure*. It is for them alone to point out what we ought to do, as well as to determine what we shall do. On the one hand the standard of right and wrong, on the other the chain of causes and effects, are fastened to their throne. They govern us in all we do, in all we say, in all we think: every effort we can make to throw off our subjection will serve but to demonstrate and confirm it. In words a man may pretend to abjure their empire: but in reality he will remain subject to it all the while. The *principle of utility* recognizes this subjection and assumes it for the foundation of that system the object of which is to rear the fabric of felicity by the hands of reason and of law. Systems which attempt to question it deal in sounds instead of sense, in caprice instead of reason, in darkness instead of light.[9]

[9] *Works*, Vol. 1, p. 1.

Then, impatiently, as if ashamed of grace in style, "But enough of metaphor and declamation: it is not by such means that moral science is to be improved."

The first thing that strikes us about this opening is the bold way Bentham admits to an attempt to unite the is with the ought. Granted his premises, a factual judgment and a value judgment are identical. Pleasure and pain determine not only how we live but how we ought to live. If they are also "sovereign masters," it would seem to follow that man is incapable of doing other than he does and a fatalistic pantheism would appear the only logical conclusion. But being roundly irritated by theological questions Bentham was incapable of seeing these implications and preferred instead to do battle with the "caprices" of those who disagreed with him. For despite the alleged sovereignty of pleasure and pain, the "fabric of felicity" is for some reason not yet generally understood. The "felicific calculus" theme must be erected to the position of a standard tool for the determination of public policy. This, in turn, implies the "addibility of happiness" as a practical operation. In 1822 Bentham added a footnote to the above reference to the principle of utility and noted that the greatest-happiness or greatest-felicity principle is an acceptable if not preferable substitute for the original term, for "the word *utility* does not so clearly point to the ideas of *pleasure* and *pain* as the words *happiness* and *felicity* do."

What this means is that every action, whether private or governmental, should be judged by the degree to which it augments or diminishes the happiness of the parties in question. Benefit, advantage, pleasure, good, and happiness are all regarded as synonyms, as are, on the opposite side of the scale, "mischief, pain, evil, or unhappiness." These terms must have reference to individuals, for apart from such concretions they have no meaning: "The community is a fictitious body. . . . The interest of the community then is—what? The sum of the interest of the several members who compose it."

Bentham is the pure nominalist. Words have no intrinsic meaning and do not refer to any universal entities. Their meaning is wholly from usage and is, in a sense, arbitrary.[10] The central concept of interest, upon which almost everything else hangs, is deliberately left undefined: ". . . not having any superior *genus,* [it] cannot in the ordinary way be defined." Other value words, as we might call them, have meaning only within the system of utility. When related to it, "the words *ought,* and *right* and *wrong,* and others of that stamp, have a meaning: when otherwise, they have none." But Bentham is at least honest enough and perceptive enough to grant that the structure is assumed rather than validated: "Is it susceptible of any direct proof? It should seem not; for that which is used to prove everything else cannot itself be proved: a chain of proofs must have their commencement somewhere."

With considerable cleverness, Bentham shows how arguments supposedly opposed to the principle of utility are actually drawn from that very principle, as he conceives it. Asceticism, for example, a supposed alternative to utility, merely tries to demonstrate that a good many pleasures are purchased at too high a cost in pain to be worth fooling with. Then, using a technique probably borrowed from Hume, Bentham challenges his reader: if there is any principle superior to utility by which to judge what a man should pursue, show us what it may be!

After this somewhat satirical review of "principles adverse to that of utility" Bentham leads us into the marvels of the felicific calculus. His taxonomic gyrations leave us breathless. For example, there are, he tells us, fourteen simple pleasures: sense, wealth, skill, amity, good name, power, piety, benevolence, malevolence, memory, imagination, expectation, association, and relief. There are as well twelve simple pains: privation, sense, awkwardness, enmity, ill name, piety, be-

---

[10] Bentham thought "happiness" was such a good word on which to base an ethical system because it was so unequivocal. On one occasion, noting that the authors of *The Federalist* had tried to make justice the end of government, he argued that justice was always a matter of dispute whereas "what happiness is every man knows." *Constitutional Code,* in *Works,* Vol. 9, p. 123.

nevolence, malevolence, memory, imagination, expectation, and association. Each of these is subdivided into its components. Sense, for example, is broken down into taste, intoxication, smell, touch, ear, eye, sex, health, and novelty; privation includes desire, disappointment, and regret; and so forth. The inclusion of some terms as both pleasures and pains merely means, for example, that the sense of touch can provide pain, as with an itching skin, or pleasure, as with a warm bath. Likewise benevolence: it sometimes hurts, sometimes feels good to give. Each simple pleasure or pain can be mixed with another to comprise a complex pleasure or pain. The simple forms are supposedly irreducible. They are also supposedly equal. In an often-quoted tribute to this equality, Bentham somewhere says that "pushpin is the same as poetry if it gives the same pleasure." To help in the comparing, weighing, measuring, and drawing and quartering of all these lumps of pleasure and pain, Bentham gives us seven criteria: intensity, duration, certainty or uncertainty, propinquity or remoteness, fecundity (i.e., the tendency to repeat), and purity (i.e., the chance of not being followed by opposite reactions). The seventh is transpersonal, extent (i.e., the number of persons affected). Armed with these categories, one can judge the worth of all things.[11]

Much fun can be made of all this—and has been. Bentham asked for ridicule by calling himself the Newton of the Moral World. But let us see if we cannot make a case in his behalf. As psychology, Bentham's "addibility of happiness" is absurd. To make mechanical the subtlest and most subjective of feelings is pathetic. But the system did force Bentham to assume the equality of each in-

dividual with every other individual in the sense of the equal worth of his interest. Despite the memory of Hobbes, this kind of thoroughgoing egalitarianism stood in sharp contrast to the assumptions of the age, indeed of perhaps any age. Moreover, once this assumption is granted, it is not so far fetched to talk of at least a crude equation of pleasures and pains distributed among members of a given society. It is at least possible to ask whether the amount of pleasure from security distributed to a large number of people, brought about by the execution of a poor sheep-stealer, is equal to the amount of pain inflicted upon him and his family. It can be asked whether the pleasures of a millionaire landlord are intense enough to balance the pain of several hundred agricultural laborers kept in abject poverty. Perhaps these were questions that needed to be asked.

By his crude equalizing of all pleasures Bentham sought to avoid the problem of values and the question of whether some values are not more fundamental than others. But in any concrete application of the system it is not surprising that Bentham's solid middle-class virtues crept into positions of priority. Benevolence turned out to be an uncommonly important pleasure. Property was a remarkably useful interest. Moreover, Bentham was no utopian. Contrary to what some writers have said of him, his object was not to eliminate all pain. In *Traités de legislation* he recognized that some pleasures must be bought with pain. "We are searching only for the possible," he wrote.[12]

The calculus, though hopeless as psychology, was not hopelessly unsuited for the task for which it was designed—legislation. The aim of Bentham was always the rationalization—in the non-Freudian sense—of the proc-

---

[11] See Bentham's modest *Table of the Springs of Action Shewing the Several Species of Pleasures and Pains of which Man's Nature is Susceptible together with the Several Species of Interests, Desires & Motives Respectively Corresponding to Them and the Several Sets of Appellatives, Neutral, Eulogistic, and Dyseopistic by which each species of Motive is wont to be Designated* (1815). The full title is even longer—by eighty-five words! See *Works*, Vol. 1, pp. 195–218.

[12] Sheldon Wolin has tried to correct the view that liberal theory was infected throughout with utopian optimism: ". . . the liberal's desperate insistence on the privacy of the pleasure-principle as the dominant motivation was meant to compensate for the real source of his worries: the predominance of pain in the world" (*Politics and Vision* [Boston: Little, Brown, 1960], p. 326). Bentham, he argues, was closer to this position than he was to Condorcet or Godwin.

ess of lawmaking. If a lawmaker attempts, as lawmakers must, to weigh the pain of a slight increase in taxes inflicted on a large number of people against the pleasures of a new public-housing project benefiting relatively few, he is at least analogically going through Bentham's felicific calculus. How many people will be affected? How much do these people desire this project? By what amount will their average income be reduced? What percentage of the population is unemployed? These are not mathematical questions but they are quantitative and they illustrate the kind of question the legislator must ask in his effort to get at something more solid than mere whim. Bentham could be called a rationalizer of the welfare state long before the welfare state came into existence.

Although a listing of pleasures and pains such as Bentham's would logically involve an examination of the motives of each individual, in practice the list was nearly always used to assess the *general* felicific consequences of given social actions. Hence we have a bad psychology in the service of a not-so-bad social policy: examine in as much detail as possible the effect of proposed policies and justify them always in terms of these effects rather than by a priori, abstract principles. Surely here is a forerunner of contemporary pragmatism. If the assumption that understanding by itself produces agreement was no more valid for Bentham than for Dewey, this is not to deny the value of first looking unblinkingly at the consequences of a proposed action before seeking agreement.

ETHICAL DIFFICULTIES

To say that Bentham provided a stimulus for legislative action based upon a rational calculation of general numerical happiness is not to say that he provided a philosophically tight rationale for such calculation. Despite his elaborate *Table of the Springs of Ac-*

tion he never overcame the gap between the understanding of motives and the evaluation of consequences, a pitfall for most systems of social ethics. If one grants, as Bentham did, that the same motive could be bad or good depending upon the consequences of the action it induced, then it would seem incumbent upon the legislator to ignore motives altogether and evaluate only the consequences of actions. But in *Morals and Legislation* Bentham notes that the legislator in measuring the "mischievousness" of acts must distinguish between "primary" and "secondary" effects. Loss of useful goods is a primary effect of robbery. But a secondary effect is the suggestion of the possibility of robbery to others, which has a weakening influence on the "tutelary motive" of respect for property. At this point one's judgment on consequences gets mixed up with the change in motives that constitutes the consequence. This is why the administration of justice can never be wholly mechanical. The dilemma is not at all novel. But Bentham did not see that it was a dilemma.

He blithely felt that he could capture goodness in a code. His whole system of ethics was, like most of what he did, wrapped up in his passion for codifying. In *Chrestomathia* (1817) he applied what he called the "dichotomous," or "bifurcate," or "bipartition," method, in which, as if he were classifying crustaceans, he would divide ethical actions into two mutually exclusive but exhaustive classes, then subdivide each of these, and so forth. He granted that it might take centuries to compile in this way a perfectly adequate and accurate catalogue of the ethical life but he believed that it would come. No wonder that he considered metaphysics to be but a minor branch of logic.

Hence a major failure of Bentham was that he confused what was essentially a legal doctrine with a system of private ethics. This confusion, in turn, was possible only because Bentham could rather simple-mindedly and single-mindedly assume that a single motive could be separated from the welter of human drives and inclinations and attached to a single action. He did not deny, of course, that a bundle of intentions could create a predis-position to act that might never be realized in action; but an understanding of such po-tential action was only background data for the legislator. Neither law nor morals really came into play until there was action.

Now private ethics has happiness for its end: and legislation can have no other. Private ethics concerns every member; that is, the happiness and the actions of every member of any com-munity that can be proposed: and legislation can concern no more. Thus far, then, private ethics and the art of legislation go hand in hand. The end they have, or ought to have, in view, is of the same nature. The persons whose happiness they ought to have in view, as also the persons whose conduct they ought to be occupied in directing, are precisely the same. The very acts they ought to be conversant about, are even in a *great measure* the same.[13]

What, if anything, is the difference be-tween ethics and law? There is no case, Ben-tham continues, in which the individual should not seek his own happiness "and that of his fellow creatures." But there are some cases in which the legislator ought not ("in a direct manner at least") to interfere. These are the cases discussed in an earlier chap-ter, in which such interference would be "groundless . . . inefficacious . . . unprofita-ble . . . needless." They include cases when punishment is badly timed; when infants are involved; when evil acts of minor conse-quence are inconveniently mingled with good acts of major consequence; when the sim-plest possible punishment would exceed the magnitude of the offense; when, as in the case of fornication, the possibility of future detection is too slight for present punishment to have much effect; when, as in the case of offenses such as rudeness, any punishment is likely to involve the innocent "in the fate de-signed only for the guilty"; and so forth.

What all this adds up to, then, is that the division between private morality and public law is created only in that realm of behavior the legislator finds inconvenient to bother with. In this conclusion there is a kind of

Hobbesian deference to omnipotent legisla-tive authority, but without the limitation of a contractual myth.

Are there any limitations upon this cen-tral figure of the legislator in Bentham? The answer of course is, yes. Three seem espe-cially worth notice. First, despite the unreal-ism of many aspects of the felicific calculus, there is nevertheless in Bentham a certain earthly realism that, at least in a true Ben-thamite legislator, would keep him from running wild. The sensibly noted inconven-iences mentioned above are an example. The best touches of reality often appear in Ben-tham's footnotes, although even here me-chanical quantification will time and again make Bentham appear a bit silly. At one point he says that a man should not receive the same punishment for giving another man ten blows as for giving him five blows, since he then has the pleasure of giving the second five blows "for nothing." Making the pun-ishment fit the crime is, not illogically, a fe-tish with Bentham.[14] But the reverse of this precept is that punishment must never be more than what is absolutely necessary to bring behavior into conformity with the de-sired social behavior. There is not a trace of vindictiveness in Bentham's system. Neither is there much compassion. But there is enough humanity to impose some self-deny-ing qualities upon the legislator. He is not to concern himself with intimate, private matters in which each man must be assumed to know what best conduces to his own hap-piness but rather to confine himself to "those broad lines of conduct in which all persons, or very large and permanent descriptions of persons, may be in a way to engage." Even here his "interference" can and should be open to dispute: "At any rate he must never

[13] *Morals and Legislation*, p. 144.

[14] Bentham was not unaware of possible reactions to this mechanization: ". . . my fear is, that in the ensuing model, I may be thought to have carried my endeavors at proportionality too far. Hitherto scarcely any atten-tion has been paid to it. Montesquieu seems to have been almost the first who has had the least idea of any such thing. In such a matter, therefore, excess seemed more eligible than defect. The difficulty is to invent: that done, if anything seems superfluous, it is easy to retrench."

expect to produce a perfect compliance by the mere force of the sanction of which he is himself the author. All he can hope to do is to increase the efficacy of private ethics, by giving strength and direction to the influence of the moral sanction." Bentham is quite aware, as we would expect, that a man often knows too little of what would conduce to his own happiness, that is, of what would produce the good; "but is it so certain that the legislator must know more?" At this point Bentham reminds any would-be legislator to remember the story of the oculist and the sot. The former, while himself drinking, prescribes that the latter give up drink if he is to save his eyes. When reminded of the discrepancy in his own behavior, the oculist replies, " 'That's very true, my friend . . . but you are to know I love my bottle better than my eyes.' " If Bentham has a defective sense of moral community, at least he has some respect for the sanctity of moral choice in the individual. This respect may not square with his psychology, but we like him the better for it.

Second, like all his fellow liberals, Bentham did not conceive of a government capable of regulating an entire economic system. Since Bentham did not believe in natural rights, he could not erect natural rights of property as a barrier against governmental action. But he did not need to. The happiness of men was so obviously advanced by leaving them free to borrow, spend, save, invest, and scramble for wages that socialism and utilitarianism could scarcely be spoken of in the same breath. In his *Defense of Usury* (1787) Bentham adopted almost completely the fundamental economic ideas of Adam Smith. What Halévy calls "the principle of the natural identity of interests"—the view, that is, that there is an "invisible hand" that sums up individual egoisms into a social harmony—was as compatible with Bentham's economics as with Smith's. Given this assumption, the government's function in the economic sphere was simply that of enabling men to know their own self-interest better. Hence Bentham spoke of the government publish-

ing new processes and lists of prices, giving prizes for new technological discoveries, protecting inventors through patents, and so forth. Beyond this, the government had no special competence and was too solitary and cumbersome to invest capital in industrial enterprises itself.

On the question of usury, Bentham went even beyond Smith, who felt that usury laws were permissible as long as they did not impinge upon the going market rate of interest. Bentham once wrote, "You know, it is an odd maxim of mine, that interest, as love and religion, and so many other pretty things, should be free."[15] While the language had made "usurer" an ugly word, in fact, argued Bentham, the usurer makes an important contribution to the progress of the economic system and is envied mainly because he has sacrificed in order to save as others have not. The exemption of usury from Bentham's long list of crimes may be taken as symbolic of the distinction Bentham made ironclad: the juridical function of the state was exalted almost in proportion as its economic function was minimized. It seems inconsistent to give the legislator a crucial role in consciously educating the individual through penal laws to a consciousness of his own (and therefore society's) true interest, while at the same time the legislator is denied such a role with reference to the individual's economic interest. Here the identity of individual with social interests was presumed to take place spontaneously. It seems inconsistent and it is inconsistent, and the failure to assimilate economic activity into its view of politics can be regarded only as a major failure of liberal thought. Yet it is too simple to chalk up this lapse to Bentham's unrealism and let it go at that. Or perhaps we could say that, though Bentham is unrealistic, he is not utopian. He carries over into the political sphere the idea of an economy of scarcity—a scarcity of pleasures. The failure of the individual to buy future pleasures with present pain is automatically punished by the

[15] Quoted in Halévy, p. 110.

economic system. In the more vaguely defined political system a legislator is needed to provide the punishment.

Third, the legislator is not unchecked in Bentham's system, at least not in his later system, because there are elections to contend with. With his penchant for elaborate terminology, Bentham could not simply call this the principle of elections. He had to call it the principle of the "universal dislocability of officials." Even earlier he had revealed himself as a somewhat uncertain and qualified democrat. At the time of the French Revolution he had written *An Essay on Political Tactics,* a handbook of essentially English parliamentary procedure intended for the guidance of the new Estates-General. And later in the same year he had written for the French a code of judicial procedure that featured a qualified system of elected ("amovable") judges. One of the interesting qualifications was the principle of "patriotic auction," in which the candidates are invited before the election to offer to pay a sum of money to the state, a sum determined by their own estimate of how much this will impress the voters. This is supposed to assure disinterested judges; but it also weighs the scales on behalf of the rich. Yet in this code Bentham notes, "I have not that horror of the people. I do not see in them the savage monster which their detractors dream of. . . . When the Athenians were cruel and unjust, were the Dionysuses and Artaxerxeses less so?"[16] If Bentham never had a thoroughgoing faith in the wisdom of the common man, at least he also had a healthy distrust of uncommon men who held power.

CONCLUSION

Bentham is still important because utilitarianism is still important. As philosophy and psychology its force has dissipated; as a practical criterion for legislation in democratic countries, however, the maximization of pleasure and minimization of pain for the greatest number of people is demonstrably alive. Much of the argument for such welfare measures as Medicare, rent subsidies, and so forth is couched in latter-day utilitarian terminology. And even college students have been known to declare with reverent voices their faith in the principle of the greatest happiness for the greater number.

In adapting Bentham's eighteenth-century mechanisms to the nineteenth century's belief in process, John Stuart Mill, it is true, succeeded mainly in vitiating utilitarianism's emotional appeal. Unable to live with Bentham's oversimplifications, Mill was forced to make what were, in effect, qualitative distinctions between short-run and long-run utility. The pleasure of poetry was placed on a different plane from the pleasure of pushpin. Too sensitive to be mechanical about majority rule, Mill worried about the "tyranny of the majority" and its psychological effect on the free expression of critical ideas.

But even in Mill the utilitarian distrust of metaphysical abstraction and respect for the concrete fact remain, as does the willingness to use law for educational and reformist purposes. And, finally, the autonomous individual, the man able to decide and act on the basis of his own calculation of self-interest, is still there. The last-named is the most troublesome, for despite Bentham's praise of security when threatened by equality[17] and despite Mill's eventual appreciation of the role of groups in political society, utilitarianism has tended to beg one basic question: can every individual be permitted to seek his own happiness, and that alone,

---

[16] *Works,* Vol. 4, pp. 262–63.

[17] Bentham, we often forget, was never a thoroughgoing egalitarian, least of all in property matters. The legislator should seek to maintain the existing distribution of property lest the security of all be attacked: "When security and equality are in opposition there should be no hesitation: equality should give way. . . . The establishment of equality is a chimera: the only thing which can be done is to diminish inequality" (*Principles of the Civil Code,* Ch. 11, in *Works,* Vol. 2, p. 311).

without utterly destroying the social fabric? Perhaps Hume alone among utilitarians did not avoid this question. But Bentham's vigor is nowhere better shown than in the way he eclipsed Hume in conventional histories of the movement. Although Bentham made an ambiguous distinction between self-regarding and nonself-regarding motives, both of which were part of self-interest rightly understood, this was no way out of the conflict we see between individual welfare and the social good. Bentham simply assumed that in the long run the pursuit of self-interest clarified by a legislator would coincide with the greatest happiness of the greatest number. And so, in essence, did Mill.

Perhaps the problem of individual and society is irresolvable in philosophic terms; but we would like our political philosophers to agonize over the problem as Rousseau did. That Bentham did not feel it was necessary is a clue to his early influence and also to his eventual fall from grace.

20

HEGEL

What shall we do with Hegel? He is too systematic to summarize, too cumbersome to quote, and too influential to ignore. Most chapters and many books that presume to simplify Hegel for the casual reader are doomed to failure. So be it. Let us bravely dare to fail together, for without knowing something about Hegel one can scarcely understand how fully he has penetrated into contemporary thinking about politics, economics, and history and how much the mood of present-day nationalism owes to his categories.

LIFE

Georg Wilhelm Friedrich Hegel, the son of a fiscal official for the Kingdom of Württemberg, was born in Stuttgart in 1770. He attended grammar school at Stuttgart, where his record was adequate but not distinguished, and in 1788 entered the University of Tübingen as a theological student, receiving a Doctor of Philosophy degree in 1790 and a certificate in theology in 1793. Along with his fellow students Hölderlin, the poet,

and Schelling, the philosopher, he tended to neglect the prescribed theological studies in favor of reading the classics. Hence he was early knowledgeable in Platonic metaphysics and attracted to the *polis* as a model of the ethical community. It was the disunity of the German peoples, the particularity of existing political institutions, that made the Greek ideal so attractive to Hegel and his contemporaries. Yet Hegel was determined to correct the failure of the Greeks to make freedom the central attribute of man as man. This same disunity had for Hegel, therefore, religious dimensions as well. Though disillusioned by formalistic, ecclesiastical religion, Hegel was concerned even at this time about the divisive political effects of secularism and, at the personal level, bothered by its egocentric influences. His essay, "The Positivity of the Christian Religion" (1796), praised the simple religion of Jesus while criticizing institutionalized dogma. "The Spirit of Christianity" (1799) showed a shift toward the philosophical as he attempted, now in a somewhat pessimistic mood, to synthesize Christianity with Greek philosophy and Kant.

After leaving Tübingen, Hegel went as a private tutor first to Berne and then to

Frankfurt but, when in 1799 his father died and left him a small inheritance, he set himself up in Jena and plunged into the intellectual life of the university in hopes of qualifying for a university position. In 1801 he was licensed as a *Privatdozent* (a recognized but unsalaried tutor dependent on student fees) and began lecturing on logic and metaphysics. Finally in 1805 he won the professorship he had long sought. Scarcely had his professorial career begun, however, when the armies of Napoleon invaded the area and the great general himself rode through the streets of Jena. "The Soul of the World" commented Hegel on Napoleon, after seeing him. It is doubtful that Hegel so admired Napoleon that his philosophy was touched by that man's affection for power, as some have suggested. The groundwork of the philosophical system was already laid and Hegel soon changed his mind about Napoleon. Perhaps more significant was Hegel's respect for Machiavelli, a theorist who understood the nature of power and the role of great men in the integration of peoples. It is certain, however, that the French Revolution had a profound effect on Hegel, as on most of his German contemporaries. The Revolution constituted an intellectual and ideological challenge to the hierarchical organization of German social life. It symbolized the possibility of reorganizing society on a rational basis, of liberating the individual from the last remnants of feudal authority and establishing his autonomy. However critical he was of the Terror, Hegel felt deeply the need for coming to grips with the French claims of having rationalized society. He did so while affected by German romantic intuitionism, converting both rationalism and intuitionism into a magisterial vision of the world. The multiplicity of interpretations of the Hegelian system is an index of its scope and complexity. Hegel has been called everything from inspiring to dangerous. Schopenhauer repeatedly called him a charlatan. Yet his significance is indisputable and his influence far reaching, and nowhere more so than in political theory. Every major political thinker discussed in the remainder of this book will show the mark of Hegel's conception of history and the political order.

In 1807 came Hegel's first major work, *Phaenomenologie des Geistes (The Phenomenology of Spirit*[1]), an analysis of the consciousness of the self in which "spirit" is seen as the essence of man and history. Close on the heels of this academic success Hegel was forced by the disruption of Jena by the Napoleonic wars to take a job as editor of a newspaper. From 1808 to 1816 he was headmaster of a *gymnasium* in Nuremberg. While there he married the charming and well-educated Marie von Tucker, twenty-two years his junior. Always a "good family man"—he was addicted only to snuff—his affection for wife and children perhaps gave him a keener appreciation of the organic elements in society than that held by the long line of British bachelors we have been studying.

In 1816 Hegel published the last volume of his greatest work, *The Science of Logic,* which contained the systematic working out of the dialectic. The success of the *Science of Logic* was so great that Hegel was immediately offered professorships from Erlangen, Berlin, and Heidelberg. He accepted the Heidelberg position but remained there only until 1818, when the death of Fichte left a vacant chair at Berlin, which Hegel gladly filled. In 1821 he published *The Philosophy of Right.* By this time he was a prominent and noted man. More and more conservative as he aged, he was in high favor with the Prussian government and was decorated by the King of Prussia in the year of his death. Made rector of the university in 1830, he died in November, 1831, after a one-day's illness of cholera. The conservative tendencies of Hegel's later life may have been more than a matter of age. Since he was a believer in the ultimate rightness of historical development it was only consistent that he

[1] John Baillie's noted translation is entitled *Phenomenology of Mind,* 2nd ed. (New York: Macmillan, 1931), but "spirit" is often considered a more appropriate translation of *Geist.* Hegel had published two works prior to this time, *The Constitution of Germany* (1802) and *The History of Philosophy* (1805).

should accept the verdict of history as his earlier enthusiasms—liberal Christianity, Napoleon, classical romanticism—lost out to an authoritarian ethos. Consistent, but also full of tragedy.

Published posthumously were *The Philosophy of History,* a series of lectures delivered between 1822 and 1831; *Lectures on the Philosophy of Religion;* and *Lectures on Aesthetics,* first delivered in 1818. Though he was worshiped by many as a scholar and teacher, Hegel's lectures were apparently delivered in a weak-voiced, painful manner with a broad Swabian accent. Nor was he particularly admired as a person. He was, it is said, "a hard dry man" but, even so, the greatest philosopher of his century.

THE DIALECTIC

It is impossible to review secondary materials on Hegel without being struck by the diversity of "key concepts" that are offered as aids to understanding the system. Reality, spirit, and dialectics, says one. Hegel's six attitudes of consciousness toward reality (simple consciousness, self-consciousness, reason, spirit, religion, and absolute knowledge), says another. Thesis, antithesis, synthesis—terms Hegel did not actually use[2]—says still another. Freedom, mind, subject, and notion, says a fourth. It is a tribute to the richness —some would say the ambiguity—of the system that so many thoughtful men could accentuate such different aspects of it. Actually, everything in the Hegelian system is related to everything else and, if one is concerned with the overall cohesiveness of the whole, he can break into the chain at many different places. But all commentators would agree that Hegel's great methodological contribution is the new logic of the dialectic. It will be helpful if we go back to the problem Hegel was trying to solve. From the first it

[2] See Gustav E. Mueller, "The Hegel Legend of 'Thesis-Antithesis-Synthesis,'" *Journal of the History of Ideas,* Vol. 19 (1958), pp. 411–14.

was a problem with both political and metaphysical dimensions.

A philosopher usually begins by correcting someone else. In the case of Hegel it was primarily the Greeks and Kant. The pursuit of the "empty" abstractions Hegel associated with the idealism of Plato and Kant was, he felt, as ultimately disillusioning as the drive of private egoism. He much admired Kant's ethical philosophy but was determined to transcend its hypothetical character. Dissatisfied with the static logic of mathematics and the geometrical philosophizing of Descartes and Spinoza, he was determined to invent a logic that could capture the ebb and flow of life itself. The result was the Hegelian dialectic.

The dialectic of the Platonic dialogues was simply a method of discourse whereby truth was approached through questions and answers and the repeated examination of the diametrical opposites of any given statement. It was a winnowing-out process directed toward the single center of the Idea of the Good, from which all other categories were a deduction. In the even more rigorous logic of "abstract universals" by which Aristotle attempted to classify all things into genus and species, it was necessary to assume absolute dichotomies. *A* and not-*A* were necessarily in a fixed position of complete opposition. Kant felt that he had reduced the problem of human knowledge to more manageable proportions by working out the twelve irreducible epistemological categories through which all is known.

Hegel's logic of "concrete universals," however, denied the monistic center of Plato's Good, denied the principle of contradiction in Aristotle's logic, and denied that Kant's epistemological categories were fixed in number. Hegel made the seemingly impossible contentions that all categories of thought could be deduced from any one category and that anything that is could be an example of any category. "Hegel found that a concept may contain its own opposite hidden away within itself, and that this opposite may be extricated or deduced from it and made to do the work of the differentia, thus converting genus into species."[3] Traditional logic, Hegel granted, was suitable for analysis, the breaking up of wholes. This produces "understanding" (*Verstand*), a valuable but limited form of knowledge. The higher logic of the identity of opposites was required for synthesis, the restoration of wholeness. This logic produces "reason" (*Vernunft*). "Understanding meets every question with an inflexible 'either . . . or.' . . . A thing either is, or is not. Reason breaks up this hard and fast schematism of the understanding, sees that *A* and not-*A* are identical in their very difference, that the truth does not lie, as understanding supposes, either wholly in *A*, or wholly in not-*A*, but rather in the synthesis of the two."[4]

Hence the form of human knowledge is triadic. A concept (called by some the "thesis") contains and gives birth to its opposite ("antithesis"), both of which are known by analysis and both of which are overcome, absorbed, and transformed by "reason" in the stage of "synthesis." But not only did Hegel claim this triad to be the form of human knowledge, he claimed it to be the form of the world itself, that which knowledge knows. From the beginning, epistemology and the philosophy of history are one for Hegel and are made one by a more fundamental ontology.

Like all ontologists, Hegel began with the concept of Being—that which is, that without which nothing can be. His dialectical interpretation of Being served as a model for the dialectical interpretation of all categories. At the lowest level, Being, mere "isness" purged of all specific determinations, is so minimal that it "passes over" into Nothing. If one can say of an object only that it is, one is saying nothing about it. Being passing into Nothing is "decease" and Nothing passing into Being is "origination." Taken together the two terms describe Becoming. The synthesis of Becoming absorbs and tran-

scends but does not annul Being and Nothing.

On the basis of this elemental triad Hegel attempted the magnificently ambitious task of embracing all the forms of knowledge known to man, a vast and complicated network of triadic processes each flowing into the others. The simplest description is found in Part I of Hegel's *Encyclopedia of Philosophic Sciences* (1817), often referred to as the "Smaller Logic." The most extensive treatment is in the *Science of Logic*. But subsequent works, such as the *Philosophy of Right,* concerned with political and historical subjects, built upon the system in such a way that later commentators were able to outline in tabular form the interrelationships of all the various parts of the Hegelian system. Some idea of these interrelationships may be obtained by studying the diagram on pages 474–75,[5] incomplete though it may appear to some Hegelian experts.

In trying to make sense of the following table, it is important to understand that these triads are not simply a set of building blocks. Each triad represents a process wherein the synthesis absorbs and completes the two prior terms, following which the *entire* triad is absorbed into the next higher process. Moreover, every term of every triad is itself the culmination of lower processes, so that in a sense it serves a dual function: it is simultaneously part of two networks. It must be noted that in what is probably the basic chain, that from Being-Nothing-Becoming to Being-Essence-Notion, the term Being appears at three different levels. The reader of Hegel is forced to remember—in such ways Hegel sometimes seems to be deliberately obscurantist—that these are three different terms—even though each is partly the same as the others! Finally, we should recognize that Hegel himself would probably have disowned a diagram like this as an oversimpli-

---

[3] W. T. Stace, *The Philosophy of Hegel* (New York: Macmillan, 1924), p. 90.

[4] *Ibid.,* p. 101.

[5] For further details see G. R. G. Mure, *A Study of Hegel's Logic* (Oxford: Clarendon Press, 1950), p. 370; the table of *Encyclopedia* categories in Stace, p. 526; and the table of contents in Hegel's *The Science of Logic,* trans. and ed. by W. H. Johnston and L. G. Struthers (London: Allen & Unwin, 1929), Vol. I, pp. 20–24.

fication. However triadic Hegel's thought, he preferred to refer to the dialectic as a system of negations rather than a system of triads. His aim was to overcome what is static in thought and thereby to see into the dynamics of both thought and actuality.

Let us return to the basic dialectic of the logic and try once again to clarify its essentials. It is, first of all, not traditional logic at all. It is a new mode of thought, adapted to and reflecting the continual movement of the world. It is neither a series of set, mathematical relationships nor a manner of a priori deductive reasonings. Hegel firmly believed that it was descriptive of the way thought must apprehend the real world. In this sense there is in the dialectic something of the intuitive quality lauded by the German romantics. The history of human thought, Hegel believed, was in fact a manifestation of the dialectic, with the power of negation asserting itself again and again to contradict what its authors regarded as settled systems of thought and by that "contradiction" lifting them to higher and higher levels:

> there are no traces in [traditional] Logic of the new spirit which has arisen both in Learning and in Life. It is, however (let us say it once for all), quite vain to try to retain the forms of an earlier stage of development when the inner structure of spirit has become transformed; these earlier forms are like withered leaves which are pushed off by the new buds already being generated at the roots.[6]

Being, at its first beginning, at the bottom of the far-left triad in the foregoing diagram, is most barren and least determinate and therefore, as we have seen, passes over into Nothing; both then move on into Becoming. The whole triad then moves on, or rather is transformed into the thesis of a new dialectical triad, the first term of which is also called Being. At the lowest level Being is most immediate, that is, it most stands by itself and does not mediate between itself and other categories. Actually, Hegel is interested in showing this mediacy at all levels,

but it varies in degree. Without trying to explain the subsequent triads of Being–Determinate Being–Being for Self, and Quality-Quantity-Measure—political theory must leave *something* for the philosophers—we can look at the key arch in the edifice of the *Logic,* the triad of Being-Essence-Notion (some would translate *Begriff* as "Conception" rather than "Notion"). At this level, Being, which includes all its subcategories, becomes the symbol for immediacy (despite the fact that Hegel has been attempting to show that the immediacy of all the subcategories was in part illusory, since they did not in fact stand apart but flowed into each other). Essence is the factor of mediation. And Notion is the unity of immediacy and mediation that swallows them both by virtue of the conception of self-mediation.

Absolute Idea, the unity of subjectivity and objectivity, is alone fully self-mediate. It transcends the whole logic and is the first term of the most exalted triad of all, Idea-Nature-Spirit. The dialectic of course operates in the world of nature and spirit as well as idea. It is in the realm of spirit, which is "thought in the full sense, knowing itself not merely as thought, but as thought-of-object," that we come at last to political thought.

Criticism of Hegel's logic is frequent. A succinct example:

> Hegel assumed that because thought is dynamic, logic also must be dynamic. It is as if we were to suppose that because (in Locke's phrase) we have difficulty in adjusting a "standing measure" to a "growing bulk" a running measure would do better. . . . The trouble is that Hegel tried to do two things in a single operation. On the one hand, he wanted to give a systematic and logically structured account of the basic categories or concepts by means of which we understand our world. On the other hand, he wanted to describe the self-transcending character of meaning. Each of these was an entirely proper undertaking, but put together as Hegel put them together they resulted in confusion. First, he attributed self-transcendence to the various categories of logic; then he turned around and attributed logical formality to the

[6] *Science of Logic,* Preface, p. 35.

The Hegelian System

NOTE: This diagram is limited to one of many possible chains of triads—a limitation arising from Hegel's incompleteness and the constraints of two-dimensional illustration. The dotted arrows indicate linkages with other triads.

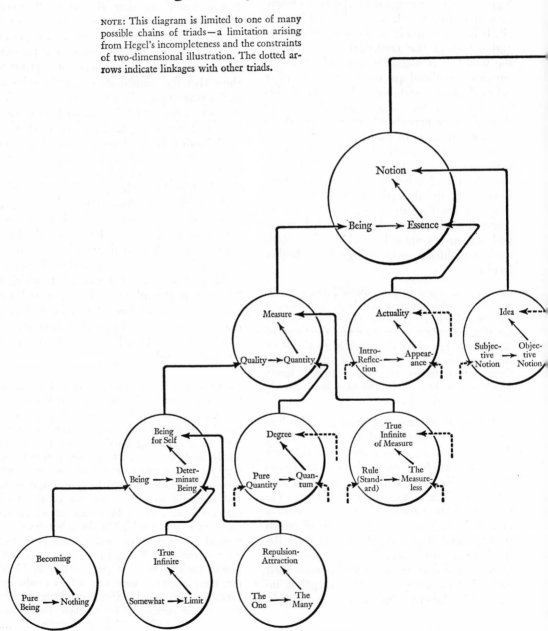

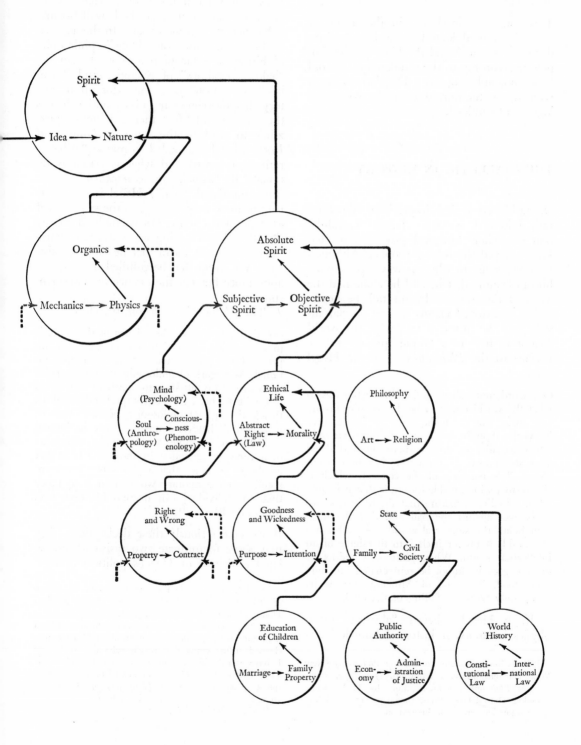

process of self-transcendence and expansion of meaning.[7]

This confusion is shown in the imprecise way Hegel used logical terms like "contradiction," "negate," and the like—at least imprecise according to the standards of the old logic and, unless one is a Hegelian to begin with, this is the only standard by which his logic can be judged.

THE DIALECTIC IN HISTORY

Old-fashioned logical imprecision, however, little inhibited one who claimed as validation the whole historical process. Not that Hegel played the role of prophet. Although there is a sense in which it was necessary for him to assume that he and he alone had the secret of the universe by the tail, he nevertheless disavowed claims to any special insight into the future or into what the world "ought to be." In a famous passage in the Preface to the *Philosophy of Right* Hegel says:

One word more about giving instructions as to what the world ought to be. Philosophy in any case always comes on the scene too late to give it. As the thought of the world, it appears only when actuality is already there cut and dried after its process of formation has been completed. The teaching of the concept, which is also history's inescapable lesson, is that it is only when actuality is mature that the ideal first appears over against the real and that the ideal apprehends this same real world in its substance and builds it up for itself into the shape of an intellectual realm. When philosophy paints its grey in grey it cannot be rejuvenated but only understood. The owl of Minerva spreads its wings only with the falling of the dusk.[8]

If, as Hegel believed, "abstract" metaphysics is empty, if historical knowledge is

all the knowledge we can command, it follows that we can know only what history gives us. The future is a blank wall because it has not yet become history. In this respect, as Friedrich points out, Hegel's philosophy of history was far more profound than the "bald generalities" of Spengler and Toynbee.[9] If "reason" is a name for all in history that overcomes negativity and recreates the substance of life,[10] then it is not so puzzling to read in the same *Philosophy of Right* what has puzzled so many: "What is rational is actual and what is actual is rational." By "actual" (or, as *wirklich* is sometimes translated, "real") Hegel is not referring to mere existence but to the synthesis of existence and essence. For example, if we say that President Harding was not a real statesman, we do not mean that he had no existence. We mean that he fulfilled the external appearance but not the essence of statesmanship.

The *Philosophy of Right,* therefore,

containing as it does the science of the state, is to be nothing other than the endeavor to apprehend and portray the state as something rational. As a work of philosophy it must be poles apart from any attempt to construct a state as it ought to be. . . . To comprehend what is, this is the task of philosophy, because what is, is reason. Whatever happens, every individual is a child of his time; so philosophy, too, is its own time apprehended in thoughts. It is just as absurd to fancy that a philosophy can transcend its contemporary world as it is to fancy that an individual can overlap his own age, jump over Rhodes.[11]

If we take seriously these declarations, they may serve to mitigate two insistent and related criticisms of Hegel's political philoso-

---

[7] W. T. Jones, *A History of Western Philosophy* (New York: Harcourt, Brace, & World, 1952), p. 879.

[8] *The Philosophy of Right,* trans. by T. M. Knox (London: Oxford Univ. Press, 1942), pp. 12–13. Subsequent quotations are from this edition.

[9] Carl J. Friedrich, in the Introduction to his edition of *The Philosophy of Hegel* (New York: Random House, Modern Library, 1953), p. III.

[10] The sovereignty of reason amounts to an article of faith for Hegel and he so recognized it: "I have proclaimed at the outset that reason rules the world and I have stated this as our presupposition and faith" (*The Philosophy of History,* in Friedrich, p. 16. Subsequent quotations from the *Philosophy of History* are from this edition unless otherwise noted).

[11] *Philosophy of Right,* Preface.

phy: first, that he seemed to stop the dialectic with the ascendancy of the German nations in his own time—much as Marx would stop the dialectic with the triumph of the proletariat—and second, that because he could envision no higher form of political life than the sovereign nation-state, he glorified the wars that result from conflict between sovereign nation-states.

It is quite true, as we shall see, that Hegel regarded the Germanic nations as the high point of a long cultural development. But a high point is not necessarily a terminus. If Hegel was correct in believing that no philosophy can "transcend its contemporary world," perhaps the glories of German culture were all that he could know fully enough to praise. The dialectic did not stop with Prussia, and certainly it is an error to accuse Hegel in one breath of defending both Prussian bureaucracy and German nationalism, for one could scarcely have defended them simultaneously. The Germanic people (*volk*) was at this time a cultural not a political concept, with little relationship to later varieties of nationalism. It is no doubt ironic that Hegel sought to explain more with his historically bound philosophy than did half a dozen run-of-the-mill philosophers without such a limitation. Historical relativism ought to induce humility; but perhaps this is asking too much of one who virtually invented historical relativism.

There was certainly a romantic strain in Hegel's treatment of war. It is by war that "the ethical health of peoples is preserved," as the wind preserves the sea from foulness. The sacrifice of oneself to the higher purposes of the state is a "universal duty." But if we remember that Hegel's avowed purpose was not to change the world but to understand it, we recognize that he was trying to *justify* war rather than to *glorify* it. Indeed, in contemplating the violence and passions of historical conflict, in "looking upon history as this butchery," Hegel noted in the *Philosophy of History* that "we can end up by feeling sorry for this vainglory." War is just *there,* in the world as a fact of life. If national unity is regarded as a good and if

war generates national unity—as it certainly does—then war has within it elements of good. It must also be noted that Hegel's view of war was nothing like twentieth-century conceptions of total war. In the *Philosophy of Right* he invoked "the proviso of the *jus gentium* that the possibility of peace be retained (and so, for example, that envoys be respected), and, in general, that war be not waged against domestic institutions, against the peace of family and private life, or against persons in their private capacity."[12] To be "rational," war must be within the framework of law.

It is not inconsistent with the dialectic to see wholes and the conflict of parts simultaneously. On the contrary, this is the essence of the dialectic. And that Hegel, speaking out of history and for history, could not see as did Kant the possibility of a world state does not by itself invalidate the dialectic or even make it irrelevant to such a possibility. All of this makes Russell's statement that Hegel's doctrine of the state "if accepted, justifies every internal tyranny and every external aggression that can possibly be imagined"[13] rather absurd.

Hegel began by taking seriously the Christian problem of theodicy, that is, how a good God can permit evil in the world, and sought to find the good that came out of evil rather than to deny the reality of evil. He also took the Incarnation seriously and accepted what it implied about the meaningfulness of history. Hegel's view of history was consequently Christian at least with respect to the conclusion that the ultimate good in history is not always coincident with the pleasure of individuals: "The History

---

[12] ". . . apart from the question whether Hegel has supplied us with an *adequate* philosophical explanation of war, it must be maintained that, on the other hand, he did not supply arguments from which the nationalist case for war could be sustained. . . . Hegel did not speak the language of nationalism or expansionist militarism" (Shlomo Aveneri, "Problems of War in Hegel's Thought," *Journal of the History of Ideas,* Vol. 22 [1961], p. 474). See also Aveneri's "Hegel and Nationalism," *Review of Politics,* Vol. 24 (1962), pp. 461–84.

[13] Bertrand Russell, *A History of Western Philosophy* (New York: Simon & Schuster, 1945), p. 742.

of the World is not the theater of happiness. Periods of happiness are blank pages in it, for they are periods of harmony—periods when the antithesis is in abeyance."[14]

It is manifestly unfair to make Hegel a totalitarian in the twentieth-century sense. In his constitutional writings Hegel favored trial by jury, local self-government, at least partial freedom of the press, and other conditions identified with liberal constitutionalism. Unlike reactionaries of the stamp of De Maistre, he favored separation of Church and state—in our sense of the word. Art, philosophy, and religion, though *in* the state, were not subordinate to it. He had a basic confidence in the capacity of public opinion to support good laws. On grounds similar to those of De Tocqueville he was sympathetic with the Americans and hopeful for their future. He sought to obtain the release from a Prussian jail of the French liberal Victor Cousin. In a long and famous footnote to the *Philosophy of Right,* Hegel attacks with remarkable vigor and lucidity the "might makes right" views of K. L. von Haller and stresses "how infinitely important and divine it is that the duties of the state and the rights of the citizens, as well as the rights of the state and the duties of the citizens, should be defined by law." We should not conclude from all this that Hegel was a "liberal." It might be more accurate to call him a postliberal in a preliberal society,[15] or perhaps a socialist without socialism.

14 *The Philosophy of History,* trans. by J. Sibree (London: Bell, 1905), p. 26.

15 This observation and a good many others on Hegel I owe to Professor John Rodman. The portrayal of Hegel as an enemy of liberalism characterizes the writings of Karl Popper and Sidney Hook. See the former's *Open Society and Its Enemies* (Princeton: Princeton Univ. Press, 1950), Vol. 2, Ch. 12. See the latter's *From Hegel to Marx* (Ann Arbor: Univ. of Michigan Press, 1960), and "Hegel and the Perspective of Liberalism," in D. C. Travis, ed., *A Hegel Symposium* (Austin: Univ. of Texas Press, 1962). Opposing views to these may be found in John Plamenatz, *Man and Society* (New York: McGraw-Hill, 1963), Vol. 2, Chs. 3–4, and Z. A. Pelozynski, Introduction to *Hegel's Political Writings,* trans. by T. M. Knox (London: Oxford Univ. Press, 1964). See the exchanges between Hook and Pelozynski in *Encounter,* January, 1965 (Vol. 24), and March and May, 1966 (Vol. 26).

Another misconception about Hegel is that his concern for history was purely abstract and categorical. In fact his *Philosophy of History* is studded with considerable historical detail, though less so in the often-reproduced Introduction than elsewhere. Man's thinking, says the author, which includes "feeling, knowledge, and insight, desire and will," is what distinguishes him from animals. History is past events, what has been. The philosophy of history is merely thinking about history. Hegel finds, as one might expect, a contradiction between the tasks of history and philosophy that must be overcome. It is overcome in the "only thought philosophy brings along" in approaching the materials of history, "the very simple thought of reason, namely that reason rules the world. . . . history is the rational and necessary way of the world spirit which is the substance of history." Hegel sagely asserts that people do not study history simply for information but for rational insight, yet many historians for this reason necessarily do precisely what they criticize the philosophers for, "namely the imparting of a priori inventions to history." Marcuse has pointed out how remarkable it is that an idealistic philosophy should proceed empirically. The hypothesis developed (and in one sense validated) in the *Logic* is here applied to the data of history. But the structure of the dialectic transcends both: "the 'negativity' that, in the *Logic,* determined the process of thought appears in the *Philosophy of History* as the destructive power of time."[16]

The task of the philosophy of history was, as we have seen, a deeply religious task for Hegel. He acknowledged the commandment of the Scriptures that it is a duty not only to love God but to know him. He sought the penetrations of eternity within "the destructive power of time." Moreover, it is not enough to know God merely as a theological abstraction; indeed, "philosophy must guard religion against certain kinds of theology." Regarding nations and states as the individ-

16 Herbert Marcuse, *Reason and Revolution; Hegel and the Rise of Social Theory* (Toronto: Oxford Univ. Press, 1941), p. 224.

uals with which history deals, "we must make an earnest effort to understand the concrete as the means and ways of providence which are spread out openly before us as the phenomena of history." Hegel felt that his own time was "now at last . . . the right time to comprehend this rich production of creative reason which is world history."[17] The unfolding of creative reason (the world spirit) was inextricably bound up with enlarging conceptions of freedom—freedom that is simultaneously self-limitation and self-realization.

Hence, in *The Philosophy of History,* Hegel reviews the order of civilizations and tells his audience that the Orientals, who had only an external morality and were able to make of government only a coercive organ, did not know that "the spirit is free in itself, or that man is free in himself." For the Oriental, past and present, only one is free and that one is the ruling despot, who, because he is only one and affected by "arbitrariness, ferocity, obtuseness of passion," is not really free and therefore not really a man. The Greeks and the Romans "knew only that a few are free, and not man as such" for they were tied to their slaves and could not rise above the accidental and contingent, which made their freedom a "passing and limited flower."

"Only the Germanic nations have in and through Christianity achieved the consciousness that man *qua* man is free and that freedom of the spirit constitutes his very nature." The task of extending this principle to the secular realm is, however, not even yet completed. Hegel asserts his theological proposition despite and not in ignorance of the various qualifications that could be made:

what constitutes the final end of the world we claim to be the spirit's consciousness of its freedom and thus the actualization of its freedom. That this [concept of] freedom is still indeterminate and ambiguous in definitions; that free-

dom, being the highest [good] implies infinitely many misunderstandings, confusions, and errors; that it involves all kinds of commotions—this one has never known better nor experienced more clearly than in our time. But right now we shall be content with the general notion, just the same.[18]

The *Philosophy of History*—of which, unfortunately, only the Introduction is read with frequency—was a brilliant but unsuccessful attempt to combine into one package philosophy and history, concept and existence, values and facts, what can be conceived in the mind and what actually happens. The rationality of everything that happens in history is scarcely apparent to all the actors in history, so Hegel was led to suggest that there is a "cunning of reason," which

sets the passions to work for itself while that through which it develops itself [i.e., the individual person] pays the penalty and suffers the loss. . . . The particular in most cases is too trifling as compared with the universal; the individuals are sacrificed and abandoned. The Idea pays the tribute of existence and transience, not out of its own funds, but with the passions of the individuals.[19]

Hartman, straining a bit, finds four types of men portrayed in Hegel's *Philosophy of History:* (1) the citizen, whose morality is in harmony with that of the state; (2) the hero, who leads the state; (3) the victim, who, having a wholly private morality, is crushed by history; and (4) the "person."[20] Of these four, only the "person," through infrequent and intangible identification with what is "essentially eternal and divine," transcends the cunning of reason working in history. In Hegel's own words, such personhood is

[17] See also Richard Kroner, ed., *Hegel on Christianity: Early Theological Writings,* trans. by T. M. Knox (New York: Harper & Row, 1961).

[18] *Philosophy of History,* pp. 12–13. See I. L. Horowitz, "The Hegelian Concept of Political Freedom," *Journal of Politics,* Vol. 28 (1966), pp. 3–28.

[19] Hartman, p. 44. The Idea is the "warp," human passions the "woof" of history's tapestry.

[20] *Ibid.,* the Hartman typologies are developed in his Introduction, pp. xxx–xl.

"one aspect of human individuality" rather than a given type of individual.

SPIRIT

Spirit has been referred to many times in the foregoing. As with many other Hegelian terms, to define spirit in a brief phrase, such as "self-contained existence," helps hardly at all; nevertheless, if we are to do justice to the overall unity of the Hegelian system, we must see how spirit at the personal level is related to spirit at the level of world history and hence world politics. For this we must look briefly to the *Phenomenology of Spirit*. It is beyond the competence of the writer and the proper scope of this inquiry to attempt a summary of the *Phenomenology*. It was for Hegel his "voyage of discovery." Royce compared it to Goethe's *Faust*. Walter Kaufmann compares it to Dante's journey through hell and purgatory. Kroner calls it an "epic of the human mind" and describes the reader's reaction:

> The reader often feels completely lost. Clouds of contradiction and dialectic obscure the course, and he does not know which way to go. He may well guess that a passage refers to certain facts of history or of literature, but to what facts he is at a loss to discover. At times long, dry discussions are suddenly interrupted by stormy outbreaks which defy understanding. At times everything is clear, and the reader enjoys the splendor of truth shedding light on human perplexities; but again the sky clouds over, and everything is lost in the darkness of obscurity.[21]

The influence of Plato and Aristotle on Hegel is much in evidence in this work. From Plato comes a sense of the distinction between surface appearance and the reality lying beneath and beyond, the world of philosophical knowledge that is truth. The "we" Hegel uses, as Marcuse notes, is addressed to philosophers and not to ordinary readers.

Plato's *Parmenides* is suggested by Hegel's concern for consciousness and otherness, that by which consciousness knows itself. But like Aristotle, Hegel saw a continuity rather than an unbridgeable gulf between the material and the nonmaterial worlds. Sense leads to thought. Going beyond both the Greeks and Kant, Hegel sought to transcend the subject-object dichotomy. It is spirit (comparable to the Platonic soul, the self-moved mover) that accomplishes this transcendence through its own self-consciousness, which is the true reality. We begin with pure subjectivity, a self not conscious of itself. To become self-conscious, spirit must go outside itself, so to speak, and make the objective world its own in order that it may know itself and its own power.

Since the process of becoming fully self-conscious involves these reciprocal relationships of self and the other and of subjectivity and objectivity, there are no fixed limits to the sources of knowledge and "The process of knowledge becomes the process of history. . . . Hegel links the epistemological process of self-consciousness (from sense-certainty to reason) with the historical process of mankind from bondage to freedom."[22] But this movement from bondage to freedom is not without its ironies. As self-consciousness is forced to recognize another self-consciousness outside itself in order to become itself, conflict results. The self—Hegel would say self-consciousness—trying to defend selfhood as the center of all that is, denies, or "suspends," the other self—out there. But this does not work, for self-awareness requires the existence of that other self—out there. We know ourselves only as we are known as selves. Hence in suspending the other, the self "thereupon proceeds to suspend its own self, for this other is itself." Such action is aimed at destroying the other but in a sense it gives selfhood back to the other, too, for "the other is also a self-consciousness; an individual makes its appearance in antithesis to an individual."[23]

[21] Kroner, p. 44.

[22] Marcuse, p. 95.
[23] The "its" reminds us that Hegel is not speaking merely of human self-consciousness, though he is more

Every action of recognition or suspension has, thus, a double meaning; every consciousness "is and is not another consciousness . . . has self-existence only in the self-existence of the other." One struggles to negate the external, objective form of self-consciousness, for that externality is "bound . . . by the particularity everywhere characteristic of existence as such." One naturally seeks freedom from dependence on the particularities of existence, the seemingly arbitrary and transient, in order to make a pure, unfettered "presentation" of the self, which, in Socratic terms, might mean to "Know thyself" as a separate person. Such negation "aims at the death and destruction of the other"; but the interdependence of self and other is so complete that by adopting such an aim the self risks its own life: ". . . it is solely by risking life that freedom is obtained."

In what amounts to a synthesis of Aristotelian aristocratic virtue with the Christian virtue of service, Hegel goes on to argue that in these risky confrontations of self with self, one will dominate, another will be subordinate. The master (*Herr*) achieves independence and lives for himself. The servant (*Knecht*) remains dependent and lives for the other. His only "independence consists in his being a thing." Yet, ironically, the supposedly independent master becomes more and more dependent on the work of the servant and the servant, able by his labor to shape and fashion external material reality, achieves in it a kind of permanence and hence independence denied the master.[24] Hegel's relatively short discussion of master and servant has been a powerful influence on a wide variety of subsequent speculation, from Marx's ideas on class and alienation to Sartre's on death and nothingness.[25]

Hegel's treatment of the French Revolution in terms of history, freedom, and consciousness is instructive. It will be remembered that the *Phenomenology of Spirit* was written in the midst of the Thermidorian reaction to the French Revolution. Hegel called the Revolution the symbol of self-destructive freedom because the state created by it was merely external. Law freely willed by man, involving a unity of the subjective and the external, had not yet been achieved. Hence the promise of a more genuine internalized freedom of the German idealist-romantic school loomed all the more attractively on the horizon. Hegel's politics were inescapably related to his whole philosophical system. Some critics have charged Hegel with the confusion of mixing historical and philosophical concepts indiscriminately. Hegel did indeed mix them, but not indiscriminately. All post-Hegelian attacks on conventional epistemology for its failure to take into account the historical (and therefore continually shifting and relational) character of knowledge (e.g., the attacks of Dilthey, Collingwood, and Mannheim) owe a great deal to Hegel.

The gap between epistemology and history Hegel bridged brilliantly, but a parallel or at least related gap he did not bridge. In the *Phenomenology of Spirit* he is looking primarily at the absorption of historical knowledge by the spirit manifest in the human individual's psyche. In the *Philosophy of History* the individual is replaced by nations and states—in the special Hegelian sense of state, which we will discuss in a moment. To Hegel, no doubt, spirit cannot be confined to one or the other but absorbs them both; a purely individualistic philosophy is, for Hegel, a contradiction in terms. So far so good. But there is a concreteness about the human individual that is not pos-

easily understood if we imagine that he is. The conflict of states is also implied. See Pierre Hassner, "Hegel," in Leo Strauss and Joseph Cropsey, eds., *History of Political Philosophy* (Chicago: Rand McNally, 1963), pp. 630–31.

[24] See Walter Kaufmann, *Hegel: A Reinterpretation* (Garden City, N.Y.: Doubleday, Anchor, 1966), pp. 136–38.

[25] See Louis Dupré, *The Philosophical Foundations of Marxism* (New York: Harcourt, Brace & World, 1966), Chs. 1–4; Erich Fromm, *Marx's Concept of Man* (New York: Ungar, 1961); Jean-Paul Sartre, *Being and Nothingness,* trans. by Hazel Barnes (New York: Philosophical Library, 1956); and Robert Tucker, *Philosophy and Myth in Karl Marx* (Cambridge, Eng.: Cambridge Univ. Press, 1961), p. 126.

sessed by nations or states and there is an arbitrariness about the selection of the latter as bearers of the world spirit that Hegel never seems to face up to. He disparages what he calls the "retail" view of Providence acting through individual persons alone and says the "totalities which are states" are the true bearers of the world spirit. From the point of view of the almost Godlike stance Hegel is required to take, it is not at all clear why nations are more significant groupings of human beings than families, or towns, or religious groups, or occupational groups, or happy people, or right thinkers, each of which (even granting the reality of some kind of collective will) could be as "natural" a collectivity in the eyes of God as a nation or nation-state. If history is national history to Hegel, should he not be somewhat more modest in his belief that history is national history to God? Still, twentieth-century man, for whom nation has in many respects become God, is ill-prepared to judge Hegel on the point and has reason to feel some kinship with one who felt that true freedom could only exist within the nation-state.

THE STATE

The concept of the State—with a capital "S" —is the heart of Hegel's political philosophy but it can scarcely be understood if pulled out of its elaborate context. If we turn back to the diagram of the Hegelian system, we note that the State is within the dialectical chain leading to Objective Spirit. The first term of the triad of which this concept is a part is Subjective Spirit, spirit in its inwardness and immediacy, the subcategories of which pertain to what we might call psychology in its broadest sense. Subjective Spirit "passes over" to Objective Spirit, spirit in its otherness, its mediateness. The latter pertains to the whole area of sociology, politics, economics, law, and ethics—the subjects discussed in the *Philosophy of Right*. And so on into the synthesis of Absolute Spirit con-

taining the highest expressions of art, religion, and philosophy.

But the State is two levels below the triad Subjective Spirit–Objective Spirit–Absolute Spirit. The triad of which it is a part feeds into Ethical Life, which is the third term of the triad Abstract Right (Law)–Morality–Ethical Life. Abstract Right is the sphere of rights and duties that attach to persons as *persons,* or those who are conscious of their consciousness, considered singly, abstractly, and in isolation from their capacity as citizens. The law with which it is concerned is that of property, contract, and external right and wrong. Morality (*Moralität*) is higher than this—though why more mediate is not clear—and includes acts properly motivated along with the individual's inner awareness of conflict between law and the desire to break it. Instead of abstract right and wrong, it involves concrete goodness and wickedness. Finally there is a synthesis in Ethical Life (*Sittlichkeit*), in which the lower forms merge into a larger conception of the good of the whole, which is symbolized by the State. It may be significant that Hegel devotes about thirty pages to Morality and one hundred and twenty pages to Ethical Life.

The State is the apex of the triad that begins with the family as an immediate form, passes over into the mediate form of "civil society" (a crude translation of *burgerliche Gesellschaft*), and proceeds to the ethical community that is the State. Unless one understands that what we today generally understand by the word "state" largely corresponds to Hegel's conception of the civil society, great confusion results. The civil society includes all that we would place in the political system and more, including the economy, the administration of justice, and bureaucratic officialdom.

The relationship between property—which Hegel discusses in the *Philosophy of Right* under the heading of Abstract Right—the civil society, and the concept of freedom is difficult to grasp but important.[26] Man's will

[26] It has been illumined for us in Marcuse's fine study, Ch. 6.

has simultaneously universal and particular aspects. Property is identified with the particular aspect of man's will because it is the result of the individual's appropriation of the "other." Even though directed toward particular ends, this assertion is nevertheless the "first phase of freedom." The resulting situation is paradoxical. Private property is essential to the freedom of the subject; but the competitive claims of private property tend toward anarchy and work against the higher freedom of a truly unified social order. The first is negative freedom; the second is positive freedom. They work against each other, but the first must be experienced before the second can be understood. Man must have some freedom in order to want any freedom. This is what Hegel means by "the free will which wills the free will." In the civil society the free play of private interests must be tolerated; their integration, if any, is a matter of chance and not rational choice. To this extent Hegel is strictly middle class in his economic orientation. But at the same time he sees the consequences for civil society as fortuitous necessity rather than true freedom. Hegel shares none of the liberals' easy optimism about a "natural" harmony between individual and general interests. Hence there is the need for the higher power of the State, which exists in a relationship of tension with the civil society. The State must dominate the civil society for the sake of the free individual—which, incidentally, is quite at odds with fascist theory. De Ruggiero deals with the same issue in a different way:

Society is the intermediate factor between the individual and the State. That is Hegel's great discovery and the turning point of all German nineteenth-century political science. The social organism, inserting itself between the two extreme terms which revolutionary theory had brought too perilously face to face, makes it possible not only to place the idea of the State in a region secure against the assaults of the individual, but also to canalize into that idea in an organic and disciplined form, all the claims and aspirations that spring spontaneously out of the individual life. It parts the two protagonists in the struggle, and at the same time unites them by a firmer bond. It destroys the Revolu-

tionary fancy that the State is a product of convention and caprice, but it equally rejects the reactionary fallacy that the State is identical with the prince and stands over against the consciousness of the people as an external object.[27]

Whether the civil society most usefully separates State and individual or whether the State saves the individual from civil society, the distinction is not irrelevant, even today. Some such distinction as that between State and civil society permits present-day patriots to love America while hating the government and also permits constitutionalists to question the Supreme Court without questioning the rule of law.

Hegel's State as an ethical community has obvious parallels with the *polis* in Plato's ideal state. In a brilliant comparative study of the two, Foster has shown the degree to which Hegel has improved upon yet confused the issue in Plato's formulation. As one capable of assimilating the liberating effect of the Enlightenment, Hegel both criticized and confused the relation of "subjective freedom" to Plato's *polis*. Plato's ruler has the subjective freedom to grasp universal forms. To this end, he is denied property and all that may conduce merely to sensual desire. Plato's subject does not have, in the ideal state, the subjective freedom to direct his soul toward any particulars, that is, toward the gratifications of sensuous desire. He has only the objective freedom derived from being tied to an all-wise ruler by external duty. In attacking Plato's exclusion of "subjective freedom" from the *polis*, Hegel, says Foster, confused this distinction. In claiming for his own state the capacity to assimilate subjective freedom for everyone he seems to be asking for incompatibles—the freedom that comes from following universal law and freedom seen as independence from universal law.[28] In his powerful drive to transcend and unite categories of subjective and objective, freedom and determination, law and liberty,

[27] Guido de Ruggiero, *History of European Liberalism*, trans. by R. G. Collingwood (Boston: Beacon Press, 1959), p. 231.
[28] Michael Foster, *The Political Philosophies of Plato and Hegel* (Oxford: Clarendon Press, 1935), Ch. 3.

Hegel undoubtedly sought to be more systematic than is humanly possible and, as we shall see, was at points forced to come down on the side of preferred positions for rulers.

This general dilemma is illustrated especially in the problem of the relationship between the civil society and the State. Once again we can refer to the illuminating study by Foster.[29] In his concept of Absolute Right Hegel tried to subsume two quite disparate entities, both of which in earlier thought went under the name state of nature. (The juxtaposition of both meanings in the same writer and under the same label appeared most conspicuously in Hobbes.) On the one hand, it referred to a condition in which the laws of passion—"natural" in the sense of universally operative, such as economic laws—dominated. On the other hand, it referred to a condition in which the laws of reason dominated either actually or potentially. In this case, "natural" meant universally valid. The sphere in which both of these conditions obtained was for Hegel the civil society.

But how, then, does one get from the civil society to the State? Civil society is still a sphere of particularity. Law may be fulfilled, but not necessarily as a result of the conscious intention of the subjects to fulfill it. Civil society can, then, be seen as the level of operative economic laws, and the State as the ideal level at which ethical will dominates, the same ethical will that is only latent in civil society. Seen in this way, the mistake of comparing the relationship between Hegel's civil society and State to, say, the relationship between Locke's society and his state is obvious. It would be more correct to think of civil society as an empiricist conception of society and State as a rationalist conception of society. Through moral education, members of the empirical society can be lifted from the level of economic necessity and sensual gratification to a higher level of voluntary obedience to law as a system of reason. In this way they achieve true freedom.

Hegel, however, did not explain the relationship of civil society to State in quite this way and, indeed, was not a consistent rationalist. The action of concrete will, quite apart from abstract reason, was important in moral choice to Hegel, and there remained the ambiguity as to whether both ruler and subject must participate in this exercise of moral will before the State is achieved. In his discussion of the role of police powers (broadly conceived) and guilds and corporations in the *Philosophy of Right,* Hegel suggests that the understanding of the moral order and the will to control affairs in its service is the basic requirement of leadership. But, says Foster, "This will which wills the universal and is therefore free, is the will which regulates, not which submits to regulations; a ruler's and not a subject's will."[30] This interpretation would suggest that the governing class alone has a life in the State, and if so, Hegel had no grounds for trying to lift anyone else out of the life of material passion in civil society.

Certainly in one sense the distinction between civil society and State is metaphysical and not physical and the division of classes is that of logical rather than historical classes. Yet in the *Philosophy of Right* Hegel does go beyond Plato in that he tries to relate his logical distinctions to existential historical classes and divisions. He does try to identify the State with existing power. He does discuss such concrete institutions as parliament, parties, public opinion, and free speech. He tries to relate them to the possibility of "subjective freedom" for subjects. He takes public education very seriously and favors extensive publicity for parliamentary debate. But, here as elsewhere, Hegel displays a fascination for the mixture of opposites that is the heart of the dialectic, coated over with the affection for moral oneness associated with Plato, Rousseau, and Kant:

The formal subjective freedom of individuals consists in their having and expressing their own private judgements, opinions, and recommendations on affairs of state. This freedom is collectively manifested in what is called "public opinion" in which what is absolutely

[29] *Ibid.,* Ch. 5.

[30] *Political Philosophies of Plato and Hegel,* p. 158.

universal, the substantive and true, is linked with its opposite, the purely particular and private opinions of the Many. Public opinion as it exists is thus a standing self-contradiction, knowledge as appearance, the essential just as directly present as the inessential.

Public opinion, therefore, is a repository not only of the genuine needs and correct tendencies of common life, but also, in the form of common sense (i.e., all-pervasive fundamental ethical principles disguised as prejudices), of the eternal, substantive principles of justice, the true content and result of legislation, the whole constitution, and the general position of the state. At the same time when this inner truth emerges into consciousness and, embodied in general maxim, enters representative thinking . . . it becomes infected by all the accidents of opinion, by its ignorance and perversity, by its mistakes and falsity of judgement. . . . because the bad is that which is wholly private and personal in its content.[31]

The fearfulness Hegel had about the political bargaining and compromise we would associate with "free" political institutions suggests that he was thinking in terms quite alien to our free-wheeling democratic tradition. On the other hand, his hope that the wide dissemination of public information could give the citizen understanding not only of the historical situation but of the philosophic conception of the State strikes us as excessiveely optimistic, perhaps even more liberal than the liberals. In both emphases the influence of Rousseau is evident. Here is a simple antithesis of pessimism and optimism concerning "the people" implicit in Hegel's political theory, which he did not successfully synthesize. But with it he drove to a central question that plagues us even more in an age of mass democracy: are there philosophic prerequisites for self-rule? Actually, despite the amount of attention Hegel paid to his crowning idea of the State, its derivation within the framework of the dialectic is one of the least satisfying aspects of Hegel's work. The family represents unity and universality, which passes over into the particularity and diversity of the civil society, which culminates in the unity-in-diversity of

the State. But, as Stace notes: "We see that *if* we advance from the idea of civil society to that of the state a reconciliation of the particular and the universal is found. But we cannot see any logical necessity why we *must* advance."[32]

We know from the *Philosophy of Right* that the State is "the actuality of the ethical Idea" and "mind objectified." We know that it exists immediately in custom, mediately in individual self-consciousness, and essentially as "substantive freedom." But we do not know exactly *how* power and ethical idea become one. This gap lays Hegel open to the criticism that his doctrine is one "that misses the tragedy of history and is the equivalent to Napoleon's dictum that God is on the side of the heaviest artillery."[33] There is enough of a sense of tragedy elsewhere in Hegel to make us wonder why he seemed to lose it in discussing the State. Even at the end of the *Philosophy of Right,* after making the victorious nation-state the bearer of the World Spirit and making world history the final court of judgment, Hegel nevertheless feels obliged to assure us that "world history is not the verdict of mere might."

INSTITUTIONS OF THE STATE

It remains to look briefly at Hegel's constitutional views, as explained in the *Philosophy of Right,* examining them as parts of an elaborate system but also evaluating their empirical realism. In taking up the constitution "on its internal side," Hegel picks from "amongst current ideas" discussed with much "babble" and "undigested chatter" the idea of separation of powers. It is, says Hegel, "if taken in the true sense" the "guarantee of public freedom." But a dangerously static equilibrium, a denial of "living unity," results if "abstract Understanding handles it" and "reads into it the false doctrine of the

---

[31] *Philosophy of Right,* secs. 316–17.

[32] *The Philosophy of Hegel,* p. 424.
[33] Cohen, p. 313.

absolute self-substance of each of the powers against the other."

The three powers have, however, quite different purposes. The Legislature is to "establish the universal." The Executive is to "subsume single cases and the spheres of particularity under the universal." And the Crown is to represent the "power of subjectivity" to bind into an individual unity all powers and thus constitute at once the base and the apex of the whole. Hegel's belief in constitutional monarchy was demonstrated by his assertion of the necessity to symbolize, as only a solitary individual can do, the moment of individuality, of subjectivity, in the notion of the State. Yet it is by a quite unconvincing deduction that this single figure is more "naturally" a hereditary monarch than one chosen by other means. (The philosophic science of the *Phenomenology,* moreover, would seem to deny validity to such a deduction.) Constitutional monarchy nevertheless "is the achievement of the modern world, a world in which the substantial Idea has won the infinite form [of subjectivity] . . . the history of this genuine formation of ethical life is the content of the whole course of world-history." The ancient distinctions between monarchy, aristocracy, and democracy are merely quantitative and therefore superficial. Hegel pays tribute to Montesquieu for his insight into the qualitative substance of different forms but disparages his feudal conception of monarchy, in which not duty but honor holds the state together.

Hegel's view of representation as it comes out in his discussion of the Idea of the Corporation nevertheless turns out to be feudal in character—even though he has, unlike some figures in the Reaction, accepted the irreversible transformation of feudal institutions by the rising middle class. The three estates receiving representation are the "substantial," or agricultural, class, which lives within "concrete universals"; the "reflected," industrial and service groups and the business class, which are directed to the particular; and the "thinking" estate, which is the determiner of the general interest. The last seems to endow with special prerogatives

the professors, the bureaucrats, and the Junker class in general.

Hegel views the question of framing an original charter or constitution, the question that took on so much significance for the contractualists almost with indifference. His discussion, he says, presupposes an existent constitution. And, then, in a passage that reminds one of the myths of Plato and of Rousseau's civil religion, he says, "In any case, however, it is absolutely essential that the constitution should not be regarded as something made, even though it has come into being in time. It must be treated as something existent in and by itself, as divine therefore." In fact, the constitution of any nation is a product of history and depends upon the development of that nation's self-consciousness. "Hence every nation has the constitution appropriate to it and suitable for it."

CONCLUSION

The flaws in the Hegelian system are many. We have examined some and can glance again at them here:

(1) Hegel asked too much of his new logic when he presented it not only as a new descriptive language but as a new view of the life that the language was supposed to describe. Nothing, not a scrap of reality, was left outside the system.[34]

(2) Without explicit defense, Hegel simply identified the more general with the more good and the more private and particular with the more bad. If general motivations are the prerequisite of greatness, it

---

[34] "[Hegel's] system must be pantheistic precisely on account of its finality. Existence must be revoked in the eternal before the system can round itself out; there must be no existing remainder, not even such a little minikin as the existing Herr Professor who writes the system" (Søren Kierkegaard, *Concluding Unscientific Postscript,* trans. by David F. Swenson [Princeton: Princeton Univ. Press, 1941], p. 111). Kaufmann shows, however, that Kierkegaard's image of a humorless Hegel is something of a caricature (pp. 62–63).

is questionable whether he will find any great men to lead the State.

(3) The recognition of the desirability of "subjective freedom" for subjects as distinguished from rulers was left ambiguous.

(4) The conditions whereby a union of subjective freedom and objective freedom could be achieved never became concrete.

(5) The transition from civil society to the State remained ambiguous.

(6) The union of power and right in the State—as, indeed, the whole attempt to fuse is and ought—remained so unstable as to be hardly a union, and some of Hegel's references to the Crown were not reassuring to enemies of despotism.

(7) The selection of nation-states as the only true bearers of the World Spirit was certainly arbitrary and ultimately probably idolatrous.

Many more criticisms and a good many rebuttals could no doubt be made. But we should not at this point care too much about Hegel's shortcomings, inasmuch as virtually all his disciples had more. His contribution to our processes of thought about political questions is what is important. He contributed great quantities of raw material for lesser minds to exploit as ideologies—the fascistic "myth of the state," the romantic glorification of war, the Marxian faith in the clash of opposites, the nationalistic fever that still rages around the globe—all have affected our recent history and our recent thinking and all owe much to what Hegel did.

But beyond the level of ideological expropriation Hegel gave us new and profound insights without which it would be virtually impossible to speak as we do of ideologies. The impact of historicism and relativism has been felt especially in the social sciences and philosophy and more recently, perhaps, in theology and science. In a sense, the completeness and abstractness of Hegel's system, when taken together with his epistemological historicism, puts him in a class by himself. He can be regarded as progressive or reactionary depending upon the society to which his system is applied.

Finally, the new logic of the dialectic, whatever its shortcomings, was a brilliant invention. In the nineteenth century the search for geometric laws of society stopped and the search for processual or biological laws of society began. The gap between the Bentham of the preceding chapter and the Marx of the following chapter is appropriately filled by our discussion of Hegel. But Social Darwinists, lawyers of the historical school, evangelizing Social Gospel men, and many others as well felt the tug of "creative evolution" set loose in the world by the hard, dry Herr Professor of Jena and Berlin.

21

MARX

That the work of Karl Marx is relevant to twentieth-century politics scarcely requires labored demonstration to the present-day reader. Indeed, an overwhelming sense of this relevance may for many actually be a barrier to understanding what Marx did and did not say. There are a good many theoretical deviations along the path that runs between the *Communist Manifesto* and communism today. Not all that is important as theory in Marx is today politically relevant; and not all that is today politically relevant in Marx is important as theory. Let us attempt a proper scholarly attitude, one that places the value of understanding a theory ahead of the value of outwitting an enemy—although the latter, needless to say, is not in all cases to be disparaged.

LIFE

The Early Years

Karl Marx, the eldest son and second of eight children in his family, was born in May, 1818, in Trier, in the German Rhineland. The area had been occupied by the French under Napoleon but was now, following the Congress of Vienna, part of Prussia. Marx's parents were Jews who had been segregated and discriminated against until the imposition of the Napoleonic Code introduced a new era of egalitarianism. During the period of new-found freedom Heinrich Marx, Karl's father, built up a successful law practice and lived the life of the respectable, liberal bourgeoisie. Then Napoleon withdrew some of the liberties granted to the Jews and finally the Prussian princes cut off the rest with the anti-Jewish laws of 1816. The abrupt retreat to a position of inferior legal status was psychologically more damaging to the Jews than constant repression might have been. Karl was thus born in the midst of a period of intense frustration. Due to his close relationship with his father, he undoubtedly absorbed much of the latter's bitterness toward authority. Shortly after Karl's birth, his father and later his mother became Christians, possibly to achieve a kind of security. When Karl was sixteen, his father made a speech advocating certain mild governmental reforms. The Prussian police descended upon the home. The elder Marx recanted and begged forgiveness. Apparently this behavior was a source of great shame to

Karl and further stimulated his attitude of resentment.

Young Marx was a precocious and brilliant student, especially in literature. Ahead of his years, he entered the Faculty of Law at the University of Bonn in 1835, at the age of seventeen. There he led the "gay and dissipated life of the ordinary German student"[1] and was once arrested for riotous behavior. Even at this time the powerful self-assurance that would later impress his followers was apparent. Reflecting a turn toward the serious, Marx transferred from Bonn to the University of Berlin in the autumn of 1836 to study jurisprudence. The attractions of Berlin were many: it was a big city, the center of the government, the hub of intellectual radicalism, and the fount of Hegelianism. Marx absorbed Hegel's system as deeply as anyone but his interest in materialism, through which he came to refashion Hegel, was in early evidence. His doctoral dissertation, written after a move to Jena in 1840–41, was "The Difference Between the Natural Philosophy of Democritus and Epicurus."

Marx had planned to follow an academic career but instead in 1841 took a job as a reporter for the *Rheinische Zeitung*. The next year he became editor. The paper was bourgeois but critical of the Prussian government, and Marx found himself writing radical but strictly capitalistic editorials, for which the journal was suppressed by the authorities in 1843. Ironically, Marx was tagged with the epithet communist long before he could rightfully claim the label or, indeed, even before it had much meaning for him. The suppression of the paper embittered Marx but stimulated his interest in politics and economics. An article written in 1844 is one of the first to reveal the germ of Marx's idea of the economic interpretation of history:

legal relations and political forms cannot be conceived as autonomous phenomena, nor as manifestations of the so-called general unfolding of the human spirit. They are, rather, rooted in

the material conditions of life. . . . the anatomy of . . . civic society is to be sought in its economics.[2]

Marx went to Paris to study economics and found there a job with the Paris magazine for German exiles, *Deutsche-Französische Jahrbücher*. While in Paris he met Friedrich Engels, a young German radical and son of a wealthy cotton manufacturer. Here began a close friendship and a great collaboration. So intertwined was the intellectual activity of Marx and Engels from this point on that when most people today speak of Marxism they are speaking of the joint output of Marx and Engels. Engels did not have as creative a mind as Marx but he possessed a vast historical knowledge and a forceful, driving character. Moreover, Engels' periodic loans enabled Marx to write with greater concentration and at greater length than would otherwise have been possible, for Marx was to be frequently on the edge of poverty.

At the request of the Prussian government, France expelled Marx in 1845. He went to Brussels to study until the fateful year 1848. While in Brussels Marx and Engels reorganized the German Workers Educational Association (*Deutscher Arbeiterbildungsverein*), which allied itself with a secret federation called the Communist League (*Bund der Kommunisten*). Michael Bakunin, in Brussels at the time, could not understand why Marx and Engels were wasting their time with a group of ignorant workmen, filling their minds with obscure theories they could not understand. The reaction was symbolic of Bakunin's anarchist impotence and Marx's powerful sense of the necessity for joining theory and practice. As Marx said in his famous comment on Feuerbach, "[Until now] philosophers have only *interpreted* the world in various ways; the point, however, is to *change* it."[3] At the re-

---

[1] Isaiah Berlin, *Karl Marx* (New York: Oxford Univ. Press, 1959), p. 33.

[2] Quoted in *Encyclopaedia of the Social Sciences*, Edwin B. A. Seligman and Alvin Johnson, eds. (New York: Macmillan, 1933), Vol. X, p. 172.

[3] *Theses on Feuerbach*, XI, in Marx and Engels, *Basic Writings on Politics and Philosophy*, Lewis S. Feuer, ed. (Garden City, N. Y.: Doubleday, Anchor, 1959), p. 245. This collection is the handiest source for basic Marxian

quest of the Communist League, Marx and Engels wrote, in 1848, one of the most important documents of modern times, the *Communist Manifesto.*

The *Communist Manifesto* and Beyond

Though written in a passionate rhetorical style, the *Manifesto* contained in nascent form many of the theoretical principles that, taken together, were to comprise the Marxian system. "A spectre is haunting Europe," it began, "—the spectre of Communism." And after thus trying—perhaps with some success—to strike terror into the hearts of respectable readers, it went on to explain why and how "The history of all hitherto existing society is the history of class struggles" and how "The executive of the modern state is but a committee for managing the common affairs of the whole bourgeoisie."[4] The bourgeoisie has served its useful purpose in the history of class struggles but its time is now past, and through exploitation of the very proletariat it has created it is blindly trying to hold onto its out-of-joint power, not realizing that "What the bourgeoisie therefore produces, above all, are its own grave-diggers. Its fall and the victory of the Proletariat are equally inevitable."

On the grounds "that intellectual production changes its character in proportion as material production is changed. . . . The ruling ideas of each age have ever been the ideas of its ruling class," Marx and Engels laid out what the new ruling class, the proletariat, had in store for the world. Some

planks of their platform—for example, the abolition of the family—would become an embarrassment to the cause. Others, such as the progressive income tax and free public education, seem less shocking to our day than to theirs. But abolition of private property in land, state ownership of basic instruments of production, and abolition of inheritance remain radical and remain communist planks today. When, as a result of these measures, class distinction shall have disappeared, politics as it has been known will disappear and "we shall have an association in which the free development of each is the condition for the free development of all." Following a critique of what they regard as spurious alternatives to their valid socialism —feudal socialism, "true" socialism of the German *literati,* Christian socialism, and utopian socialism—Marx and Engels end with the ringing words: "The proletarians have nothing to lose but their chains. They have a world to win. Workingmen of all countries, unite!" The assumptions underlying this great tract furnish us with more than enough problems to deal with in one chapter.

Even tolerant Belgium was obliged to expel Marx when the *Manifesto* came to light. But revolution was breaking out in Paris, so Marx felt safe in returning there. Revolts sprang up in Milan, Rome, Venice, Berlin, Vienna, and Budapest. To some this looked like the great proletarian revolution Marx had predicted. But Marx took no part in the formation of a legion of revolutionaries to fight in Germany and coolly said they would be mercilessly beaten by the Royal Prussian Army. They were. Later in the year Marx went back to Berlin and persuaded some liberal industrialists to back a new version of his old paper, to be known as the *Neue Rheinische Zeitung.* Again the journal was probourgeoisie and antigovernment, and again (May, 1849) it was suppressed by the authorities. Marx—who had been participating in secret Communist League activities while editing this business-oriented paper— printed the last issue of the *Zeitung* in red ink. He was arrested for sedition but made

---

materials but Émile Burns, ed., *A Handbook of Marxism* (New York: Random House, 1935), is still immensely valuable. See also *Marx on Economics,* Robert Freedman, ed. (New York: Harcourt, Brace & World, 1961).

[4] *The Communist Manifesto,* authorized English trans. (New York: International Publishers, 1932). Subsequent quotations are from this edition. The *Manifesto* was immediately translated into English, French, Italian, Flemish, and Danish but not, interestingly enough, into Russian.

a long and powerful speech at his trial that led, to everyone's surprise, to his acquittal. Marx's position at this time is crucial for the exegesis of later Marxians. The right-wingers pointed to this time to show that violent revolution was not necessarily the first consideration of Marx; he could and did work for reform with groups other than the proletariat. Such was the view expressed by the so-called revisionists, Eduard Bernstein and Karl Kautsky. Lenin and the left-wingers pointed out that Marx had not let his right hand know what his left hand was doing and that the logic of the dialectic required a bourgeois revolution before a true proletarian revolution could take place. Hence Marx was conscientiously encouraging a bourgeois revolution while also secretly keeping the proletarian revolution simmering. Marx's later writings would seem to confirm this interpretation. In *The Eighteenth Brumaire of Louis Napoleon* (1852) he spoke of the Paris situation in 1848: "Upon the *bourgeois monarchy* of Louis Philippe, only the *bourgeois republic* could follow. . . . The demands of the Parisian proletariat are utopian tom-fooleries that have to be done away with."[5]

Expelled from Prussia in July, 1849, Marx had only one place left to go: England. He expected to spend only a few weeks there but instead spent the rest of his life. He lived with his large but devoted family in London, in what was frequently miserable squalor. Mainly he lived off loans from Engels, though in the fifties and sixties he was a correspondent for the New York *Tribune*. His typical day from 10 A.M. to 7 P.M. was spent in the reading room of the British Museum, where he ground out his heavy prose. In one two-year period he produced 1,472 pages organized into twenty-three books, only two chapters of which were published. Sometimes he lacked money for postage to send his manuscripts to the publishers. Proud, contentious, uncompromising and af-

flicted with boils, eye trouble, and liver trouble, he was not a prepossessing sight during his last years. Virtually unknown in England, he nevertheless enjoyed a tremendous reputation on the Continent, participating in the formation of the First Workers International in 1864. In 1867 the first volume of Marx's greatest work, *Das Kapital* (*Capital*), was published. The second, third, and incomplete fourth volumes did not come out until after Marx's death in 1883.

HISTORICAL MATERIALISM AND THE DIALECTIC

Irritated by the convolutions of his disciples, Marx once said in the later years of his life, "I am not a Marxist." Most founders of systems are to some extent betrayed by their progeny. But in another sense the Marxian system was really built by those who followed, for Marx never worked out a complete, well-rounded theoretical "system." The theory of dialectical materialism upon which all of Marxism seems to rest was given very little direct attention by Marx. *Das Kapital,* his great theoretical work, assumed dialectical materialism and worked instead on the theories of surplus value and capitalist accumulation. He left to Engels, in *Socialism, Utopian and Scientific* (1892) and *The Origin of the Family* (1884), speculation on a theory of the state.

Marx's tendency to bypass philosophical questions makes Hegel's influence all the more relevant for us. From Hegel came the dialectic. It is not enough to say that Marx took the Hegelian dialectic (see Chapter 20) and by substituting the materialist concept of class for the idealist concept of spirit made it explain historical process materialistically rather than idealistically. This explanation is not altogether wrong; it is merely too simple. For one thing, Hegel, we may remember, had not thought of himself as an idealist, if this term implies a simple dualism between matter and idea. Marx spoke of

[5] *The Communist Manifesto with Selections from The Eighteenth Brumaire of Louis Napoleon,* trans. by Daniel DeLeon, in Samuel Beer, ed. (New York: Appleton-Century-Crofts, 1955), p. 53.

finding Hegel on his head and proceeding to "set him the right way up"; but no such either/or would have satisfied Hegel. The dialectic transcended and absorbed idea *and* nature *and* spirit.

Moreover, Marx differed from Hegel not only with reference to the object of philosophic discourse but with reference to its function as well—although the two were bound together. For Hegel, philosophy "always comes too late." It can only understand the world, not change it. But the point of philosophy for Marx was precisely to change the world, for all philosophy was class philosophy and classes were the fulcrum of history. In the day when classes would be no more, Marx believed that social philosophy would literally cease and become descriptive social science.

In criticizing Hegel, Marx and Engels adopted many of the arguments of Ludwig Feuerbach (1804–72), a "Young Hegelian" who, with *Zur Kritik der Hegelschen Philosophie* (*A Criticism of Hegelian Philosophy,* 1839) and other books published in the following decade, became a prominent philosophical materialist. Feuerbach incisively demonstrated that in deducing the ideal from the real, Hegel ended with nothing but what he had been forced to assume at the outset. Feuerbach charged that Hegel's disregard for the problem of sense perception had been cavalier; rejected traditional theism and traditional philosophy ("My philosophy is no philosophy," he said rather misleadingly); and sought to unite the scientific with the speculative, to theorize about the ordinary experience of ordinary men. Especially useful to Marx and Engels was Feuerbach's penetrating analysis of the psychology, sociology, and anthropology of religion. But Marx criticized Feuerbach for neglecting the concrete historical analysis his own assumptions seemed to require and for lacking appreciation of the dialectic itself.[6]

In breaking with idealism, Marx did not go back to a simple materialism that could evade the question of the nature of human thought. Idealists from Kant to Hegel had struggled with the problem of the extent to which thought is an activity of the mind depending upon preexisting consciousness as well as mere external stimuli, and Marx could not dismiss it. He agreed with Feuerbach that Hegel's identification of this preexisting consciousness with a timeless divine Subject was mythological nonsense. But having said that, Feuerbach, confined, as Marx thought, to academic speculations, was up a blind alley. Marx tried to get out of the blind alley by turning to history unencumbered by Hegel's metaphysical trappings and there solved the problem of consciousness by finding that it was not preexisting at all but was itself a part of the historical process. "In direct contrast to German philosophy, which descends from heaven to earth, here the ascent is made from earth to heaven. . . . men, developing their material production and their material intercourse, change, along with this their real existence, also their thinking and the products of their thought. It is not consciousness that determines life, but life that determines consciousness."[7]

The process of thought, in other words, is a part of the process of nature, a hypothesis that cannot be proved by speculation but can be proved by practice (*Praxis*). Feuerbach's "contemplative materialism" failed to see this. We do not discover the truth; history proves the truth for us through "human, sensuous activity, practice." *Hegel saw the role of activity in thought but not in sense. Feuerbach saw the role of sense in thought but not in activity. The insights of the two are combined in Marx's "dialectical materialism."*

Compared to this fundamental tenet, the dialectical "laws" of Hegel—for example, the transformation of quantity into quality, the

---

[6] For a much fuller examination of these questions, see Sidney Hook's *From Hegel to Marx* (Ann Arbor, Mich.: Univ. of Michigan Press, 1962), especially Chs. 1–3, 7, and 8, and Louis Dupré, *The Philosophical*

Foundations of Marxism (New York: Harcourt, Brace & World, 1966), Chs. 3–4.

[7] Marx and Engels, *German Ideology* (1846), in Burns, pp. 212–13.

unity of opposites, the negation of the negation—were important but subsidiary propositions.[8] They were invoked, sometimes metaphorically, more by Marx's followers than by Marx himself. Engels in *Anti-Dühring* (1877) tried to apply the dialectic to biology, using the life cycle of barley seed—as Hegel had done—to demonstrate the "negation of the negation." Marx himself was not much interested in these biological excursions and preferred to stay in the realm of social theory, where his heart was.

ALIENATION

Although from his editorial days Marx was interested in social and economic theory, the younger Marx had somewhat different interests than the older Marx. In the 1840s psychological and ontological problems were, if not prominent, at least present in his thought. The later Marx focused his attention on more impersonal and collective categories— what we might call the categories of social science. Scholars have recently made much of a set of manuscripts written by Marx in Paris in 1844, manuscripts that were not published until 1927 and were not available in English until 1961.[9] A term that appeared frequently in the *Economic and Philosophic Manuscripts,* as these 1844 documents are called, was "alienation," a term that has become important in the vocabulary of a variety of twentieth-century social critics.[10]

Marx was never to abandon his concern for alienation but his early discussions of this problem were more direct and perhaps more comprehensible than anything in his later years.

In Hegel's *Phenomenology of Spirit,* we recall, the development of human consciousness was held to require that a man become divided against himself as his subjective spirit within confronts the objective spirit of the external world. The process of knowing is the overcoming of this strangeness outside ourselves. Hegel called this condition self-alienation (*Selbstentfremdung*).[11] Marx criticized Hegel's neglect of the evils of private property in *Critique of Hegel's Philosophy of the State* (1843) and questioned there Hegel's conception of alienation, though not by name. The explicit attack came in the *Economic and Philosophic Manuscripts.* What Hegel had conceived as a process in the production of thought only, argues Marx—a bit unfairly—is in fact bound up with the production of all things, including thought. Marx wrote that Hegel "has only discovered the abstract, logical and speculative expression for the movement of history, but not yet the *real* history of man as a presupposed subject."[12] Man is alienated from the world not only in thinking but in his whole being and the alienation of his labor from the process of economic production is of primary importance in this process. Marx had been reading the capitalist economics of writers like Adam Smith and J. B. Say and concluded that the whole subject of political economy with such doctrines as the iron law of wages was unconsciously designed to fit the conditions of alienated labor. This process of alienation, this externalization and objectification of the self, is not confined to workingmen. It affects

[8] See the discussion of Marx's use of these laws in R. N. Carew Hunt, *The Theory and Practice of Communism,* 5th ed. (New York: Macmillan, 1957), Ch. 4.

[9] See Erich Fromm, *Marx's Concept of Man* (New York: Ungar, 1961). Fromm both translates and comments upon the manuscripts.

[10] See Daniel Bell, *The End of Ideology* (New York: Free Press, 1960), pp. 337–42; Erich Fromm, *The Sane Society* (New York: Holt, Rinehart and Winston, 1955); Erich Fromm, ed., *Socialist Humanism* (Garden City, N Y.: Doubleday, Anchor, 1966), Part IV; Eric and Mary Josephson, eds., *Man Alone: Alienation in Modern Society* (New York: Dell, 1962), and J. O'Neill, "Alienation, Class Struggle and Marxian Anti-politics," *Review of Metaphysics,* Vol. 17 (1964), pp. 462–71.

[11] See Robert Tucker, *Philosophy and Myth in Karl Marx* (New York: Cambridge Univ. Press, 1961), for an excellent discussion of the influence of these conceptions on Marx. Tucker also shows how Hegel's conceptions are foreshadowed in Kant's distinction between a noumenal self and a phenomenal self. See especially Chs. 1–7.

[12] *Historisch-Kritische Gesamtausgabe,* Vol. 3. Quoted by Tucker, p. 127.

all who exist within a money-oriented system. Man becomes cut off from his natural self and is enslaved not merely to the capitalist but to capital itself:

The less you eat, drink and read books; the less you go to the theater, the dance hall, the public-house; the less you think, love, theorize, sing, paint, fence, etc., the more you *save*—the *greater* becomes your treasure which neither moths nor dust will devour—your *capital*. The less you *are,* the more you *have;* the less you express your own life, the greater is your *externalized* life—the greater is the store of your alienated being. Everything that the political economist takes from you in life and in humanity, he replaces for you in *money* and *wealth;* and all the things that you cannot do, your money can do. . . . All passions and all activity must therefore be submerged in *greed*.[13]

The moral passion embodied in such passages affects us with its force even today. It is direct, vibrant, and personal. Marx is attacking a blind social system that is dehumanizing man and estranging him from his personal identity. By contrast, the tone of the later Marx does not jab us but puts us to sleep. His writings become increasingly abstract and scientific as he pursues the goal of demonstrating that the primacy of economic factors in this process of alienation is necessary and universal, an essential element in a historical dialectic as sweeping and all-inclusive as Hegel's.

Feuerbach's criticism of Hegel in his *Das Wesen des Christentums* (*Essence of Christianity,* 1841) had also been a criticism of Christianity. The alienation of the self that Hegel described was for Feuerbach an inevitable consequence of the Christian religion. He would have demystified religion and returned philosophy to nature: "Philosophy is the science of reality in its truth and totality. But the sum total of reality is *nature.* . . . The return to nature is the only source of salvation."[14] But for Marx, as we have seen, Feuerbach's view of nature was too static, too abstract, and too individualistic: "Feuerbach resolves the religious essence into the *human* essence. But the human essence is no abstraction inherent in each single individual. In its reality it is the ensemble of the social relations."[15] Feuerbach would seem to make a false view of religion a cause of alienation, whereas for Marx religion itself was but one compensatory result of man's alienation, which arose out of a dynamic economic-social process. Salvation for Marx was not to be found in a philosophic return to nature nor in thought at all but in human action. But salvation is nevertheless probably the right word to use, for Marx's impulse seems itself religious, or at least redemptive, in character.

Scholars are not agreed on the significance of this youthful religious impulse in Marx. Is the Marx of the early years, the semireligious prophet, or the Marx of the later years, the social scientist, the *real* Marx? As stated, the question may seem sterile, yet one's answer can affect the way one looks at the whole of Marx's prodigious output: should we value Marx for his moral-prophetic indictments of a sick society or should we seek from him valid scientific or philosophical propositions?[16] The answer each of us gives to this question probably stems from one of the same pair of impulses found in Marx. That is, if one is concerned with man as an alienated creature in the religious or psychological sense, he will find the early Marx fruitful and the later Marx tedious. If one is concerned with man as an alienated creature in the sociological sense, he will find the later Marx more significant. In neither case, however, does Marx make man into a mechanical automaton, as a good many caricatures have suggested.

---

[13] *Ibid.,* pp. 138–39.
[14] Feuerbach, *Zur Kritik der Hegelschen Philosophie.* Quoted by Dupré, p. 73.

[15] Marx, *Theses on Feuerbach,* V, in Feuer, p. 244.
[16] Although other issues would divide these men along other lines, the scientific Marx receives emphasis in the writings of Sidney Hook, George Lukacs, Herbert Marcuse, and Karl Popper, while the humanistic Marx is stressed by Louis Dupré, Erich Fromm, C. Wright Mills, and Robert Tucker.

THE THEORY OF OBJECTIVE DEVELOPMENT

Marx did not deny the capacity of men to think. He denied the autonomy of thought and felt that he had discovered the hitherto unrecognized power of economics to shape it. In the famous words of the Preface to *The Critique of Political Economy* (1859):

I was led by my studies to the conclusion that legal relations as well as forms of state could neither be understood by themselves, nor explained by the so-called general progress of the human mind, but that they are rooted in the material conditions of life, which are summed up by Hegel . . . under the name "civic society;" the anatomy of that society is to be sought in political economy. . . . In the social production which men carry on they enter into definite relations that are indispensable and independent of their will; these relations of production correspond to a definite stage of development of their material powers of production. The sum total of these relations of production constitutes the economic structure of society—the real foundation, on which rise legal and political superstructures and to which correspond definite forms of social consciousness. The mode of production in material life determines the general character of the social, political, and spiritual processes of life. It is not the consciousness of men that determines their existence, but, on the contrary, their social existence determines their consciousness.[17]

We may note in passing that the *general* and not the special character of social, political, and spiritual processes of life is determined by the mode of production. Marx is talking here about men in general in the broad sweep of history. What is important in this passage is the distinction between the "relations" or the "mode" of production—men working with men—and the "powers" or, in the sentence that follows, the "forces" of production—men working with coal, ships, and machines, that is, technology in general. In the course of history there arise between these

two complementary systems a lag and eventually conflict. But let Marx continue in his own behalf, for this is the heart of Marxism:

At a certain stage of their development, the material forces of production in society come in conflict with the existing relations of production, or—what is but a legal expression for the same thing—with the property relations within which they had been at work before. From forms of development of the forces of production these relations turn into their fetters. Then comes the period of social revolution. With the change of the economic foundation the entire immense superstructure is more or less rapidly transformed. In considering such transformations the distinction should always be made between the material transformation of the economic conditions of production which can be determined with the precision of natural science, and the legal, political, religious, aesthetic or philosophic—in short, ideological forms in which men become conscious of this conflict and fight it out. Just as our opinion of an individual is not based on what he thinks of himself, so can we not judge of such a period of transformation by its own consciousness; on the contrary, this consciousness must rather be explained from the contradictions of material life, from the existing conflict between the social forces of production and the relations of production. No social order ever disappears before all the productive forces, for which there is room in it, have been developed; and new higher relations of production never appear before the material conditions of their existence have matured in the womb of the old society. Therefore mankind always takes up only such problems as it can solve; since, looking at the matter more closely, we will always find that the problem itself arises only when the material conditions necessary for its solution already exist or are at least in the process of formation.[18]

The stages of history that this theory requires—each producing its own grave-diggers, each jerking itself through revolutions to the next "higher" stage—bear a striking resemblance to Hegel's stages, or Comte's, or even, for that matter, Condorcet's. In the Marxian view of history, the primitive agrarian economy was followed by the slave econ-

[17] *The Critique of Political Economy,* 2nd ed., trans. by N. I. Stone (Chicago: Kerr, 1904), pp. 11–12.

[18] *Ibid.,* pp. 12–13.

omy of the ancient world, then by the feudal economy, then by the bourgeois economy, and finally by the socialist economy, now in the throes of being born. It is Enlightenment progressivism made "objective" by being attributed to inevitable and ultimately uncontrollable material forces rather than to human thought and initiative. As has often been pointed out, the classical laissez faire economists, without the same sense of historical development, also had a faith in an economic system not controlled by conscious individual discretion. As is frequently the case, here a theorist and his enemies shared a basic presupposition. Another shared belief was that "better" meant "more efficient." The periodic disjunctions between the technology and the social system that ran it were presumably intolerable because the social system ("relations of production") could no longer efficiently run the technology ("forces of production"). To be sure, there was in Marx's analysis, as we shall see, a half-hidden moral judgment against continuing in the lower stage when the higher stage was ripe for birth, but the praise Marx heaped upon the efficiency of early capitalism indicates that he shared some of the economic biases of the class he denounced—which, of course, only tends to confirm what he was saying about social existence determining consciousness.

Marx can be said to have expressed simultaneously a potent ideology and an acute theory of ideology. In *Die Deutsche Ideologie* (*The German Ideology,* 1846) Marx and Engels compare the way we see the world to the way the lens of a camera inverts images and records them upside down. Our inner eye records a set of beliefs determining action in the material world. But the "actual life process" is action in the material world determining a set of beliefs. The grandiose edifice of German philosophy is but an inverted reflection of material relations in Germany, a delusion encouraged by the division of mental labor from material labor: ". . . consciousness *can* really flatter itself that it is something other than consciousness of existing practice, that it is *really* conceiving something without conceiving something real."[19] The proletariat, who do not live on words as philosophers do, are not so afflicted with ideological delusions. Communism is not, thus, an ideal but a "real movement" and the truth of the writers' words is confirmed not by more words but by action. What is disjunctive in all this is that Marx and Engels are so obviously outraged by the results of a process they claim to be inevitable and inherent in the world. There may indeed be some self-hatred in the bitterness with which Marx the philosopher denounces philosophy.

Nevertheless, the conception of "legal, political, religious, aesthetic or philosophic" enterprises as nothing more than superstructures built upon the economic substructure is as close to a wholly original contribution as one is likely to find in social theory. Its effect on our thinking is demonstrated every time an anti-Marxist historian decides to include a few statistics on diamond-mining in a chapter on the Boer War. Before Marx, the decisions of kings and generals tended to be the stuff of history. Today we all apologize for our economic biases and even the unlettered know that oil has something to do with our foreign policy in the Middle East. Similarly, Marx can take no small amount of credit for our concern with the problem of ideology. The present age has been called the age of ideology. Even Christianity, an "opium of the people" to Marx, has been examined as ideology. We now go back and look anew at settled figures of past scholarship. We ask how Locke's position as a Whig landlord affected his epistemology, a question no one had thought to ask before. Some fear, and with justification, that we have grown accustomed to regarding all classical theory as mere ideology, that is, as mere rationalization, so that the most sophisticated of us are afraid to theorize in the grand manner of the past and become instead narrow technicians of language. The sense that politics is but the visible part of a deeply submerged iceberg carried by little-known tides may also be partly responsible for the political apathy

[19] Feuer, p. 252.

characteristic of citizens in some of our most culturally advanced democracies.

But why this concern with economics in the first place? Marx, the methodological enemy of apriorism, presumably did not set out to prove that economics was a more fundamental determinant of thought than age, nationality, blood chemistry, musical training, annual rainfall, or any other of an infinite number of "fundamentals." Hegel at least pretended to have surveyed and synthesized all human knowledge. Not so Marx. The empirical pragmatism of his methodology was both his strength and his weakness: his strength in that scholars could not and did not disregard his monumental research, his weakness in that the correlations he discovered between economic class and ideology could not properly be regarded as a primary historical cause until the same monumental research had been applied to all other possible causes in all periods of history. This, of course, was impossible and, though analogies were drawn from ancient and medieval times, major Marxian analysis was confined to the modern period.

It is often said that Marxism fails most conspicuously in being unable to explain the class position of its own advocates. Marx, like Engels, Lenin, Trotsky, and many others, was of middle-class, not proletarian, background. Actually, this is not a great difficulty for Marx. The theorist is always to some extent the exception to the social generalizations he produces. In seeing the system he stands outside of it. Marx was not at all concerned to prove the power of class consciousness with individual psychology. He was interested in the large-scale social forces that move history, forces powerful enough to tap as spokesmen persons who, by a legalistic definition, are outside the emerging class. In the course of discussing the French peasantry in *The Eighteenth Brumaire,* Marx reveals his sensitivity to this problem. The French peasantry, he says, both is and is not a class:

Insofar as millions of families live under economic conditions that separate their mode of life, their interests and their culture from those of the other classes, and that place them in an attitude hostile toward the latter, they constitute a class; insofar as there exists only a local connection among these peasants, a connection which the individuality and exclusiveness of their interests prevent from generating among them any unity of interest, national connections, and political organization, they do not constitute a class. Consequently they are unable to assert their class interests in their own name, be it by a parliament or by convention. They cannot represent one another, they must themselves be represented. Their representative must at the same time appear as their master, as an authority over them.[20]

Although such empirical modifications of the theory of class and class ideology solve one problem, they create another. In showing how it is that external interpreters of class interest may see historical reality more clearly than members of the class itself, Marx comes close to saying that *only* such trained "scientific" interpreters as himself can know true class interest. Although Lenin was to develop it much further, there was an incipient elitism in Marx himself. His vicious personal attacks on theoretical deviates and former friends such as Bauer and Ruge suggest a closed circle of dogmatism by which the true criterion of class and class interest was known only to the insiders. The claim to scientific validity for his interpretation was and is weakened as long as large numbers of reputable but independent scholars find the criteria of class either ambiguous or esoteric.

Marx's conception of class interest, said Schumpeter, was "nearly as valuable as was the economic interpretation of history itself." Yet,

Curiously enough, Marx has never, as far as we know, worked out systematically what it is plain was one of the pivots of his thought. It is possible that he deferred the task until it was too late, precisely because his thinking ran so much in terms of class concepts that he did not feel it necessary to bother about definitive statement at all. It is equally possible that some points about it remained unsettled in his own mind, and that his way toward a full-fledged theory of classes was barred by certain difficulties he created for himself by insisting upon a

[20] In Beer, pp. 63–64.

purely economic and over-simplified conception of the phenomenon.[21]

Without objective scientific criteria of class, it can hardly be established that class is a fundamental motive force in history—not that this is all that is required. Marx's theory of the objective development of history is marred by factors of subjective interpretation. Indeed, "class" in the Marxian scheme may turn out to be just as metaphorical as *der Weltgeist, das Volk* or the American Way of Life.

If class is the key to the economic interpretation of history and the concept of class is ambiguous, we are brought back to the earlier question: why was economics itself so important to Marx? We find, paradoxically, that economics was important to Marx because capitalism had made economics too important. Beneath his veneer of scientific detachment—a thick veneer, and useful—we find a deep, bitter, and possibly confused moral indignation that human beings were being used in the industrial process as mere economic commodities. Although in the earlier Marx this indignation was unvarnished, in the later Marx the evidence for such dehumanizing mistreatment was presented in the form of the most technical and sometimes abstruse economic language. The argument was given the name of the theory of surplus value.

THE THEORY OF SURPLUS VALUE

The first thing to be said about the theory of surplus value is that, while it depends upon the labor theory of value, it is not the same thing as the labor theory of value. Students are frequently confused on this point. The labor theory of value dates back to Locke and found full expression in Ricardo and the so-called classical economists. It holds that the value of every commodity is proportional to the quantity of labor necessary to produce it, quantity being measured in man-hours and the labor assumed to be "socially useful" (i.e., a tree chopped down in the middle of a dense forest, if it cannot be removed or used on the spot, has no economic value however many hours were devoted to the felling). The theory also assumes, of course—and this is its weakness—perfect competition in the labor market and in the commodity market.

As a tool for economic analysis the theory was never very good. Even assuming perfect competition, it would work only where labor was the only significant factor in production (for what happens if weather and soil conditions mean that one hour of labor produces five boxes of luscious strawberries in one place and two boxes of scrawny inedibles in another? Will their economic value be the same?); and where different types of laboring activity were similar enough to be comparable (for what happens if we try to compare a diagnosing doctor with a pig-iron-shoveling laborer?). Time spent in training could of course be made to explain wage differentials between skilled and unskilled workers ("skilled labor counts only as simple labor intensified"[22]) and even a labor-replacing machine could be viewed as the embodiment of labor, but these adjustments did not meet the basic difficulties.

Marx, then, began with a strictly orthodox and rather inadequate economic doctrine that was rapidly becoming irrelevant to the real conditions of imperfect competition. Evidently Marx wanted to show up the capitalists using their own favorite theory, to build a model they could not ignore because it was based on their own assumptions. Perhaps he also clung to the labor theory of value because it was a necessary foundation for his truly inventive theory of surplus value. According to the latter, labor is a commodity like any other commodity; therefore, following the labor theory of value, it must be valued by the man-hours devoted to its "pro-

[21] Joseph A. Schumpeter, *Capitalism, Socialism, and Democracy*, 3rd ed. (New York: Harper & Row, 1950), pp. 14–15.

[22] *Capital*, Vol. 1, Ch. 1, trans. by Samuel Moore and Edward Aveling (Chicago: Kerr, 1919), p. 51.

duction"—that is, to feeding, clothing, and sheltering the worker in order to maintain life at subsistence level—which was, as a matter of fact, the level at which many workers were living in Marx's day. It could be said that labor is bought just as any other commodity is bought and valued in the same way. Marx meant it as almost more than a metaphor, therefore, when he spoke of "wage slavery." But, unlike other commodities, labor is not consumed in a clearly determinable period of time. A worker is "bought"—or more precisely his "labor force" or "labor potential" (*Arbeitskraft*) is bought—for the price of sustaining him physically, prorated in hours or days or weeks. But he may produce the equivalent of this price in economic value in six or eight hours of work, whereas the factories of Marx's day kept men going for ten, twelve, or fourteen hours a day. The difference between what the worker does (set by arbitrary standards of the work day) and what he is paid for (set by competition) is surplus value (*Mehrwert*), the source of all capitalist profits.[23] The labor power consumed has produced value in excess of its own replacement value.

Please note that surplus value is not just a matter of "cheating." The aim of Marx was to avoid such crass moralistic charges—at least in *Das Kapital;* the *Communist Manifesto* may be another matter. Given perfect competition, the capitalist can pay workers at the *correct* value of their labor potential, charge the customer the *correct* price for producing the commodity, and still have a margin left over—a thin layer of cream he skims off the top of the economic system. The system is at fault and not the employer, who, given the ideological basis of all social thinking, can literally conceive of no other way of operating, for no other way of operating can succeed within the capitalistic system. Marx eats his cake and has it too. He has inferentially revealed the injustice heaped upon the workers but he has shown it to be the result

not of bad men but of a particular system. Reform within the system, therefore, however well-intentioned, is doomed to failure. The state, being but the "executive committee of the ruling class," is powerless. Only revolutionary overthrow of the whole system can succeed. Only a new synthesis can overcome the contradiction between thesis and antithesis.

ACCUMULATION, IMMISERIZATION, REVOLUTION

Capitalists accumulate surplus value not because they enjoy champagne and yachting on the Riviera but because they need to accumulate in order to remain capitalists. Capitalist accumulation is both necessary and, by the rather unreal logic of perfect competition, in the long run disastrous. The continual pressure of competition means that firms must always be expanding production and producing technological innovations if they are to maintain income and keep ahead of their competitors. To do this they must accumulate capital. The best way to accumulate capital is through surplus value. Since what Marx called "constant capital" (machinery, plant, and so forth, produces no surplus value, the pressure is toward hiring more and more exploitable workers, whose labor is "variable capital." As the pace of competition in the consumer's market quickens, prices go down; as the pace of competition in the labor market quickens, wages go up—but only for the short run, as we will see.[24]

To meet the crisis of lower prices and higher wages, capitalists try to economize by introducing labor-saving machinery but this, while it may produce a temporary gain in the market, only accelerates the drying up of the surplus value that is needed for subsequent expansion. It is as if a cruel and mock-

---

[23] It must be noted that Marx did not deny to managerial talent its proper share of labor costs. Surplus value was over and above legitimate managerial reward.

[24] If Marx had not rejected Malthus' theories of population pressure, wages would not have gone up at this point.

ing Fate wheedles the capitalist into building his own trap without knowing what he is doing. The firm lags behind, struggling, and, when it can no longer survive in the desperate life of the economic jungle, it is swallowed up by a larger firm that is capable of consolidating units of control and increasing the size of plants. This theory of "expropriation" is but a corollary of the theory of "concentration," as the many become the few in the capitalist elite. The uneven progress of consolidation and collapse means alternating periods of boom and bust, which come with increasing rapidity and cause greater and greater panic.

The denouement of all this is described in the theory of *Verelendung* (which Schumpeter, with admirable literalness, translates as "immiserization"). The introduction of labor-saving machinery means that men are laid off, unemployment results, and wages fall. Now, when he needs a substitute for Malthus' population pressure, Marx invents the term "industrial reserve army" to describe the unemployed. As workers become more miserable, as they are herded into larger and in a sense "socialized" work units, the breaking point approaches. There is a "contradiction between the socialized organization in the individual factory and the social anarchy in production as a whole."[25] Let Marx describe the process:

As soon as this process of transformation has sufficiently decomposed the old society from top to bottom, as soon as the labourers are turned into proletarians, their means of labour into capital, as soon as the capitalist mode of production stands on its own feet, then the further socialisation of labour and further transformation of the land and other means of production, as well as the further expropriation of private proprietors, takes a new form. That which is now to be expropriated is no longer the labourer working for himself, but the capitalist exploiting many labourers. The expropriation is accomplished by the action of the immanent laws of capitalistic production itself, by the centralisation of capital. One capitalist always kills

many. Hand in hand with this centralisation, of this expropriation of many capitalists by few, develop, on an ever extending scale, the co-operative form of the labour-process, the conscious technical application of science, the methodical cultivation of the soil, the transformation of the instruments of labour into instruments of labour only usable in common, the economising of all means of production by their use as the means of production of combined, socialised labour, the entanglement of all peoples in the net of the world-market and this, the international character of the capitalistic regime. Along with the constantly diminishing number of the magnates of capital, who usurp and monopolise all advantages of this process of transformation, grows the mass of misery, oppression, slavery, degradation, exploitation; but with this too grows the revolt of the working-class, a class always increasing in numbers, and disciplined, organised by the very mechanism of the process of capitalist production itself. The monopoly of capital becomes a fetter upon the mode of production, which has sprung up and flourished along with it, and under it. Centralisation of the means of production and socialisation of labour at last reach a point where they become incompatible with their capitalist integument. This integument is burst asunder. The knell of capitalist private property sounds. The expropriators are expropriated. . . . It is the negation of negation.[26]

In this way the forces of production and the relations of production are brought back into harmony.

There is a difficulty if not an inconsistency in this process. Earlier Marx had said that factory owners were reluctant to introduce new machinery, since it produces no surplus value. Now he is saying that they *must* add new machinery in order to compete, even though they are dooming themselves in so doing. At several turns in the Marxian system we seem to find the equivalent of Adam Smith's "invisible hand" skillfully manipulating the vast congeries of forces to assure not, this time, that things will get better and better but that they will get worse and worse. Marx has a cataclysmic view of history: things must get worse be-

[25] Engels, *Socialism: Utopian and Scientific*, trans. by Edward Aveling (New York: International Publishers, 1935), p. 74.

[26] *Capital*, Vol. 1, Ch. 32, pp. 836–37.

fore they can get better. Eventually, they will get very good indeed.

Despite all his empirical evidence, despite his vast historical researches into the world wide depredations of capitalistic enterprise, Marx's over-all economic system rested upon deduction rather than induction and in the course of time turned out not to fit the real world very well. Workers' wages did not go down and down;[27] more machines did not mean fewer workers; and, finally, the predicted revolution never came —anywhere. What happened in Russia in 1917 or China in 1949 has very little similarity to the revolution Marx described. And the industrially advanced countries—England, Germany, the United States—where by Marx's logic the proletarian revolution would be most likely to occur, now seem to be the least likely environment for such an event.

Marx's prediction, however, of the growth of big business at a time when most enterprise was quite small and widely expected to stay that way was remarkably prescient. Nor was his general assumption that recurring slumps, panics, and depressions would become a chronic problem for a free-market economy too far off the mark. The pressing need for continual growth and expansion to prevent such depressions is now accepted by almost all economists and departure from the unregulated market in order to stimulate such growth by government expenditures is, in greater or lesser degree, today accepted by most. Though Marx's abstract, theoretical system was built on assumptions of perfect competition that never prevailed in actuality

and even became irrelevant as business consolidations brought about the imperfect competition of oligopoly, we must remember that Marx was relying on the Hegelian dialectic in more than a technical way and expected the capitalist system, both as a theoretical model and as a set of practices, to contradict itself—hence, the "negation of the negation." If he offered next to nothing by way of an adequate economic theory of monopoly, he did not feel obliged to offer anything. In a sense, his self-destructive economic theory had done its work. By the time he was talking about the final stages of capitalistic monopoly he had left economic theory behind and was once again immersed in the philosophy of history.

Belief in the inability of class-conscious capitalists[28] and their political representatives either to prevent the demise of unfettered competition or to abandon their ideological affection for such a system rests not upon economic theory but upon social and political theory; and in this, too, Marx was not completely in error. If capitalism did not, as he predicted, perish by violent revolution, neither did it survive in the form in which its nineteenth-century defenders knew it.

COMMUNISM AND THE CLASSLESS SOCIETY

Neither Marx nor Engels had much to say about what happens after the revolution. Engels said the most in *Anti-Dühring*—and in *Socialism: Utopian and Scientific,* which included one section relevant to this problem among the three lifted *in toto* from *Anti-Dühring.* Comes the revolution and:

[27] In time, workers' wages went up and up. Even in his own lifetime Marx had to explain how this could be. He tried the tricky way out of saying that, though concrete wages had risen, still, relative to the capitalist, the worker was worse off: ". . . although the comforts of the labourer have risen, the social satisfaction which they give has fallen in comparison with those augmented comforts of the capitalist. . . . Our wants and their satisfaction have their origin in society, and not in relation to the objects which satisfy them. Since their nature is social, it is therefore relative" (quoted in Abram L. Harris, "The Social Philosophy of Karl Marx," *Ethics,* Vol. 53 [1948], Part II, p. 25). If our "social satisfactions" are this far divorced from material reward, what happens to economic determinism?

[28] One of the major weaknesses of Marx's view was his failure to make a clear distinction between the "capitalist," who puts up the money to run the show, and the "entrepreneur," who may also put up some money but actually manages the business. In time, of course, the investing and managerial functions would become much more distinct than they were in Marx's day.

The proletariat seizes the State power and transforms the means of production in the first instance into State property. But in doing this, it puts an end to itself as the proletariat, it puts an end to all class differences and class antagonisms, it puts an end also to the State as the State. Former society, moving in class antagonisms, had need of the State. . . . [Now] The interference of State power in social relations becomes superfluous in one sphere after another, and then ceases of itself. The government of persons is replaced by the administration of things and the direction of the process of production. The State is not "abolished," *it withers away.*[29]

It is apparent that the word "state" has such evil connotations for Engels that a proletarian state is not even a rational possibility for him. Yet, evil though the state may be, its meaning is never made precise in either Marx or Engels, suggesting that political theory was not their primary interest. In *The Origin of the Family, Private Property and the State* Engels discusses the growth of institutions beginning with primitive communalism (relying heavily on Lewis Morgan's *Ancient Society,* [1877]). Whether a state even existed in that stage of history remains ambiguous in Engels' treatment. In general terms, the rise of the state is identified with the rise of private property and the whole network of law that constitutes the sinews of the modern state is regarded as an instrument of the ruling class.

Whether or not Hegel can be said to have stopped the dialectic with the Prussian state of his day, Marx and Engels certainly stopped the dialectic with the statelessness of proletarian triumph. The state, insofar as it suggested coercive class power, could logically have no existence in a condition of classlessness. Marx and Engels undoubtedly deserve to be placed with the utopians in their apparently sincere belief that coercive social power was tied to a particular culture and would disappear when that culture disappeared. To speak of the "administration of things" and the "direction" of production as if no human conflict and hence no politics

were involved can be regarded as nothing less than naive. Of course coercive regulatory power could not be wished away all at once, so Marx and Engels in a few places referred to the transitional stage as "the dictatorship of the proletariat." Marx apparently regarded the concept as one of his basic contributions:

no credit is due to me for discovering the existence of classes in modern society, nor yet the struggle between them. . . . What I did that was new was to prove: (1) that the *existence of classes* is only bound up with *particular, historic phases in the development of production;* (2) that the class struggle necessarily leads to the *dictatorship of the proletariat;* (3) that this dictatorship itself only constitutes the transition to the *abolition of all classes* and to a *classless society.*[30]

In Lenin, as we shall see, the phrase "dictatorship of the proletariat" became a basic concept for the strategy of practical politics. It did not have such a precise meaning for Marx and Engels. It did not mean the dictatorship of a small cadre of the party elite but simply the coming into its own of the proletarian class as a whole, crushing out in all areas the remnants of bourgeois mentality. The *Communist Manifesto* implied that the proletariat did not need to be organized into one centralized party to gain victory. Later Marx and Engels supported the idea of a worldwide Communist Party, but they did not conceive of it as the disciplined action group that Lenin made it. To Engels the dictatorship of the proletariat would be without "exploitation" and therefore without the oppression of the bourgeois state, but it would not be free of all coercion; therefore it would be "a half-state," "not a state in the proper sense of the word."[31] In *Anti-Dühr-*

[29] In Burns, pp. 295–96.

[30] *Letter to Georg Weydemeyer* (March 5, 1852), in *Selected Correspondence of Marx and Engels 1846–95,* trans. by Dona Torr (New York: International Publishers, 1942), p. 57.

[31] Quoted in Henry B. Mayo, *Introduction to Marxist Theory* (New York: Oxford Univ. Press, 1960), p. 158. Engels was not utopian enough to identify classlessness with complete equality: "There will always exist a certain inequality in the conditions of life. . . . the notion of socialist society as the realm of equality is a superficial French idea resting upon the old "liberty,

ing Engels suggests that during this period the slum-ridden industrial cities as they were in his day would be taken apart, piece by piece, and industry decentralized all over the landscape.

Looking at much more concrete, short-run aims, Marx in his *Address to the Communist League* (1852) told his hearers how they must beware of the "bourgeois democrats" who, after the revolution, would try to give land to the peasants as private property. Marx would nationalize the land and organize it into "settlements for the associated groups of the landed proletariat."[32] He would in every way attack the "reactionaries" and go one step further on every reform proposal of the "democrats." Workers' clubs should be centralized under an Executive Committee with headquarters in Germany. All workers should take immediate steps to insure that the "trickery" of local authorities does not deny them the vote. Apparently Marx accepted some usage of parliamentary machinery, for he talked of putting up working-class candidates in all constituencies. But he also spoke of arming the workers and of confiscating factories and railways. At any rate, there was enough flexibility in his words so that Lenin could make much expedient use of them. In fact, the basic problem of the status of state power in the dictatorship of the proletariat can be deferred to Chapter 24, for it was Lenin who from necessity took these fragments of political theory in Marx and made the most of them.

Suffice it to say that this transition period —as seen by Marx in *Critique of the Gotha Program*—would be a hard but glorious period for the faithful, eventuating in the establishment of an ideal communism, when the rule of "from each according to his ability, to each according to his work" would be replaced by the traditional communist goal of "from each according to his ability, to each according to his needs."[33] Bakunin had accused Marx of wishing to impose a new form of repressive state on the workers and perhaps Marx was at this point attempting to show that he, too, envisioned a free, libertarian order—in the long run. But he qualified this long-run utopianism—which had also flavored the *Communist Manifesto*— with some short-run realism suggesting that inequalities in both effort and reward would persist for some time under the new socialist rule. Lenin was most grateful, later, to be able to fall back on this concession to reality by the old master.

CONCLUSION: IDEOLOGY AND IDEALS IN SOCIAL CHANGE

As economist, Marx was brilliant but unsuccessful. The theory of surplus value was an ingenious but faulty construction and with the passage of time Marxian economics, as a technical science, has become not so much empty as irrelevant.

As theologian, Marx was naive but notoriously successful—even to the point of suggesting a correlation between naiveté and success. The comfort of dogmatic belief in an absolutely inevitable process is not unre-

---

equality, fraternity' " (*Letter to August Bebel* [March 28, 1875], in *Selected Correspondence of Marx and Engels,* p. 231). In his essay "On Authority" (1874), Engels ridiculed those who thought socialism meant the end of authority. The factory system itself, he said, creates an inescapable need for authority. Moreover, "A revolution is certainly the most authoritarian thing there is; it is the act whereby one part of the population imposes its will upon the other part." But after the revolution, *political* authority will be progressively "transformed into simple administrative functions" (Feuer, p. 485).

[32] In Burns, p. 69.

[33] *Critique of the Gotha Program,* in Feuer, p. 119. In this work Marx vehemently attacked what he regarded as the sentimental vagaries of the unity program adopted by two German socialist parties at Gotha in 1875. The quoted phrase is enshrined in the present Soviet Constitution as the ultimate Marxist goal. The period of the dictatorship of the proletariat is not a period of "communism," even though we popularly call the Soviet Union a communist system. To the orthodox Marxist, communism is the end condition; the means is "socialism." Like the communists, right-wing spokesmen frequently employ this verbal distinction in trying to discredit noncommunist socialism.

lated to the religious loyalty with which Marxists cling to their system. Marx's eschatology accounts for no small part of his historic success, even though from the standpoint of the outside his utopian theology must be regarded as a thin and emaciated myth by comparison with, say, the robust images of the Book of Revelation.

As social theorist, Marx was both provocative and influential. His fundamental conviction that class is the basic determinant of modes of human thought stimulated generations of scholars to look at social causation in a new light. Was Marx right? Few independently minded persons today would say yes. We can look at the bourgeois class that was the target of Marx's critique and find that many of its characteristic ideas—an atomistic conception of society, limited government, and so forth—far antedated the existence of the class as such. And some of what are taken to be its characteristic ideas will undoubtedly persist long after the class itself has dissolved or been transformed by historical forces into something else. In fact, to speak of two and only two classes, bourgeois and proletariat, toward which everyone and everything is being pushed is to make a statement with no empirical basis then or now. Like every philosophy of history, Marx's grand explanatory principle required an oversimplification of the infinitely complex pattern of action and response that is the substance of history. Communists to this day are victims of this oversimplification when they say, in effect, "If you're not for us, you're against us." Yet the dramatic way in which Marx pointed to class as a determinant of thought has made us realize that class is important. If not a determinant of thought, it is at least a conditioner.

That broad ideals familiar to many classes at many different times in history have af-

fected the worldly success of Marxism seems indubitable. Apart from all the trappings of economic analysis, there was in Marx's treatment of the theory of surplus value an underlying passion that bubbled to the surface from time to time. It was the sense of injustice born of contemplating the treatment of men as mere commodities. Exploitation in Marx's sense was inefficient, yes; but worse, it was dehumanizing. Yet bourgeois liberals like William Cobbett and John Stuart Mill also spoke out against the dehumanizing evils of an irresponsible factory system. As against this negative ideal, Marx briefly flashed to his readers a positive ideal of a classless society where social harmony and individual fulfillment would characterize an entire epoch. Yet the much-ridiculed utopian socialists had a no less striking vision of what the future might be and for a time struck a response in members of almost every class and station as widespread as that of Marxism.

Finally, Marx stood for one ideal more powerful, perhaps, than justice or social harmony, an ideal implicit in everything he wrote. It is what has sometimes been called the need to "get in step with history." To this day the great emotional appeal of Marxism is its own conviction of historical truth, the negation of finitude contained in its assurance that the "scientific" key to the historical process has at last been discovered. Hence it gives to its advocates the self-satisfying dogmatism of those who know they are right and know they will win. This is what has made Marxism one of the great "secular religions" of modern times. Without such nonmaterial and nondialectical aspirations, aspirations that cannot be understood simply by ideological analysis, dialectical materialism, paradoxically, would not have become the powerful ideology we know it to be.

22

NIETZSCHE

Of all the writers to whom we give special attention, Nietzsche is the most apolitical, the least concerned with governmental policies for a whole public. Two justifications may be offered for his inclusion in a political study. First, we may note that many lesser minds who were intensely interested in what we commonly call politics were profoundly interested in Nietzsche. We may rightfully look, therefore, to the source of their inspiration. Second, we sometimes find even in relatively apolitical writers—Augustine would be another—so fundamental a challenge to existing political norms that our understanding of those norms is clarified by examining the challenge. Such is singularly the case with Nietzsche.

LIFE

Friedrich Wilhelm Nietzsche was born in 1844 in the village of Rocken, Saxony, which was then in Prussia. His father was a successful and respected Lutheran pastor who died from a fall off a horse when Friedrich was still an infant. The family background

was Polish but Nietzsche was never able to substantiate his claim that his ancestors were Polish noblemen.

Nietzsche was brought up in an atmosphere of great piety and overwhelming femininity provided by a grandmother, a mother, a sister, and two aunts. They all meant well but the poor boy never had a chance. His classmates at school ridiculed him as the "Little Minister." In 1864 he went to the University of Bonn to study philosophy and, ostensibly, theology. Using up more of the family funds than was prudent, he made his last great effort to be one of the boys and threw himself into the gay social life of one of the *Burschenschaften*: going on excursions up the Rhine, drinking beer, singing lusty songs, even engaging in what turned out to be a mockery of a duel. According to one theory, during this time he picked up a case of syphilis that explains his later insanity. At any rate, it was largely a lost year as far as studies were concerned and not really a happy year, for student revelry was not natural to Nietzsche's temperament.

The next year he went to Leipzig, where the great classicist Friedrich Ritschl had just been appointed to a chair. Ritschl was not only a great scholar but a great teacher who knew that his duty, as Nietzsche was later to express it, was to "find [the] chief talent in his pupil, and to assist the latter in organizing his whole life by means of it."[1] With only his love of music and solitary walks for diversion, Nietzsche buried himself in classical philology. With Ritschl's encouragement he wrote and published learned articles. Already his Lutheran orthodoxy had left him and he had set upon the lonely course suggested in a letter to his sister written at the end of his year at Bonn: "Certainly faith alone saves. . . . Every true faith is indeed infallible: it accomplishes that which the believer concerned hopes to find in it; it does not offer the least support for the establishment of an objective truth. It is here then that the ways of men divide: do you wish to strive after peace of mind and happiness, well then believe; do you wish to be a disciple of truth, then inquire."[2] The alternatives were too sharply posed but the quest of honesty at all costs was to become a Nietzschean trademark.

More important than Ritschl's influence on Nietzsche, at least during his first year at Leipzig, was his discovery of Schopenhauer,[3] whose Eastern quietism resulting from his pessimistic philosophy of blind will that rules the world seemed to the young Nietzsche the height of wisdom. Having accidentally come across *The World as Will and Idea* (1818) in a bookstore, Nietzsche took it home and devoured it, finding it a mirror of himself.

Serving his year of required military service, Nietzsche, in the autumn of 1867, fell off a horse as his father had and was severely injured. He was given a medical discharge and was never again in good health. Affected with migraine headaches and weak eyesight, he became more and more hypochondriac

and more and more dependent upon drugs. He went back to Leipzig, indulged his musical tastes, and was blessed with a meeting with Wagner, whose music he loved. The meeting led to a great but short friendship, a romance with Wagner's wife Cosima, and a long and bitter quarrel over Wagner's violent racism and nationalism.[4]

Thanks to the reputation of his articles and the support of Ritschl, Nietzsche was asked to become professor of Greek at the University of Basel in 1869. At not quite twenty-five, Nietzsche accepted a position that many older men coveted. He held the post until 1879, when ill health forced his resignation, and he was reasonably successful as a teacher. When the Franco-Prussian War came in 1870, Nietzsche was eager to fight for his fatherland against the "cursed French tiger" but, since he was now a Swiss national, the most he could do was serve as a volunteer ambulance attendant. His service was brief but bloody and ended when he picked up dysentery and diphtheria from his wounded patients. Despite his patriotism, he wept when he heard of the Germans burning the Louvre in Paris and openly questioned whether Prussia might be a danger to culture.

Nietzsche returned to Basel, gave some widely heralded public lectures, and on the last day of 1871 held in his hands the first copy of the newly published *Die Geburt der Tragödie* (*Birth of Tragedy*). This began a series of memorable publications. According to Andler,[5] Nietzsche's work can be put into two cycles, each consisting of a period of mystical intuition followed by a period of rigorous analysis. The first period, which he calls "Wagnerian revaluation," lasted from 1869 to 1876. During this time Nietzsche felt

---

[1] H. A. Reyburn, *Nietzsche* (London: Macmillan, 1948), p. 44.

[2] June 11, 1865. Quoted in Reyburn, p. 36.

[3] Arthur Schopenhauer (1788–1860) of Danzig, Hamburg, and Frankfurt. Independently wealthy, Schopenhauer studied at several universities and wrote his philosophy untroubled by the need of gainful employment. He was a brilliant linguist.

[4] The Wagner Circle of racist intellectuals, later called the Bayreuth Circle, lasted with scarcely a break in continuity into the 1920s, when Eckhart, Hitler, Goebbels, and Rosenberg were members.

[5] Charles Andler, in *Encyclopaedia of the Social Sciences,* Edwin B. A. Seligman and Alvin Johnson, eds. (New York: Macmillan, 1933), Vol. XI, pp. 373–75; see also Andler's *Nietzsche: Sa vie et sa pensée* (Paris: Bossard, 1920–31).

Nietzsche as Philosopher

that the great age of Greek tragedy and philosophy was being reborn in Germany. The music of Wagner and the philosophy of Schopenhauer were, to him, symptomatic of this rebirth. Nietzsche felt that neither science nor the state had done anything to promote the arts and he advocated the establishment of a new institute of culture. There followed a period of "intellectualistic evolutionism" (1876–81). During this period, says Andler, Nietzsche seemed to turn against the state as an institution of force and to seek instead a "society of free spirits" created as a work of art by some transcendent genius, a pan-European rather than a nationalistic society.

Next came the period of "lyrical affirmation" (1882–85), during which was produced the best known of Nietzsche's works, *Thus Spake Zarathustra,* a poem with great poetic imagery and not a small amount of nonsense. The final period was "critical reflection on the values of decadence and renaissance" (1885–88). This time critical reflection seemed to confirm rather than dissolve Nietzsche's mystical insights.

After 1879 Nietzsche, living a drab, impoverished life, wandered from Sils-Maria in the Alpine valley of the Engadine in the summer to Genoa or Nice in the winter. In 1889 he cracked up. Embracing a horse being flogged in the street, he prayed for its beatification by God and then collapsed. A Basel friend, church historian Franz Overbeck, came to get Nietzsche and found him, shrieking, pounding a piano with his elbow. Going by train to a clinic in Basel, Overbeck could not prevent the usually soft-spoken Nietzsche from shouting out his poetry. From the clinic he was taken to an asylum in Jena and finally to Weimar, where he died half paralyzed by a stroke and "sunk in a docile imbecility." It was only after his insanity that has fame grew and then it was impossible to prevent exploitation of his name by his sister.

After Nietzsche's insanity came *Anti-Christ* (1885) and, published posthumously, *Der Wille zur Macht: Versuch einer Umwertung aller Werte (The Will to Power: Attempt at a Transvaluation of All Values,* Vol. 1, 1901; Vol. 2, 1906) and *Ecce Homo* (written 1888, published 1908).[6] Nietzsche's sister had much to do with *The Will to Power,* to its detriment. A woman of great zeal but limited intelligence, she married a rabid anti-Semite named Förster, who committed suicide after trying to organize a Teutonic colony in Paraguay. Changing her name to Elizabeth Förster-Nietzsche, the sister became a dedicated manager of her brother's reputation. She cornered and hoarded his manuscripts and in an arbitrary and biased way put together the fragments that were published as *The Will to Power.* She lived to know Hitler and was in large part responsible for Nietzsche's spurious reputation as an anti-Semite and for the attempts to link him to Nazism.

Nietzsche had a gentle laugh and a fragile politeness that attracted people yet kept them at a distance. He always seemed to feel alone and to convey that feeling. He wore a very long military mustache almost as a mask to hide his inner turmoil. The most introspective of philosophers—in this lay the essence of his contribution—and an advocate of painful candor, he nevertheless probably failed to see the degree to which his praise of noble bestiality concealed his own effeminate reserve and his role of Anti-Christ mirrored a deep spiritual longing.

NIETZSCHE AS PHILOSOPHER

One scholar, as we have seen, finds that Nietzsche's work fits into a neat pattern of cycles. Another, however, finds only a pattern of irrational patternlessness:

[6] *Ecce Homo,* Nietzsche's autobiography, features as opening chapters "Why I Am So Wise," "Why I Am So Clever," and "Why I Write Such Excellent Books." These titles are more cynical than vain, claims Kaufmann, and take their inspiration from Socrates in Plato's *Apology. Ecce Homo* is Vol. XVII of Friedrich Nietzsche, *The Complete Works,* trans. by Anthony Ludovici and others, in Oscar Levy, ed. (London: Allen & Unwin, 1910–11). Hereafter cited as *Complete Works.*

Try the following experiment: take any one of his [Nietzsche's] works and open it at random. Start reading. Aphorism *n* has an electrifying effect. With enthusiasm we approve the correctness of what it says. Aphorism *n* plus 1 also calls forth our vivid assent. This goes on for a while until suddenly, while reading Aphorism *nn′*, we realize that somewhere something has got out of control, that the author has started raving, that something must have happened. . . . The solution of the puzzle is that we are dealing with a man who is seriously ill.[7]

Another scholar sees in Nietzsche a subtle, truly philosophic mind at work. Although granting Nietzsche's disdain for the pretense of "objectivity" and his dislike of scientific dogmatism, Morgan sees his work as that of a "growing system" that could attain a completeness, if at all, only at the end. "In his last self-comments Nietzsche not only affirms but specifies the essential identity in his thinking. . . . the problem of good and evil occupied him continually from his fourteenth year. . . . Nietzsche of course does not claim an absolute identity in all his writings; rather, his ideal of philosophy as a fruit of life implies change, including the discard of things outgrown." Morgan, too, acknowledges different periods of Nietzsche's development, with dramatic turning points, but he claims they were not accidental but "a dialectical pattern with cumulative effect." Morgan concludes that "there can be no doubt that he deserves to be read seriously as a philosopher."[8] Likewise, Kaufmann says, "he embodied the true philosophic spirit."[9]

Arendt, on the other hand, sees Nietzsche, along with Kierkegaard and Marx, as a symbol of the end of philosophy. Although it was, in Arendt's view, twentieth-century totalitarianism that shattered the Western philosophical tradition, Nietzsche's

"leap from the non-sensuous transcendent realm of ideas and measurements into the sensuousness of life, his 'inverted Platonism' or 'trans-valuation of value,'" was the means whereby he "tried desperately to think against the tradition using its own conceptual tools."[10] Jaspers attributes to Nietzsche the same radical position but sees it as a new beginning rather than an end to philosophy:

The contemporary philosophical situation is determined by the fact that two philosophers, Kierkegaard and Nietzsche, who did not count in their times and for a long time remained without influence in the history of philosophy, have continually grown in significance. . . . They stand today as the authentically great thinkers of their age. . . . Their thinking created a new atmosphere. They passed beyond all of the limits then regarded as obvious. It is as if they no longer shrank back from anything in thought.[11]

In the tradition of philosophy from Parmenides to Hegel, says Jaspers, Being is discovered in thought. With Kierkegaard Being is discovered in faith and in Nietzsche it is discovered in the "will-to-power." But beyond this surface definitional distinction is the methodologically significant point that neither faith nor will-to-power are concepts in the traditional sense but mere *signa*. They do not connote but point to and are hence "capable of endless explication."[12]

Obviously, estimates of Nietzsche's philosophical significance turn on judgments not only of the nature of philosophy but of what he was trying to do. And he himself was perhaps not too sure of this. To say that he

---

[7] Robert Rie, "Nietzsche and After," *Journal of the History of Ideas*, Vol. 13 (1952), p. 353.

[8] George Allen Morgan, Jr., *What Nietzsche Means* (Cambridge: Harvard Univ. Press, 1941), pp. 25, 26, and 29.

[9] Walter A. Kaufmann, *Nietzsche: Philosopher, Psychologist, Anti-Christ* (Princeton: Princeton Univ. Press, 1950), p. x.

[10] Hannah Arendt, "Tradition and the Modern Age," *Partisan Review*, Vol. 21 (1954), pp. 63 and 60.

[11] Karl Jaspers, *Reason and Existence*, trans. by William Earle (New York: Noonday Press, 1955), pp. 23–24.

[12] *Ibid.*, p. 27. Thus, Nietzsche refers to morality as a "sign-language of the feelings." See Jaspers, *Nietzsche; An Introduction to the Understanding of His Philosophical Activity*, trans. by Charles F. Wallraff and Frederick J. Schmitz (Tucson: Univ. of Arizona Press, 1965), Bk. II, Ch. 1. Nietzsche's "great politics"—great in the sense of being beyond the purview of any single state—is discussed in Bk. II, Ch. 4. Nietzsche "never glorifies the 'state as such.'"

was in "revolt against reason" is suggestive but too simple. What people mean when they say that Nietzsche was not a philosopher is that he was an impulsive artist with words who strung no beads of logical propositions. He communicated to his select followers by allusion and metaphor rather than by definition and demonstration. He tried, not to transcend sensation as did Plato or to unite sensation and thought as did Hegel, but to burrow into sensation as far as he could go—beyond reflection and beyond thought. Through his discussion of guilt and dreams and instinct he was a contributor to Freudian psychology. Through his subjectivism he was a strong influence on contemporary existentialism. He was also a moralist, though a perverse one. He was perplexed by the problems of good and evil and inspired if incautious in studying the cultural origin of social values. He believed in and practiced the use of etymology to teach us about ourselves—as individuals and as societies. In these respects surely he can be called a philosopher.

THE DIONYSIAN MYTH

In *The Birth of Tragedy* Nietzsche highlights, by striking leaps of imagination, the interrelationships of the Apollonian and Dionysian myths in ancient Greece, relationships generally confirmed by later scholarship. Both Apollo and Dionysus were art-sponsoring deities but, says Nietzsche, Dionysus was closer to the primal urges expressed in music and in the transport of intoxication. Apollo was the sponsor of the visual, plastic arts, whose spirit appeared in the more detached, personalized imagery of dreams. Apollo spoke for individuation and separateness and quiet balance. Dionysus symbolized a wild plunge into the flux of life, the unity and community of all things. The Apollonian, as in Doric art, tended to discipline the Dionysiac, somewhat at the latter's expense, according to Nietzsche. Already in this, his

first book, Nietzsche is revealing his nihilistic bent, or perhaps more accurately his "immoralist" bent. The high point of Greek culture, he says, came in the great amoral art— all art for him was amoral by any conventional standard of morality—of Aeschylean tragedy, which was the union of Dionysian and Apollonian elements. Philistine interpreters saw tragedy as justifying a moral order. Aristotle saw tragedy as a purgative for pity and fear. Schopenhauer saw tragedy as a lesson in resignation. Nietzsche rejected all these. He saw tragedy as a tonic for life, an affirmation of joy in existence, which included evil as well as good. In a sense therefore, tragedy justified evil: "We may express the Janus face, at once Dionysiac and Apollonian, of the Aeschylean Prometheus in the following formula: 'Whatever exists is both just and unjust, and equally justified in both.' What a world!"[13]

Tragedy began to perish with Euripides, who was infected with the optimistic, rationalistic spirit of Socrates, "the great exemplar of the theoretical man." This spirit tried to make reasonable everything that was beautiful, held that virtue is knowledge and that only the virtuous are happy, and tried to overcome death with this cheery faith. Hence real tragedy was gone. The grand illusion of Socrates "that thought, guided by the thread of causation, might plumb the farthest abysses of being and even correct it,"[14] persists to the present day, weakening the hold of nonrational myth, without which every culture loses its creativity. But the dark powers of Dionysian feeling are still latent and spring forth in every truly artistic act and the memory of great tragedy lingers in and gives "supreme significance" to dissonance in modern music.

[13] *The Birth of Tragedy*, Ch. 9, in *The Birth of Tragedy and the Genealogy of Morals*, trans. by Francis Golffing (Garden City, N. Y.: Doubleday, Anchor, 1956), p. 65. Subsequent quotations from *The Birth of Tragedy* and *The Genealogy of Morals* are from this spritely, useful, and convenient translation.

[14] *Ibid.*, p. 93. In later years Nietzsche came to have greater respect for Socrates' position.

ETERNAL RECURRENCE
AND SUPERMAN

Convalescing in the Alps in 1881 Nietzsche was struck with an idea of such emotional force that he wept in great gushes. It was the idea that came to be known as "eternal recurrence." In brief it is simply that, since there is only so much energy in the universe, all possible combinations of it have occurred in the past and will recur in the future. Life, in short, is not a matter of infinite expansion but an endless cycle. There is nothing very precise in this concept. It is a matter of mood rather than hypothesis and the physical questions raised by such a theory, the nature of space and matter, are pushed aside or ignored. What was more important for Nietzsche was that it removed purpose from the world but also created a kind of timelessness that has been called Christian immortality in a new form.[15] Man makes his own purposes but they are not trivial, for one's own "highest feeling" and the means necessary to achieve it are in a way part of nature's plan. The doctrine of eternal recurrence was for Nietzsche a substitute for the religion and the universalistic ethics he had thrown out.

The great expression of the idea of eternal recurrence was made by Nietzsche in his most popular book, *Thus Spake Zarathustra* (1883). Also introduced in *Zarathustra* was the idea of the Superman, the one who could take the empty freedom of the universe and by sheer exertion of courage make of it what he would, thereby surpassing the ordinary timid breed of man:

I teach you the Superman. Man is something that is to be surpassed. What have ye done to surpass man?

All beings hitherto have created something beyond themselves: and ye want to be the ebb of that great tide, and would rather go back to the beast than to surpass man? . . .

Lo, I teach you the Superman!

The Superman is the meaning of the earth. Let your will say: The Superman *shall be* the meaning of the earth!

I conjure you, my brethren, *remain true to the earth* and believe not those who speak unto you of superearthly hopes! Prisoners are they, whether they know it or not.[16]

The comic-strip character Superman is a testament to the perverse effect of literary appropriation; but he may also have rendered more difficult an American's understanding of Nietzsche. *Übermensch* is literally "overman" but *über* has at least two meanings in this context. One is "ruling over" and the other is "higher than." We could with justification, therefore, translate *Übermensch* as "looked-up-to-man," a higher creation because it is a self-creation, one who has overcome man because "man is something that must be overcome." The implausibility of this "answer" to the despair Nietzsche found in life is matched only by the depth of that despair, for even the great men of the past were miserable creatures:

Ah, man returneth eternally! The small man returneth eternally!

Naked had I once seen both of them, the greatest man and the smallest man: all too like one another—all too human, even the greatest man!

Ah, Disgust! Disgust! Disgust![17]

It is not fair to say of Nietzsche or his Superman, as Brinton does, "A thousand Nietzsches have written a thousand appeals to create the Superman, and a thousand more will write again the same appeal, world without end and words without end. But no Nietzsche will ever have the slightest memory of another Nietzsche."[18] Nietzsche's memory was more acute and his Superman was less unoriginal than this implies. As a

---

[15] See Jacob Taubes, "Community—After the Apocalypse," in Carl J. Friedrich, ed., *Community* (New York: Liberal Arts Press, 1959).

[16] *Thus Spake Zarathustra*, Prologue, sec. 3, trans. by Thomas Common (London: Allen & Unwin, n.d.), pp. 6–7. Subsequent quotations from *Zarathustra* are from this edition.

[17] *Ibid.*, Part 3, Disc. 57, sec. 2, p. 268.

[18] Crane Brinton, *Nietzsche* (Cambridge: Harvard Univ. Press, 1941), pp. 140–41.

figure apart, the Superman can appear only excruciatingly paradoxical: Godlike, yet wholly of this earth; wholly new, yet eternally recurring; a man set apart, yet, because he is needed, somehow a cultural creation. That he is wholly different from ordinary men, even "great" men of the past, becomes more apparent when we note how, in his aphorisms, Nietzsche can penetrate human foibles with an almost cynical clarity: "One uses one's principles to tyrannize or justify or honor or affront or conceal one's habits." "Who has not at some time or other sacrificed himself in order to save his reputation?" "A great man, did you say? All I ever see is the actor creating his own ideal image."[19]

The Superman cannot be God, for "God is dead" as Nietzsche many times says.[20] Kant and Hegel, with their elaborate reconciliations of technical philosophy with Christian theology, were merely "procrastinators" of atheism. The death sentence imposed on God is more than a personal judgment. It was, for Nietzsche, the end of a civilization. Yet Nietzsche knew that life is not possible without illusion, that "the sincere person ends by realizing that he always lies."[21] And so he deliberately created and gave us an illusion born of his own experience of reflection six thousand feet high in the Alps. He called it *Übermensch*. The term points to a man apart who is also not apart. The *Übermensch* is not only some future race of giants; it is also the higher selves in each of us. Original as its form may be, Nietzsche did not claim newness for the idea itself. In essence it comes from classical literature and may be found in the earliest Dionysian joy in life as it is. Thus Superman and "eternal recurrence" are not as antagonistic as they might seem at first.[22]

Nietzsche's Superman is explicitly distinguished from the historical-political heroes of Carlyle—"that great counterfeiter," as Nietzsche called him. If Superman is apolitical and ahistorical yet does not reside in some transcendental sphere, he must reside in us as individuals. That he is not a political leader is clear from *Zarathustra:*

> Somewhere there are still peoples and herds, but not with us, my brethren: here there are states. . . . the coldest of all cold monsters. Coldly lieth it also; and this lie creepeth from its mouth: "I, the state, am the people."
> It is a lie! . . .
> There, where the state ceaseth—there only commenceth the man who is not superfluous. . . . Do ye not see it, the rainbow and the bridges of the Superman?[23]

NIETZSCHE AS CRITIC

During the writing of *Zarathustra,* Nietzsche broke away to write *Die Fröhliche Wissenschaft (The Gay Science,* 1882),[24] which was aphoristic, worldly wise, and autobiographical, forming a sequence with the earlier *Menschliches Allzumenschliches (Human All Too Human,* 1878) and *The Dawn of Day* (1881). In a more mordantly practical approach than that of *Zarathustra,* Nietzsche in *The Dawn of Day* suggests that one way the individual may lift the weight

---

[19] *Beyond Good and Evil*, Art. 4, Nos. 77, 92, and 97, trans. by Marianne Cowan (Chicago: Regnery, Gateway, 1955), pp. 76 and 78. Subsequent quotations from *Beyond Good and Evil* are from this edition.

[20] *Zarathustra*, Prologue, sec. 2, p. 5. See also Nietzsche, *Nachgelassene Werke, Gross-oktav Ausgabe* (Leipzig: Kröner, 1901–26), Vol. 5, pp. 147 and 271; Vol. VI, p. 12; Vol. XIII, p. 316; and Morgan, pp. 36–42. Nietzsche is speaking of the Christian God. About other gods, he seems to agree with Epicurus: "If there are gods, they do not care for us."

[21] *Nachgelassene Werke*, Vol. 12, p. 293. Cited in Morgan, p. 51. Hans Vaihinger puts great importance on Nietzsche's "doctrine of conscious illusion" in the development of his own "philosophy of 'as if.'" See *The Philosophy of "As If,"* trans. by C. K. Ogden (London: Routledge & Kegan Paul, 1935), pp. 341–42.

[22] The evidence for this interpretation of *Übermensch* is well stated by Kaufmann, Ch. 11.

[23] *Zarathustra*, Part 1, Disc. 11, pp. 54 and 57. Note that it is not a bridge *to* Superman but a bridge *of* Superman. The metaphor suggests that we may use the illusion-myth-symbol of the Superman to move up out of our lesser selves.

[24] This is sometimes translated *The Joyful Wisdom,* a less revealing title.

of customary morality with which society oppresses him is to achieve the great prestige of madness. In *The Gay Science* a calmer Nietzsche brings the doctrine of eternal recurrence once more to the fore and at the end brings in the prophet Zarathustra, who now deigns to leave his solitary height and go down into the world of men to distribute his riches—not, however, as an exercise of charity but as an exercise of power. The "gaiety" of the science Nietzsche approved of lay in its willingness to experiment fearlessly and to take lightly any settled opinion. Nietzsche was not hostile to science, only to dogmatic science.

After the great effort of finishing *Zarathustra,* Nietzsche was again full of dejection. But he bounced back and set aside his next six years to write *Zarathustra*'s prose counterpart, his great work of philosophy, which was to be called *The Will to Power.* As we have seen, it was not completed in his lifetime. Again he kept breaking off to include portions of the greater work in smaller versions, some of which overlapped and some of which were written at high speed. The best known is *Jenseits von Gut und Böse (Beyond Good and Evil,* 1886), which was followed by *Genealogie der Moral (The Genealogy of Morals,* 1887), *Der Fall Wagner (The Case of Wagner,* 1888), *Götzendämmerung (The Twilight of Idols,* 1889), and *The Anti-Christ.*

By the time of *Beyond Good and Evil* Nietzsche seemed somewhat less the scholarly philologist and more the colorful essayist, although he had never been colorless. Here he plays with the reader, purposely leaving crucial thoughts in midair, toying with words, making tongue-in-cheek exaggerations. Almost surreptitiously he notes that most of the time when he is saying terrible things about "women as such," he is talking about himself. Even the form is playful. The 296 paragraphs are divided into nine scholasticlike articles with faintly ironic titles: "We Intellectuals," "Our Virtues," "Peoples and Fatherlands," and "What Does 'Distinguished' Mean?" Article 4 is "Aphorisms and Entr'actes," pithy and powerful

assertions ranging all over the landscape; and elsewhere as well, the sudden, barely relevant insight flashes before the eye: "It was a masterpiece of *British* instinct to sanctify and dullify the Sunday to such a degree that the Briton quite unnoticeably begins to yearn for his workaday week."

If the work is impossible to summarize, the themes are clear enough. They have appeared before and will appear again: what is often taken to be morality is merely timidity, an inability to face up to the fact that one's guidelines to life are based upon illusion; comprehension is but the tool of desire, reason a pawn of instinct; the self-deception of philosophers is one of the most amusing phenomena of intellectual life. Kant's categorical imperative mainly tells us that Kant wanted to be a dutiful person. Schopenhauer could not be a consistent pessimist because he enjoyed playing the flute too much. Descartes was "superficial" in claiming that reason was his only authority. Spinoza "naively recommended destruction of the passions through analyzing and vivisecting them." Aristotle with his golden mean would tone down the passions "till they reach a harmless mediocrity." Much of this was *ad hominem* forensics but Nietzsche's wild slashes at the stupid arrogance of those who claim a "science of morality" come close to the jugular. When he much too briefly draws upon linguistics to demonstrate how much of our supposedly hard knowledge depends upon uncontrollable intuitive leaps, we have the feeling that he could, if he would, take everyone apart analytically as he has done rhetorically.

As he criticized everything else, Nietzsche criticized German culture. No nationalist, he. And the opposite of an anti-Semite, saying that "the Jews are beyond doubt the strongest, toughest, purest race now living in Europe." It is a sign of the weakness and insecurity of German nationhood that Germans are "afflicted now by the anti-French stupidity, now by the anti-Semitic, now the anti-Polish. . . . I hope that I shall be forgiven if I, too, during a brief reckless sojourn in this infected country, did not remain entirely free of the disease; if I too, like everybody else, began to have thoughts about things which are none of my business—the first symptom of political infection." "It would be useful to banish from the country the anti-Semitic crybabies." Nietzsche thought of national political problems as petty problems, beneath his gaze, and after discussing this one, he quickly jumps back to "my *serious* problem: the European problem as I understand it: the breeding of a new caste which is to rule Europe."[25]

The thrust of disillusionment once more having dissolved politics, we are confronted again with the necessity of a Superman, the "natural master" who knows what he wants, takes it, and holds it. ". . . when such a man feels compassion, then such compassion is worth something! But of what use is the compassion of those who suffer? Or even worse of those who *preach* compassion?" But as disillusionment dissolved politics, so also in the end it dissolves philosophy and even the counterpart of Zarathustra's Superman here adumbrated does not evoke great conviction. Candor seems to be the only virtue left, says Nietzsche, and laughter the only action. Though Hobbes tried to ruin the reputation of laughter, "I should permit myself an ordering of the ranks of philosophers according to the quality of their laughter—all the way up to those who are capable of *golden* laughter. And if the gods, too, philosophize . . . I do not doubt that they also know how to laugh in superhuman and original fashion—and at the expense of all serious things!" There is more consistency in Nietzsche than one might think. The tragicomic symphony never stops.

GOOD AND EVIL, GOOD AND BAD

The prose work of Nietzsche that is most compelling to contemporary readers is proba-

[25] Although there are passages that suggest the literal eugenic breeding of a new caste, Nietzsche here must be taken to mean "breeding" in a metaphorical sense.

bly *The Genealogy of Morals.* The thesis of the work still has the power to shock. Nietzsche raises the questions of the value of values and how man has come to invent judgments of good and evil. He boldly asserts that in the dim dawn of history the strong simply created those conceptions of "good" that would be of most use to them and imposed them on the weak. But from time to time the weak outsmart the strong and sell their ideas to civilization, a maneuver most notably illustrated by the history of Christianity. The crisis of the present age, which is really the crisis behind everything Nietzsche wrote, is the decay of judgmental language, the irrelevance of moral standards, and the lack of strong men to impose a new standard. Nietzsche was a nihilist not in the sense that he was one who said men do not need moral standards, but rather in the sense that he was one who said moral standards have no intrinsic morality. The many, the vulgar, will never be able to understand this.

After a swipe at the English utilitarians' lack of historical sense, Nietzsche concedes the relevance of their criterion of practicality to morals, even though they do not understand what this relevance is. Nietzsche does turn to history in general and etymology in particular to demonstrate that the word "good" almost invariably originated from a word meaning "noble" in the class sense. Or, to put it another way, "Political supremacy always gives rise to notions of spiritual supremacy." Two qualifications need to be thrown into this equation. While the noble were basically the strong, Nietzsche did not make sheer physical force alone the determinant of right. Class power, even the power of military conquerors, existed in a context that imposed conditions. Secondly, the sometimes subtle modes of resistance of the weak, especially the admonitions of priests and seers, are what have most contributed to making man an "interesting" creature. Had there been nothing to contend with in history but the depredations of the powerful, man could not have become profound as well as evil: "The greatest haters in history—but also the most intelligent haters—have been priests.

Beside the brilliance of priestly vengeance all other brilliance fades. Human history would be a dull and stupid thing without the intelligence furnished by its impotents."

The most brilliant case of the weak outsmarting the strong was what the Jews did with Jesus. They first dared to invert all the basic values: the good became not the powerful, the noble, the privileged, and the healthy but the weak, the ignoble, the poor, and the suffering. Then they took the most conspicuous prophet of this doctrine, Jesus of Nazareth, and nailed him to a cross "like a mortal enemy, so that 'the whole world' (meaning all the enemies of Israel) might naively swallow the bait." As a result, the slaves, the mob, the herd, democrats, Christians, Jews—they are all very much the same for Nietzsche—have more and more taken over from aristocrats and imposed their cringing, negative ethics. They are not necessarily stupid. Their kind of life breeds a kind of sharp-wittedness. But such a person's "soul squints."

The noble classes or races live by a distinction between good and bad by which the good (what they want) is uppermost and its opposite, the bad, is almost an afterthought. The slave morality pervading the modern world is that of good and evil, in which a deified evil born in rancor, bitterness, vengeance, and *ressentiment,* dominates the whole mentality and good is only the passive, sugar-coated restraint of these feelings. The true noble spirits bear no grudges. They are positive thinkers. They can return "from an orgy of murder, arson, rape, and torture, jubilant and at peace with themselves as though they had committed a fraternity prank."[26]

The phrase "beyond good and evil" has at least three meanings in Nietzsche. It means first, as appears here, that true noble spirits are unconfined by conventional morality. But it also suggests that the role of the critic, that is, Nietzsche, is to conduct inquiries without regard to current moralisms, to penetrate be-

hind and beyond them. Finally, there is, standing by itself as a reminder of the tender side of Nietzsche, Aphorism 153 of *Beyond Good and Evil:* "What is done out of love always happens beyond good and evil." Here we find a special morality not apart from but deeper than ordinary morality.

The noble spirit of *The Genealogy of Morals* is called the "autonomous" man, one who is "more than moral." Here more clearly than elsewhere in Nietzsche's writings the autonomous man is recognized as the end product of a long and pain-racked history, pain-racked because it is only through the infliction of great pain that ordinary men could be made to remember their race's history and to do what society demanded of them. In modern times the rack, boiling in oil, and flaying alive have been abandoned; but punitive and festival cruelties have now simply been replaced by psychological ones. As a community becomes full of pride and power, its penal code becomes more lenient; but when the community is threatened, the code becomes harsh again. Justice itself may be canceled out under the name of mercy but mercy as well as justice is still defined by the man outside the law—the strong, the autonomous, the "active man" rather than the "reactive man."

Nietzsche ridicules the historians of law for their easy acceptance of the original purpose of laws as exhaustive of their present meaning. These historians tend to ignore the constant transmutations of function as legal institutions are used differently by each ascending generation. He loosely links this distortion with "The democratic bias against anything that dominates or wishes to dominate." Spencer's faith in progressive adaptation of the species "misjudges the very essence of life; it overlooks the intrinsic superiority of the spontaneous, aggressive, overreaching, reinterpreting and re-establishing forces, on whose action adaptation gradually supervenes." The spontaneous expression of instinct is creative; its repression as encouraged by religion produces a sense of indebtedness to higher powers, the "bad conscience" that is "the wellspring of all altruistic values."

---

[26] Such admirably uninhibited fellows could be found almost anywhere. Nietzsche mentions the Roman, Arabian, German, Japanese, and Scandinavian nobles, as well as the Homeric heroes, who, one suspects, were his models.

Therefore "Atheism and a kind of 'second innocence' go together."

The third part of *The Genealogy of Morals* is an examination of the "ascetic ideal," which concludes that man's capacity to suffer, to be cruel to himself, has been a part of all the great cultural achievements upon which lesser men today complacently feed: ". . . learning today is a hiding place for all manner of maladjustment, lukewarmness, self-depreciation, guilty conscience. Its restless activity thinly veils a lack of ideals, the want of a great love." Yet beneath the falsity and hypocrisy of society persists a driving human will not so much troubled by suffering as by its meaning. *The Genealogy of Morals* concludes:

the ascetic ideal arose to give it [suffering] meaning—its only meaning, so far. But any meaning is better than none and in fact, the ascetic ideal has been the best stopgap that ever existed. . . . It signifies, let us have the courage to face it, a will to nothingness, a revulsion from life, a rebellion against the principal conditions of living. And yet, despite everything, it is and remains a *will*. Let me repeat, now that I have reached the end, what I said at the beginning: man would sooner have the void for his purpose than be void of purpose.[27]

In spite of himself, Nietzsche was a social theorist, concerned with the values which can give meaning not to one man but to all men.

WILL–TO–POWER

"Will-to-power" is on a par with eternal recurrence and Superman as a basic concept—or, remembering Jaspers, *signa*—for Nietzsche. It served in Nietzsche's later writings as a unifying agent, bringing together earlier dualisms, such as Dionysus and Apollo, nature and value, and empirical self and true self. As Kaufmann explains,[28] this duality persists in Nietzsche's first explorations with

the will-to-power. On the one hand, he seems to see will-to-power as a craving after worldly success, which Nietzsche deplored; on the other, it was a basic psychological drive, by which even pity and humility could be explained as the assertion of self and the desire to hurt others. In neither sense, then, is will-to-power at this point a virtue to Nietzsche.

The term itself first breaks onto the scene, as did "eternal recurrence," in *Zarathustra*. Beginning with assertions of the relativism of all values, the Prophet says that nevertheless "A table of excellencies hangeth over every people. Lo! it is the table of their triumphs; lo! it is the voice of their Will to Power." But the crucial transition comes in *Dawn of Day,* where Nietzsche acknowledges that power itself ennobles even though the will-to-power may lead to degraded behavior. At this point there is still a trace of dualism, which *Zarathustra* seems to resolve in favor of making quantity of power a measure of value.

Actual power, it would seem, was for Nietzsche neither physical nor material; nor was it metaphysical. It was, rather, a capacity for self-discipline, a capacity of "giving style to one's character," probably what Nietzsche meant in *The Genealogy of Morals* by an "instinct of freedom." ". . . one thing is needed: that a human being attain his satisfaction with himself . . . only then is a human being at all tolerable to look at. Whoever is dissatisfied with himself is always prepared to revenge himself therefore: we others will be his victims."[29] The effect of the will-to-power is thus not to pit person against person and nation against nation but to pit every person against himself and every nation against itself. "In Nietzsche's vision the globe became a Greek gymnasium where all nations vie with each other, each trying to overcome itself and thus to excel all others."[30]

The boldness of Nietzsche's concept of will-to-power poses an ironic threat to his consistency, inasmuch as he had often casti-

---

[27] Essay 3, sec. 28, p. 298.
[28] Ch. 6.

[29] *The Gay Science.* Quoted in Kaufmann, p. 367.
[30] Kaufmann, p. 173.

gated philosophers for their grand explanatory concepts and advocated piecemeal experimentation. Moreover there seemed to be a classic paradox built into the inference that the will-to-power lies behind all motivations, for then Nietzsche's own assertion of the concept would be nothing but an act of the will-to-power and it would invalidate itself. But one can say that at least Nietzsche never pretended that the concept is more than a hypothesis drawn from his own experience. He offered no deductive proofs, no claim of transcendental revelation. Perhaps his ultimate faith was not so much will-to-power as "will-to-truth": "'I will not deceive, not even myself': and herewith we are on the ground of morality."[31]

CONCLUSION

In the brief half-century since his death a fantastic collection of distortions and myths has grown up around Friedrich Nietzsche. By concentrating on what Nietzsche really said, this chapter, it is hoped, has discredited what is merely attributed to him. He was not anti-Semitic. He was not a German nationalist. He was not a statist. His Superman was not a political leader. His will-to-power had nothing to do with military might or material success. His sister helped the myths along by mistakenly attributing the birth of the will-to-power idea to Nietzsche's observation of loyal German troops in the Franco-Prussian War. But consider one who could write this:

And there comes perhaps a day when a people, distinguished by wars and victories and by the highest development of a military order and intelligence, and accustomed to make the heaviest sacrifices for all these things, will exclaim of its own free will: *"we break the sword"*—and will smash its entire military establishment down to its last foundations. *Rendering itself unarmed while one was the best armed,* out of the *height* of a feeling—that is the means to real peace

which must always rest on a peace of mind: while the so-called armed peace, as it exists now in all countries, is the lack of peace of mind which does not trust itself nor its neighbor and, half from fear, does not lay down arms. Rather perish than hate and fear, and *twice rather perish than make oneself be hated and feared*—this must also some day become the highest maxim of every single commonwealth![32]

Nietzsche's direct influence on psychoanalysis and existentialism is infinitely greater than his direct influence on fascism. His political significance stems not from what he was for but from what he was against. Existing European parties, parliaments, and laws all come under his scathing ridicule. He heaped contempt on monarchy as well as democracy.[33] They are partners in an empty, smug, false, and mediocre culture. The *Bildungsphilister* (culture philistines) were his prime target. He offered no political "solutions." According to his "hammer philosophy" destruction was better than mediocrity. His attempt at a transvaluation of all values was a radical and rather heroic attempt to overcome what he regarded as a deep crisis in civilization.[34] And this was not so much the construction of a new system of ethics as it was the creation of a wholly new personality.

We cannot say that Nietzsche succeeded in being much more than provocative in these constructive efforts. But in his attacks and prophecies he created a mood that somehow seems strangely akin to that of the twentieth century. In an apocalyptic vision[35] he prophesied that great and horrible wars would follow the rapid deterioration of basic values. Whatever one may say about the deterioration of our values, we have had great and horrible wars. Nietzsche's radical antipoliticism spoke for a moral emptiness at the root of the political order that, in Germany at least, in time led to a radical propoliticism.

---

[31] *Anti-Christ.* Quoted in Kaufmann, p. 314.

[32] *Der Wanderer und sein Schatten.* Quoted in Kaufmann, p. 160.

[33] See *The Will to Power,* Bk. III, Part III, in *Complete Works,* Vol. 15, pp. 183–238.

[34] See Eric Voegelin, "Nietzsche, The Crisis and the War," *Journal of Politics,* Vol. 6 (1944), pp. 177–212.

[35] *Ecce Homo,* in *Complete Works,* Vol. 17, Ch. 4.

Neither moral nor political anarchy is a viable condition. If nothing else, Nietzsche's historical generalization that "political supremacy always gives rise to notions of spiritual supremacy" can lead us to conclude that perhaps the reverse order can and ought to obtain. To say, as Nietzsche does, that God is dead at least implies that once He was alive.

As the liberal faith in the equal reason of independent individuals was beginning to wane and the socialist faith in the justice of the social group was beginning to burgeon, Nietzsche undercut both with a devastating critique of both individual rationality and wisdom in the mass. If he has not given us solutions, he has recognized and defined some of our problems, in particular the problem we have yet to do much with in the twentieth century: how can truths of man, without which a political order destroys its own subjects, be embodied in that order without being transformed into falsehoods by the process of political embodiment? Plato had an answer but we, like Nietzsche, seem to have none.

23

THE TWENTIETH CENTURY

Philosophy has never been popular and political theory has never been free of ideology. But the curious thing about these two subjects in the twentieth century to date is that in forms of expression they draw further apart, philosophy becoming more narrowly technical and political theory becoming more ideological. If we look at the philosophical movements, we see pragmatism, logical positivism, and existentialism, all difficult and often esoteric movements, holding the stage. In political theory, the textbook headings tend to read *fascism, communism, the new liberalism, democratic socialism, nationalism*—all "isms," patterns of thought better designed to sway crowds than to reach truth. Hobbes, Rousseau, and Hegel were simultaneously philosophers and political theorists but Heidegger and Wittgenstein are not very political and Trotsky and Laski were not very philosophical. The most imaginative conservatives—such as Michael Oakeshott[1]—verge on effete skepticism.

[1] See his *Rationalism in Politics* (New York: Basic Books, 1962).

WHO IS IMPORTANT?

Political philosophy in the grand manner is not altogether lacking on the contemporary scene. There is Eric Voegelin's *Order and History,* Hannah Arendt's *The Human Condition,* and, possibly in this category, the scholarship of Bertrand de Jouvenel and Leo Strauss. But except for Strauss,[2] these writers do not seem to evoke a following. No doubt it is too soon to look for "followings," as it is too soon for any solid judgment on the "greats" of an age that is our own. Without pretending to establish their greatness, we shall examine in subsequent chapters three figures who represent some of the dominant trends in twentieth-century political theorizing.

Though not, perhaps, qualified as a phi-

[2] See Joseph Cropsey, ed., *Ancients and Moderns: Essays on the Tradition of Political Philosophy in Honor of Leo Strauss* (New York: Basic Books, 1964). Dante Germino discusses Oakeshott, Strauss, Voegelin, Arendt, and De Jouvenel in *Beyond Ideology: The Revival of Political Theory* (New York: Harper & Row, 1967).

losopher, Lenin (Chapter 24) is an intellectual force that must be reckoned with. His election to special-chapter status should find few objectors.

John Dewey (Chapter 25) is an exception to the just noted tendency of philosophers and political theorists to part company in the twentieth century. This characteristic in itself is a mark of his distinction. Dewey in retrospect appears more conditioned by nineteenth-century ideas than he did when pragmatism flourished in the schools, but still he is a twentieth-century figure and a major theorist on anyone's list. No matter that his philosophy was antiphilosophical; he nevertheless fits the tradition of the philosopher-political theorist.

Reinhold Niebuhr (Chapter 26) is a symbol of the most serious reunion of political and orthodox Christian categories since the sixteenth century. This reunion may be a flash in the pan or it may be what the twentieth century will be known for. It is too early to tell. There are more original contemporary theologians than Niebuhr—Barth or Tillich, say; there may be more perceptive social analysts—Weber or Mannheim—or more archetypal political theorists—Voegelin or Arendt. But Niebuhr, like Lenin and Dewey, can stand for what is important in twentieth-century thought so far. He reflects, in addition to the new-found strength of theological thinking, the eclipse of liberalism, the rise of existentialism, and the transcending of the outworn categories of capitalism and socialism.

The contents of this chapter will necessarily be as arbitrarily chosen as the subjects of the three that follow. We shall look first at the theory of totalitarianism, for the fact of totalitarianism is as deep in our twentieth-century consciousness as any social fact can be. Next we shall examine some aspects of twentieth-century liberalism. Third, we shall look at the political impact of existentialism. And finally, we shall have a word to say about the new interest of the West in Eastern political thought.

TOTALITARIANISM

Some theorists explain; other theorists justify; some do both. In few cases is the line between these types of theorists sharper than in the case of totalitarianism, at least from the standpoint of the western democratic biases most of us hold. Adolf Hitler, in *Mein Kampf,* was no doubt "explaining" Nazism when he said of the masses: ". . . in view of the primitive simplicity of their minds, they more easily fall a victim to a big lie than to a little one, since they themselves lie in little things, but would be ashamed of lies that were too big." He was "justifying" it in saying, "All who are not of good race in this world are chaff."[3] While both were statements of some power, neither was of a high order of theoretical insight. The antirational tendencies of fascist brands of totalitarianism worked against first-rate theory in its behalf. And among nontotalitarian interpreters of totalitarianism there has been the widest divergence of views as to its essence. Early interpreters tended to stress the state and its role as a total entity. Cobban in 1939 linked totalitarianism to very old theories of the organic state: ". . . the liberal state proclaims itself as organic. Until recently the organic idea of the state was no more than a theory, but the progress of what we have called the internal aspect of nationalism has produced a vigourous attempt to transfer this theory into practice, and of this attempt totalitarianism is the result."[4] In the same year Lederer pointed to the destruction by the state of classes and other forms of social stratification as the essence of totalitarianism and even saw, apart from war, internal tensions ahead for totalitarianism. The bureaucratic agents of this "destruction of society" would in time themselves become entrenched and hence antipathetic to the principle of the "amorphous mass"—the "people," who, under totalitarian-

[3] *Mein Kampf,* trans. by Ralph Manheim (Boston: Houghton Mifflin, 1943), pp. 231 and 296.
[4] Alfred Cobban, *Dictatorship, Its History and Theory* (New York: Scribner's, 1939), p. 177.

ism, are denied a tradition and a social structure and hence become dependent upon raw emotion.[5]

Recent theorists of totalitarianism have moved in the direction of stressing its character as *movement,* as a dynamic emotional force that, as Lederer suggested, is antithetical to the orderliness inherent in well-established governmental forms. This view would seem to represent a consensus drawn from the many stimulating hypotheses developed and tested at a three-day conference held in Boston in 1953.[6] If the conferees agreed on totalitarianism as movement, they did not agree on much else. Some thought terror was a calculated policy for the maintenance of a position of leadership; others thought it had a more irrational basis. Some regarded totalitarian ideologies as hypocritical tools of leadership; others felt that the leaders, too, were generally infected with ideological belief. Some thought of totalitarianism as an enemy of all religion; others thought of it as a secular religion itself. Some thought fascist and communist forms of totalitarianism were quite similar, others stressed their differences —though none as much as was customary among scholars when the U.S.S.R. and Nazi Germany were fighting each other in World War II. The Sino-Soviet schism, the relaxation of Cold War rigidities, the survival of Khrushchev into genteel retirement, and assertions of independence by Poland and Rumania have all, of course, forced qualifications on some of the more doctrinaire views of what foreign totalitarianism is all about. Meanwhile, the term has been increasingly used, though without much precision, to describe certain political and, even more, social tendencies in the United States. These factors cloud but do not change the definitional problem.

On the basis of empirical evidence from those societies of recent experience that have been labeled totalitarian (Fascist Italy, 1922–43; Nazi Germany, 1933–45; the Soviet Union, 1917– ; Communist China, 1949– ; and the various Soviet satellites), Friedrich and Brzezinski list six features that, taken together, must be regarded as the typological signs of a totalitarian regime: (1) an official ideology broad enough to cover the "vital aspects of man's existence," which is usually focused on some future ideal state of mankind; (2) a single mass party, usually led by one man, the "dictator," composed of a select and small percentage of the population, organized hierarchically, and superior to or intertwined with the government organization; (3) "a system of terroristic police control"; (4) a monopoly control of the media of mass communication (press, radio, cinema) by the party; (5) a similar monopoly of all means of effective armed combat; and (6) "central control and direction of the entire economy" with bureaucratic coordination of formerly independent associations and groups.[7]

While these authors give us a carefully worked-out description of totalitarianism, they do not try long-range speculation or an inquiry into ideological genesis. The shattering newness of totalitarianism has inhibited studies along these lines. Friedrich points out that not a single one of the great scholars of social institutions at the beginning of this century was able to foresee the rise of totalitarianism in anything approximating its actual form.

The Genesis of Totalitarianism: Arendt

Undoubtedly the major work so far pro-

[5] Emil Lederer, *State of the Masses, the Threat of the Classless Society* (New York: Norton, 1940).

[6] Carl J. Friedrich, ed., *Totalitarianism.* Proceedings of a conference held at the American Academy of Arts and Sciences, March, 1953 (Cambridge: Harvard Univ. Press, 1954).

[7] Carl J. Friedrich and Zbigniew Brzezinski, *Totalitarian Dictatorship and Autocracy* (Cambridge, Mass.: Harvard Univ. Press, 1956), pp. 9–10. See also Charles W. Cassinelli, "The Totalitarian Party," *Journal of Politics,* Vol. 24 (1962), pp. 111–41; William Ebenstein, *Totalitarianism: New Perspectives* (New York: Holt, Rinehart and Winston, 1962); Alexander J. Groth, "Isms in Totalitarianism," *American Political Science Review,* Vol. 58 (1964), pp. 888–901; Richard Lowenthal, "Totalitarianism Reconsidered," *Commentary,* Vol. 29 (June, 1960); and R. Reinitz, "The Totalitarian Potential of American Society," *Contemporary Review,* Vol. 205 (1964), pp. 14–20.

duced that does attempt to move back into the historical, philosophical, and ideological roots of the subject is Hannah Arendt's *The Origins of Totalitarianism*. At the descriptive level Arendt would agree with much of the foregoing but stresses especially the transvaluation of values inherent in the totalitarian way of life. For example, totalitarian regimes deliberately seek out the innocent for abuse, punishment, and even death, while the guilty go free or are treated more respectfully. This tactic shatters the sense of order and the reliability of law, creating a helpless insecurity and dependence even in those who are not punished, and giving the latter, in addition, a collective guilt that binds them together into an amorphous mass. She notes that the common criminal, as against political and racial prisoners, was in almost every Nazi and Soviet concentration camp part of the elite group because the common criminal had at least the status of a conviction under law. He had not been deprived of his "juridical person." The whole paraphernalia of Nazi repression—the uniforms, the shaving of heads, the shipment of masses of persons by boxcar, and finally the factorylike process of execution in gas chambers—were well suited to the destruction of any sense of uniqueness in individual persons, again not only in the victims but in the population as a whole, who were aware of the boxcars moving through the night.

More than being indifferent to moral values, totalitarianism tends to establish a new, inverted morality. "Thou shalt not kill" gives away to "Thou shalt kill." Whereas older forms of tyranny imposed an order resistant to change, totalitarianism has been dependent upon disorder and continual change. It is expansiveness of power for no rational end, elevated to a principle. Whereas followers of pragmatism and even of Leninism believed that reality could be known only by action rather than by thought, Arendt's model of totalitarianism goes further: the search for reality ceases. The belief that literally "everything is possible" leads totalitarian rulers to invent a policy and force social conditions to conform to it, rather than the reverse. Legis-

lation tends to mean nothing and offers no guide to the populace or administrators. Survival in a totalitarian regime depends upon the development of a sixth sense as to which order or official to follow and which to disregard. In this way every individual tends to be isolated from every other individual by a veil of suspicion. It is "a permanent state of lawlessness."[8]

Arendt is more successful in capturing the acrid flavor of totalitarianism[9] than in explaining its historical genesis, but her ambitious attempt to do the latter is filled with brilliant insights and juxtapositions. Her strength is at the point of interpenetration between historical events, articulate theories, and subconscious popular moods. The historical tendencies that "crystallized" into totalitarianism came, she finds, out of the racism and imperialism of the late nineteenth century and from the growing irrelevance of abstract conceptions of human rights. As long as economies were largely confined within the nation-state system, the bourgeoisie tended to leave politics to others. As economics in the age of imperialism (1885–1914) moved abroad, the bourgeoisie found it necessary to involve themselves with politics in order to influence domestically minded statesmen like Richter, Gladstone, and Clemenceau. The supposedly "interntional" Jews, who had been identified as moneylenders to the absolute monarchs of the past, became convenient targets of resentment. But anti-Semitism was not the only racism to contend with:

When the Europeans discovered what a "lovely virtue" a white skin could be in Africa, when

[8] Hannah Arendt, *The Origins of Totalitarianism*, 2nd ed. (New York: Noonday Press, Meridian, 1958), p. 394. Subsequent quotations are from this edition.

[9] See also Elie A. Cohen, *Human Behavior in the Concentration Camp* (New York: Norton, 1953); Raul Hilberg, *The Destruction of the European Jews* (New York: Quadrangle Books, 1961); Eugen Kogon, *The Theory and Practice of Hell*, trans. by Heinz Norden (New York: Farrar, Straus & Giroux, 1950); Ceslaw Milocz, *The Captive Mind* (New York: Random House, Vintage, 1953); and David Rousset, *The Other Kingdom*, trans. by Ramon Guthrie (New York: Reynal, 1947).

the English conqueror in India became an administrator who no longer believed in the universal validity of law, but was convinced of his own innate capacity to rule and dominate . . . when the British Intelligence services began to attract England's best sons, who preferred serving mysterious forces all over the world to serving the common good of their country, the stage seemed to be set for all possible horrors. Lying under anybody's nose were many of the elements which gathered together could create a totalitarian government on the basis of racism."[10]

Imperialism incorporated a mood of continual expansionism justified by mysterious forces of history, which became the heart of both Nazi and communist totalitarianism.

The growing nationalistic feeling attending this imperialist thrust was a sign not of the strength of the nation-state system but rather of its weakness, for "the nation-state cannot exist once its principle of equality before the law has broken down" and the attempt to rule "inferior nations" was destroying this principle. Without the advantages of a Roman *imperium* of law, the imperialist states were equipped only with very troublesome doctrines of consent of the governed, which they did not care to apply to native populations. From this loss of community and the context of free speech that community provides followed a loss of humanity. The supposedly inalienable Rights of Man that had been intended to replace the security of feudal station proved unenforceable outside a national context. Paradoxically, human rights are lost at that moment when one becomes a human being in general, without citizenship, a profession, or group support. When nothing but equality as a human being is left, one's humanity is destroyed. Hence the terrible plight of contemporary "stateless" persons ("displaced persons," thinks Arendt, is a euphemism), who are the peculiar products of totalitarianism:

Denationalization became a powerful weapon of totalitarian politics, and the constitutional inability of European nation-states to guarantee

human rights to those who had lost nationally guaranteed rights made it possible for the persecuting governments to impose their standard of values even upon their opponents. Those whom the persecutor had singled out as the scum of the earth—Jews, Trotskyites, etc.—actually were received as scum of the earth. . . . a practical demonstration of the totalitarian movement's cynical claims that no such thing as inalienable human rights existed.[11]

Hence, thinks Arendt, Burke was right in his attacks upon the abstract rights of the French Revolution. We are not born equal; we are *made* equal by political organization, by the protections of law. The private realm of uniqueness and difference is always something of a threat to the public realm, the political. But the private realm needs the protection and encouragement of the public if human uniqueness is to be maintained. In totalitarianism the public realm not only absorbs the private, it seeks to destroy it and thereby transform human nature itself, to prove "everything is possible." It seeks to produce a system in which "all men [are] equally superfluous"—even the leaders of the system. The most terrifying of Arendt's many pessimistic conclusions is that totalitarianism cannot finally prove itself until it has global control and all men are equally dehumanized.[12]

Italian Fascism

Athough going beyond the limits of empirical data,[13] Arendt is rich and compelling by contrast with most of the theorists who have tried to justify totalitarianism, since the

---

[10] Arendt, p. 221.

[11] *Ibid.*, p. 269.

[12] Arendt observes that totalitarianism works only in very large countries, where there are large undifferentiated masses of people. Totalitarian regimes in smaller countries like Yugoslavia or Albania tend to revert to old-fashioned tyranny and dictatorship.

[13] Empirical studies of phenomena peculiar to mass societies have become more available. See William Kornhauser, *The Politics of Mass Society* (New York: Free Press, 1959), and the bibliography therein. The psychiatrist Bruno Bettelheim draws on his own experience in a concentration camp in *The Informed Heart: Autonomy in a Mass Age* (New York: Free Press, 1960).

movement rides so heavily on nonrational assumptions. For intellectual nourishment the Italian Fascists leaned heavily on Giovanni Gentile (1875-1944), professor of philosophy at Pisa and Rome and Mussolini's Director of the Institute of Fascist Culture. An almost mystical disciple of Hegel, Gentile made the "State" the embodiment of all things good, its force a mode of discipline not only consistent with individual well-being but necessary to achieve the citizen's "true" personality and freedom. Another theorist, Alfredo Rocco (1875-1935), stressed "society" more than the "State," but, using a biological analogy, he meant by this term national society, which had unity, purpose, and direction transcending the lives of its individual members. The appeal of the Fascists was to a public interest painted in bright hues, contrasted with petty, competing private interests, and to an expansive national pride that glorified war and the will to dominate. What the Fascists were against may have been more important than what they were for. They opposed flabby and decadent liberalism that pandered to individual comfort and license. They opposed parliamentarianism, with its indecent welter of conflicting groups. After his march on Rome in 1922, Mussolini tried to bring these groups under control with what he called the corporate state. Before this time he had fooled around with Marxist socialism and the French syndicalist ideas of Sorel. His economic positions were inconsistent; yet inconsistency itself was supposed to be consistent with the spontaneity and antirationalism upon which Fascist men of power—and even philosophers like Gentile—prided themselves. Nothing could have been further from the truth than Mussolini's assertion that "Fascism has a doctrine, or, if you will, a particular philosophy with regard to all the questions which beset the human mind today."[14]

---

[14] Quoted in Rocco, *The Political Doctrine of Fascism*, trans. by Dino Bigongiari (Washington: Carnegie Endowment for International Peace, International Conciliation Bulletin No. 223, 1926), p. 7. For Gentile's ideas see *Genesis and Structure of Society*, trans. by H. S. Harris (Urbana, Ill.: Univ. of Illinois Press, 1960), and

Nazism

In any narrow sense of "political," the Nazis scarcely had a political theory at all, since what they glorified was not the state but the nation (*das Volk*). Perhaps the most sophisticated of Nazi theorists was Carl Schmitt (1888-   ), a professor of law and from 1933 to 1945 a Prussian State Councilor. In the essay "The Concept of the 'Political' " (1927) he makes the distinction between friend and enemy the core distinction of politics, comparable to that between good and evil in morals or beautiful and ugly in aesthetics. We find in Schmitt the previously mentioned totalitarian tendency to make everything of importance public in that he defines "enemy" not as those we may individually hate but as that collectivity of men who as a real possibility will fight one's nation: "Enemy is only the public enemy, because everything that relates to such a collectivity, especially a whole nation, becomes *public*." And he later continues, "The genuine concept of the enemy thus implies the eventual reality of a struggle." The antagonistic relationship is essential to any political order, for "Political unity presupposes the real possibility of an enemy."[15] Compared to Schmitt, the wild Nordicism of the Nazis' "official" philosopher, Alfred Rosenberg (1893-1946), is very superficial. His *Myth of the Twentieth Century* (1930) is a mishmash of Treitschke, Nietzsche, Chamberlain,

---

Benito Mussolini, *The Political and Social Doctrine of Fascism*, English trans. (London: Hogarth, 1933). See also Herbert W. Schneider, *Making the Fascist State* (New York: Oxford Univ. Press, 1928), and *Readings on Fascism and National Socialism* (Denver, Colo.: Swallow, n.d.).

[15] The quotations are from William Ebenstein's translation, reprinted in his *Modern Political Thought* (New York: Holt, Rinehart and Winston, 1954), pp. 327-28. To overcome what he regards as the unresolved dualisms of anarchic liberalism (state/individual, state/society, law/politics, and legislative/executive), Schmitt substitutes what Barker has called a "trialism": ". . . the party stands at the centre of the common life, reaching out on the one hand into the state . . . and reaching out on the other into the People or Volk" (Ernest Barker, *Reflections on Government* (New York: Oxford Univ. Press, Galaxy, 1958), p. 289. See entire Part IV on totalitarianism.

and Gobineau. And even Rosenberg never really understood the purposefulness of Hitler's policy of extermination.

Though theory must come to grips with totalitarianism and contemporary scholarship has only begun to probe its depths, it is action and not theory that gives totalitarianism its character. Hitler's policy of living space (*Lebensraum*) needed only a mystique of German expansionism and not fancy geopolitical rationalizations to keep the Wehrmacht pushing on. His leadership principle (*Fuehrerprinzip*) evoked but did not ennoble the self-selection of power-wielders and their disregard for the traditional forms of election and majority vote. The interesting theoretical justifications for totalitarian rule are found in communist theories. But these we shall leave until we look at what Lenin did to Marx (see Chapter 24). For the moment it is enough to reflect that anti-intellectual ideologies of action often have special appeal to intellectuals and others caught in a social bankruptcy of traditional ideals. Above all, we must not think that totalitarianism as a phenomenon is relevant only to other places and other times. Insofar as its legacy is the evisceration of human rights and the derangement of orderly relationships between public and private categories, totalitarianism as a problem is likely to be distressingly close to us for some time to come.

LIBERALISM IN THE TWENTIETH CENTURY

As the twentieth century began, political liberalism was riding high. Now, in the mid-twentieth century, it is in retreat. Liberalism as a belief in the ultimacy of individual conscience and as a movement directed to freeing the individual from archaic social restraints and his own irrationalities had and still has many forms. To William Graham Sumner, the free individual was the economically unrestricted individual, at liberty to compete in a dog-eat-dog world. At the other extreme, in the writings of idealists like Bernard Bosanquet or William Hocking, the free individual was one whose potentialities could be developed only within the framework of a state or social order that evoked his higher loyalties. In between we find Hobhouse, defending greater state activity but in the name of essentially utilitarian values, or Holmes, for whom duty to nation could take on almost mystical overtones but who was nonetheless a champion of the maximum of individual liberty and tolerance of diversity, for reasons that were based on the too literal economic analogy of the "free marketplace of ideas." There were in the first decades of the twentieth century few new philosophical inquiries dedicated to undergirding the liberal faith. Intellectually, liberalism was riding on the momentum of Locke, the Enlightenment, and Adam Smith. But the faith was still there.

The twentieth century has seen a continual battering of this liberal faith.[16] The hard, inescapable fact of totalitarianism is no doubt the greatest of all challenges to the hopefulness that liberalism blended into the politics of Western democracies. Not all pre-World War I liberals were bland optimists, by any means, but the mood of that time was indubitably progressive: science, industry, popular education, and government by the people were moving us toward a better, freer life for all. Totalitarianism shattered that mood.

The shock of totalitarianism turned theologians from liberal preachments of the social gospel to reinterpretations of original sin. The political significance of the irrational in man was freshly demonstrable and Freudian psychology became a tool of political analysis.

Meanwhile the disastrous economic conditions of the twenties, which helped make totalitarianism in Germany possible, were

[16] See Judith Shklar's study of the decline of Enlightenment faith as revealed in the philosophy, poetry, and theology of the late nineteenth century, in *After Utopia: The Decline of Political Faith* (Princeton: Princeton Univ. Press, 1958).

making the tenets of laissez faire liberalism increasingly irrelevant. *Socialism* (meaning the nationalization of productive units) did not fare well in all places but the *welfare state* (meaning redistribution of income and a managed economy) moved ahead without let across the Western world. Politically, the welfare state has been defended mainly with mellow clichés about liberty and equality drawn from the old liberal arsenal. But attackers of the welfare state[17] were forced to draw their clichés from the same warehouse and with them did poorly in elections. The deep thinkers, meanwhile, seemed to be working on other issues.

Granting the wisdom of selecting Dewey as the most philosophically eminent representative of twentieth-century liberalism, we may look briefly here at four men chosen not because they are great political theorists and not even because they span the range of contemporary liberalism but simply because they suggest its diversity and uncertainty. The four are Laski, Keynes, Galbraith, and Lippmann.

Laski

Harold J. Laski (1893–1950) may at first glance appear far more a critic of liberalism than a liberal. A lifelong activist in the Labor Party and an inveterate crusader against the injustices of capitalism, he became in the 1930s an avowed though unorthodox Marxist. But in 1920, the year he returned to England from a dazzling teaching stint at Harvard, he criticized Fabian socialist Sidney Webb for an excessive faith in governmental regulation and attacked Fabian and Marxist socialists alike for assuming that the nationalization of industry was a cure-all.

Laski at this time[18] occupied a position reflecting both the syndicalists and the guild socialists on one side and the pluralists of the historical school of jurisprudence on the other side. That is, he held with the former that workers ought to have a greater direct say in the determination of industrial policy and held with the latter that the state should be viewed as but one association among many associations. Consequently sovereignty became for Laski merely the ability of the state to induce the obedience of members to its rules, a relationship present in other associations as well. One difficulty of the former position was frequently the vagueness of the proposals to increase popular participation in industrial control. A difficulty of the latter position was the easy assumption that in case of a conflict arising from differing loyalties to state, church, union or other group, a harmonious ordering could be worked out without the superior imposition of one group's will on the others. Laski's thought shared these difficulties.

The pluralist position emerges from the precocious Laski's four earliest and most intellectually rigorous books: *Studies in the Problem of Sovereignty* (1917), *Authority in the Modern State* (1919), *Foundations of Sovereignty and Other Essays* (1921), and *A Grammar of Politics* (1925), which is probably his most significant book. Accepting the Benthamite formula of the greatest good for the greatest number, Laski rejected the egoism of its earlier applications: "If man is to live in community with his fellows it is a necessary condition of his life that what he attains should, at least in the long run, involve benefit also to others."[19]

Yet by 1930, when the second edition of the *Grammar of Politics* and Laski's *Liberty*

---

[17] For example, Milton Friedman, *Capitalism and Freedom* (Chicago: Univ. of Chicago Press, 1962); Friedrich von Hayek, *The Road to Serfdom* (Chicago: Univ. of Chicago Press, 1944) and *The Constitution of Liberty* (Chicago: Univ. of Chicago Press, 1960); Ludwig von Mises, *The Anti-Capitalist Mentality* (Princeton: Van Nostrand, 1956); and Henry C. Simons, *Economic Policy for a Free Society* (Chicago: Univ. of Chicago Press, 1948).

[18] At Harvard "Laski was a liberal in the American sense. He was for the underdog, for trade unions, and collective bargaining, mildly socialist in a fashion that lay between a liberal pluralism, tinged with Fabian ideas, and the Guild Socialism then fashionable among progressive intellectuals in Britain" (Kingsley Martin, *Harold Laski* (1893–1950), *A Biographical Memoir* [London: Gollancz, 1953], p. 33).

[19] *A Grammar of Politics* (London: Allen & Unwin, 1925), p. 25.

in the Modern State appeared, he had moved away from the pluralist conception of the state and also—though there seems to be no logical connection between the two—toward an older, more individualistic view of liberty: "Let me remind you of the essence of my argument. I have taken the view that liberty means that there is no restraint upon those conditions which, in modern civilization, are the necessary guarantees of individual happiness."[20]

From the first edition of the *Grammar of Politics* on, Laski became more and more busy with popularizing ventures and more and more eclectic; and his intellectual powers declined.[21] The conscious adoption of a watered-down Marxism in the 1930s was more a sign of flagging originality than a conversion. Laski's consistency was in his passionate concern for social justice, the freedom to express ideas, and the opportunity for ordinary people to have a decent existence. That he did not harness these concerns to a systematic theoretical position is a failure of the man but also a failure of contemporary liberalism, for, as Deane says, "Marxism and classical liberalism are philosophies poorly equipped to deal with the central political issues of our times. Both are fundamentally concerned with the society and the economy rather than the polity."[22]

Keynes

John Maynard Keynes (1883–1946) was one of the most versatile men of his age— British public official, scholar, essayist, patron of the arts, businessman, speculator, and theater director. As prophet he gave the world a grim insight into disaster in *The Economic Consequences of the Peace* (1919), "bursting into international fame when men of equal insight but less courage and men of equal courage but less insight kept silent."[23] As economist, in *The General Theory of Employment, Interest and Money* (1935), he gave capitalism a theoretical and highly technical rationale for accepting the governmental intervention it needed to survive after the disaster of depression struck.

But he was not a political philosopher, even though a liberal—in ideas and in party registration. Beyond his monumental role as economic innovator, a role that ranks him with Adam Smith and Karl Marx, his political ideas were perhaps most substantial in their negative aspect, that is, in their corrosive impact on outworn doctrines still appended to Western industrial activity:

Let us clear from the ground the metaphysical or general principles upon which, from time to time, laissez-faire has been founded. It is *not* true that individuals possess a prescriptive "national liberty" in their economic activities. There is *no* "compact" conferring perpetual rights on those who Have or on those who Acquire. The world is *not* so governed from above that private and social interest always coincide. It is *not* so managed here below that in practice they coincide. It is *not* a correct deduction from the Principles of Economics that enlightened self-interest always operates in the public interest. Nor is it true that self-interest generally *is* enlightened; more often individuals acting separately to promote their own ends are too ignorant or too weak to attain even these. Experience does *not* show that individuals, when they make up a social unit, are always less clear-sighted than when they act separately. We cannot therefore settle on abstract grounds, but must handle on its merits in detail what Burke termed "one of the finest problems in legislation, namely, to determine what the State ought to take upon itself to direct by the public wisdom, and what it ought to leave, with as little interference as possible, to individual exertion." We have to distinguish between what Bentham, in his forgotten but useful nomenclature, used to term *Agenda* and *Non-Agenda,* and to do this without Bentham's prior assump-

[20] *Liberty in the Modern State,* rev. ed. (New York: Viking, 1948), p. 129.

[21] Herbert Deane has documented this decline in his excellent *The Political Ideas of Harold J. Laski* (New York: Columbia Univ. Press, 1955).

[22] *Ibid.,* p. 342.

[23] Joseph A. Schumpeter, *History of Economic Analysis* (New York: Oxford Univ. Press, 1954), p. 1170.

tion that interference is, at the same time, "generally needless" and "generally pernicious." Perhaps the chief task of Economists at this hour is to distinguish afresh the *Agenda* of Government from the *Non-Agenda;* and the companion task of Politics is to devise forms of Government within a Democracy which shall be capable of accomplishing the *Agenda*.[24]

In his affirmative declaration "Am I a Liberal?" (1925), he moved away from economic issues with some reluctance and aligned his liberal faith with such broad goals as stability and justice. At bottom, it was experimentalism to which he was committed: "Our programme must deal not with the historic issues of Liberalism, but with those matters—whether or not they have already become party questions—which are of living importance and urgency today."[25]

But Keynes did express some hope that altruistic impulses natural to man would increasingly find expression at a level between that of the strictly individual and that of the state as a whole, namely in the modern corporation—which had in fact long ago become a nonindividualist, nonprivate enterprise—a possible bearer of a new public spirit. Government, he felt, should not try to replace corporations or to do what individuals were already doing but it should do what no one in the 1920s was doing: manage the whole economy through fiscal and monetary controls.

A generation later this new but no less "true" liberalism—antisocialist but progovernmental regulation—found expression in another economist, less brilliant in the technicalities of the discipline but somewhat more willing to theorize about the political whole.

Galbraith

The writings of John Kenneth Galbraith (1908–   ) have an edge of irony reminiscent of Thorstein Veblen or Thurman Arnold.[26] Especially in his *American Capitalism* (1952), *The Affluent Society* (1958), and *The New Industrial State* (1967), he challenges Americans to look again at the stereotypes of capitalism and socialism. In the first, he substitutes a concept of "countervailing power" for traditional price competition in the market. In the present-day welfare state, economic and political policy alike are, he feels, resultant from the bargaining between the big power blocs of government, labor, business, and sometimes agriculture. Between the oligopolistic conditions of modern industry and the unrestricted price competition presumed to be normal under classical economic theories the former is much to be preferred, says Galbraith. In *American Capitalism,* he chides economic thinkers for not taking the problem of power seriously. In *The Affluent Society* he chides the makers of public policy for not taking seriously the productivity of the economic system. In effect, he is saying to Americans that we have not learned how to live with, and use, wealth. Our past thinking has been so oriented first toward production goods and then toward consumer goods marketable individually that important expenditures on such public works as schools, hospitals, and urban renewal have been neglected. We have been bound by the conception of how an individualistic society works long after an individualistic society is impossible. The net effect of all this is that the union of business and government turns out to be more than a temporary antidepression expedient. It is here to stay, even in a United States that is regarded as the last bastion of private-enterprise capitalism.

In *The New Industrial State* Galbraith argues that American society is dominated by a new corporate "technostructure" that feeds upon a scientific-educational elite, makes decisions by committee, and has subordinated profit-making to other values, especially organizational security, autonomy,

[24] *The End of Laissez-Faire* (1926), in Alan Bullock and Maurice Shock, eds., *The Liberal Tradition from Fox to Keynes* (Edinburgh: Black, 1956), pp. 254–55.

[25] "Am I a Liberal?" in Bullock and Shock, p. 284.

[26] See Thurman Arnold, *Folklore of Capitalism* (New Haven: Yale Univ. Press, 1937).

and growth. In *American Capitalism* the concept of countervailing power is an optimistic view of what replaced the restraints of the market. Here again, Galbraith's conclusion is more optimistic than his analysis would warrant, for he leans a bit too heavily on the hope that the scientific-educational fraternity can save the body politic from domination by the bland corporate leadership.

Galbraith's movement is away from traditional liberal assumptions about the priority of individual choice and the priority of economic over political considerations. This may account for some of the coolness displayed toward him by the economic profession. But Galbraith is still a liberal in the way he values economic well-being and political pluralism. The full-scale subordination of economic to political values appears in those who are neither liberal nor socialist. They cannot simply be called conservatives, for the varieties of conservatives are too numerous. Perhaps "antiliberals" or "half-liberals" will do.

Lippmann

One such "half-liberal" is Walter Lippmann (1889–   ). The ambiguity of the label is doubly appropriate, for Lippmann has never been easy to pigeonhole. A socialist as an undergraduate at Harvard, he has been called conservative by some, liberal by others. He is neither a philosopher for the ages nor a mirror of his times. He is a philosophic journalist who has carved a unique niche for himself halfway between the political arena and the ivory tower. His writings have displayed a countervailing tendency: in the optimistic and idealistic 1920s his *Public Opinion* (1922) and *Phantom Public* (1925) were penetratingly realistic about mass opinion. In the heyday of New Deal planning his *The Good Society* (1937) defended the unplanned society. During the complacent modernism of the mid-50s he spoke for traditional and aristocratic values in *The Public Philosophy* (1955). It is, says Schlesinger, "as if he were impelled always to redress the balance against

the dominating suppositions of the day—sometimes after he himself had given those suppositions their most clear and trenchant statement."[27]

From his precocious *Preface to Politics* (1913) to the present Lippmann has illumined the intractable public illusions that inhibit creative leadership. His role as intermediary has allowed him to tug at the reins of reason, pulling both majoritarian radicals and authoritarian elitists toward the center. Probably the best of his more than twenty books is *Public Opinion*, notable for its descriptions of how stereotypes of reality form in the minds of mass-media consumers and how the manipulation of symbols can pass for political leadership. Modest in its claims, it nevertheless employs psychological analyses that are relevant two generations later. Lippmann also suggests specific reforms for bridging the informational gaps left by commercially minded interpreters of the news. In its conclusion the book stubbornly clings against considerable odds to a democratic hope. We must live by intuition, "But we can make belief in reason one of those intuitions. We can use our wit and our force to make footholds for reason. . . . the demand upon reserves of mere decency is enormous, and it is necessary to live as if good will would work."[28]

The editors of Lippmann's anthologized writings in political philosophy call him "perhaps the most important American political thinker of the twentieth century."[29]

---

[27] Arthur M. Schlesinger, Jr., "Walter Lippmann: The Intellectual versus Politics," in Marquis Childs and James Reston, eds., *Walter Lippmann and His Times* (New York: Harcourt, Brace & World, 1959), pp. 191–92.

[28] *Public Opinion* (New York: Penguin, 1946), pp. 314–15. Eulau called this work "the liberal Lippmann's farewell to liberalism" (Heinz Eulau, "From Public Opinion to Public Philosophy: Walter Lippmann's Classic Reexamined," *American Journal of Economics*, Vol. 15 [1956], p. 450). But see Lippmann's "Conservative, Liberal, Progressive," *The New Republic*, Vol. 146 (January 22, 1962), pp. 10–11.

[29] *The Essential Lippmann; A Political Philosophy for Liberal Democracy*, Clinton Rossiter and James Lare, eds. (New York: Random House, Vintage, 1965), p. XI.

This is surely overly generous—not because Lippmann is unworthy of accolades but because his strengths lie in the area of public policy rather than public philosophy, despite his book by that title. Lippmann's admirable willingness to prescribe solutions as well as to criticize unfortunately produced in *The Public Philosophy* an inadequately stated conception of natural law. The book begins with a problem that had long bothered Lippmann, the ponderous emotionalism by which democratic publics tie the hands of executive leaders trying to cope with crises in foreign affairs. But with much less precision than he displayed in his earlier philosophical writings Lippmann attributes this and the widest variety of other social evils to what he calls the philosophy of "Jacobinism"—Rousseau, Andrew Jackson, Marx, Sartre, and progressive education are all included in this category—and proposes as an antidote an eclectic brand of natural law that rather indiscriminately encompasses such diverse views as those of Cicero, the American founding fathers, C. S. Peirce, and Ernest Barker.

A Preface to Morals (1929) is a more coherent philosophic work than *The Public Philosophy*. It expresses what comes close to a Stoic view of life: a child does not become a man "until and unless he feels the vast indifference of the universe to his own fate." We require the functional presence of a "high religion," which "is a prophecy and an anticipation of what life is like when desire is in perfect harmony with reality."[30] Even here, however, Lippmann ends ambiguously, sympathetic with both religion and reason but unable to affirm one at the expense of the other: "The choice is at last a personal one. The decision is rendered not by argument but by feeling."[31] Lippmann affirms a "religion of the spirit" that "the world is able at last to take seriously." The "at last" suggests a progressive, modernist view of history, yet the content of the position is traditionalist. Once again, Lippmann

is in the middle. Put into concluding words, this old-new faith sounds platitudinous: "It is that only the regenerate, the disinterested, the mature, can make use of freedom. That is the central insight of the teachers of wisdom."[32]

Lippmann's concern in *The Public Philosophy* with the "language of accommodation" whereby higher law becomes operative suggests that orderly government and the conditions conducive to rational debate remain his overriding aims. True to his lifelong practice of following diagnosis with prescription, Lippmann offers the public philosophy as a means to an end. Its philosophic limitations are less a reflection on Lippmann, who does not pretend to be a philosopher, than a reflection on the paucity of philosophic resources upon which contemporary liberalism can draw.[33]

That liberalism in the twentieth century has had so few spokesmen of profundity must be taken as a sign of its decline as a political philosophy.

Freudian Liberalism

To speak of Freud and liberalism in the same breath may seem to many a contradiction. But Freud himself was more of a liberal than many who link his name with dark and irrational passions will concede. He was liberal in that a liberated individual was the *raison d'être* of his work. He was liberal in that he believed in the power of reason—not, to be sure, reason disembodied as rational idealists had tended to conceive of it but reason as an aspect of man's emotional life, an ego controlling an id.[34] As a scientist,

---

[30] *A Preface to Morals* (New York: Macmillan, 1929), pp. 187 and 193.

[31] In *The Public Philosophy* Lippmann seems to reject this same point as it is made by Sartre.

[32] *A Preface to Morals*, pp. 326 and 327.

[33] On the decline of liberalism as a philosophy see Ch. 17, *n.* 13, above.

[34] It is barely possible that the reader is unfamiliar with Freudian terms like *id, ego,* and *superego; Eros* and *Thanatos;* and *Oedipus* and *Electra complexes.* It is even imaginable that he might not know that Sigmund Freud (1856–1939), Viennese psychiatrist, was the founder of psychoanalysis. If so, it is suggested the reader consult the family magazine section of a Sunday newspaper, any issue. Then again, *The Basic Writings*

he was obliged to operate on deterministic assumptions but he was not far from Kant in the seriousness with which he took the problem of personal moral obligation. In the Freudian view character is formed early in life. Men are not remade as adults. Yet Freud never doubted that knowledge could contribute to any man's therapy. His one unshakable faith was in science, and a progressive science at that. This, surely, was liberal.

His liberalism did not, however, lead Freud to become an optimist or a sentimentalist. He stopped short of cynicism, but he had few illusions and courted none. As he somewhere put it, his aim was to "transform neurotic despair into the general unhappiness which is the usual lot of mankind." Concerned as he was with individual patients, he had little sympathy with grand, overarching nationalistic or class explanations of human behavior as given by a Hegel or a Marx. As many commentators have observed, his pessimism shared something with that of Hobbes: in the views of both it was the misery of men that required and possibly was sufficient to sustain a social order. In Hobbes it was a more or less rational fear of death that showed men the inexorable need for authority. In Freud it was an irrational death wish, the basis of aggression, that created the need for authority. In one the myth of the social contract rationalized political power; in the other the myth of Oedipus' slaying his father rationalized the guilt that binds men to their brothers.

On this basis Freud was more of an elitist and less of an egalitarian than Hobbes. But Freud's natural elite, the strong and self-knowledgeable, were cut down to human size by the drive of sex, which stamped all men with a biological commonality; and even the most pathetic, self-deceiving neurotic was granted some capacity for rational control. If man was not blessed with innate goodness, neither was he cursed with innate

depravity. The neurotic might not be free but even the normal man did not have *much* freedom.

Freud, of course, was not a political theorist at all and not much of a social thinker. His early explorations into primitive anthropology[35] have been much criticized. His study of religion[36] misunderstands elemental doctrines of the Judeo-Christian tradition. Yet all this testifies to the power on Freud of nineteenth-century historicism and its search for genetic roots. Although concerned with the problems of individuals, Freud wanted to explain essences by primitive origins. Faced with an individual who knew no father, he could fall back on "racial memory" to provide Oedipal feelings.[37] On the occasions when he does speak of whole cultures, he leaps if anything too easily from the individual to the mass. After discussing the struggle between Eros and Thanatos, the life urge versus the death instinct, Freud observes, "When . . . we compare the cultural process in humanity with the process of development or upbringing in an individual human being, we shall conclude without much hesitation that the two are very similar in nature, if not in fact the same process applied to a different kind of object."[38]

In *Das Unbehagen in der Kultur (Civilization and Its Discontents,* 1939) Freud discusses guilt and conscience, that part of guilt stimulated by the superego. The *superego* is the internalization of the moral demands of society, what Riesman has called "the walking delegate from ideology." Contrary to some vulgarizations of Freud, the liberation of the life force in the dark places of the id from the restraint of guilt was not Freud's

---

of Sigmund Freud, trans. by A. A. Brill (New York: Random House, Modern Library, 1938), might be more helpful.

[35] See *Totem and Tabu* (1913) in *Basic Writings.*

[36] See *The Future of an Illusion,* trans. by W. D. Robson-Scott (London: Hogarth, 1928). See also the essays by Will Herberg and Reinhold Niebuhr in Benjamin Nelson, ed., *Freud and the Twentieth Century* (New York: Noonday Press, Meridian, 1957).

[37] See David Riesman, "Authority and Liberty in the Structure of Freud's Thought," in *Individualism Reconsidered* (New York: Free Press, 1954).

[38] *Civilization and Its Discontents,* trans. by Joan Rivière (London: Hogarth, 1939), p. 133.

primary object. Indeed, "the price of progress in civilization is paid in forfeiting happiness through the heightening of the sense of guilt."[39] But this is not an easy progress. Though disclaiming a prophet's role, Freud raises the question of whether a whole people ("possibly even the whole of humanity") can become neurotic under the pressure of these civilizing trends. And so at the very end he returns to the struggle between the life force and the death force and, in a statement even more appropriate to the postatomic age, says:

Men have brought their powers of subduing the forces of nature to such a pitch that by using them they could now very easily exterminate one another to the last man. They know this— hence arises a great part of their current unrest, their dejection, their mood of apprehension. And now it may be expected that the other of the two "heavenly forces," eternal Eros, will put forth his strength so as to maintain himself alongside his equally immortal adversary.[40]

The important contributions of Freud to twentieth-century political thinking were not made directly through his own semipolitical writings but indirectly through the change he wrought in the prevailing conception of man. A certain tolerance and flexibility in penal procedures accompanied the recognition that the *ego,* or the rational self, is not unlimited in its capacity to control the *id,* or the subconscious. This affected standards of responsibility in law and expectations of self-direction in education and in some respects led to a reduction in the perfectionist moral demands made by the *superego,* or the culture, on the individual. Our dependence upon parents as authority figures and our capacity to transfer this dependence to surrogates who may be political leaders have been observed, and the observation has affected not only our understanding but our leadership. Though many Freudians are, in common parlance, liberals, nevertheless, as Rieff writes, "The conservative implications of Freudian psy-

chology are clear: nothing qualitatively different happens in history. With the leader forced to play father-imago because his followers are children, politics becomes an unchanging strife between the generations."[41] The biologically equalizing tendencies of the Freudian approach probably have inhibited the possibility of regarding leaders as truly noble figures in any classical sense of the word "noble." Finally, the Freudian insight into the rationalizing propensities of the human being, transferred to politics, makes ideology as compared to "pure" ideals all the more pervasive and, as well, suggests the possibility of "subliminal" manipulations, which has been lost on neither advertisers nor political manipulators. The capacity of individuals for the repression, suppression, and displacement of aggressive feelings, whatever it has suggested by way of mass manipulation, also has revealed to us the depth of the problem of rational social control.

Neo-Freudianism: Fromm

Freud, of course, is not the only contem-

---

[39] *Ibid.,* p. 123.
[40] *Ibid.,* p. 144.

[41] Philip Rieff, *Freud: the Man and the Moralist* (Garden City, N. Y.: Doubleday, Anchor, 1961), p. 261. Rieff's analysis of Freud is probably the most penetrating of those analyses that stress social and political implications. See also Norman O. Brown, *Life Against Death* (New York: Random House, Vintage, n.d.) and Thomas Johnson, *Freud and Political Thought* (New York: Citadel, 1965). On parental-political authority figures, see Sebastian DeGrazia, *The Political Community: A Study in Anomie* (Chicago: Univ. of Chicago Press, 1963) and Robert E. Lane, "Fathers and Sons: Foundations of Political Belief," *American Sociological Review,* Vol. 24 (1959), pp. 502–11. For Marxian interpretations see Herbert Marcuse, *Eros and Civilization* (New York: Random House, Vintage, 1962) and Reuben Osborn, *Freud and Marx* (New York: Equinox Cooperative Press, n.d.). Perhaps the most notable application of Freudian concepts to political studies has been in the work of Harold Lasswell. See *Psychopathology and Politics* (Chicago: Univ. of Chicago Press, 1930), *World Politics and Personal Insecurity* (New York: McGraw-Hill, 1935), and *Power and Personality* (New York: Norton, 1948).

porary psychological influence[42] and the so-called Freudian revisionists have departed from the master in many respects. Perhaps the most politically minded of these neo-Freudians is Erich Fromm (1900–), whose reputation was made by *Escape from Freedom* (1941).[43] In that work, well timed to confront readers when the Nazis' power was at its height, he reminded liberals of the negative possibilities of freedom. Tracing the alienation of the individual from his primary social groups since the Renaissance and the Reformation, Fromm analyzed the sadistic and masochistic feelings generated by the loneliness of a competitive industrial society. Modern man finds that he has negative freedom, freedom *from,* but he does not know what to do with it. He yearns to be a unique and different self and to be accepted as a whole person. But a fragmented and mechanical culture treats him as a cog in a machine. He is like everyone else. "The despair of the human automaton is fertile soil for the political purposes of Fascism." He needs somehow to achieve positive freedom, freedom *to,* which is synonymous with "the spontaneous activity of the total integrated personality."[44]

In pursuit of this laudable goal Fromm explicitly criticized Freud for his narrow biologism and, like his psychiatric colleague Sullivan, stressed the importance of interpersonal relations in shaping character well beyond childhood. He also emphasized the affirmative and unifying rather than the cathartic side of love.

If Freud can be criticized for neglecting social institutions, Fromm can be criticized for making the community responsible for almost everything. Like the nineteenth-century utopian socialists, Fromm takes an extremely optimistic view of natural man, and the way in which he offers his "humanitarian communitarianism" as a solution to "robotism" and the most complex socio-psychological problems is engagingly naive. On man: ". . . the striving for mental health, for happiness, harmony, love, productiveness, is inherent in every human being who is not born a mental or moral idiot. Given a chance, these strivings assert themselves forcefully, as can be seen in countless situations."[45] On solutions: "Changes in ownership must be made to the extent to which they are necessary to create a community of work. . . . Man must be reinstituted to his supreme place in society, never being a means, never a thing to be used by others or by himself. Man's use by man must end, and economy must become the servant for the development of man. Capital must serve labor, things must serve life."[46]

---

[42] See, for example, C. G. Jung, *Modern Man in Search of a Soul* (London: Routledge and Kegan Paul, 1933) and Ira Progoff, *Jung's Psychology and Its Social Meaning* (New York: Grove Press, Evergreen, 1957).

[43] *Escape from Freedom* (New York: Holt, Rinehart and Winston, 1941). See also Fromm's *Beyond the Chains of Illusion* (New York: Simon and Schuster, 1962) and Karen Horney, *The Neurotic Personality of Our Time* (New York: Norton, 1937). A highly critical study of Fromm's political thought is John Schaar, *Escape from Authority* (New York: Basic Books, 1961).

[44] *Escape from Freedom,* pp. 256 and 258.

[45] *The Sane Society* (New York: Holt, Rinehart and Winston, 1958), p. 275.

[46] *Ibid.,* p. 361. With more thoroughness than any other recent writer Christian Bay has taken the liberal tenet of the free individual and has tried to work out a set of propositions appropriate to a social policy based on this ideal, postulating a "humanitarian loyalty" that is "compatible with a maximal level of *psychological* freedom." In *The Structure of Freedom* (New York: Atheneum, 1965), he employs the latest findings of psychology, social psychology, and sociology and tries, with some difficulty, to follow a "value-free" methodology in so doing. See Walter Berns, "The Behavioral Sciences and the Study of Political Things: The Case of Christian Bay's *The Structure of Freedom,*" *American Political Science Review,* Vol. 55 (1961), pp. 550–59. The concern for the political *as* the political in Berns' criticism of Bay represents a new and essentially nonliberal, or transliberal, tendency in contemporary political thinking. Liberals have generally thought of politics as the resultant of conflicting "interests," either individual or group, a kind of superstructure built on nonpolitical forces. This assumption is challenged in such writings as Joseph Cropsey, "On the Relation of Political Science and Economics," *American Political Science Review,* Vol. 54 (1960), pp. 3–14; Norman Jacobson, "The Unity of Political Theory: Science, Mor-

EXISTENTIALISM

Existentialism is a much misunderstood but highly important twentieth-century phenomenon, perhaps the most significant philosophic movement yet to rise up in this century.[47] Its forms are various and subtle and, insofar as it has common tenets, they are apolitical, if not antipolitical. Yet its political consequences are tremendous.

Kierkegaard

The starting point of contemporary existentialism is in the Platonic distinction between existence and essence, more particularly in the reaction of the Danish theologian Søren Kierkegaard (1813–55) against Hegel's attempt to make rational essence embrace all that is. The search for essence is both a rational and a definitional exercise. Existence does not need to be (indeed, cannot be) defined, analyzed, plotted out, or reduced to abstractions: it is simply *there*. We know it not by intellectual inquiry but by a transrational "encounter." It is concrete rather than abstract, spontaneous rather than predictable,

---

als, and Politics," in Roland Young, ed., *Approaches to the Study of Politics* (Evanston: Northwestern Univ. Press, 1958), pp. 115–24; Sheldon Wolin, *Politics and Vision* (Boston: Little, Brown, 1960); and works by Hannah Arendt cited above.

[47] The bibliography of existentialism is already immense. See Kenneth Douglas, *A Critical Bibliography of Existentialism* (*The Paris School*) (New Haven: Yale Univ. Press, Yale French Studies Special Monograph No. 1, 1950) and Victor Vanitelli, S.J., "A Bibliographical Introduction to Existentialism," *The Modern Schoolman*, Vol. 26, No. 4 (May 1949). Some important studies since these dates are Hazel E. Barnes, *Humanistic Existentialism* (Lincoln: Univ. of Nebraska Press, 1963); William Barrett, *Irrational Man* (Garden City, N. Y.: Doubleday, Anchor, 1962); H. J. Blackham, *Six Existentialist Thinkers* (London: Routledge and Kegan Paul, 1953); Marjorie Grene, *Introduction to Existentialism* (Chicago: Univ. of Chicago Press, 1959); Frederick Heinemann, *Existentialism and the Modern Predicament,* 2nd ed. (New York: Harper & Row, 1958); and Paul Roubiczek, *Existentialism* (Cambridge, Eng.: Cambridge Univ. Press, 1964).

---

free rather than determined, subjectively rather than objectively known.

According to Kierkegaard, the separation of existence from essence is most apparent to a man in moments of personal crisis. At such a time definitions, abstract concepts, and "principles" seem especially unreal. They do not satisfy. Yet man's intellect is trapped within the sphere of essences, for that is all intellect can know. We depend upon our intellectual constructions even in times of crisis but they are found wanting and great tension and frustration result. This is the anguish (*Angst*) Kierkegaard described as "metaphysical sickness," which was for him the precursor of religious faith, for, when one is at the end of his intellectual rope, he is forced either to dangle helplessly or to take the "leap of faith" and grasp "the absurd," which is beyond reason but restores wholeness of spirit. The paradox—among the many that delighted Kierkegaard—is that, until one knows he is sick, he cannot be well.

From the preleap outlook, the leap is made into darkness and can be in any direction. Hence, the freedom that liberals once prized so highly now becomes terrifying. It is a "dizziness." The optimistic view of freedom that had become part of modern man's inheritance was shattered in Kierkegaard—and Dostoevsky and Nietzsche. The incidence of personal crises that makes freedom so terrifying may be more characteristic of twentieth-century life than of nineteenth-century life. This may help to explain why Kierkegaard's writings lay in limbo for the second half of the nineteenth century only to be rediscovered and spread over the globe in the twentieth.

Jaspers

One of many influenced by Kierkegaard is Karl Jaspers (1883–   ), psychiatrist and professor of philosophy at Heidelberg and, since 1948, Basel. More directly concerned than many other existentialists with the political environment as a matter of theory,

Jaspers outlines the present historical condition of man in *Die geistige Situation der Zeit* (*Man in the Modern Age,* 1957).[48] Jaspers finds a threat to the selfhood of every man in the giant impersonal machine of modern mass society. The Nietzschean influence is obviously cast over the following passages, yet their content seems as fully relevant to the 1960s as to the Weimar Republic days when Jaspers wrote them:

Essential humanity is reduced to the general; to vitality as a functional corporeality, to the triviality of enjoyment. The divorce of labour from pleasure deprives life of its possible gravity: public affairs become mere entertainment; private affairs, the alternation of stimulation and fatigue, and a craving for novelty whose inexhaustible current flows swiftly into the waters of oblivion. . . . Youth as the period of highest vital efficiency and of erotic exaltation becomes the desired type of life in general. Where the human being is regarded only as a function, he must be young; and if youth is over he will try to show its semblance. . . . Great men pass into the background as contrasted with the efficient. . . . Without the support of the mass will he [the human being] is of no account. What he can be is not measured by an ideal, is not related to a genuinely present Transcendence, but is based upon his conception of the fundamental qualities of mankind as manifested in the majority. . . . Now the result of "leadership" of this kind is inextricable confusion. . . .

With the unification of our planet there has begun a process of levelling-down which people contemplate with horror. That which has today become general to our species is always the most superficial, the most trivial, and the most indifferent of human possibilities. Yet men strive to effect this levelling-down as if, in that way, the unification of mankind could be brought about. . . . People dress alike. . . . the same dances, the same types of thought, and the same catchwords.[49]

Politics is always, says Jaspers, a concrete activity, full of obscure motives, taking place within a vast and incomprehensible whole. But political claims are couched in terms of abstract generality and drilled into citizens "with the fixity of religious dogmas." The concept "nation" is one of the best, that is, worst, examples of this and the bolsheviks and fascists are the most adept at the drilling.

How does Jaspers help us overcome these suffocating forces? His means obviously cannot be construction of a new system. In his gigantic three-volume *Philosophy* (1932) he noncommittally examines the possibilities of transcending material knowledge and the realm of objects. Being more "representational" than other existentialists would approve, Jaspers surveys a variety of philosophical world views. He is trying to help man become aware of himself and to help him face his free decision. After his enforced "inside exile" under the Nazis, he came up with a massive volume that was supposed to be the first of three in a new *Philosophical Logic.* Its title is *Von der Wahrheit* (*Of Truth,* 1947). Despite its name, it was not a logic; in spite of himself, Jaspers had now produced a system of sorts; and, also in spite of himself, he had come close to a religious faith. Seeing him move from Nietzschean defiant doubt to Kierkegaardian faith, some critics marked this as a sign of strength, others as a sign of weakness.[50] If one contribution of Jaspers stands out, it is his treatment of the problem of communication between persons beyond the limits of rational knowledge, that is, beyond the realm of the essential. He speaks of a "rise into transcendence" where by "evocation" one recreates in another a crisis similar to one's own. Transrational "signs" are in this way "decoded" and a meeting of the minds is achieved. This is the level of being Jaspers calls "The Encompassing" (*das Umgreifende*) and it is with this level that authentic philosophy deals.

---

[48] *Man in the Modern Age,* trans. by Eden and Cedar Paul (Garden City, N. Y.: Doubleday, Anchor, 1957).

[49] *Ibid.,* pp. 48, 55, and 85. See also Jose Ortega y Gasset, *The Revolt of the Masses* (New York: Norton, 1932).

[50] Compare Heinemann, p. 76, with Walter Kaufmann, ed., in the Introduction to *Existentialism from Dostoevsky to Sartre* (New York: Noonday Press, Meridian, 1956), p. 33.

Although The Encompassing is transrational, reason is man's best instrument for a "new politics" above self-interest and expansionist aims. Jaspers' *Die Atombombe und die Zukunft des Menschen* (*The Future of Mankind*) takes a grim look at the political realities of the atomic age and is stamped with Jaspers' characteristic nobility and hopefulness in the face of acknowledged danger. But it is also frustratingly diffuse in its explication of the role of reason. Jaspers' reason, like Hegel's, has a life of its own; we are never quite sure whether it belongs to man or God:

Reason is more than the sum of acts of clear thinking. These acts, rather, spring from a life-carrying basic mood, and it is this mood we call reason. . . .
    It is the essential human trait—whatever else is human shines by its light alone. It is the lofty mood of humanity itself.
    It is as strong in youth as in old age, but in all phases of life it is in danger of failing. It is never perfected.
    It exists only in common. The individual cannot be rational by himself. . . .
    Reason is essential to politics because it should prepare the ground for the community of all men in the state and in its institutions. At first, however, the community formed by reason is always one of individuals who find each other and—without agreements, without organization, without expression—embody the hidden rational solidarity. This reality is suprapolitical. It must take political action if politics is to become constructive and enduring, but it cannot be drawn into politics itself.[51]

Later Jaspers says, "The cause of all things is not reason but the incomprehensible reality above us, the symbolic term for which is God."

Like other existentialists, Jaspers would bring philosophy back from technicism to the central moral concerns of concrete living. But his message is muffled by Germanic abstractness and a deep distrust of political conflict.

[51] *The Future of Mankind*, trans. by E. B. Ashton (Chicago: Univ. of Chicago Press, 1961), pp. 218–19.

Sartre

Possibly the most difficult of twentieth-century philosophers of existence is Heidegger. Utterly neglectful of the problem of community, he has been absorbed by the ontology of man's "encounter with nothingness." Heidegger's thought need not detain us here, but the name serves to introduce his more politically minded student, Jean-Paul Sartre (1905–), one of few contemporary philosophers who willingly accepts the name "existentialist" (Jaspers is an advocate of *Existenzphilosophie*). Sartre tries to bring Heidegger's detached ontologizing down to the problems of the subjective self.

Heidegger, Jaspers, and Sartre all agree that the philosophy of existence must be lived to have meaning. All agree that man makes himself by his choices. It is doubly interesting to note, thus, the divergent courses they followed when faced with the crisis of Nazism. Heidegger joined the Nazi party to keep his university post. Jaspers, who had a Jewish wife, lost his professorship but continued working in seclusion. Sartre fought in the French resistance. (During the Korean war he publicly aligned himself with—but did not join—the Communist Party as a protest against the status quo.)

The relationship of Sartre's practical Marxism to his ontology of nothingness is a problem for both Sartre and his interpreters. How can the objectivism of dialectical materialism be reconciled with the subjectivism of man making himself? The former is determinist, the latter ardently antideterministic. How can social thought with any scientific *or* moral content emerge from a base of individual isolation and despair? We must, to sketch an answer, look briefly at Sartre's major philosophic work, *L'être et le néant* (*Being and Nothingness*, 1943).

One of the basic distinctions of *L'être et le néant* is that between "being-in-itself," or unconscious being (*l'être-en-soi*) and "being-for-itself," or conscious being (*l'être-pour-soi*). There is here a close parallel to Hegel's distinction between *an-sich* and *für-sich*.

From the viewpoint of the conscious, which is the only viewpoint we can articulate, being-in-itself has neither possibility nor impossibility, neither reason nor justification; it just *is*. As far as we can see, its isness is identical with nothingness. Yet conscious being must be an aspect of being-in-itself; hence conscious being is derived from nothingness. Indeed, being-for-itself is absolutely dependent upon being-in-itself, while being-in-itself, which is a plenitude, is not at all dependent on being-for-itself. There is, thus, no reciprocity in this relationship. There is no law of necessity, no other being (e.g., God), no possibility that can explain how consciousness comes to be. There is no such thing as human nature.

being can neither be derived from the possible nor reduced to the necessary. Necessity concerns the connection between ideal propositions but not that of existents. An existing phenomenon can never be derived from another existent qua existent. This is what we shall call the *contingency* of being-in-itself. But neither can being-in-itself be derived from a *possibility*. The possible *is* a structure of the *for-itself*. That is, it belongs to the other region of being. Being-in-itself is never either possible or impossible. *It is*.[52]

The basic Sartrean paradox is that, though being-for-itself comes out of nothingness, it knows itself as nothingness and in so knowing finds a revelation of being.

Because being-for-itself comes blindly out of this contingency, it is absolutely free and the humans who embody it are terrifyingly alone. This aloneness, this feeling of being superfluous (*de trop*) is illustrated in a vast range of Sartre's literary works: people have difficulty communicating (e.g., *No Exit*); even the world of nature is alien (e.g., *Nausea*). Nevertheless, external factors do seem to impinge on this freedom. Something outside ourselves makes us aware of our bodies, our senses, other people. These facts are "out

there" and realists call them real. We cannot change our looks, our race, our family. These are surely facts with reference to which we cannot be free. They are what Heidegger refers to as "brute existents." Sartre speaks of the problem of "facticity" and argues that to being-for-itself all such things are wholly neutral. A man does not choose to be born a cripple but, being so born, he can choose his attitude toward the infirmity—humiliation, defiance, exhibitionism, or whatever. We choose ourselves not in our physical being but in our manner of being. The same thing applies to the past. Though it seems fixed, we can transform its meaning by our attitude toward it. Freedom for Sartre is really the attitude we take toward anything.[53] Even the natural world has meaning only after we assert our intentions. Objects are heavy only because we want to lift them; an incline is steep only because we want to ascend it. If we try to climb a mountain crag and fail, we may say that it cannot be climbed: ". . . let us note that the crag is revealed as such only because it was originally grasped as 'climbable'; it is therefore our freedom which constitutes the limits which it will subsequently encounter."

A link between Sartre's ontology and his political thought opens up at this point. Just as nature comes into being because we choose it, society comes into being and reveals its complexity only because we want to change it. But before looking at the problem of other people as society, let us look at the problem of other people as persons. Both problems raise complications for Sartre's thought.

We bring other people into being only by choosing to regard them. They are objects to us: ". . . the relation of my body to the Oth-

---

[52] Hazel E. Barnes, in the Introductiton to her translation of *Being and Nothingness* (New York: Philosophical Library, 1956), p. LXVIII. Subsequent quotations are from this edition.

[53] Freedom understood as a yielding to the nature that "flows through us at the borders of consciousness and the unconscious" is, says Barrett, unknown to Sartre (William Barrett, *Irrational Man*, Ch. 10). Read attacks the same problem in a different way and shows that, etymologically, "free" and "friend" come from the same root. A communitarian "liberty" is what is really concrete and existential, he says; the "freedom" existentialists brood over is really abstract and essential (Herbert Read, *Existentialism, Marxism, and Anarchism* [London: Freedom Press, 1950], pp. 21–24).

er's body is a relation of pure, indifferent exteriority." But in looking at us, others give us the experience of being objects, too. This experience of "being-for-another" (*le pour-autrui*) is, like the birth of being-for-itself, an "absolute event." The mere look of another can threaten our subjectivity, can give our private world an "internal hemorrhage." Fear and shame are the two immediate responses when another breaks into our world like this. We feel reduced, looked down upon, guilty. This, says Sartre, is his version of original sin. To preserve ourselves we fight back, so to speak, by looking at the other, by making him an object. Thus, as Hegel argued, conflict is endemic to the human condition. Love, sexual or otherwise, cannot overcome this conflict, for love is but the attempt to absorb another's freedom in oneself: "What I aim at in the other is nothing more than what I find in myself." A personal union of sorts comes when a third person fixes his objectifying gaze on two partners in an enterprise. They are united by the need for common resistance; but this union is only temporary. Basically, we are alone.

That our own values are *ipso facto* values for mankind ("My commitments commit all men") appears to have ethical implications in Sartre's widely translated and reprinted speech *"L'Existentialisme, est-il un humanisme?"* ("Existentialism: Is It Humanism?" 1946),[54] where he implies that personal responsibility carries with it social responsibilities. But the roots of Sartre's social ethics must remain undernourished because he fails to establish any other than a negative basis for human communication. Ethically, what is to be avoided is "bad faith," the pretence that we did not choose the course of action we are following. Persons of bad faith are either cowards (*les lâches*) or aggressors (*salauds*—literally, dirty fellows). The authentic man—a Heideggerian rather than Sartrean term—knows who he is and lives out his existential nothingness with dignity. The function of existential psychology, in

Sartre's view, is to help a patient clarify what his actual life "project" is. Sartre tells of counseling a boy who was struggling during the German occupation of France to decide whether to stay in France to protect his mother or to flee to England to fight the Germans. Sartre's only counsel was and is: you are free to choose, you must trust your instincts, you must act without hope.

Sartre's ontology of freedom is a tour de force, impressive but not convincing. Many of us may know the fear and shame, dread and estrangement that Sartre so searchingly adumbrates, but what is the logic by which any of these should be given an ontological status more fundamental than, say, joy or compassion? We may be separated from our fellow men as hostile, warring objects, united only in resistance, but what is the logic by which the analysis of consciousness itself must begin with separation rather than with a sense of union with our fellows? Sartre's elevation of despair into a principle fits very well an age of totalitarian anxiety and dehumanized urbanism, but, as Grene writes, "if we have lost those activities—part work, part ritual—in which men genuinely stand together to wrest the goods they need from a co-operative, yet unwilling, nature, we have no right, in consequence, to call our sophisticated loneliness a universal condition of mankind."[55]

We have yet to state how Sartre's Marxism fits into his philosophic thought—if it does. How can the interior meanings of existentialism be reconciled with the exterior meanings of Marxism? Sartre has always rather self-consciously identified with the underdog and the oppressed. In *Roads to Freedom* Brunet the communist is the most sympathetic figure. In *The Respectful Prostitute* the Negro and the prostitute are the only honest persons. The middle class, Sartre has long claimed, is doomed. In the essay "Marxisme et Revolution" (1946), however, Sartre is merely able to affirm that Marxism is right because it is the philosophy of the proletariat. Its materialism, as philosophy, is but a "use-

---

[54] The American edition is titled *Existentialism*, trans. by Bernard Frechtman (New York: Philosophical Library, 1947).

[55] *Introduction to Existentialism*, p. 92.

ful myth." Socialism is basically humanistic; therefore, "a materialistic socialism is contradictory."[56]

Sartre's ponderous *Critique de raison dialectique* (*Critique of Dialectical Reason*, 1960),[57] in its first volume, *Theorie des ensembles pratiques* (*Theory of Practical Wholes*), undertakes the ambitious task of setting forth the structures whereby the individual is related to society. Sartre justifies writing in a Marxist framework by invoking the Marxist concept of ideology: Sartre is the self-professed and rather too humble ideologue writing in an era so dominated by Marxism that it is "unsurpassable" (*indépassable*). Though as a philosophical base it may have defects, Marxism is held to be indispensable for social action. Sartre does not, however, seriously consider alternative systems. His aim is to help Marxism "take on human dimensions," for when it has done so existentialism will have done its job, "empirical anthropology" will have been established, and "existentialism will no longer have a reason for being."

The body of the work follows familiar existentialist terminology in discussing how an individual's "project" can be moved beyond his "situation." But Marxist terminology is also employed. Part I is titled "From Individual Praxis to the Practical Inert" and Part II, "From Group to History." Sartre argues that the key factor that drives people together into society is scarcity: there is never enough of anything to go around. Society is primarily a "serial group," a mere collectivity, a "plurality of solitudes." He gives the example of people waiting for a bus in which there may not be enough seats. They line up in an orderly fashion, without reference to individual differences or merit, because the alternative is violent struggle for the scarce

seats. The persons in line become "general individuals"—anonymous, impotent, "inert material." Their group is the "practical inert."

In revolution the serial, or collective, group can become a "group in fusion," or dynamic group—curiously for a Marxist, Sartre does not speak of class nor deal much with economics. The group is united by oath, so that its members may know each other, and by terror, without which the oath is empty. This sounds very much like the French resistance movement but Sartre says that terror is the "ontological rule" that the group must make use of in its praxis. Political authority and sovereignty have meaning only for members of groups-in-fusion because members of serial groups cannot internalize their membership. What happens to freedom in a terror-ridden group? In a very Hobbesian note Sartre says, "if I recognize myself as a member of a group, I rediscover my freedom in one way or another in that of the sovereign."

All this is supposed to pertain to what Sartre calls "totalization," the movement of understanding from the individual consciousness to the plane of history; but we must wait for the second volume of the *Critique,* which will deal with the possibility of a comprehensive meaning for history as a whole, before we can be sure what "totalization" leads to. For now we are confined to a rather old "new dialectics" of the revolutionary group, which requires "for practical unity" the assumuption that "freedom and necessity are one and the same."

So far, despite his powerful psychological insights, Sartre has failed to give us either the method of rational dialectics that he promised or the criteria for a social ethics that would complete his ontology of freedom.

Camus

Sartre's literary, political, and philosophic works share a common moral vision; this wholeness of commitment probably accounts for much of his influence. The same could be said for the less philosophically oriented

[56] *Literary and Philosophical Essays,* trans. by Annette Michelson (New York: Criterion, 1955), p. 230.

[57] *Critique de raison dialectique* (Paris: Gallimard, 1960). Subsequent quotations are from this edition. There is no English translation yet, but the work is discussed in Wilfred Desan, *The Marxism of Jean-Paul Sartre* (Garden City, N.Y.: Doubleday, 1965). See also the review by Edouard Morot-Sir in *Journal of the History of Ideas,* Vol. 22 (1961), pp. 573–81.

Albert Camus (1913–60). The two men were friends but broke publicly in 1952 over Sartre's Marxism.[58] Camus shared Sartre's atheism and his vision of the absurd but he could be distinguished from his older compatriot by his hostility to all forms of ideology—including Marxist ideology—and to philosophical abstraction used as a cloak for inhumane action. Nor was despair an ultimate category for Camus, as it is for Sartre. Camus objected to being labeled an existentialist and was more a man of letters than a political theorist.

In the well-known essay "The Myth of Sisyphus" (1942), the condemned Sisyphus, who must roll a great rock to the top of the mountain only to have it fall back of its own weight, is referred to as "the absurd hero." Yet he is a tragic hero because, unlike many modern workmen whose task is no less futile, Sisyphus is *conscious* of his absurdity. He learns that "There is no fate that cannot be surmounted by scorn." His discovery of the absurd is enough by itself to bring happiness ("Happiness and the absurd are two sons of the same earth"), for at least Sisyphus' "fate belongs to him. His rock is his thing."[59]

The illustrative heroes of "The Myth of Sisyphus"—Don Juan, the actor, the adventurer, and the creative artist—are nonsocial creatures. *L'homme révolté,* by contrast, is a political activist. This book, Camus's most political work, is a manifestation of his response to the torture and killing of innocents in World War II and to the "logic of destruc-

tion" that led to administrative murder. He condemns the individual act of suicide in "The Myth of Sisyphus." He condemns the social act of murder in *L'homme révolté.*[60] Yet the work is not simply negative. Camus makes a case for the view that by rebelling we assert the worth of the society against which we rebel. It is the very act of rebelling that creates the value society has for us. "I rebel, therefore we exist." This is Camus's equivalent of *Cogito ergo sum.* Rebellion, like religion, affirms the solidarity of the human race. If it tries to destroy this solidarity, it "loses simultaneously its right to be called rebellion and becomes in actuality an acquiescence in murder." Camus explicitly distinguishes his position from nihilism through the idea of "limits," for rebellion without a sense of limit is a form of slavery and is self-defeating. Inherent in Camus's rebellion are the ideas of restraint and the rejection of absolutes, for absolute justice is always unfree and absolute freedom is always unjust. Only through restraint can rebellion be kept alive and constant and pertinent, which it must be to be meaningful.

Along the way Camus throws off dazzling critiques of, among others, Rousseau, Saint-Just, Sade, Hegel, Marx, Nietzsche, and the entire socialist movement. He gives us many vignettes of what in contemporary society can be rebelled against: authoritarianism, systematic violence, the centralized state, colonization, human misery, and the persecution of innocents. But any such checklist is superficial in relation to the deeper thrust of Camus's attack: the utopian valuing of the future over the present and the use of ideology to delay human decency:

---

[58] The occasion was a review of *L'homme révolté* (*The Rebel,* 1951) by Francis Jeanson in *Les Temps Modernes* and subsequent letters by Camus and Sartre. See Sartre's "A Reply to Albert Camus," in *Situations,* trans. by Benita Eisler (New York: Braziller, 1965). The feud is discussed in Raymond Aron, *The Opium of the Intellectuals,* trans. by Terence Kilmartin (New York: Norton, 1962), pp. 51–58; Germaine Brée, *Camus* (New Brunswick: Rutgers Univ. Press, 1961), pp. 55–57 and Ch. 22, *passim;* and Roy Pierce, *Contemporary French Political Thought* (New York: Oxford Univ. Press, 1966), pp. 76–78.

[59] "The Myth of Sisyphus," in Kaufmann, pp. 314–15. See also Fred H. Wilhoite, Jr., "Albert Camus' Politics of Rebellion," *Western Political Quarterly,* Vol. 14 (1961), pp. 400–14.

[60] Camus's vigorous opposition to capital punishment was part of this stance: the finality of a planned death cannot be justified by the "unverifiable possibility" that an execution deters crime. The only conspicuous motive for capital punishment is revenge. Unless executions are public, the state confesses that it acts without public authority; yet the tacit suppression of eyewitness accounts shows that the brutal facts of executions are not really believed to be exemplary ("Reflections on the Guillotine" [1957], in *Resistance, Rebellion, and Death,* trans. by Justin O'Brien [New York: Knopf, 1961]).

The men of Europe, abandoned to the shadows, have turned their backs on the fixed and radiant point of the present. They forget the present for the future, the fate of humanity for the delusion of power, the misery of the slums for the mirage of the Eternal City, ordinary justice for an empty promised land. They despair of personal freedom and dream of a strange freedom of the species; reject solitary death and give the name of immortality to a vast collective agony. They no longer believe in the things that exist in the world and in living man; the secret of Europe is that it no longer loves life. Its blind men entertain the puerile belief that to love one single day of life amounts to justifying whole centuries of oppression. That is why they wanted to efface joy from the world and to postpone it until a much later date. Impatience with limits, the rejection of their double life, despair at being a man have finally driven them to inhuman excesses. Denying the real grandeur of life, they have had to stake all on their own excellence. For want of something better to do, they deified themselves and their misfortunes began; these gods have had their eyes put out. . . . [Others] refuse, on the contrary, to be deified in that they refuse the unlimited power to inflict death. They choose, and give us as an example, the only original rule of life to-day: to learn to live and to die, and in order to be a man, to refuse to be a god.[61]

Thus, finally, the struggle to keep rebellion alive yet within limits is a struggle within man and not outside him. In the face of the hard fact that in twenty centuries the sum total of evil has not diminished and probably will not diminish, one understands why "rebellion cannot exist without a strange form of love." But the love Camus asks is not a form of resignation. Indeed, his final words are an exultant clarion call of hope: ". . . it is time to forsake our age and its adolescent rages." For the "love of the earth" we must fit a new arrow to the bow, "the bow bends; the wood complains. At the moment of supreme tension, there will leap into flight an unswerving arrow, a shaft that is inflexible and free."[62]

A NOTE ON EASTERN AND WESTERN POLITICAL THOUGHT

This is a book on the history of *Western* political theory not because the West alone is important but because the book is written by a Westerner for Westerners in the conviction that we must first know what we are before we can know what we may be. So far, at least, "the West can interpret the West; it can only describe the East."[63]

While Western man has been aware of Eastern thought for centuries, it has taken the world-shrinking conflicts and technological revolutions of the twentieth century to give it common relevance. Culturally, and especially technologically, Eastern nations—nation is itself a Western concept—are becoming Westernized at an accelerating rate. The newer constitutions of Asia reflect Western political ideas far more than Eastern. And, insofar as the great political struggle of the present in Asia may be described as that between liberal democracy and communism, it must be noted that both are Western importations.

The reverse—East-to-West—influence is hardly equivalent. However, no commerce can be wholly unilateral and a new interest, especially among Americans, in Eastern religion, art, and culture may be detected. The so-called hippie movement is only the most conspicuous, not necessarily the most important, evidence of this influence. Mukerji has argued that ancient Hindu philosophy integrated socio-political theory more successfully with "a morally valid . . . view of life" than Western thinkers have ever done, a fact Westerns are only beginning to recognize.[64] Without question we can and shall learn much from Eastern concepts of "community without collectivism" and "personality without individualism."

The outcome of this commerce is, how-

[61] *The Rebel*, trans. by Anthony Bower (New York: Random House, Vintage, 1956), pp. 305–06.
[62] *Ibid.*, p. 306.
[63] John Lukacs. Quoted in Norman D. Palmer, "Indian and Western Political Thought: Coalescence or Clash?" *American Political Science Review*, Vol. 49 (1955), p. 748.
[64] K. P. Mukerji. *Ibid.*, p. 757.

ever, by no means clear. The consequences for political theory are clouded by the fact that typical Eastern philosophy is generally apolitical and often antipolitical. Eastern philosophy still has a dominant purpose: escape from the miseries of worldly existence and a loss of self in mystical detachment. As worldly miseries become less miserable—if they do—no one can be quite sure what will happen. Meanwhile it is not to be wondered at that the worldly and politically expansive West has contributed more to a consistent body of political doctrine. Ironically, part of the current American interest in Zen Buddhism undoubtedly stems from a general disenchantment with the political, a disenchantment of which existentialism may be another expression.

Another factor worth noting is that Eastern modes of thought at their roots are so different from Western modes of thought that significant communication in political or other theory remains difficult and frustrating. Western thought, even that employed against the dominance of logic, is geared to logical progression. It zeroes in on its object. As Abegg observes in her rewarding *The Mind of East Asia,* Eastern thinking is "envelopmental thinking," taking the form of a series of encircling thrusts around its object, trying to open up as many avenues to comprehension as possible, trying to intimate a wholeness that can never be encapsuled in propositional and logical form. To the Westerner, Eastern thought, even at its most erudite, often seems meandering, undisciplined, and inconclusive. To the Easterner, Western thought, even when most diligently in search of some kind of *Gestalt,* often seems incomplete and pedantically constricted.[65]

We can agree with India's great scholar and former President, Sarvepalli Radhakrishnan, when he says: "Mankind stems from one origin from which it has figured out in many forms. It is now striving toward the reconciliation of that which has been split up. The separation of East and West is over. This history of the new world, the one world,

has begun."[66] But we are not yet capable of the intellectual and spiritual leap necessary to ratify the end of this separation by a serious history of the political thought of the world. Not yet; but undoubtedly soon in this century of phenomenal cultural assimilation.

CONCLUSION

We have not attempted in this chapter a systematic survey of twentieth-century political thought. Rather we have looked at certain themes and schools of thought that illustrate what is old and what is new in the twentieth century. We began and ended with developments so new that we hardly know how to assess them: the experience of totalitarianism and the experience of large-scale East-West interactions. In the middle we looked at liberalism, at patterns of thought still lively yet so old as to require, perhaps, gerontological prescriptions. Freudianism, by contrast, may be old hat to the fashionable but it is not yet old and the sexual revolution rightly or wrongly associated with it is still very much with us. It is a revolution against male dominance as much as anything and, since political authority tends to be bound up with paternal authority, this revolution may be as significant as any other in this century. It is more revolutionary at least than existentialism, the next-to-last item considered in this chapter. Existentialist thought is a symptom both of heroic despair and of the longing for authenticity that despair cannot drown.

None of the three men whom next we study was a despairing man. The positive seems to have more durability than the negative, at least in the realm of ideas. But all three, as we shall see, were responding to the conditions of unusual turbulence we still live with.

[65] Trans. by A. J. Crick and E. E. Thomas (London: Thames & Hudson, 1952).

[66] *East and West, Some Reflections* (London: Allen & Unwin, 1955), p. 131. Other works on the same theme are F. S. C. Northrop, *The Meeting of East and West* (New York: Macmillan, 1946); Arnold Toynbee, *The World and the West* (New York: Oxford Univ. Press, 1953); and Barbara Ward, *India and the West* (New York: Norton, 1964).

24

LENIN

We need not try to prove that Vladimir Ilich Ulianov, more commonly called V. I. Lenin, was one of the most skillful revolutionists in history. Many detailed histories of the Bolshevik Revolution do that. It is enough to assert that Lenin was a rare combination of theorist and activist without whose efforts the Bolshevik Revolution would probably have failed. Most theorists are uncomfortable organizing people. Most organizers are impatient with theory. Lenin was neither. By no stretch of the imagination could he be called a major philosopher. He was invariably too close to action decisions to be thoroughly reflective. His one work devoted to philosophic subjects, *Materialism and Empirio-Criticism* (1908), was written for political purposes and contained a number of deviations from ideas expressed in private writings. But there is no question that Lenin took seriously the theoretical problems of Marxism, especially the nature of the dialectic of history. Again and again he went back to the works of Marx and pored over them, setting a pattern for subsequent generations of Marxists and Maoists.

LIFE

His father and his brother contributed a good bit to Lenin's seriousness of purpose, revolutionary zeal, and theoretical inventiveness. His father had been a Councilor of State and a director of schools in Simbirsk, a practicing Christian who had worked against considerable odds to build schools and spread education. Though frequently away from home, the father imposed on the household his reformist liberalism and solid middle-class virtues. He died after seeing his lifework go down the drain with the surge of feeling against popular education that followed the assassination of Czar Alexander II in 1881. The brother, Alexander, whom Lenin had emulated as a child, went away to the university in St. Petersburg, was involved in a plot to assassinate the new Czar, Alexander III, and was hanged for his involvement. The older brother was twenty-one at the time; Vladimir was seventeen. The event, according to his sister, noticeably "hardened" Vladimir. A short while later he was expelled from the University of Kazan, largely because he was the brother of "the other Ulianov."

Lenin now began to read Marx. Thanks to his mother's efforts, he was permitted to take the law examination at the University of St. Petersburg and, though his only training was a limited amount of self-education, he passed ahead of all the other examinees. His legal career was short and unsuccessful, for he soon found himself a political prisoner and was later exiled to Siberia. There he married Nadezhda Konstantinova (in later years simply "Krupskaya"), a fellow Marxist he had met in St. Petersburg, and spent a happy honeymoon copying the text of *The Development of Capitalism in Russia,* his first major work. In 1899 he went abroad and began to publish, in Munich, *Iskra* ("The Spark"), at which time he began to use the name N. Lenin.

For seventeen years Lenin was in exile—writing, talking, and thinking. Through the vehicle of *Iskra,* printed on onionskin paper and smuggled into Russia, Lenin waged relentless war on the various other groups seeking the leadership of revolutionary sentiment in Russia, groups such as the People's Will (*Narodnaya Volya*), whose chief policy was assassination, and the Economists, who ignored Marxism to concentrate on attaining free speech and the right to strike. Lenin, of course, was not alone in editing *Iskra.* Among the exiled Social Democrats, as they were called, Lenin, Julius Martov, and A. H. Potresov regarded themselves as a *troika,* a three-man editorial team. Helping with *Iskra* from Switzerland, Georgi Plekhanov, with his followers Pavel Axelrod and Vera Zasulich, served as an inspiration to Lenin's group by virtue of Plekhanov's rigorous application of Marxist principles to Russia. By 1903 dissension had risen between the Lenin group, which was by that time in London, and the Plekhanov group in Switzerland. This was neither the first nor the last of the almost infinite number of schisms and divisions within the Marxist movement.

While in London, Lenin had met and was impressed by Lev Davidovich Bronstein, who would be known to the world as Leon Trotsky. Plekhanov did not like Trotsky very much but, when the division over the editing of *Iskra* became so deep that Lenin resigned, Trotsky stayed with Plekhanov, as did almost everyone else. Lenin was cut off and alone. But he had a remarkable capacity for believing himself right even in these circumstances; this was a basic factor in his subsequent strength. Lenin wrote feverishly, attacking his old friends publicly and privately. This period produced *One Step Forward, Two Steps Back* (1904), which stands with *What Is To Be Done?* (1902) as one of Lenin's greatest organizational monographs. Although his fortunes were at a low ebb, Lenin was tremendously heartened when the Marxist writer Bogdanov came over to his side. Together they published in Switzerland *Proletarii,* a counterpart of *Iskra.*

Because of early majorities in the tempestuous voting at the 1903 Social Democratic Party Congress in Brussels, Lenin's faction had been called the Bolsheviks (from *bolshinstvo,* or majority) and the group that grew up around Martov (which Plekhanov later joined) was called the Mensheviks (from *menshinstvo,* minority). The Bolsheviks held their own Third Party Congress in London in 1905 while the Mensheviks were holding their session in Geneva. Two months later Lenin tore into the Mensheviks in *Two Tactics of Social Democracy in the Democratic Revolution.*

Meanwhile a general strike in Russia had led to the Revolution of 1905. Determined to be a part of it, Lenin slipped back into the country with a forged passport. A first Russian Duma, or parliament, was called. Lenin would have nothing to do with it and, when in 1907 the Duma was finally dissolved and its Social Democratic members were arrested and incarcerated, the Bolshevik faction was in a position to dominate the party. But Lenin was forced to flee to Finland, then to Switzerland, and finally, in 1909, to Paris. The intrigues of this ten-year exile are intricate and fascinating. The plots and the counterplots, the arrests and the escapes provide a treasury of melodramatic material. All the while Lenin was writing. In Zurich in 1916 he wrote *Imperialism*. *State and Revolution* was written during the summer of 1917, while its author was in hiding in Helsingfors. Shortly thereafter, through the assistance of the German authorities, who knew that a Lenin in Russia was infinitely more troublesome to their enemy the Czar than a Lenin out of Russia, he was returned to his homeland aboard a special train. Preaching "Peace, Bread, and Land" to the Petrograd proletariat and surrounding peasantry, Lenin was in a position to make the Petrograd Soviet of Workers' and Soldiers' Deputies the seat of authority when Kerensky's Provisional Government collapsed.

The rest of Lenin's story is too familiar to need detailed repeating here: the vigorous pursuit of "war communism" until the White Russian armies were defeated; the retreat into the "New Economic Policy" (NEP) of modified capitalism that Lenin had to defend against the purists of Marxist theory; the would-be assassin's bullet that accelerated the breakdown of Lenin's already failing health; the ultimate doubts about Party Secretary Stalin, who was now dug-in in preparation for his forthcoming battle with Trotsky. Lenin died of a massive sclerosis of the brain on January 21, 1924. Even in death his image continues to inspire the faithful, for his embalmed body is still on display at the Kremlin.

Lenin is a herald not only of communism but of the age of ideology itself. For, facile as was his mind, ideas were for him weapons and only weapons. He took Marxism with utter seriousness—as a set of axioms to be applied rather than as a set of propositions to be examined. He was bright, ruthless, and single-minded and his task was to lead and to train in the manner of the stern headmaster to whom Wilson compared him.[1]

[1] Edmund Wilson, *To the Finland Station* (New York: Harcourt, Brace & World, 1940), Part III. See also Louis Fischer, *The Life of Lenin* (New York: Harper & Row, 1964); Stefan T. Possony, *Lenin* (Chicago: Regnery, 1963); Leon Trotsky, *Lenin,* authorized trans. (New York: Minton, Balch, 1925); and Bertram D. Wolfe, *Three Who Made a Revolution* (New York: Dial, 1948).

Few have demonstrated more convincingly how philosophy can become an instrument in the struggle for political power.

LENIN AS PHILOSOPHER

Lenin's major contributions to Marxist theory are three in number: (1) his theory of the organization and functioning of the party as an integral part of the revolutionary occurrence, (2) his concept of capitalistic imperialism, and (3) his concept of the dictatorship of the proletariat. With his typically hollow air of profundity, Stalin wrote in *The Foundations of Leninism* (1924), "What, then, in the last analysis, is Leninism? Leninism is Marxism of the era of imperialism and of the proletarian revolution."[2]

A fourth contribution, though not a major one, was represented by Lenin's writings on the philosophy of materialism per se, especially his attack on the Russian philosopher Bogdanov in *Materialism and Empirio-Criticism* (1908). Like virtually all of Lenin's works, the book was politically inspired. Bogdanov's philosophy had been expounded in *Empiriomonism,* which appeared in three volumes from 1904 to 1906. Lenin read the books as they came out but waited to attack them until 1908, when for factional reasons he broke with Bogdanov. (Plekhanov, by contrast, had attacked Bogdanov's works at the time of their publication.) Lenin had made common cause with Bogdanov and his poet and philosopher friends in the face of the turmoil surrounding the 1905 revolution. But now, in 1908–09, Lenin was impatient with this group for its ostensible deviation from hard Marxist materialism. He accused them of *fideism,* or the substitution of faith for knowledge, on the grounds that some of them—least of all, ironically, Bogdanov—were flirting with religion and religious met-

[2] Josef Stalin, *The Foundations of Leninism,* new trans. (New York: International Publishers, 1939), p. 10. See Z. A. Jordan, "The Dialectical Materialism of Lenin," *Slavic Review,* Vol. 25 (1966), pp. 259–86.

aphor. Bogdanov was the principal target because Lenin was trying to oust him from the editorial board of *Proletarii*. In April, 1909, when the book was in process of publication, Lenin wrote: "It is hellishly important for me that the book should come out at the earliest possible date, not only for literary but also for political reasons."[3]

Lenin's principal thrust was against the Machians, supposed followers of the Viennese physicist and positivist Ernst Mach. In a rather strange juxtaposition, the Machians and the "god-builders" were regarded as "one essential whole." As against Engels, who argued that the reality of the external world was provable by the continual application of science and industry, the Machians postulated a realm of the unknowable, a factor of indeterminacy that precluded categorical knowledge of the reality of the material world. This presumably enabled them to be classed with the agnostics, who became religious in Lenin's eyes simply because they had rejected pure materialistic atheism.

The polemical character of Lenin's work is apparent throughout. He constantly refers to various arguments as "tricks" or "betrayals" and impugns the motives of those he criticizes. He helps the reader to "see with what sophistry 'recent' empirio-critical philosophy operates. We shall compare the argument of the idealist Berkeley with the *materialist* argument of Bogdanov, as a kind of punishment for the latter's betrayal of materialism!"[4] The arguments of his opponents he variously labels as "trash," full of "indecency," "extremely naive," "a cunning and refined form of fideism," and "destined to find their way into the museum of reactionary exhibits manufactured by the German professordom." To the inference drawn from "the humanitarian Philistines in Europe with

their freethinking sympathies and their ideological slavery" that philosophy is properly above partisan strife, Lenin answers: "Nonpartisanship in philosophy is only a contemptible cloak of servility to idealism and fideism." The statement is not only polemical; it is parochial.

The book is also authoritarian in the sense that the final appeal in almost every case is to a quotation from Friedrich Engels. Marx is frequently mentioned but Engels provides the text. Engels, it is true, offers a more substantial case for dialectical materialism than Lenin was apparently capable of, a case designed to prove that those who questioned the externality of "objective" matter were in a solipsistic trap; but Lenin seems unable to cope with the necessity of a fundamental reexamination of Marxist tenets. When he rather self-consciously raises the question of his appeals to authority, he almost pathetically tries to down it with one more appeal to authority:

And do not cry out, you Machians, that I resort to 'authorities'; your clamour against the argument from authority is only a screen to conceal the fact that you substitute for the socialist authorities Marx, Engels, Lafargue, Mehring, Kautsky, the bourgeois authorities (Mach, Petzoldt, Avenarius, and the immanentists). It would have been much better if you had not raised the question of 'authorities' and 'authoritarianism.'[5]

Perhaps the most substantial and fair-minded chapter in the book is Chapter 5, in which Lenin summarizes current developments in physics and shows how the conclusions of some physicists that "matter has disappeared" when conceived as the particles heretofore postulated does no damage to the Marxist assumption of a "world existing and developing independently of the mind," which appears to be the heart of Marxist materialism.

All in all, *Materialism and Empirio-Criticism* is significant not so much for the technical philosophy it tosses violently around as for the evidence it gives of Lenin's intense

---

[3] Quoted in Wolfe, p. 509. Later in 1909 Bogdanov and his followers were just outside the "faction" but explicitly not outside the "party." In 1912 Lenin's faction would declare itself the party!

[4] All quotations in this paragraph are from *Materialism and Empirio-Criticism*, trans. by David Kvitko (New York: International Publishers, 1927), pp. 30, 132, 183, 179, 311, 179, and 308, respectively.

[5] *Ibid.*, p. 210.

dedication to the goal of organizational and ideological unity. Lenin spent considerable time and mental energy in studying philosophical and scientific writings. But he did so not so much out of the love of learning and speculation—though this motive was no doubt present—but in order to use philosophy for nonphilosophical ends.

PARTY AND REVOLUTION

Lenin's theory of the party was developed in the continuous outpouring of tracts, pamphlets, and articles that occupied so many of his prerevolutionary days. A synthesis of most of his early ideas on the subject appears in the monograph *What Is To Be Done?* It still stands as a monument to the tenets that came in time to be called Leninism. The need for a hard, dedicated, disciplined party, flexible in action but inflexible in lines of authority: this was and is the essence of Leninism. The first chapter is an attack on the idea of "freedom of criticism" within a revolutionary party and is directed against the "English Fabians, the French Ministerialists, the German Bernsteinists" as well as the Russian "Critics." Lenin expresses gratitude for the new international flavor of the basic conflict between his position and that of all other socialists, a gratitude eventually turned to bitterness by the latent nationalism that World War I brought out in European socialists.

Already the problem of the supposed spontaneity of the dialectical process was creating psychological and philosophical problems that Lenin felt obliged to meet. He attacked "following in the tail" (*khvostism*), the view that regarded the party as a mere passive force following in the wake of the predetermined events of history. The party must be, he said, not in the tail of history but in the vanguard. The party as the "vanguard of the proletariat" henceforth became a symbol of great force in the communist movement. The intelligentsia, who, Lenin

frankly conceded, did not come out of the proletariat, were vitally necessary to keep the communist movement related to Marxist theory, the railroad into the future: "Without revolutionary theory there can be no revolutionary movement. This cannot be insisted upon too strongly at a time when the fashionable preaching of opportunism is combined with absorption in the narrowest forms of practical activity." By themselves, peasants and workers at the present stage, he wrote, could at best achieve a consciousness of the need for low-level, trade-union reformism. Only those trained to see further into history could grasp the full sweep of the required revolution, "the task of emancipating the whole people from the yoke of autocracy," and develop the organizational means to carry this through, for "the role of vanguard can be fulfilled only by a party that is guided by an advanced theory."[6]

What may be the most fundamental Marxist characteristic, the tendency to dichotomize everything, is apparent throughout *What Is To Be Done?*: ". . . the only choice is: Either bourgeois, or Socialist ideology. There is no middle course (for humanity has not created a 'third' ideology, and, moreover, in a society torn by class antagonisms there can never be a non-class or above-class ideology). Hence, to belittle Socialist ideology *in any way,* to *deviate from it in the slightest degree* means strengthening bourgeois ideology."[7] The target of this outburst was the group called the Economists, those who, favoring the line of least resistance, believed that, while the proletariat could be successful with forays into politics in the West, this was a fruitless course in Russia. Their faith in the spontaneous working out of the Marxian dialectic led them to urge, instead, the gradual building up of worker strength through trade-union organization. Lenin was infuriated by expressions of this position and led what he himself called "a desperate struggle against sponta-

[6] *What Is To Be Done?* Ch. 1, sec. D, in *Collected Works,* authorized trans. (New York: International Publishers, 1929), Vol. 4, p. 110.

[7] *Ibid.,* Ch. 2, sec. B, p. 123.

neity." At this date Lenin was still able to welcome as an ally the scholarly Karl Kautsky (1854–1938), German Marxist and editor of *Neue Zeit*. Both had attacked the conciliatory "revisionism" of the German Social Democrat Eduard Bernstein (1850–1932), and now Bernstein was linked to the Economists.[8]

Nowhere is Lenin's prose stronger than in the passage where, gibing at "infantile playing at 'democracy,'" he calls for a greater sense of "professional" party work— the first time he uses the word in this connection—that is, finding able agitators, seeing that they are put in the kinds of jobs where they can do the most good (or damage), and paying for their subsistence from party funds if necessary. The organizational discipline and self-sacrificial zeal that later generations would associate with Communist Party activity were already apparent in *What Is To Be Done?* But it is fair to say that the quotation on the title page, an excerpt from a letter of Lassalle to Marx, which says, "A party becomes stronger by purging itself," did not in 1902 have the ominous overtones that in time would come to be identified with the word "purge."

The battle continued with the publication of *One Step Forward, Two Steps Back*. But this time the object of attack—always there was an object of attack—is not the Economists but the Mensheviks who came out of the Second Party Congress (1903), "the opportunist wing of our party," as Lenin unabashedly called them. Through a close examination of the minutes of the Second Congress, Lenin brings to light a tangle of factional conflict that can only fill the present-day reader with bewilderment. Forty-three delegates representing twenty-six different organizations cast fifty-one votes. There were Bundists and *Rabocheye Dyelo*-ites and the *Yuzhny Rabochy* group and many others. Thirty-three delegates supported *Iskra* to begin with. But, as Stalin's official *History of the Communist Party of the Soviet Union (Bolshevik)* quaintly puts it, "not all those who considered themselves *Iskra*-ists were real Leninist *Iskra*-ists."[9] To maintain the ideological offensive against the articulate Mensheviks, Lenin lashed out at their broad conception of party membership, which would allow every striker to consider himself a member. Such looseness would only lower the party's vitality and ultimately destroy its effectiveness, argued Lenin. The party must not lose its connections with the whole working class, it must not become an ivory-tower elite, Lenin agreed. But it appears that the constant connection with the proletariat he called for was not to be so much for the sake of nourishing the party on new ideas and challenges as to provide an avenue whereby the right answer already possessed by the party could be transmitted to the masses.

Lenin's excursions into the theory of the dialectic are but shallow dips that season the essentially practical argument:

the great Hegelian dialectics which Marxism made its own, having first turned it right side up again, must never be confused with the vulgar trick of justifying the zigzags of politicians who swing over from the revolutionary wing to the opportunist wing of the Party. . . . Genuine dialectics does not justify individual errors, but studies the inevitable turns, proving that they were inevitable by a detailed study of the process in all its concreteness. The basic principle of dialectics is that there is no such thing as abstract truth, truth is always concrete.[10]

---

[8] Bernstein held that evolution rather than revolution would lead to communism, and over a much greater time span than Marx had assumed. He repudiated the predestinarian implications of the early materialist conception of history. He criticized the theory of surplus value not only on the grounds that it too simply explained an entire economy in terms of one phase of industrial production but on empirical grounds: industries with a high rate of surplus value in fact often had the highest-paid workers. In general, Bernstein faced the uncomfortable un-Marxist fact of a growing differentiation of industrial function that did not confirm the prophecy of the poor getting poorer while the rich got richer.

[9] *History of the Communist Party of the Soviet Union (Bolshevik)* (New York: International Publishers, 1939), p. 40. The Second Party Congress began in Brussels but moved en masse to London when the Brussels police became troublesome.

[10] *One Step Forward, Two Steps Back*, sec. R, in *The*

The principle of the "negation of the negation" was used to explain how, in the Second Party Congress, majorities become minorities and vice versa, and the offensive position became the defensive position.[11] But the underlying circularity of Lenin's reasoning is never overcome, for the right side in the struggles that make up this inevitable process is ultimately defined as the side represented by the Party, and the Party is that faction of the Social Democrats led by Lenin. Despite his praise of concreteness, Lenin could not accept even revolutionary success as a test of rightness:

there are revolutions which are more like reaction. . . . We must know whether it was a revolutionary wing or the opportunist wing of the Party which was the actual force that made the revolution, we must know whether it was revolutionary or opportunist principles that inspired the fighters, before we can determine whether the "world" (our Party) was moved forward or backward by any concrete revolution.[12]

How truly revolutionary principles may be distinguished from merely opportunist principles never becomes clear. Indeed, given such an intense dedication to "concreteness," it is not clear how principles enter into the matter at all.

The last monograph worth mentioning that belongs to this period and this genre is *Two Tactics of Social Democracy in the Democratic Revolution*. This work was addressed to the difficult problem of the relationship between the bourgeois revolution and the proletarian revolution as applied to backward Russia. There were two basic positions, as we have seen above, on the nature of the party. There were three basic positions

on the nature of the forthcoming revolution.[13] The Mensheviks, on the one hand, believing that a proletarian revolution would have to wait until an authentic bourgeois revolution had occurred, were closest to Marxian orthodoxy. They recognized that the proletariat in Russia was nowhere near a majority and in no position to take over the government. The Social Democratic Party, they felt, should stay out of any provisional government. Trotsky and his followers, on the other hand, felt that the bourgeois and proletarian revolutions could be telescoped into one. The weak Russian middle class could manage no revolution on its own. Socialist-proletarian leadership would have to make a "bourgeois" revolution that almost simultaneously would become the proletarian revolution. This was Trotsky's "permanent revolution" predicted on the basis of his own inventive modification on Marx, the "law of combined development," as he called it.

Lenin's was a shifting, intermediate position. "In formulae, Lenin sounded much like the Mensheviks; in spirit he was forever attracted to the Trotskyist pole."[14] Ironically, as Trotsky had warned Lenin in 1904 of the dangers of factional dictatorship and the need for democracy within the party, Lenin was warning Trotsky in 1905 of the dangers of party dictatorship—though not put in these words—and the need for democracy within the state. Lenin's uncertainty is revealed in the *Two Tactics*. The question, he says, is not whether there will be a revolution but whether the party can "put a proletarian imprint" on it in order to overcome the "half-heartedness and treachery" of the

Essentials of Lenin (London: Lawrence & Wishart, 1927), Vol. 1, pp. 344–45.

[11] Lenin was no doubt recalling the crucial 28–22 defeat he suffered in the Second Party Congress concerning what seemed to many a minor difference with Menshevik Martov over the broad versus the narrow definition of party membership. To the detached observer, Lenin's reversal of this defeat seems much more a matter of his own tenacity and cleverness than an inevitable process.

[12] *One Step Forward, Two Steps Back*, p. 345.

[13] See Wolfe, pp. 289–93.

[14] *Ibid.*, p. 291. The theory of "permanent revolution" was a joint product of Trotsky and his friend and mentor Parvus (Alexander L. Gelfand), though the concept was used by Marx in his *Address to the Communist League* (1850). Implying as it did the necessity of sustaining an ever expanding network of revolutions around the world, it became anathema to Stalin, whose idea of "socialism in one country" was a useful shibboleth in the expedient persecution of Trotsky. See Thornton Anderson, *Masters of Russian Marxism* (New York: Appleton-Century-Crofts, 1963), pp. 120–24, 135–40, and 226–30.

democratic bourgeoisie. Should the work of the party in the present moment emphasize organizing trade unions and educating the masses or should it move immediately to the building up of a revolutionary army? Both are necessary, says Lenin, seeming to hedge. But the weight of his remarks is clearly on the side of moving rapidly ahead with militant organization and action so that the bourgeoisie will not be able to stop the revolution short of socialist goals. To this end, Lenin focuses the whole monograph on the proper formulation of "correct tactical slogans" in order to keep the revolution on the right track and to keep the initiative in the hands of the Bolsheviks.

The essence of the tactics proposed was a deft management of a simultaneous attraction-repulsion effort. The peasantry was to be attracted, for the Bolsheviks needed an ally if they were to be successful in this not-yet-industrialized country. The repulsion was directed to the liberal bourgeois democrats, who were not to be trusted with the leadership of the revolution even though, in one sense, it was their revolution:

Marxism has irrevocably broken with the ravings of the Narodniks and the anarchists to the effect that Russia, for instance, can avoid capitalist development, jump out of capitalism, or skip over it, along some path other than the path of the class struggle on the basis and within the framework of this same capitalism. . . . the idea of seeking salvation for the working class in anything save the further development of capitalism is *reactionary*. In countries like Russia, the working class suffers not so much from capitalism as from the insufficient development of capitalism. . . . The bourgeois revolution is precisely a revolution which sweeps away the survivals of the past, the remnants of serfdom (which include not only autocracy but monarchy as well) and which most fully guarantees the broadest, freest and most rapid development of capitalism.

That is why a bourgeois revolution is *in the highest degree advantageous to the proletariat*. A bourgeois revolution is *absolutely* necessary in the interests of the proletariat. The more complete, determined and consistent the bourgeois revolution, the more assured will be the proletarian struggle against the bourgeoisie for Socialism. Such a conclusion will appear new, or strange or paradoxical only to those who are ignorant of the rudiments of scientific Socialism.[15]

Since Marxism prescribed that the bourgeois revolution precede the socialist revolution, Lenin was stuck with the sequence. But he was determined not to let the bourgeois manage such a bourgeois revolution. Some would call this brilliant theorizing. Others would call it ideological rationalizing. Still others would say Lenin wanted to eat his cake and have it, too. The amazing thing is that he did.

IMPERIALISM

Following his formulation of a new and more crucial role for the party as the "vanguard of the proletariat," Lenin made a second major contribution to Marxist theory in *Imperialism, The Highest Stage of Capitalism*, written in Zurich in the spring of 1916. In a preface to the Russian edition of 1917, Lenin complained about the need to write in 1916 "in that cursed Aesopian language" of indirection and allusion necessary to get by the Czarist censors. "It is very painful, in these days of liberty, to read these cramped passages . . . crushed, as they seem, in an iron vise, distorted on account of the censor."[16] In the text he gives Japan as an example of how "social-chauvinist deserters . . . lie on the question of annexations" but in the preface he says he was really talking about Russia.

Like Lenin's other writings, *Imperialism* was a *pièce d'occasion*. But such was his skill that he could write a work of compelling directness that also spoke to several different problems simultaneously. Lenin was explain-

---

[15] *Two Tactics of Social Democracy*, sec. 6, in *The Essentials of Lenin*, Vol. 1, p. 376.

[16] *Imperialism, The Highest Stage of Capitalism*, new rev. trans. (New York: International Publishers, 1939), p. 7. Subsequent quotations are from this edition.

ing World War I in the light of Marxist doctrine ("I proved that the war of 1914-18 was imperialistic."). He was explaining how it was possible during the war for workers in belligerent countries to abandon the cause of the proletariat in a mood of patriotic nationalism. He was attacking the "revisionist" theories of former ally Kautsky (and, in passing, scoring thrusts against leaders of labor in various countries: Otto Bauer in Austria, Ramsay MacDonald in England, and Samuel Gompers in the United States).

Lenin's primary task was to account for the refusal of workers to put class above country. Although Lenin was capable of becoming technical at times, the heart of his argument was quite simple: a handful of states, less than one-tenth of the world's population, "very rich and very powerful," were plundering the whole world "simply by clipping coupons." Out of "such enormous super-profits" drawn off colonial lands over and above what is made by the exploitation of workers in their home country, "it is quite *possible to bribe* the labour leaders and the upper stratum of the labour aristocracy." Capitalists "bribe them in a thousand different ways, direct and indirect, overt and covert."

Imperialism is loaded with statistics demonstrating the growing concentration of productive facilities in the hands of a few, the sharp increase in the export of capital abroad, and the economic division of the world into cartels by the political division of the world into areas ruled by a few great powers. Above all, Lenin emphasized that old-fashioned bank capital had more and more been merged with industrial capital to create what he called "finance capital," the control of which, as symbolized by the J. P. Morgan interests, led to new and hitherto undreamed-of power.

Much of this had already been described by non-Marxist scholars, foremost of whom was the English economist J. A. Hobson (a "bourgeois social reformer" from Lenin's view), whose *Imperialism* had been published in 1902. Lenin at least gives him a reasonable share of the credit. The real issue as far as Lenin is concerned is how this development was to be interpreted within the framework of the Marxist world view. Hence, Lenin is far more vituperative in discussing Kautsky, with whom he shared basic theoretical positions, than he is in discussing Hobson, who was, presumably, beyond saving. Lenin accuses Kautsky not of failing to see the facts but of failing to see what they meant. Kautsky, according to Lenin, saw the expansion of finance capital around the world as a matter of national policy by which more advanced nations annexed less advanced countries. Lenin saw this process not simply as a matter of governmental policy but as a necessary stage of capitalist development, an inexorable phase of the Marxist dialectic.

In a 1919 article Kautsky had defined imperialism as "the striving of every industrial capitalist nation to bring under its control and to annex increasingly big *agrarian* regions."[17] Lenin, in a 1920 preface, is enraged by this seemingly innocuous definition: "Kautsky's definition is not only wrong and un-Marxian. It serves as a basis for a whole system of views which run counter to Marxian theory and Marxian practice all along the line." It is "a mockery of historical concreteness."[18] It seems that to emphasize the acquisition of agrarian areas by industrial states is to minimize unduly the inevitable conflict between industrial states and to overlook the forces driving them to absorb one another. Kautsky, claims Lenin, does not see that industrial states are inexorably led to devour one another and hence that World War I had to come. Lenin also charges Kautsky with the failure to attach sufficient significance to the new dominance of the financier over the producer and merchant—although in fact Kautsky did recognize the role of finance capital.

[17] Quoted in *Imperialism*, p. 91.

[18] To the end Kautsky adhered to the basic tenets of Marxism: historical materialism, class struggle, the concentration of capital, and the rest; but he argued cogently against the necessity or desirability of violent revolution. The revolution could and should come through democratic processes, he maintained. After the Bolshevik Revolution, Kautsky became an outspoken critic of Soviet autocracy.

Because, from his viewpoint, imperialism is only one and not the essential policy of modern capitalism, Kautsky thought the world might see an era of "ultra-imperialism," in which the big powers unite peacefully for the sake of joint exploitation. Lenin cannot abide "Kautsky's silly little fable about 'peaceful' ultra-imperialism. Is this not the reactionary attempt of a frightened philistine to hide from stern reality?" In short, there *must* be wars and capitalism *must* be the cause.

International war was in this way made to be a kind of substitute for inevitable internal revolution in those countries where the internal revolution that Marx predicted seemed less and less likely to occur. In England, contrary to every prophecy based upon Marxist tenets, the standard of living was rising. But Lenin was able to note that both immigration into and emigration out of England were declining, in effect contributing even among English working people themselves to a sense of being a privileged class because they were members of a privileged nation. The bribery earlier referred to now becomes understandable: it was the seduction of the workers into a kind of proletarian bourgeoisie by virtue of their participation in the exploitation of less fortunate brethren overseas. The explanation is ingenious and not without a certain amount of truth. The sense of national superiority in workers, and especially civil servants, was an essential part of nineteenth- and early twentieth-century imperialism. Lenin managed to find three letters of Engels that commented upon the special bourgeois attitudes of English workers, so it was possible to invoke the blessing of the highest—or next to the highest—authority to bolster Lenin's orthodoxy.

Lenin's fighting spirit carries through on every page. He concludes *Imperialism* like a football coach speaking to his team or a general admonishing his troops. Those people are "dangerous," he says, who do not understand that the "fight against imperialism is a sham and humbug unless it is inseparably bound up with the fight against opportunism." To **Lenin**, neglect of the war against

capitalism on either the home front or the foreign front or the attempt to make this war less warlike was opportunism.

THE STATE AND THE DICTATORSHIP OF THE PROLETARIAT

Lenin's third theoretical contribution was his handling of the transition period between capitalism and communism and the role of the state in this transition period. We have already seen to what extent the party was the center of all decision-making power during this transition; but not until *State and Revolution* was it clear to what extent Lenin identified the state with coercive power and regarded it as a transitional institution that would disappear once the revolution was fully consummated. Indeed, *State and Revolution* stands in some degree of isolation from Lenin's thought both before and after its writing.

In this work the party as a causal force is scarcely mentioned. Lenin speaks rather of the necessity of smashing the bourgeois state in order that power may be not so much transferred as eliminated. Following Engels, Lenin portrays the elimination of the state as the elimination of coercion of man over man. Government gives way to the administration of "things" and the working people are set free. *State and Revolution* represents a sharp swing to the left by Lenin, at least partly due to the influence of Bukharin during the winter of 1916–17.[19] A swing to the left meant a swing to utopian categories. A strong factor affecting the tone of this book was the imminence of the Revolution itself, which forced Lenin to turn from thoughts of undercover revolutionary activity to questions of what happens after revolutions. His answers are fairly unoriginal as well as utopian. He apparently consulted in some haste

[19] See Robert V. Daniels, *"State and Revolution*: A Case Study in the Genesis and Transformation of Communist Ideology," *American Slavic and Eastern European Review,* Vol. 12 (1953), pp. 22–43.

Engels' *Origin of the Family* and Marx's *Critique of the Gotha Program,* for he repeats many of their vague postrevolutionary formulations.

The ostensible purpose of *State and Revolution* was to *"resuscitate* the real teachings of Marx on the state." Mainly on the basis of Engels' *Origin of the Family,* Lenin concludes that "the state is a product and the manifestation of the *irreconcilability* of class antagonisms. The state arises when, where and to the extent that the class antagonisms *are* irreconcilable."[20] There are, to Lenin's way of thinking, two distortions of this truth about the state, one gross and one subtle. The gross distortion is that of "petty-bourgeois politicians," who see that the state brings about order but cannot see that it does so only by suppressing class antagonisms. The subtle distortion is that of Kautsky and the "Kautskyists," who gloss over the implication of the doctrine that the state is an instrument for the suppression of class antagonisms, namely the implication that the apparatus of state power is necessarily so contaminated by its function of suppression that after the revolution the apparatus itself must be destroyed. Even the institution of universal suffrage shares in this contamination and must be destroyed. Lenin simply postulates that it is a "wrong idea that universal suffrage 'in the *modern* state' is really capable of expressing the will of the majority of the toilers and of assuring its realization."

Lenin must reconcile this position with Engels' famous statement in *Anti-Dühring* that "The state is not 'abolished,' it *withers away.*" The popular conception of this is "the crudest distortion," says Lenin. What Engels really means is that the proletarian semistate, the "special repressive force" that takes over in the transition period, withers away. The bourgeois state, the real state, is "done away with" by the revolution.

In place of the bourgeois state, the "dictatorship of the bourgeois," we shall find the well-known "dictatorship of the proletariat." But by contrast with its earlier identifications with the party, Lenin here curiously omits mention of the party and speaks of the political rule of the proletariat as "power shared with none and relying directly upon the armed forces of the masses." But shortly thereafter there is a passage that sounds like the Lenin of old, in which the party as the vanguard is seen as "leading the whole people to Socialism" and acting as "teacher, guide, and leader of all the toiling and exploited."

Considering the fierce realism of his conspiratorial activities, it comes as a surprise to find Lenin as utopian and as anarchistic as he appears to be in *State and Revolution.* He states that the growth of literacy and the training and discipline required in an industrialized society have already created the conditions whereby the whole mass of the people can govern themselves, since most of the functions of an industrialized society are mechanical and routine:

It is perfectly possible, immediately, within twenty-four hours after the overthrow of the capitalists and the bureaucrats, to replace them, in the control of production and distribution, in the business of *control* of labour and products, by the armed workers, by the whole people in arms. (The question of control and accounting must not be confused with the question of the scientifically educated staff of engineers, agronomists, and so on. These gentlemen work today, obeying the capitalists; they will work even better tomorrow, obeying the armed workers.) . . . *All* citizens become employees and workers on *one* national state "syndicate." All that is required is that they should work equally, should regularly do their share of work, and should receive equal pay. The accounting and control necessary for this have been *simplified* by capitalism to the utmost, till they have become the extraordinarily simple operations of watching, recording and issuing receipts, within the reach of anybody who can read and write and knows the first four rules of arithmetic. . . . The whole society will have become one office and one factory, with equal work and equal pay.[21]

[20] *State and Revolution* (New York: International Publishers, 1932), p. 8. Subsequent quotations are from this edition.

[21] *Ibid.,* pp. 83–84.

This vision of technocratic paradise seems to us absurdly simple and romantic, somewhat like the quaint Victorian narratives of Edward Bellamy. Surely Lenin could not have believed all this; surely he must have been writing consciously hypocritical pap for the consumption of emotionally volatile revolutionaries; surely he could not place so much trust in the people as to think that an armed and unfettered mass of them would be models of decorum.

We underestimate the power of the nineteenth-century faith in industrial progress if we do not concede that Lenin could very well have believed some of this nonsense. If we think back on Owen, Fourier, Comte, and many others, we recall a similar faith that the right organization of society would liberate an essentially good human nature and that scientific management would virtually eliminate the need for the hard moral choices among competing alternatives, which we call politics. The difference between Lenin and the other utopians was that, partly because of his own propensities and partly because of historic circumstances, he found himself with a government to run and could not in the long run remain content with simple formulas.

CONCLUSION

Lenin demonstrates at once the force and weakness of ideas. Less paradoxically, we can say that Lenin demonstrates the instrumental but not the substantial force of ideas. Because he was skillful with words, because he could sniff out the crux of a factional dispute and neatly fit the Marxist categories to his own position, we can call him a theorist of influence. But, inasmuch as he failed to push beyond the urgent to the enduring issue, failed to construct a standard of governmental reality and purpose of truly general applicability, he was no political theorist at all.

The development of Marxism since Lenin has not been much more auspicious. Once Marxists gained massive blocs of political power, they made of Marxism an orthodoxy hardly stimulating to creative thought. Even in countries far removed from the Kremlin the weight of this orthodoxy could be felt, in large part because its institutionalization transformed Marxism into a creedal religion. At the same time the hostility of traditional institutions to Marxism made it a religion embroiled in a political fight. And from our own experience it is easy to conclude that political fights over religion are not conducive to philosophical creativity.

One thing Lenin accomplished was to create a tradition of "theorist leaders," which dictated that Stalin should be known as a theorist even though in many respects he was the antithesis of the man of thought. So from his pen, or those of his ghostwriters, came Stalin's *Marxism and the National and Colonial Questions,* written before the Revolution; *Dialectical Materialism,* written as part of the official history of the Communist Party and published in the mid-thirties; and *The Foundations of Leninism* (1924). These works, primerlike in tone, now stand as useful guides to some of the inarticulate preconceptions of the Marxist. But as theory they are anemic. In China in the 1920s and after, Mao Tse-tung, with a more facile mind than Stalin's, took up the old Marxist problems and tried to fit them to a feudal agrarian society even less developed than Russia.[22]

In underdeveloped countries the appeal of Lenin, especially in those of his writings that justify the simultaneous existence of capitalist and socialist institutions, is not due so much to his intrinsic merits as a theorist as to the usefulness of his thought in meeting the psychological demand for rebellion against colonial institutions. Paradoxically, the most economically backward nations

[22] See Anne Freemantle, ed., *Mao Tse-tung: An Anthology of His Writings* (New York: New American Library, 1962); Arthur A. Golden, *The Communism of Mao Tse-tung* (Chicago: Univ. of Chicago Press, 1964); Stuart A. Schram, *The Political Thought of Mao Tse-tung* (New York: Praeger, 1963); and Benjamin I. Schwartz, *Chinese Communism and the Rise of Mao* (Cambridge, Mass.: Harvard Univ. Press, 1951).

have become the most "advanced" agencies of "proletarian class consciousness."

Marxism is a product of the industrial age, and all its ideas about society arise from an acceptance of the machine as the most basic fact of modern life. At the same time, it is radically critical of the social institutions and relationships of the industrial age. Transformed into the theory of imperialism, this ambivalence toward industrial capitalism turns into an ambivalence toward the West, and this mixture of hostility and admiration develops naturally among politically conscious men in underdeveloped areas. In espousing Leninism, such men can advocate a program of westernization without abandoning their hatred and fear of the West.[23]

The use of a theory of advanced industrialism as a rationale for nationalist-agrarian revolt is but one example of the theoretical confusion that afflicts our ideological age.

[23] Alfred G. Meyer, *Leninism* (Cambridge, Mass.: Harvard Univ. Press, 1957), p. 267. See also Leonard Schapiro, "Lenin's Contribution to Politics," *Political Quarterly,* Vol. 35 (1964), pp. 9–22, and David G. Smith, "Lenin's Imperialism: A Study in the Unity of Theory and Practice," *Journal of Politics,* Vol. 17 (1955), pp. 546–69.

25

DEWEY

John Dewey has often been called a typical American with a typically American philosophy. How typical he and his philosophy were may be questioned but he was one of the first scholars to get a Doctor of Philosophy degree in the United States and one of the last native philosophers to have a widespread public reputation.

LIFE

John Dewey was born and educated in Vermont—and got out as soon as he could, as he later told a friend, displaying a certain earthiness that Americans like to think is typical. The year of his birth was 1859, the year of Marx's *Critique of Political Economy*, Mill's "On Liberty," Darwin's *Origin of Species*, and the birth of Bergson and Ellis. Nothing close to home foreshadowed the distinction that was later to come to Dewey. His father ran a general store in Burlington. As a boy, John delivered newspapers, worked in a lumber yard, and made an unexceptional record in the local grammar and high schools. Even after entering

the University of Vermont at the age of fifteen, Dewey did not give promise of great academic prowess until his senior year, when Thomas Huxley's physiology textbook aroused his interest in science and jarred his complacency by creating concern for the supposed conflict between revealed religion and scientific method. Dewey received his Bachelor's degree at the University, then taught high school in Pennsylvania and in a country school in Vermont. Meanwhile he was reading philosophy, ever more voraciously. His first published journal article came out the year that he entered Johns Hopkins University to begin work on the doctorate. The article was entitled "The Metaphysical Assumptions of Materialism." Two years later, in 1884, he had his degree and was off to the University of Michigan as a young instructor.

After a year at the University of Minnesota in 1888, Dewey returned to Michigan as head of the department of philosophy. In 1895 President Harper asked him to come to the newly established University of Chicago to head the departments of philosophy, psychology, and education. With the help of Mrs. Dewey he there established what later would be famous as the Experimental, or

Laboratory, School, starting progressive education on its long and controversial career. The University was not as happy as the Deweys over their experiment and in 1904 Dewey resigned to go to Columbia as professor of philosophy, a post he held until his retirement in 1930.

Before his death in 1952 at the venerable age of ninety-two, Dewey had written more than thirty books and had worked in behalf of many liberal political causes. His name had become widely known for his advocacy of child-centered, democratic, nonformal education. He spoke out against the conviction of Sacco and Vanzetti. He worked in the League for Industrial Democracy and supported the American Civil Liberties Union. He helped found the Liberal Party of New York and the New School for Social Research. In 1937, at the age of seventy-eight, he went to Mexico to investigate the guilt of Leon Trotsky, who had been exiled there by a Soviet tribunal. As a result of his investigations, he roundly denounced the Soviet government, upon whose experiments he had at one time looked with considerable interest. In 1941, along with several others, he produced an angry defense of Bertrand Russell against the bigots who kept him out of The College of the City of New York.

At Johns Hopkins, studying under G. S. Morris, Dewey was introduced to Hegel. The latter's opposition to dualism and his emphasis on process and the historical approach to knowledge had immediate appeal for Dewey. Hegel's influence remained with Dewey all his life, despite his specific rejection of the Hegelian dialectic early in his career. At the same time, the down-to-earth, problem-solving orientation of what came to be called instrumentalism led Santayana to regard Dewey as typifying the spirit of modern industrial enterprise. Dewey never cared much for this description. And, indeed, Dewey's challenge to tradition included a departure from traditional American thought, even though the spirit of his antiphilosophical philosophy indubitably was American to the core.

ANTIFORMALISM

Dewey was a leader in what Morton White has called the "revolt against formalism," expressed not only in philosophy by Dewey but in law by Holmes, in history by Beard and Robinson, and in economics by Veblen. On the theoretical level the revolt was hostile both to the scientific rigidities of British empiricism and to the dogmatic abstractions of traditional metaphysics. On the political level the revolt was directed against the excessively legalistic interpretations of American political society characteristic of the late nineteenth century.

The central theme of the revolt, and especially Dewey's part in it, was growth. Dewey is said to have said that the statement in *Reconstruction in Philosophy* (1920 and 1949) "Growth itself is the only moral end," was central to his whole intellectual life.[1] There was in this emphasis a good bit of Hegelian process and Darwinist natural selection. It is not irrelevant that Dewey was a youthful admirer of Hegel and that one of his early books was entitled *The Influence of Darwin on Philosophy* (1910). By lifting Social Darwinism out of the realms of atomistic competition and adapting it to the idea of problem-solving communities, Dewey was able to transform it from an ideology of laissez faire to an ideology of the welfare state.

At the level of epistemology, this processual emphasis led to the substitution of the concept of inquiry for that of truth. "Inquiry," wrote Dewey in his best known epistemological work, *Logic: The Theory of Inquiry* (1939), "is the controlled or directed transformation of an indeterminate situation into one that is so determinate in its constituent distinctions and relations as to convert the elements of the original situation into a unified whole."[2] Russell, whose epis-

[1] Cited by James T. Farrell in Corliss Lamont, ed., *Dialogue on Dewey* (New York: Horizon Press, 1959), p. 53.
[2] *Logic: The Theory of Inquiry* (New York: Holt, Rinehart and Winston, 1939), pp. 104–05. Subsequent quotations from *Logic* are from this edition.

temological realism always put him at odds with Dewey in these matters, commented snidely that this definition would fit a brick-layer converting a pile of bricks into a wall. Russell, representing a correspondence theory of truth, was interested at getting at the reality of the facts "out there," which were assumed to exist independently of the observer. Dewey, representing a coherence theory of truth, was interested in the mutual adjustment between an organism and its environment; this relationship rather than something wholly outside the observer or, for that matter, wholly within him, was the basic factor to be considered. The test of any proposition was the consequence of following it. This, not something more ultimate or unchangeably real, is what gave it "warranted assertability." "An idea is true so long as it is profitable to our lives," said William James, who had an unfortunate habit of using monetary metaphors. Dewey preferred not to use the word "truth" at all, but rather "inquiry." The quest for certainty, he often said, was incompatible with the self-corrective process of scientific method. When the indeterminate situation has been transformed into a determinate situation, inquiry is simply terminated. This is as close to knowledge—or "warranted assertability"—as we can get.

The revolt against formalism, the new emphasis upon process, adjustment, problem-solving, and indeterminacy—or, better, always provisional determinacy—that we associate with Dewey had its most conspicuous impact in the rejection of a good many traditional philosophic dichotomies, among them theory-practice, percept-concept, learning-doing. We shall look especially at four: subject-object, value-fact, past-present, and individual-society.

SUBJECT AND OBJECT

Much of Dewey's position on subjective-objective relationship and indeed much of his whole technical philosophy came from

Charles Sanders Peirce (1839–1914; pronounced "purse"), now generally credited with being the founder of pragmatism although little known during his lifetime. Peirce held a university chair only briefly and published no books while he was alive; his thought is contained in a vast and exceedingly diverse array of journal articles, most of which were published in six volumes by Harvard University (1931). His paper "How To Make Our Ideas Clear" (1877) attracted little attention until William James made much of it in a lecture at the University of California in 1898. After some of his ideas were picked up and distorted, Peirce publicly denounced "pragmatism" and coined "pragmaticism," a term, he said, "ugly enough to be safe from kidnappers."

In the essay "How To Make Our Ideas Clear" Peirce attacks Leibnitz's method of abstract definition and Descartes' a priori appeal to self-evidence. One does not learn anything new, he argues, simply by refining and analyzing definitions. In the past, philosophers mainly have disputed meanings and have been led into nothing but disagreement. Scientists conduct investigations rather than disputations and their method has led to wider and wider areas of agreement. This, then, is the course that philosophers ought to follow. The rationalist conception of "true ideas" as some kind of "mind stuff" is useless. With such a method there is an inevitable confusion between what seems clear subjectively and what *is* clear objectively. By focusing on the consequences of an idea or concept one can overcome this dilemma. Hence the "pragmatic maxim" formulated by Peirce: "Consider what effects, which might conceivably have practical bearings, we conceive the object of our conception to have. Then, our conception of these effects is the whole of our conception of the object."[3]

It is important to note that this emphasis upon effects as the test of validity had little in common with the merely "practical" in the sense of the expedient, or what is con-

[3] *Values in a Universe of Chance, Selected Writings of Charles S. Peirce*, Philip Wiener, ed. (Garden City, N. Y.: Doubleday, Anchor, 1958), p. 124.

ducive to success. Some of Peirce's friends wanted him to call his methodology "practicalism" but he vigorously repudiated the implication. The Kantian terms *praktisch* and *pragmatisch,* observed Peirce, "were as far apart as the two poles," the latter referring to controlled, purposeful experimental observation.[4] William James was largely responsible for the materialist overtones given some of the tenets of pragmatism, and this more by inadvertence than by intent.

Pragmatism tended to lead away from concern for the problem of subjectivity and objectivity. The concepts in themselves were of course abstract and could be placed in the catalogue of empty symbols of the past, such as mind, matter, and substance. But in fact the pragmatists, Dewey as well as Peirce, could be said to have evaded the old problem simply by assuming that out of observation, experiment, and an operational orientation the agreement of observers would emerge.

FACTS AND VALUES

Pragmatism was also an assault upon the dichotomy between facts and values. It is important to note that this union of the is and the ought was quite different from the comparable union in the natural-law tradition. There, reason liberated from the drag of appetite and passion was assumed to be capable of glimpsing the nature of ultimate reality, which included a simultaneous vision of the good and the true. Dewey and the pragmatists, as we have seen, made no such assumption about universal goodness or universal truth. Dewey, like Hume, believed thought was stimulated by the nonintellectual side of man. Moreover, there is no Good or True, only goods and truths that are invariably relative to a particular historical situation. Dewey was a thoroughgoing "contextualist." Neglect of the historic situation, the concrete problem at hand, in pursuit of a

standard supposedly set by pure, abstract reason is, he thought, illusory and dangerous. He sought always to serve "ends in view" rather than ends so exalted as to be out of view.

In a practical way, there is much to recommend this attitude. It is the pragmatist's contention that intellectual and social conflicts are unarbitrable if the arguer on each side (or for that matter on only one side) of a dispute asserts that his position stems from a true perception of reality or if he asserts, in a manner consistent with the emotive-imperative school of ethics, that his position stems from a wholly subjective emotion that can have no rational defense. The logic of either position, the pragmatist argues, is that social disputes can be settled only by violence or superior power, since genuine conciliation requires a modification of the values of both sides. The pragmatic alternative is to apply the test of a critical examination of the probable consequences of proposed policies and let the needs of each ongoing situation, as determined by scientific methodology, decide the best policy:

the idea of actively adopting experimental method in social affairs, in the matters deemed of most enduring and ultimate worth, strikes most persons as a surrender of all standards and regulative authority. But in principle, experimental method does not dignify random and aimless action; it implies direction by ideas and knowledge. . . .

Where will regulation come from if we surrender familiar and traditionally prized values as our directive standards? Very largely from the findings of the natural sciences. . . . a moral that frames its judgments on value on the basis of consequences must depend in a most intimate manner upon the conclusions of science. For the knowledge of the relations between changes which enable us to connect things as antecedents and consequences *is* science. . . .

Another great difference to be made by carrying the experimental habit into all matter of practice is that it cuts the roots of what is often called subjectivism, but which is better termed egoism.[5]

---

[4] "What Pragmatism Is" (1905), in *Values in a Universe of Chance,* p. 183.

[5] Dewey, *The Quest for Certainty* (New York: Min-

The critic may well ask: can social conflicts really be expected to wait until all the evidence is in? In the face of ambiguity will not decisions have to be made upon the basis of the subjective (or objective) standards of the participants? And are these not in every case assertions of what they feel to be ultimately important? To this Dewey would undoubtedly say that, since the truly ultimate cannot in any case be reached with certainty, it is not necessary to pursue problems that far. Consensus on the desirability of certain consequences over other consequences can hold for the sake of solving a particular concrete problem about which all are agreed, after which we all move on to the next problem requiring solution. This may, in fact, be the way society tends to deal with its problems, whether or not it is scientific about the determinattion of consequences. But this method must be regarded as an evasion of the question above, which turns on the validity of one's grounds for moral choice in the face of ambiguity—perhaps the inevitable condition of moral choice.

Dewey was conscious of the problem and recognized the need for some kind of ethical theory to bridge the gap between what is desired (which might include "the free play of impulse") and what ought to be desired. "The fact that something is desired only raises the *question* of its desirability," wrote Dewey, "it does not settle it." He proposed the application of scientific tests to help people determine if what they seemed to desire was what they really desired. In the last analysis, however, he was still forced to equate the desirable with the desired; this is the flaw in all naturalistic theories of ethics. Dewey did not wish to be simply a naturalist in ethics. He did not wish to recognize raw emotion as a self-validating source of value. Neither could he honestly hope to eliminate emotion from values. What he hoped to do was purify values by subjecting them to a rigorous test of consequential relevance. He put his faith, then, more in a process of han-

dling values than he did in any particular acknowledged value. He never did, indeed never tried to, work out a hierarchy of scientifically approved values. The pragmatic orientation to values is as opposed to hierarchies of values as it is to the dichotomy between facts and values:

Most conflicts of importance are conflicts between things which are or have been satisfying, not between good and evil. And to suppose that we can make a hierarchical table of values at large for once and for all, a kind of catalogue in which they are arranged in an order of ascending or descending worth, is to indulge in a gloss on our inability to frame intelligent judgments in the concrete. Or else it is to dignify customary choice and prejudice by a title of honor.[6]

Dewey is never willing to say what values we should follow, because he does not believe that valid values can be meaningfully expressed in the abstract. He gives us, rather, a method for the refinement and improvement and validation of whatever values presently exist or will exist in the concrete situation to which the method will be applied. The method is, of course, the method of Deweyan "inquiry" already referred to. Perhaps the only abstract value Dewey explicitly assumes is "intellectual honesty." Beyond that, he says, "inquiry should follow the lead of subject matter." But, in general, it can be said that this is the experimental, scientific method: ". . . an idea [we could as well substitute "value"] in experiment is tentative, conditional, not fixed and rigorously determinative. It controls any action to be performed, but the consequences of the operation determine the worth of the directive idea; the latter does not fix the nature of the object."

In the phraseology of his critic Morton White,[7] Dewey recognizes that "X is desired" is not a synonym for "X is desirable." But in the long run he comes out with a

ton, Balch, 1929), pp. 273–74. Subsequent quotations from *The Quest* are from this edition.

[6] *Ibid.*, p. 266.
[7] See Morton G. White, "Value and Obligation in Dewey and Lewis," *Philosophical Review*, Vol. 53 (1949), pp. 321–29, and *Social Thought in America: The Revolt Against Formalism* (New York: Viking, 1949), Ch. 13.

position by which "X is desirable" *is* the equivalent of "X is desired under normal conditions" where normal conditions suggest full and rational reflection on the causes and consequences of the particular act in question. In this way, says White, the factual statement slips confusingly over into the normative statement, somewhat in the manner of traditional natural-law theories: *de facto* becomes *de jure*.

Hook, a defender of Dewey, contends that this is not a careless slip but a significant move. White, he says, tries to put Dewey's dynamic, concrete analysis into static and abstract terms. The *de facto* becomes *de jure,* the desired becomes the desirable, not by abstract rationalization of its consequences but by being rationally examined in a context of actual choice, a context that can never be fully anticipated. "The normative element in the conclusion is in a sense provided by that which distinguishes the situation as a practical one from one that is purely logical or theoretical. The underlying premise is: that should be done which appropriately meets the needs and requirements of the situation, broadly conceived to include the demands and expectations of the community or traditions in which we find ourselves."[8]

From this excellent statement of the pragmatic position in ethics we may draw several not altogether reassuring conclusions: (1) In repeatedly deferring to the "needs" of a not-yet-arrived "situation" the issue of the ground of moral choice is evaded rather than met. Perhaps this is to say only that one cannot make a satisfactory abstract ethical statement demonstrating that ethical statements can never be abstract. (2) When asked what the needs of some future situation might be, pragmatists usually defer to the "demands and expectations of the community or traditions in which we find ourselves." While they rarely draw this implication, such an approach can result in not merely a conservative bias but a frightfully reactionary position.

[8] Sidney Hook, "The Desirable and Emotive in Dewey's Ethics," in Sidney Hook, ed., *John Dewey, Philosopher of Science and Freedom, A Symposium* (New York: Dial Press, 1950), pp. 204–05.

tion. Reason and scientific method become prisoners of the situation rather than masters of it.

An excursion into technical ethical theory may seem out of place in an examination of political theories; but Dewey's ethic is fundamental to his orientation toward public policy and, indeed, to the whole character of his influence. His was a profound rationale for avoiding profound moral discourse. It seemed to fit an optimistic nation more interested in doing than in thinking. Certain constant values, even abstractions, if you will, do emerge from Dewey's language, despite their possible inconsistency with his desire to close no doors and his hope to bring immediate, concrete, empirical data into the very vortex of moral choice and keep them there. These values include science, community, growth, education, liberalism, democracy, openness, freedom, and "thinking which is operative." Some of these we shall examine later in this chapter.

PAST AND PRESENT

Another dichotomy battered by the pragmatists was that between the past and the present. It is not surprising that, given a dynamic and wholly interrelational union of subject and object, value and fact, we find the past seen in the light of the present and the present seen in the light of the past. Like Beard, Dewey believed that history is necessarily written from the standpoint of the present. At the same time, the validity of historical propositions could, he thought, be subjected to the same kind of evidential tests as any other kind of proposition. Indeed, history was regarded as but another medium of problem-solving and, as he wrote in *Logic,* "the writing of history is an instance of judgment as a resolution through inquiry of a problematical situation." Again, "That which is now past was once a living present, just as the now living present is already in course of becoming the past of another present.

There is no history except in terms of movement toward some outcome, something taken as an issue. . . ." And finally, "history cannot escape its own process. It will therefore, always be rewritten. As the new present arises, the past is the past of a different present."

The sense of fluidity and wholeness that characterizes other aspects of Dewey's thought is markedly apparent in his treatment of history. His view is best called contextualist, because he continually emphasizes the unity of history with other forms of inquiry and recognizes that the historian invariably plucks out of a mass of detail those facts that serve a present interest.

INDIVIDUAL AND SOCIETY

The Dewey-dissolved dichotomy most closely related to the subject matter of traditional political theory is that between the individual and society. No human mind, thought Dewey, could be completely known when separated from society:

The interaction of human beings, namely, association, is not different in origin from other modes of interaction. There is a peculiar absurdity in the question of how individuals become social, if the question is taken literally. Human beings illustrate the same traits of both immediate uniqueness and connection, relationship, as do other things. No more in their case than in that of atoms and physical masses is immediacy the whole of existence and therefore an obstacle to being acted upon by and effecting other things. Everything that exists in as far as it is known and knowable is in interaction with other things. It is associated, as well as solitary, single. The catching up of human individuals into association is thus no new and unprecedented fact; it is a manifestation of a commonplace of existence.[9]

Habits, upon which we depend for existence, are acquired functions that are picked up only through the medium of the surrounding social environment:

There are specific good reasons for the usual attribution of acts to the person from whom they immediately proceed. But to convert this special reference into a belief of exclusive ownership is as misleading as to suppose that breathing and digesting are complete within the human body. To get a rational basis for moral discussion we must begin with recognizing that functions and habits are ways of using and incorporating the environment in which the latter has its say as surely as the former.[10]

Although prior in time, instincts or—to use a term that Dewey preferred—impulses were not prior in action, but secondary, for the social medium is what gives them meaning and direction. Take anger, for example: "Human displays of anger are not pure impulses; they are habits formed under the influence of association with others who have habits already and who show their habits in the treatment which converts blind physical discharge into a significant anger." Hence, in a sense, virtually all psychology becomes for Dewey social psychology.

At times there seems to be something almost Rousseauistic in Dewey's conception of impulse shaped by a social medium, for, while he placed a higher value on society than did Rousseau, still he talked as if there were a natural man encapsuled in a crust of social convention: ". . . there are always intrinsic forces of a common human nature at work; forces which are sometimes stifled by the encompassing social medium but which also in the long course of history are always striving to liberate themselves and to make over social institutions so that the latter may form a freer, more transparent and more congenial medium for their operation." Dewey rejects with some vehemence theories of intuitional moral knowledge that set moral judgments against man's natural tendencies. There is no "separate agent of moral knowledge," Dewey insists. Even the utilitarians

[9] *Experience and Nature* (La Salle, Ill.: Open Court Publishing, 1925), pp. 174–75.

[10] *Human Nature and Conduct* (New York: Random House, Modern Library, 1930), p. 15. Subsequent quotation from *Human Nature and Conduct* are from this edition.

were guilty of this error in trying to trace morality from sensations. Morality is not a set of fixed principles, or a faculty of mind, or a dictate of innate and constant conscience. It is a matter of the adjustment of the organism to the environment in such a way that what was formerly a problem is no longer a problem. When Dewey comes at the question from a different angle it would appear that intelligence likewise is the process of satisfactory adjustment of an organism to its environment:

Deliberation needs every possible help it can get against the twisting, exaggerating and slighting tendency of passion and habit. To form the habit of asking how we should be treated in a similar case—which is what Kant's maxim amounts to—is to gain an ally for impartial and sincere deliberation and judgment. It is a safeguard against our tendency to regard our own case as exceptional in comparison with the cases of others. . . . Demand for consistency, for "universality," far from implying a rejection of all consequences, is a demand to survey consequences broadly, to link effect to effect in a chain of continuity. Whatever force works to this end *is* reason. For reason, let it be repeated, is an outcome, a function, not a primitive force.[11]

Morality and intelligence, in other words, are, for all practical purposes, synonyms.

Such a theory of morality and human nature necessarily puts a heavy burden on the environment, for what is right for an individual would seem to be determined by what is right in terms of a particular social environment. As we shall see, this conclusion has tremendous significance for Dewey's views on education and politics and the relations between the two. It also leads him to place a very high value on community as a norm. He would not like this phraseology; but what else can one say in contemplating the final words of *Human Nature and Conduct* (1930): "Within the flickering inconsequential acts of separate selves dwells a sense of the whole which claims and dignifies them. In its presence we put off mortality and live in the universal. The life of the community

in which we live and have our being is the fit symbol of this relationship." The phrasing is religious, if not mystical, and the universal that Dewey has been so concerned to avoid comes lumbering up to attach itself to the social order—one is tempted to say *any* social order, though this would hardly be fair to Dewey's intent. Religionists, however, are either amused or irritated by seeing Dewey make the secular community a "fit symbol" of the universal. He gives no reason why it should be; indeed, he cannot without throwing away the core of pragmatism.

COMMUNITY

Since Dewey is unwilling—passages such as the above apart—to come down on either horn of the individual-society dilemma, it follows that communication, the means whereby individuals become a society and society shapes its individuals, is an especially important subject for him. The political aspects of this concern are displayed most tellingly in *The Public and Its Problems* (1927). Dewey begins by showing what fallacious quests most searches for a theory of the state have been. They have drawn us away from the facts and into a labyrinth of mythological constructions. Despite their variety, they all "spring from a root of shared error: the taking of causal agency instead of consequences as the heart of the problem." The fiction of the state has tended to be a mask for private ambition and "society itself has been pulverized into an aggregate of unrelated wants and wills."[12] What the public is, or what the state (conceived as a public organized by officials) is, is a matter for empirical investigation, not abstract speculation.

Dewey goes on to sketch the outlines of what constitutes the state on the basis of what he takes to be empirical evidence; but he actually proceeds in a manner not much

[11] *Ibid.,* p. 247.

[12] *The Public and Its Problems* (Chicago: Gateway, 1946), pp. 20–21. Subsequent quotations from *The Public and Its Problems* are from this edition.

different from that of many "abstract" political theorists of the past. He then turns to the problem of the democratic state, which consists of finding a way for the public itself to make its weight felt in the determination of public policy. In practice this means overcoming the tendency for political power to be acquired by "accidental and irrelevant factors" and for officials to employ such power for private rather than public ends. (Any transactions "which affect others beyond those immediately concerned" are earlier referred to as public.) Dewey establishes the fact of a greatly broadened range of public transactions in recent times by reference to the interdependence of modern industrial society and discusses "the enormous ineptitude of the individualistic philosophy [of Locke, Adam Smith, and the utilitarians] to meet the needs and direct the factors of the new age." The primary need is to regain a sense of community: ". . . the machine age in developing the Great Society has invaded and partially disintegrated the small communities of former times without generating a Great Community." "Till the Great Society is converted into a Great Community, the Public will remain in eclipse. Communication can alone create a great community."

Dewey is generally regarded as a theorist of democracy or a democratic theorist, which may not be quite the same. The appellation is not inappropriate. His repeated emphasis upon a fluid, adaptable, problem-solving community built out of the sinews of constant communication between individuals as citizens and officials as agents of the public is little more than a description of a functioning democracy. But perhaps he gives the term more than it can carry: "Regarded as an idea, democracy is not an alternative to other principles of associated life. It is the idea of community life itself. . . . The clear consciousness of a communal life, in all its implications, constitutes the idea of democracy." This sounds both ideal and idealistic, in the popular sense, but Dewey, as always, insists upon staying close to "the facts":

Only when we start from a community of fact, grasp the fact in thought so as to clarify and enhance its constituent elements, can we reach an idea of democracy which is not utopian. The conceptions and shibboleths which are traditionally associated with the idea of democracy take on a veridical and directive meaning only when they are construed as marks and traits of an association which realizes the defining characteristics of a community. Fraternity, liberty and equality isolated from communal life are hopeless abstractions.[13]

An adequate set of community symbols is necessary, Dewey feels, to transmute the "order of energies" that is a human association into the "order of meanings" that is a human community. Intelligence, in Dewey's sense of inquiry, and education were key factors in this transformation. One is tempted to see parallels between the community of symbols Dewey calls for and many of the mythical structures used to bolster previous ideal communities: Plato's golden lie, or Rousseau's civil religion, or Comte's religion of humanity. But, though Dewey regards communication as an art, he would certainly not see it as a manipulative art: "Opinion casually formed and formed under the direction of those who have something at stake in having a lie believed can be *public* opinion only in name."

A basic assumption of Dewey, acknowledged but scarcely explored in *The Public and Its Problems,* is that the common perceptions brought about by communication will create common interest. His unwillingness to postulate any long-run ends in so many words makes it imperative for him to adopt this faith in what certain instrumental means will do. Logically it must be a rather blind faith, trusting serenely in the wisdom of a future generation liberated from past dogma and with nothing else to guide its members but the canons of science. Actually, of course, certain long-run and rather abstract values, the kind in which Dewey is not supposed to indulge himself, can be found in many of Dewey's pages. The old French ideal of fraternity seems to have spe-

[13] *The Public and Its Problems,* p. 149.

cial importance for Dewey. He speaks of utilizing government as "the genuine instrumentality of an inclusive and fraternally associated public." He speaks warmly of sustaining "fraternally shared experience." He talks of the need for the kind of face-to-face community that can grow only in small towns or in neighborly relationships.

This emphasis upon community-mindedness is consistent with Dewey's theories of education in both their narrow and their broad applications. His view of education is democratic, first, in respect to what is supposed to go on in the classroom. The experimental elementary school at the University of Chicago illustrated this. Traditional education was oriented around passive listening to authoritative exposition. Dewey wanted to make each child an active contributor. He wanted the fixed curriculum to be supplanted by projects that arose out of the "felt personal and group needs" of the children themselves, with regimentation and discipline minimized for the sake of spontaneous expression by the pupils. Dewey's view of education is democratic, secondly, with respect to the relationship between the classroom and the larger society beyond. As the growth of the individual child should be uppermost in the classroom, so should the growth and reconstruction of the social order be uppermost in society. One learns by doing and the citizen learns how to be a citizen by continually examining and questioning the political institutions of his society. The aim of the educational system should not therefore be (as it usually is) to habituate the young to the *status quo*. Even if the *status quo* is admirable, change is inevitable and "the problem is not whether the schools *should* participate in the production of a future society (since they do so anyway), but whether they should do it blindly and irresponsibly or with the maximum possible of courageous intelligence and responsibility."[14]

[14] "Education and Social Change," *The Social Frontier*, Vol. 3 (1937), pp. 235–38. Quoted in Joseph Ratner, ed., *Intelligence in the Modern World* (New York: Random House, Modern Library, 1939), p. 692.

SOCIAL PLANNING

As one who spoke of the indeterminacy of the situations to be dealt with in the future and the need for discussion, communication, and openness, it might seem that Dewey was in a poor position to be an advocate of planning. But a notable advocate of planning he was. Some would say that Dewey did not reconcile successfully the discrepancy implied in belief in indeterminacy, on the one hand, and advocacy of social planning, on the other. But at least we can say that the ubiquitous concept of consequences was the link Dewey tried to forge:

in practice, if not in so many words, it has been denied that man has any responsibility for the consequences that result from what he invents and employs. The denial is implicit in our widespread refusal to engage in large-scale collective planning. Not a day passes, even in the present crisis, when the whole idea of such planning is not ridiculed as an emanation from the brain of starry eyed professors or of others equally inept in practical affairs. And all of this in the face of the fact that there is not a successful industrial organization that does not owe its success to persistent planning within a limited field—with an eye to profit—to say nothing of the terribly high price we have paid in the way of insecurity and war for putting our trust in drift.

Refusal to accept responsibility for looking ahead and for planning in matters national and international is based upon refusal to employ in social affairs, in the field of human relations, the methods of observation, interpretation, and test that are matters of course in dealing with physical things, and to which we owe the conquest of physical nature. The net result is a state of imbalance, of profoundly disturbed moral knowledge.[15]

Dewey was concerned basically with methodology. But underlying this concern was a hearty belief that his methodology would produce a certain kind of society of which he approved. It would be a democratic society, with widespread and active

[15] *Problems of Men* (New York: Philosophical Library, 1946), pp. 26–27.

discussion of political and economic matters by all the people and where capitalistic enterprise would be restrained by intelligent centralized planning to make sure that the Great Community that had emerged out of all this discussion was moving the Great Society in the direction it ought to go. Dewey was not, supposedly, prejudging this direction; but it would seem that the old revolutionary goals of liberty, equality, and fraternity, so long as they were not treated as "hopeless abstractions," had much to recommend them. In the semipopular essays and articles collected in his *Problems of Men* (1946), we can, if we wish, point out certain highly concrete evils that Dewey sniped at; this may tell us as much as or more than the abstractions of his antiabstractionist philosophy: the evils include the Hearst press, Tammany Hall, the "spurious liberalism . . . represented by the Liberty League and ex-President Hoover," dictatorships, the educational philosophy of Robert Maynard Hutchins, the use of press and radio for "propaganda," loyalty oaths for teachers, and racial discrimination.

Dewey was in a somewhat anomalous position, although perhaps he never fully realized it. He had certain values that in practice he advanced with vigor, both through his institutional associations and through his more popular writing. But philosophically, he defended none of them; indeed, he could not consistently defend them, since his *sine qua non* was a methodology that deferred to the values of each emerging situation rather than some fixed catalogue of ends. Dewey's great contribution, it must be said, was negative rather than positive, though this is not to say it was a small one.

CONCLUSION

When we look over the bulk of Dewey's writing on political subjects, it seems clear that he stands hip-deep in the mainstream of the Western liberal tradition and that many of the values attached to it, which he espouses, not only have never been subjected to an experimental scientific test but probably could not be. In a chapter on "Democracy and America" in *Freedom and Culture* (1939) he speaks with great praise of Jefferson and the ideals of the Declaration of Independence. Because, he says, we are wary today of "self-evident truths," it is necessary to translate eighteenth-century ideals into twentieth-century symbols, for which purpose he suggests the substitution of "moral rights" for "natural rights":

Nature and the plans of a benevolent and wise Creator were never far apart in his [Jefferson's] reflections. But his fundamental beliefs remain unchanged in substance if we forget all special associations with the word *Nature* and speak instead of ideal aims and values to be recognized —aims which, although ideal, are not located in the clouds but are backed by something deep and indestructible in the needs and demands of humankind.[16]

This identification of the traditional ideals of liberal thought with certain attributes of human nature that seem to be virtually permanent would not appear to be consistent with basic pragmatic assumptions; but it cannot be dismissed as a mere lapse. Again and again Dewey makes this point. In the conclusion of *Liberalism and Social Action* (1935) he writes, "the cause of the liberty of the human spirit, the cause of opportunity of human beings for full development of their powers, the cause for which liberalism enduringly stands, is too precious and too ingrained in the human constitution to be forever obscured. Intelligence after millions of years of errancy has found itself as a method and it will not be lost forever in the blackness of night."[17]

Dewey assumed that experimentalism as method would in time validate the traditional values he already held. It would be

16 *Freedom and Culture* (New York: Putnam's, 1939), p. 156. See also Milton R. Konvitz, "Dewey's Revision of Jefferson," in Hook, pp. 169–76.
17 *Liberalism and Social Action* (New York: Putnam's, 1935), p. 93. Subsequent quotations from *Liberalism and Social Action* are from this edition.

unfair to say that Dewey did not make concrete application of these abstract ideals in his own life, for he did. The indictment runs the other way, namely that the theory of experimentalism, useful as a critical tool, was not helpful in supporting many of the values Dewey most wished to support. It permitted and perhaps made imperative begging off from the task of working out a program for practical reform that could stand on a platform of philosophically solid principles. Dewey was not unwilling to tackle the program but he could not consistently build the platform. As White has suggested, there were two Deweys, one who was opposed to any fixed ends for society and one who wanted to engineer the construction of a liberal society.

Writing in 1935, Dewey could sketch with accuracy the threat to liberal ideals posed by communism and fascism and issue a rallying cry to liberalism's banner:

The eclipse of liberalism is due to the fact it has not faced the alternatives and adopted the means upon which the realization of its professed aims depends. Liberalism can be true to its ideals only as it takes the course that leads to their attainment. The notion that organized social control of economic forces lies outside the historic path of liberalism shows that liberalism is still impeded by remnants of its earlier *laissez faire* phase, with its opposition of society and the individual. The thing which now dampens liberal ardor and paralyzes its efforts is the conception that liberty and development of individuality as ends exclude the use of organized social effort as means . . . socialized economy is the means of free individual development as the end.[18]

We may note the reification involved in the continual reference to liberalism as an "it" that can be true, and therefore presumably false, to its ideals, which are presumably justified by applying the theory of inquiry. But a few sentences later Dewey seems not so much to be justifying liberalism as taking it as a given for the sake of using it either as an example of the method of inquiry or, possibly, as a means to the higher end of unity:

[18] *Ibid.*, p. 90. See also *A Common Faith* (New Haven: Yale Univ. Press, 1934).

". . . by concentrating upon the task of securing a socialized economy as the ground and medium for release of the impulses and capacities *all men agree to call ideal* [our italics], the now scattered and often conflicting activities of liberals can be brought to effective unity." The italicized phrase is typical of Dewey's ambiguity at the crucial points, where one might determine what values he finally chooses to defend. Does he mean that all men, literally all men, agree to make liberalism their social ideal? Surely he cannot seriously mean this as a factual statement. Does he mean, then, that all men *ought* to agree to make liberalism their ideal? If so, *why* ought they? Dewey nowhere explicitly prescribes a social ought for all men, because to do so would be to violate his instrumentalist premise, namely that theories, including ideals, are products of emerging concrete historical situations good only for their own time and place, just as mechanical inventions are good only for their own time and place.

Indeed, he seems suddenly to shy away from the very activity he has entered into. In the next sentence he says, "It is no part of my task to outline in detail a program for renascent liberalism." But he begins almost immediately to berate liberals once again, this time, however, for their weakness in organization rather than for their failure to agree on socialization of the economy. This, in a sense, is a revival of a methodological issue; but it is a quite different issue, appropriate for the practical level that assumes we all agree on our objective—though he has earlier suggested that all are not agreed on the middle-level objective of socialization— and that wants to find the best way to achieve it. But all of a sudden it turns out that the cause to be served by this better organization, this hypothetical "concrete program of action," is not the socialization of the economy at all, not even liberalism in general, but "democratic ideals": ". . . without this organization there is danger that democratic ideals may go by default. Democracy has been a fighting faith. When its ideals are reenforced [not, please note, established] by those of scientific method and experimental intelligence, it cannot be that it is incapable of evoking discipline, ardor and organization." Why can it not be? All the tenets of instrumentalism would seem to indicate that it could very well not be.

Perhaps we are to dismiss all this confusion as a mere example of the hyperbole even philosophers indulge in when speaking to popular audiences. (This was a lecture given at the University of Virginia.) One would be inclined to take this way out upon reading on the same page: "I for one do not believe that Americans living in the tradition of Jefferson and Lincoln will weaken and give up without a whole-hearted effort to make democracy a living reality. This, I repeat, involves organization." But unless one can assume a duplicity wholly alien to Dewey's known character, one must take all his writings seriously and grant as well that what one says in a mood of exhortation is often more revealing of one's underlying position than arid pedagogical utterance. And, moreover, Dewey in the passage under review is not wholly forgetful of the philo-

sophic position he is bound to uphold. We push on to the next sentence: "The question [presumably of whether democracy can be a "living reality"] cannot be answered by argument. Experimental method means experiment, and the question can be answered only by trying, by organized effort." We are carried back to Peirce's contention that philosophers have only disputed and found disagreement, while scientists have investigated and found agreement.

It would seem that Dewey's basic faith is in the capacity of scientific method to bring men together into a common life of progressively revealed and shared insight. Around this faith he gathered in somewhat haphazard fashion, as befits one who does not believe in hierarchies of value, all sorts of more or less well-defined value concepts, including those of democracy and liberalism.

Dewey turns out to be an important symbol of American political existence after all. He was impatient of delay, he was willing to run some risks out of confidence in the future, and he took his thoroughly American liberalism largely for granted.

26

NIEBUHR

To say that there has been a great "return to religion" in the post-World War II period of Western civilization would, by itself, be misleading. The religious picture is rather more cloudy than such a statement implies. After the war, European and American theologians who had been writing for a number of years—Barth, Brunner, Buber, Maritain, Niebuhr, and Tillich—began to be listened to with greater interest than before. Billy Graham revivals seemed to flourish as they could not have in the 1930s. Church membership in America rose sharply and piety at times threatened to become a political necessity. The continuing spread of communist influence around the world, however, put churches, especially Christian churches, on the defensive. Although quarrels between fundamentalist churchmen and natural scientists over evolution seemed a thing of the past and more scientists than before were able to be practicing churchmen, the widespread scientific revolution of automation, space flights, and electronic social analysis elevated the scientific, "objective" mind to which religion seemed frequently irrelevant. Curiously, it was the unchurched and half-churched who seemed most interested in the small group of highly technical Christian theologians identified with the "God is dead" movement of the 1960s.

Nevertheless, it does not seem inappropriate to conclude our treatment of individual theorists with consideration of the work of a theologian, especially one who has been concerned with the effect of scientific assumptions on political thinking and who has been in touch with such contemporary currents of thought as existentialism and depth psychology. These currents may or may not lead to clear-cut alternatives to the by now traditional liberal categories. We have not yet entered a new age of faith. But most observers concede that we have begun to leave the great age of reason dominated by Enlightenment optimism.

LIFE

Reinhold Niebuhr was born in Wright City, Missouri, in 1892. His father, Gustave Niebuhr, was a scholarly German preacher who died when Reinhold and his younger brother, Helmut Richard (late professor in the Yale Divinity School) were still young. A frugal and industrious childhood preceded their enrollment in Elmhurst College in Illinois. Reinhold left that school without a degree in 1910 to enroll in Eden Theological Seminary, St. Louis, and transferred from there to the Yale Divinity School, from which he received Bachelor of Divinity and Master of Arts degrees. He has since received honorary degrees from Yale, Harvard, Princeton, Oxford, Glasgow, and other institutions.

In 1915 he was ordained in the Evangelical Synod of North America and accepted his first pastorate at the Bethel Evangelical Church of Detroit, a church with a small working-class congregation, mainly auto workers. Here he came to identify with the fight against the depersonalizing influences of modern industrial society and became involved with working-class interests. During this period he once commented that "the lowliest peasant of the Dark Ages had more opportunity for self-expression than the highest paid employee in the Ford factory." Niebuhr's championing of labor's cause led to overt conflicts with employers and the conservative churches of the area.

In 1928 he left Detroit to become associate professor of the philosophy of religion at Union Theological Seminary, New York City, and remained at Union for the rest of his active career, retiring as dean of the faculty in 1960. In his early days in New York he was an active member of the Socialist Party and editor of a Socialist publication, *The World Tomorrow*. In June of 1940 he resigned in protest against the party's pacifist position.[1]

Niebuhr has been a prolific writer, the author of seventeen books and countless articles. He was a contributing editor of *The Christian Century* and *The Nation* and editor or co-editor of *Christianity and Society* and *Christianity and Crisis*. The first of his books to attract wide attention was *Moral Man and Immoral Society* (1932), a searing

[1] See his *Christianity and Power Politics* (New York: Scribner's, 1940), Ch. 1, for a statement of his anti-pacifist position at that time.

blast at the sentimental assumptions of the social gospel. In 1939 he was named the fifth American to deliver the famous Gifford Lectures at the University of Edinburgh. In published form, the lectures became his magnum opus, *The Nature and Destiny of Man* (1941 and 1943).

Always active in practical politics, Niebuhr was one of the organizers of Americans for Democratic Action and worked for the Liberal Party in New York. For years he maintained an intensive preaching schedule, frequently appearing at eastern centers of higher education. His tone was prophetic and his pungent, slightly rasping style unforgettable. A severe stroke in 1956 ended his preaching but not his writing.

NEO–ORTHODOX THEOLOGY

Neo-orthodox Christian theologians of the twentieth century are set apart by the effort to take seriously the fundamental theological concepts that had tended to be neglected by the liberal religionists of the late nineteenth and early twentieth centuries: original sin, grace, atonement, resurrection, and last judgment. Their attempts to make the theological tradition represented by such terms relevant to the present day range from the Biblicism of Karl Barth, whose God is "wholly other" rather than immanent and who must be taken in the language of the Bible or not taken at all, to Paul Tillich, whose attempt at a rational explication of theological categories in a manner that absorbs a vast array of modern knowedge led some to call him a pantheist. Niebuhr is less architectonic than Tillich, more worldly than Barth, and probably less original than either. His method is built upon a fundamental dualism that tends toward contradiction, paradox, and irony. The dialectical tendencies of Paul, Pascal, Hegel, Kierkegaard, and Heidegger appear in his work.

Niebuhr sees "contradictions" in both the psyche of the individual and in the human historical communities of which he is a part. In the individual he finds both love and self-love. In historical existence he finds both fate and freedom. Being by inclinatiton an incisive critic, Niebuhr examines a variety of supposed attempts to find coherence and purpose in human history—Enlightenment rationalism, communism, Freudianism, and logical positivism—and argues that these attempts all fail to see or misinterpret the "contradictions" recognized by traditional Christian interpretations.

Christian faith, as Niebuhr conceives of it, does not eliminate these contradictions, for they are woven into the fabric of existence, but it transmutes them into meaningful paradox. Man's ability to "accept by faith" the Christian interpretation of human existence represents "self-transcendence," perhaps the most difficult term in Niebuhr's lexicon. Within history, within logic, within reason, there is no resolution of these basic conflicts. Niebuhr, of course, grants that there can be no formal conflict between logic and truth: "The laws of logic are reason's guard against chaos in the realm of truth." Yet he asserts that, while rationally understanding and accepting the limits of rationality, man may find in faith "that a rationally irresolvable contradiction may point to truth which logic cannot contain."[2]

A primary example of such a "dialectical" truth is the contradiction between fate and freedom, which finds its personal expression in original sin. Sin is rebellion against God and therefore rebellion against one's true self, in the form of either affirming one's animality at the expense of one's humanity (sins of the flesh) or denying one's animality at the expense of imitating God (sins of pride). Man is free not to sin. But he is fated to sin. In the origin of his being there is a "bias in the will," "something more than ignorance and something less than malice," which pulls him apparently inevitably, yet through a process of responsible choice—what psychology calls "rationaliz-

ing"—to a defiance of God's sovereignty over the world. This is a contradiction overcome not by reason but by grace.

That man has a considerable affinity with lower animals has been apparent to almost all philosophers. It has been the magnitude and character of man's dissimilarity from other animals that has caused contention. In his typical dichotomizing manner, Niebuhr classifies the efforts to understand man as basically two: those that see man primarily in terms of his animal nature and those that find in the excellencies of his rational faculties his primary character. In the former category fall those who seek in impulses, drives, instincts, and so on the key to man's fundamental nature—or, which may be more relevant today, those who by their devotion to the study of man from a psychobiological point of view imply that these are the keys to man's nature. Niebuhr welcomes the findings of modern psychology but contends that its failure to explain how subliminal factors are transmuted into "highly complex spiritual phenomena" marks the limitations of psychology as a science: "Man is never a simple two-layered affair who can be understood from the standpoint of the bottom layer should efforts to understand him from the standpoint of the top layer fail."

Niebuhr's criticism falls no less heavily upon the rationalists, those who, presumably, concentrate only upon the "top layer." They not only assume a greater emancipation from the limitations of physical nature than actually exists but fail to see that there is more to man than the rational capacity of surveying the world and forming general concepts about it. Man possesses the capacity of *self-transcendence,* that is, the capacity to stand outside his own rational processes to ask questions about the relation of rational to natural processes and the limits of his own reason. The distinction between man and animal, therefore, is not fully explained by the distinction between reason and no reason, for "animal consciousness is merely the expression of a central organic unity of an organism in relation to its immediate environment. Human consciousness invokes

[2] *The Nature and Destiny of Man* (New York: Scribner's, 1949), Vol. 1, pp. 263 and 262. Subsequent quotations from *Nature and Destiny* are from this edition.

a sharp distinction between the self and the totality of the world." It is this distinction between the self and the totality of the world, man's realization of his finitude, that is, paradoxically, the greatest clue to man's potentialities of infinitude. Man tries, however imperfectly, to stand off and look at himself self-consciously—and not only at himself but at his place in history. The rational mind can contemplate "nature" as a collection of objective phenomena but the whole self "with all its hopes, fears, and ambitions" becomes involved in any reflection on human history. This cosmic relationship, Niebuhr insists, is not encompassed by the classic Greek conception of reason. "Dialogue" is a word Niebuhr favors. The uniqueness of the human self is found in its constant dialogue with itself, with its fellows, and with God.[3]

In constructing his theory of self-transcendence Niebuhr acknowledges the work of Heidegger, who used the idea of transcendence to denote man's attempt to reach beyond rationality, and Scheler, who used the word "spirit" (*Geist*) to denote both the Greek *nous* (man's particular rational qualities, his technical intelligence) and a higher type of comprehension, requiring certain volitional capacities, that can make the whole world, including the self, an object of knowledge. The relationship would seem to be hierarchical: "What is ordinarily meant by 'reason' does not imply 'spirit,' but 'spirit' does imply 'reason.' "[4]

Reason is inadequate to satisfy man's innate quest for the "unconditioned ground of existence," since the only unconditioned

statement man can rationally make is that all human truth is relative to changing historical and cultural situations. We can say absolutely only that nothing in our rational consciousness is absolute. Reason exposes but does not overcome the ambiguities of man's nature and his historic position. Two centuries ago Western society felt otherwise but the faith in progressive revelation through reason found in the Enlightenment has been shattered by the fruits of nineteenth-century biology and psychology and by "scientific" but demonically irrational forces in the twentieth century. Today we are quicker to acknowledge that reason is used more than it uses.

Reason by itself, then, can dissolve hope but can no longer sustain it. Yet man, led by rational analysis to the "abyss of meaninglessness"—here the existentialist influence shows through—must nevertheless, Niebuhr believes, construct a world of meaning:

Implicit in the human situation of freedom and in man's capacity to transcend himself and his world is his inability to construct a world of meaning without finding a source and key to the structure of meaning which transcends the world beyond his own capicity to transcend it. The problem of meaning, which is the basic problem of religion, transcends the ordinary rational problem of tracing the relation of things to each other as the freedom of man's spirit transcends his rational faculties.[5]

Niebuhr calls himself a "Christian realist," by which he means to suggest emancipation from the naive hope of "even the most consistent naturalists" that scientific development within history will provide "an ultimate triumph of the rational over the irrational."[6] The varieties of naturalism, Niebuhr asserts, start with an avowed concern for nothing beyond causal explanation but end by elevating finite elements of existence

---

[3] *The Self and the Dramas of History* (New York: Scribner's, 1955), Ch. 1. Niebuhr defers to modern empiricists in granting that the third dialogue cannot be subject to empirical verification in precisely the same way as the first two. But at the least, he says, it can be taken as an empirical datum that the human self persistently imagines itself in dialogue with God: "The anatomy of human selfhood distinguishes itself by a yearning for the ultimate."

[4] *Nature and Destiny*, Vol. 1, p. 162n. It should be noted that Augustine and Kierkegaard were more significant influences than either Heidegger or Scheler on Niebuhr's overall thought.

[5] *Ibid.*, p. 164.

[6] *Faith and History* (New York: Scribner's, 1949), p. 67. Subsequent quotations from *Faith and History* are from this edition. The attack is here directed against Dewey. See also Paul Tillich, *Systematic Theology* (Chicago: Univ. of Chicago Press, 1951–63), Vol. 1, pp. 71–105.

—reason, sex, the survival impulse, economic relationships, biological growth, nation, or race—into ultimate explanations and hence bestowing upon them the eminence of the divine.[7] The "hidden dogmas" of social science, such as, for example, the view that the realm of history is for purposes of study virtually identical with the realm of nature, are all the more potent, he thinks, for being hidden.

The innate tendency of human beings to seek unity with greater and greater wholes would, if carried to the nth degree, destroy individuality. The natural desire to establish and protect one's individual identity thus stands in a contradictory relationship with the impulse toward the divine. The result is a tension infecting all human endeavors, a tension that constitutes a "bias toward sin" and is manifest in man's perennially uneasy conscience. (This is not, Niebuhr insists, a Rousseauistic or Hegelian dichotomy between a particular self and a universal self.) Out of this tension come not only man's rebelliousness, which manifests itself in the various forms of sin, but man's creativity. Both the sin and the creativity have collective as well as individual manifestations.

GROUP MORALITY

That groups can become extensions of the personal egos of their members is hardly a new insight. What Niebuhr has done with this phenomenon is to discuss it in terms of traditional Christian symbolism. The effect has been to make both Christians and non-Christians look anew at some old behavior patterns. The Philistine seismograph registered the highest shock waves in 1932, when Niebuhr published *Moral Man and Immoral Society*. Americans were in this year facing

the bottom of the Great Depression. Those putting inordinate hope in new forms of collective action were laced by Niebuhr's icy blast. Without in the least suggesting that we could do without collective action, indeed, suggesting the exact reverse, Niebuhr nevertheless threw cold water on any hope for an easy collective morality:

Individual men may be moral in the sense that they are able to consider interests other than their own in determining problems of conduct, and are capable, on occasion, of preferring the advantages of others to their own. They are endowed by nature with a measure of sympathy and consideration for their kind. . . . Their rational faculty prompts them to a sense of justice which educational discipline may refine and purge of egoistic elements. . . .

But all these achievements are more difficult, if not impossible, for human societies and social groups. In every human group there is less reason to guide and check impulse, less capacity for self-transcendence, less ability to comprehend the needs of others, and therefore more unrestrained egoism than the individuals who compose the group reveal in their personal relationships.[8]

The larger the group, the more selfish, by and large. The larger the group, the more difficult the achievement of a genuine moral relationship with another group. The unifying principle in large organizations is more likely to be basic but unreflective impulses. The impulse to national survival that operates in war most clearly unifies a national community and most inhibits altruistic behavior toward rival nations: "It is a rather pathetic aspect of human social life that conflict is a seemingly unavoidable prerequisite of group solidarity." Even small groups, even intimate groups like the family, characteristically display a marked selfishness in protecting their interests vis-à-vis the interests of other groups, and the leadership of even small groups (e.g., the father in a patriarchal society) is rarely as benevolent as individual persons defending purely individ-

---

[7] Whether all men or only some men share this yearning for ultimate meaning is, of course, the question that most clearly divides religionists and nonreligionists. And, in the nature of the case, neither can answer the question in terms satisfactory to the other.

[8] *Moral Man and Immoral Society* (New York: Scribner's, 1932), pp. XI–XII. Subsequent quotations from *Moral Man and Immoral Society* are from this edition.

ual interests can be. An individual may literally sacrifice himself on a heroic impulse. A group almost never does or can, figuratively or literally.

The tendency to couch group aims in the language of noble and altruistic ideals only makes matters worse. Niebuhr does not believe in a group mind existing apart from the individuals who make up the group. But the existence of the group enables persons to lose themselves, even to sacrifice themselves, in the name of a nominally laudable end, while participating in an emotional enterprise whose genuine purposes are anything but laudable.[9] The sins of the flesh may be less dangerous simply because they tend to be individual in manifestation, while the sin of pride is, above all, a collective phenomenon. American Protestant churches have often evaded the danger of the sins of collective pride, thinks Niebuhr, by overconcentrating attention on sins of the flesh. But liberal political theories generally have tended to underestimate the difficulties created by group pride:

Our contemporary culture fails to realize the power, extent and persistence of group egoism in human relations. It may be possible, though it is never easy, to establish just relations between individuals within a group purely by moral and rational suasion and accommodation. In intergroup relations this is practically an impossibility. The relations between groups must therefore always be predominantly political rather than ethical; that is, they will be determined by the proportion of power which each group possesses at least as much as by any rational and moral appraisal of the comparative needs and claims of each group.[10]

Niebuhr is not saying that all politics is unethical or that ethics is unrelated to politics. He is saying that the spokesmen of the liberal heritage, those who have been "children of light" less wise in their generation than the "children of darkness," have tended to overestimate the degree to which personal ethics can be fulfilled or at least not damaged by group action. They have underestimated the degree to which group loyalties tend to degenerate into irrational faith in "false absolutes"—the contingent norms of race, class, nation, and even religious sect, which become spuriously absolutized.

Critics of Niebuhr suggest that the gap between his impossible transcendent ideal and the realities of earthly political existence is so great that Christian ethics becomes virtually irrelevant to politics in the Niebuhrian system. He is so realistic, they say, that he slides into a Burkean conservatism in which prudence is all.[11] Niebuhr sometimes seems to invite this criticism by his stubborn penchant for rhetorical paradoxes and by his emphasis on divine perfection and human depravity. Of course his own political activism and reformism would seem to belie the quietistic or conservative implications some would draw from his thought. But the logical implication of his theory rather than his own personal behavior is the crucial factor at this point. (See, however, the concluding section of this chapter.) The question of whether Niebuhr's tension ethics results in a hopeless compartmentalization dividing Christian ethics from practical politics may, perhaps, be clarified by looking at Niebuhr's treatment of the relationship between the Christian norm of love and political justice as dealt with by courts of law.

The Christian ethic is summed up in the *agape* of Christ, a sacrificial, outward-moving, selfless, ecstatic love that regards other individuals as objects of God rather than as objects of the self. It is intensely personal.

[9] See Eric Hoffer, *The True Believer* (New York: Harper & Row, 1951).

[10] *Moral Man and Immoral Society*, pp. XXII–XXIII.

[11] See Holtan P. Odegard, *Sin and Science, Reinhold Niebuhr as Political Theologian* (Antioch, Ohio: Antioch Press, 1956), especially p. 197, and Morton G. White, *Social Thought in America: The Revolt Against Formalism*, rev. ed. (Boston: Beacon Press, 1958), Epilogue. The criticism of Niebuhr as a latent conservative can be matched by criticism of Niebuhr as a hidden liberal. Wilson Carey McWilliams, in "Reinhold Niebuhr: New Orthodoxy for Old Liberalism," *American Political Science Review*, Vol. 56 (1962), pp. 874–85, turns Niebuhr into a kind of apotheosis of the "bankruptcy" of liberalism. A more balanced view is Henry Kariel, *In Search of Authority* (New York: Free Press, 1964), pp. 180–93.

Justice in its everyday connotation is thought of as the "rightness" of the rewards and punishments a community formulates and administers to preserve its order and cohesiveness. Such justice is rational and calculating; it cannot be wholly personal, nor is it easily subject to the ecstatic illuminations of the spirit. Were legal justice dispensed by agapic individuals, unreasonable disorder would result. Even—or especially—a town full of saints would require a dispassionately administered set of traffic laws. Spontaneous love and public order are, therefore, separable if not at odds.

Seen as a norm of justice, *agape*—Christian brotherhood can be regarded as a collective approximation of *agape*—is a standard by which all earthly systems of justice are found wanting. Some such spirit of love must, however, accompany and animate rational calculation in the establishment and maintenance of earthly systems if they are not to become purely mechanical and inhuman. As Niebuhr says in *Moral Man and Immoral Society,* "justice which is only justice soon degenerates into something less than justice." Yet the rational calculation of rights and interests, which are so intrinsic a part of the judicial process, remains antithetical to the spirit of Christian ethics—at least to the ethics of the New Testament, which is not all that Christians claim but is the most that they can agree upon as authoritative. This standard is quite heedless of rights and interests and is wholly beyond the rational appeal for equal treatment:

You have heard that it was said "An eye for an eye and a tooth for a tooth." But I say to you, Do not resist one who is evil. But if any one strikes you on the right cheek, turn to him the other also; and if any one would sue you and take your coat, let him have your cloak as well; and if any one forces you to go one mile, go with him two miles. . . . Love your enemies. . . . do not be anxious, saying, "What shall we eat?" or "What shall we drink?" or "What shall we wear?" . . . Judge not that you be not judged.[12]

[12] Matthew 5:38–41 and 44; 6:31; and 7:1.

Human survival and strict obedience to these commandments are not consistent, thinks Niebuhr; but the spirit of the commandments, a spirit not derivable from the rational faculty, is necessary to prevent the deterioration of human society to a subhuman level.

But it is not enough simply to say, "We shall adopt the spirit of the New Testament while recognizing the irrelevance of its concrete standards." This would be the opposite of the more common ethical dilemma of trying to follow a set of rules without participating in the spiritual force that gives them sanction—*legalism,* or goodness by the numbers. Niebuhr insists that these commandments must be understood by the Christian as ultimately realizable even though provisionally unrealizable. Hence the Christian concern for eschatology, the doctrine of last things, has important ethical consequences. Goodness is sustained by a hope strong enough to overcome a despairing present. The Christian ethic and the perfection of the moral life are what Niebuhr calls the "impossible possibility," a possibility without which the Christian is unable to reject the normativeness of the merely normal.[13]

Critics coming out of the natural-law tradition would be inclined to say, of course, that reason is much more than prudential calculation and that, while in the last analysis revelation may sustain the norms of the New Testament, these norms are not the contradictions to reason that Niebuhr assumes. From a quite different direction the scientific humanist is apt to agree that they are, in their literal extremity, beyond rational demonstration and on these grounds to deny their validity in favor of moral norms validated by scientific inquiry, experi-

[13] See *Nature and Destiny,* Vol. 2, Ch. 3; *Faith and History,* Ch. 13; *Christianity and Power Politics,* pp. 214–18. The American Protestant Church, thinks Niebuhr, is not eschatological enough. It has participated too fully in America's naive confidence in a "redemptive history." Niebuhr's latest book, *Man's Nature and His Communities* (New York: Scribner's, 1965), is, if anything, even more critical of Protestantism and is avowedly more sympathetic to Catholicism and Judaism than the younger Niebuhr was.

ment, or some other means. More techni-cally minded students of ethics might argue that Niebuhr's tension ethics keeps in sus-pension and needlessly confuses two differ-ent types of ethical system: the ethics of proper motive, which is essentially personal, and the ethics of proper consequences, which is essentially social. To this Niebuhr would no doubt reply that the logical separation of the two, which in different language he fully concedes, is not a separation in life. There, each exists in a sort of hostile dependence on the other. Indeed, this is the problem; this is the continuous ethical tension of man in society.

The tension is reflected in Niebuhr him-self in a more acute form than is likely to occur in those able to be more consistently optimistic or pessimistic. He explicitly ac-knowledges that the "highest satisfactions of the inner life" from an aloof, ascetic view-point may be enjoyed at the expense of tragic social injustice, while attempts to maintain order through proximate norms of justice may undermine personal moral ideal-ism. The human situation is one in which it is necessary to see "love exploited to the full yet discounted."[14] There is even a note of despair in the earlier Niebuhr of *Moral Man and Immoral Society*: ". . . justice can-not be approximated if the hope of its per-fect realization does not generate a sublime madness in the soul. The illusion is danger-ous because it encourages terrible fanati-cisms. It must therefore be brought under the control of reason. One can only hope that reason will not destroy it before its work is done."

NATION, COMMUNITY, AND HISTORY

Group ethics, as we have seen, is a funda-mental concern for Niebuhr. When the

group is the modern nation-state, special fac-tors come into play. The size, the longevity, the coercive power, and the traditional sym-bolism of the nation-state are apt to make it an object of worship or an object of fear or both. Since awe and fear are basic emo-tions evoked by divinity, the state has fre-quently been one of the "false gods" wor-shipped by men. German idealism and Ger-man political practice alike are frequently mentioned by Niebuhr as examples of state worship in which the particular is absolut-ized. The United States, with its early her-itage of "that government is best which gov-erns least," is cited as an example of fear of the state, which sometimes approaches the edge of anarchy and often downgrades the valid and necessary element of majesty in government.[15] Niebuhr's German-American background is perhaps reflected in these two examples.

The exaggerations of the positive and the negative aspects, respectively, of state con-trol in these two traditions both reveal ex-cessively rigid conceptions of the relationship of the individual to his larger political com-munity, thinks Niebuhr. In *The Children of Light and the Children of Darkness* (1944), he sets forth his understanding of this rela-tionship in three propositions. In the first place the individual is so related to his com-munity that "the highest reaches of his in-dividuality are dependent upon the social substance out of which they arise."[16] A great artist like Shakespeare may achieve a per-spective approaching universal dimensions but he remains a product of his community and his community limits every choice he makes, not least through the language it pro-vides. There is freedom in history but no absolute freedom. There is self-transcendence

[14] *Christianity and Power Politics*, p. 39. See also *Be-yond Tragedy* (New York: Scribner's, 1937), Ch. 8.

[15] *The Irony of American History* (New York: Scrib-ner's, 1952). Subsequent quotations from *Irony* are from this edition. The religious factor in the majesty of state and its neglect by Western democratic theory is dis-cussed in *The Structure of Nations and Empires* (New York: Scribner's, 1959), Chs. 4 and 11.

[16] *The Children of Light and the Children of Dark-ness* (New York: Scribner's, 1944), p. 48. Subsequent quotations from *Children* are from this edition.

but no removal from social limitations. The juridical norms behind positive law may be conditioned by profound religious insights but any statement of them is conditioned to a greater extent than natural-law advocates are willing to acknowledge by the shifting historical milieu.

In the second place, "Both individual and collective centers of human vitality may be endlessly elaborated" and any premature attempt to define the limits of these vitalities suppresses the "indeterminate creativity" of man and society as well as their destructive possibilities. Such premature definitions are found, thinks Niebuhr, in the natural harmony of the economic order presupposed by classical economics and the inevitable class conflict (and harmony "on the other side of the revolution") presupposed by Marxian theory. At the level of individual vitality, Niebuhr finds similar attempts in Freudian and behaviorist psychologies in their attempt to explain man in terms of the sex impulse or various reflexes. Man's freedom allows "indeterminate elaboration" of any natural impulse, perhaps aesthetically, perhaps perversely.

Finally, "individual vitality rises in indeterminate degree over all social and communal concretions of life"[17] and is not ultimately fulfilled within the historical process. This third contention, which brings us back to the difficult problem of "self-transcendence," is probably most subject to dispute, for at this point Niebuhr himself seems to be standing outside history to speak of an ultimate that cannot be fulfilled within history. This is the position of anyone who asserts a philosophy of history, whether secular or religious—if, indeed, a secular philosophy of history is not a contradiction in terms. Such a position can never be compelling to

the skeptic. None of us has experienced or can experience more than an indeterminate part of history. "History as a whole," therefore, is a category beyond empirical knowledge and its use implies some sort of revelation.

Niebuhr uses what he regards as the Christian view of history as a fulcrum by which to pry up at their roots modern secular democratic theories. The failure to understand "the full height of . . . human self-transcendence" has led such theories to oscillate between excessively individualistic and excessively collectivistic emphases. The individualism of a democratic Bentham can eventuate in a disorder, especially in the neglected economic realm, which actually constricts individual freedoms. The communitarianism of a democratic Dewey, Niebuhr writes in *Faith and History* (1949), places such faith in political communities, whose life is "even more contingent than that of the individuals who are able to survey their relations to them," as to make possible the cutting off of the "pinnacle of individuality" by the community.

Both of these theories—indeed all those that Niebuhr would put in the category of "modern" thought as distinguished from the classical view and the Biblical view—are guilty of treating history as "redemptive." That is, they can operate only on the assumption that man and society are capable of being redeemed by the triumph of processes already at work within history: ". . . modern culture, despite its diversities, has a common confidence in the temporal process as that which gives meaning to our existence." In the time that man controls, therefore, rather than in the eternity that he does not control man's error can in some way or other be made self-liquidating.

In *Faith and History* Niebuhr contrasts the modern view with the classical view, in which reality is a fixity above and apart from the realm of historical flux and change. Niebuhr contends that the modern view is truer than the classical in seeing "that both nature and historic institutions are subject to development in time" but that from this

---

[17] In *The Self and the Dramas of History* Niebuhr employs a different terminology, speaking of the "vertical" and the "horizontal" dimensions of the individual's relationship to the community. In the former, the individual looks down on the community from a position of moral transcendence. In the latter, he is made aware of the special separateness of his community through conflict with other communities.

truth two illusions developed: "Modern culture . . . consistently exaggerated the degree of growth in human freedom and power" and made the "second mistake of identifying freedom with virtue." Both classical and modern views are, of course, contrasted with what Niebuhr identifies as the Biblical view, which recognizes historical process but does not deify is because it acknowledges a Deity outside of historical process.

The United States is the national representative par excellence of the essentially optimistic view of history as redemptive. The success of our national experiment surely helps explain this. In *The Irony of American History* (1952), Niebuhr fits the United States into the Niebuhrian system, with illuminating results for those complacent about the clichés by which America lives. He argues that America's constantly expanding economy, "a gift of providence" thanks to a small population on a large, rich continent, is primarily responsible for the fluidity of our class structure. This has enabled capitalism to take credit for economic productivity without having to take the blame for hardened class lines. The theory remains relatively unspotted and hence unexamined, while the practice of American capitalism goes its own unorthodox way. Marxism criticizes the error of a false individualism used as a rationalization for collective oppression and "substitutes a more grievous error for the error which it challenges," namely the view that class interest as interpreted by an elite party is synonymous with the interest of the whole and is the very purpose of historical movement.

Liberals in general, of whom Americans are such good examples, Niebuhr calls soft utopians. Communists he calls hard utopians. One group mistakenly regards property as the primary instrument of justice; the other mistakenly regards property as the primary instrument of injustice. The utopianism is also reflected in the impatient desire to solve political problems "once and for all." "In this debate between errors, or between half-truth and half-truth, America is usually completely on the side of the bourgeois credo

in theory; but in practice it has achieved balances of power in the organization of social forces and a consequent justice which has robbed the Marxist challenge of its sting."

Although granting a providential basis to America's material position, Niebuhr by no means equates this, as an older Calvinism might have done, with divine sanction for America's ideological position. It is precisely this erroneous equation that Niebuhr attacks in *The Irony of American History*. It is this error that liberalism and communism alike, using the secular language of "progress" (i.e., redemptive history) have committed. Niebuhr's view of history is not progressive but tragic and ironic in almost equal proportions. This view suggests not a quickness to identify historical causes as God's causes but a great reluctance to do so. In the American political past, Niebuhr finds Lincoln a rather solitary example of this kind of restraint. His Second Inaugural, with its "malice toward none, charity for all" and its reference to the God to whom South as well as North pray, Niebuhr compares with the scriptural injunction to "judge not that you be not judged." "Lincoln's model . . . rules out our effort to establish the righteousness of our cause by a monotonous reiteration of the virtues of freedom compared with the evils of tyranny. . . . it is very dangerous to define the struggle as one between a God-fearing and a godless civilization." Russia is worshipping a god, albeit a different one from ours, and we are not so God-fearing as we pretend. In the Marxist liturgy, Engels' "withering away of the state" is the

anarchistic pinnacle on top of the collectivist structure of utopia which makes the Leninist dream at once so implausible and so attractive to the victims of injustice. It provides the ideological basis for the power system which has developed in the communist world. If we remember that power is never merely force but always a combination of force and prestige it must become apparent that the ideological framework for the communist power structure has some striking similarities with—as well as differences from—the traditional power structures which are maintained through the millennia of human history. In these the gradations of authority and the centralization of power in government were presented as consonant with the cosmic order as enjoined by the divine will.[18]

CONCLUSION: THEOLOGY AND POLITICS

In rather rapid order we have now moved from the sinful nature of man to United States–Soviet relations, a movement typical of Niebuhr himself. The most perplexing question emerging from this chapter concerns the tensile strength of the links connecting these two poles.

The essence of Niebuhr's argument may be summed up as follows: The "soft utopianism" of liberal politics and religion and the "hard utopianism" of communist politics and religion alike underestimate the depth of self-love and overestimate the possibility that scientific knowledge will defeat the sinful propensities of man at some point in history. The former tends toward a sentimental view of the force of individual good will in coping with perverse institutional structures; the latter places too much confidence in institutional structures (and, after the withering away of the state, in naturally virtuous individuals). By contrast with these diverse "children of light," the cynical "children of darkness" give up all pretense of moral aspiration and yield to Machiavellian pessimism in politics.

The "Christian realist," while acknowledging the ambiguity of his own standards and actions, avoids the liberal temptation to put his faith in a redemptive history as well as the cynical temptation to disengage himself from the moral conflicts of his community. He is willing to balance power against power in the interests of a tolerable order and a provisional justice, without expecting personal or social redemption from them. The Christian realist does not look to pure democracy to overcome the ingrained short-

comings of the *demos* but finds it desirable as "a method of finding proximate solutions for insoluble problems," for "Man's capacity for justice makes democracy possible; but man's inclination to injustice makes democracy necessary."[19]

As Niebuhr readily acknowledges, there is much of Augustine in all this:

Modern realists know the power of collective self-interest as Augustine did; but they do not understand its blindness. Modern pragmatists understand the irrelevance of fixed and detailed norms; but they do not understand that love as the final norm must take the place of these inadequate norms. Modern liberal Christians know that love is the final norm for man; but they fall into sentimentality because they fail to measure the power and persistence of self-love. A generation which finds its communities imperiled and in decay from the smallest and most primordial community, the family, to the largest and most recent, the potential world community, might well take counsel of Augustine in solving its perplexities.[20]

Granted his definitions and assumptions, especially that liberals err on the side of sentimentality and "modern" realists err on the side of cynicism, it is not hard to agree with Niebuhr. It is, in fact, difficult to argue that we should be more sentimental, that we should hope for nothing less than perfection in politics, that we should be either more utopian or less moral. But who other than fools would so argue? With some justification, critics of Niebuhr accuse him of putting too many people in too few categories. His victims are too often strapped to a Procrustean bed. Rousseau gets thrown in with the liberals because he used social-contract terminology. Locke is pictured as naive about the ease of determining consent. Bentham is portrayed as unable to see the need for social controls. Hegel believed in a redemptive history and so, apparently, does Bertrand Russell. Niebuhr sometimes seems more interested in massive differences than in fine distinctions. As a matter of fact, lib-

---

[18] *Structure of Nations and Empires*, p. 227.

[19] *Children*, pp. 118 and xi.

[20] *Christian Realism and Political Problems* (New York: Scribner's, 1953), p. 146.

erals, however much they have deified nature, have frequently been much less sentimental about human nature than Niebuhr indicates.

Is it possible that Niebuhr merely provides us with a gigantic tautological system built upon the cornerstone of man's sinfulness and then gives it the semblance of empirical validity by picking and choosing among the facts of intellectual history and current events? If so, Niebuhr would not be the first philosopher to do so. Nor would his company necessarily be undistinguished. Tautological, pseudo-empirical systems can be both profound and helpful. Indeed, it may be that all philosophic thought is tautological insofar as it is truly systematic and no more than pseudo-empirical insofar as it strains for universality. A system, even one that acknowledges religious mystery, can hardly incorporate religious mystery. Niebuhr has oversold and overextended his system—but it is a good system, as systems go.

But Niebuhr is not only a system-builder. He practices what he preaches about involvement in the crucial political issues of the day and this involvement includes for him analysis, commentary, and prescription. Though they might not meet all the tenets of contemporary scientific empiricism, his analyses in a periodical like *Christianity and Crisis* of, say, the Teamsters Union, Charles de Gaulle, a Berlin crisis, or Vietnam are certainly empirical in one legitimate sense of the term. Our question, then, should perhaps be rephrased: is the system, whether or not invariably *supported by* the empirical analysis, invariably *related to* the empirical analysis? Or are there two Niebuhrs, Niebuhr the theologian and Niebuhr the political analyst?

Examination of Niebuhr's more political writings reveals a remarkable consistency of style and approach. There have been, of course, changes in point of view. But after the big changes in the 1930s, first away from pacifism then away from socialism, they have been marginal. Some articles are devoid of theological language, some are not. What makes even the former peculiarly Niebuhrian in flavor is (1) their pungency, frequently attained through the use of irony, paradox, and the close juxtaposition of logical antinomies; (2) their unblinking attention to power factors in the situation under scrutiny; (3) their uniform level of generality (instead of concentrating on factual details and local color, Niebuhr is almost always chiefly concerned with the ends decision-makers were trying to achieve and the reasons people reacted as they did to the situation); and (4) their uniform level of normativeness (Niebuhr is not only unafraid to use "value-laden" words—"freedom," "justice," "tyranny"—but he does so easily and consistently, at a level somewhere between manifestly judgmental and manifestly descriptive usages).

Let us look, for example, at two statements on race relations, the first more or less theoretical, the second more or less empirical:

Christianity's resources for approaching the problem of race relations do not stop short with a mere statement of the ideal of equality. Christian insights into the human situation afford, for instance, a much more profound illumination of the sources of racial prejudice than does the analysis of secular liberalism. Generally, American liberals have regarded racial prejudices as vestiges of barbarism, which an enlightened education was in the process of overcoming. . . . Our anthropologists rightly insisted that there were no biological roots of inequality among races; and they wrongly drew the conclusion from this fact that racial prejudice is a form of ignorance which could be progressively dispelled by enlightenment.[21]

counties which comply [with the Supreme Court decision requiring school integration] are usually those in which Negroes are a minority of 25 per cent or less. On the other hand, counties which approach the 50 per cent ratio almost invariably seek some form of evasion. . . . It is easier for a majority to be tolerant of a small minority than of a large minority. . . . This is a phenomenon of all group relations and does not apply solely to Negro-white relations. It may lead to pessimistic conclusions in regard to certain counties in the South. But it prompts to optimism when we consider the nation as a

[21] *Children*, pp. 138–39.

whole, where Negroes are in an obvious minority. The relation of morals to percentage points is a reminder to all of us of the frailty of our conscience and the limits of our tolerance.[22]

The first statement, while not wholly devoid of factual references, is essentially an assertion that race prejudice is more than ignorance (how much more is dealt with elsewhere at length) and that "Christian insights" recognize this but "secular liberalism" does not. This statement is prophetic and apologetic, in the Christian sense, and may be summed up more bluntly in Niebuhr's own words: "Race bigotry is, in short, one form of original sin."[23] This is not the conclusion of a sociologist. The statement on the correlation of the size of minorities with the intensity of racial tensions is the kind of observation a sociologist might make. But again, in prophetic fashion Niebuhr cannot help but remind us of what this suggests concerning our own frail consciences.

Whatever other purposes they serve, these two quotations do illustrate a point. Whether he is being theoretical or empirical, Niebuhr is perennially and indubitably a Christian prophet, calling men and nations to think upon the condition of their souls. What, then, do Niebuhr's critics mean when they question the relation of his theology to his politics? Perhaps all that they mean is that his prophetic conclusions do not necessarily follow from the data. Indeed, they do not *of necessity* follow, or else no nontheistic sociologist would be in a position to say anything significant about race relations, a proposition that even theologians would find hard to accept. The function of prophets may be to point a spotlight of urgency at deeply shadowed truths, while that of theologians is to switch on a floodlight of significance.

Some critics attack not so much the overconclusiveness of Niebuhr as the undercon-clusiveness. He uses theological language, yes, but mainly to show how murky and involved problems are rather than how to resolve those problems. Since Niebuhr does not offer "Christian answers" at the practical political level, so this criticism runs, he is party to a divorce between politics and theology. This argument suffers from the widespread misconception that Christianity is concerned mainly to prescribe "answers" to men's practical problems rather than to illumine the true character of these problems in their broadest dimensions. Some Christians by their evangelical excesses certainly encourage this error but, since Niebuhr's view of history is a tragic-ironic view, he can hardly be expected to apply Christian doctrine as some kind of magic formula that provides simple solutions to complex problems. The burden of his whole argument is that Christians ought to be better able to live with the ambiguities of political life without loss of hope and to endure provisional solutions, arrived at by men of many viewpoints, to intractable problems. Critics who indict Niebuhr for not providing certified Christian solutions to everyday problems, therefore, only indicate that they have not understood him.

But we must get back to the main issue. There remains a valid question about the relationship of theology to politics. It involves neither the extent to which Niebuhr employs theological language nor the extent to which he prescribes Christian answers but the degree to which his theological position enhances the value of his admittedly useful political commentaries. In a sense, all Niebuhr's political commentaries are but illustrations of the most general kind of theological propositions—about man's sin, man's fate, and God's way of working in the world. The value of the illustration is not wholly dependent upon the theological context but the full value of the illustration cannot be appreciated without sharing to some extent the presuppositions on which it is based. The non-Christians are no doubt right in suggesting that Niebuhr's political writings can stand alone; but they are not right in concluding from this that they can "just as well"

[22] "Morals and Percentages," *Christianity and Society,* Vol. 20 (1955), pp. 3–4, in Harry R. Davis and Robert C. Good, eds., *Reinhold Niebuhr on Politics* (New York: Scribner's, 1960), p. 230.

[23] "Christian Faith and the Race Problem," *Christianity and Society,* Vol. 10 (1945), p. 23, in Davis and Good, p. 232.

stand alone—that the theology is superfluous. It is superfluous to them, of course, and this is a difficulty.

Like every theologian, Niebuhr is speaking from a base of prerational commitment and can communicate fully only to those who to some extent, perhaps even half-consciously, share such a commitment. To say this will seem to some a hopeless confusion of private subjective feelings with the criteria of objective demonstration that political theory should supposedly display. There is in this criticism, however, a bias—a liberal bias?—toward viewing religion as private because subjective and therefore presumably less significant than objective, hence public, knowledge. In Niebuhr's view, religious commitment precedes and transcends categories of public and private, objective and subjective, interests and obligations, art and science, without necessarily annulling them. Every statement, "factual" or otherwise, presupposes an ultimate concern that makes it worth stating. Indeed, significant thought itself proceeds from religious commitment in this sense.

The editors of Niebuhr's collected political philosophy agree that the understandings that we label Niebuhr's political science and his political ethics are in neither case verifiable apart from highly personal involvement: "To freeze these understandings into a rigid, completely coherent system would do violence to their spirit. At the center is no sys-tem, but the concerned, searching, believing, understanding and acting person."[24] Thus even Niebuhr's action in the field of politics, his work for this cause or that candidate, is inseparable from his theorizing about man and God in history, simply because actor and thinker are one person. To point to Druid-worshippers who support the same political causes as Niebuhr or to men of other political beliefs who use similar language to describe God in history, with the implication that religious faith and politics are separable, is to miss the point. They are always logically separable and never, short of schizophrenia, personally separable.

Niebuhr is not primarily proving a set of precepts, though he may sometimes appear to be. He is describing the world, including the political world, as seen from a particular vantage point. In this he is, to use Christian terminology, witnessing to a faith; and part of the faith is that what he sees of the world of politics from his particular vantage point is not illusory. All who write of politics, whatever their viewpoint may be, all who have been discussed in this book, act from a similar ground of faith in their "given" viewpoint. And so do all who read what they have written.

[24] Davis and Good, p. xi. See also Charles W. Kegley and Robert W. Bretall, eds., *Reinold Niebuhr, His Religious, Social, and Political Thought* (New York: Macmillan, 1956), especially essays by Emil Brunner, Alan Richardson, and Kenneth Thompson.

27

POLITICAL THEORY AND
THE SCIENCE OF POLITICS

There is nothing new about the application of scientific methods to political subjects. Few would want to deny to Aristotle either the title scientist or the title political scientist. Concern for a science of politics agitated many seventeenth-, eighteenth-, and nineteenth-century thinkers, and they were not altogether unsuccessful in their efforts to this end. The "scientific" political hypotheses of, say, Hume, may possibly stand up to any yet produced in the twentieth century.

What is new in the twentieth century at the level of scholarly practice are the vastly more subtle ways in which mathematics is being used—the social science of a Comte or a Mill or a Spencer, like that of Aristotle, was more influenced by the biological paradigm. But even more fundamental for our purposes here is the twentieth-century divergence of rationale between what is claimed to be *the* scientific approach to politics and the tradition of Western political philosophy we have traced in this volume. Many political-science faculties in our larger universities know this split, and though graduate students, perhaps to alleviate an otherwise humdrum existence, like to magnify disagreement among their mentors, it is surely there.

The quantifiers may think that their historically oriented colleagues are wasting their time with grand but empty metaphors (if they are theorists) or with mere anecdote (if they are researchers). The traditionalists may think the quantifiers are wasting their time with precise but obvious formulas (if they are theorists) or with precise but trivial data (if they are researchers).

Those preoccupied with mathematics have been termed practitioners of "hard" social science; those who describe historical events and relationships in narrative form have been termed practitioners of "soft" social science. But practice is not the issue we choose to emphasize here. Careful practitioners of both "hard" and "soft" social science will find their work respected and used. It is when our brethren become theorists, it is when they enter the lists as justifiers of their methodologies, that emotions rise and questions multiply: Do survey research studies of public opinion deflect attention from the public good to the merely popular? Do they, in the name of scientific neutrality, support manipulative attitudes toward the public? Is the dichotomy between man as scientist and man as citizen tenable? Are men demeaned if they are studied by means of experiments comparable to those used in studying rats and chimpanzees? Is human nature composed of certain essential and unchanging qualities or is it infinitely malleable? Does change in history follow knowable and predictable patterns or does uniqueness of men and their communities preclude successful prediction? Are fundamental values so subjective and emotive in origin as to be irrational? Are scientists, philosophers, and prophets three separate breeds of men? Does philosophy as linguistic analysis preclude philosophy as love of wisdom? Is value-free science possible? Is socially neutral science possible? Can science tell us what we ought to do? Is traditional political philosophy necessarily obscurantist and elitist? Is it concerned more, or less, with right political action than is modern political science? Is metaphysics a subject or an illusion? Is there an ontology without metaphysics?

We can raise but we can scarcely resolve such disturbing questions here. Nor would we be well advised to assign contemporary political scientists to one of two camps based on superficial answers to them. Little is gained but militancy and false security by that course. The fact is, there are disagreements within disagreements. A behaviorist, who looks at humans through a mechanistic stimulus-response framework, will disagree with a "behavioralist," who uses Freudian developmental concepts; both will oppose natural lawyers. Natural lawyers will disagree over the relation between revealed religion and natural reason; both factions will oppose cultural relativists. Cultural relativists will fight over the transmissibility of culturally induced values or the relation of language to thought; they . . . and so on. Nor do ultimate faith, moral behavior, or qualities of temperament match up with these intellectual positions as neatly as some would like. Theists and atheists, democrats and antidemocrats, kindly men and vicious men can be found in most of the foregoing camps.

This confusing hodgepodge of positions makes us eager to put everything in order and, at the least, to clear up the other fellow's confusion. But some kinds of confusion

may be a sign of vitality. Our task as scholars—as schoolmen—is surely to save ourselves and our fellows from chaotic confusion; but not at the expense of premature certitude. If not chaotic confusion, at least fruitful confusion is the proper environment of the intellectual. Intelligence requires and consumes confusion, just the way fire requires and consumes oxygen.

Our attempt at imposing order in this chapter on the question of a science of politics involves judgments on the significance of trends not yet revealed in anything like their fulness. Yet we know that what is done in the name of science in our day gains considerable popular authority thereby. It has seemed best, therefore, to segregate somewhat our discussion of political science from our discussion in Chapter 23 of twentieth-century political thought, even though the decline of liberalism, the fact of totalitarianism, and the spread of Marxian and Freudian modes of thought examined there, have obviously affected contemporary political science. In this chapter we shall look at several intellectual influences upon American conceptions of the possibility and the nature of a science of politics: European sociology, logical positivism, legal science, behavioralism, and systems theory.[1]

---

[1] Some of the questions raised in this brief introduction are dealt with in the following works: Bernard Crick, *The American Science of Politics* (Berkeley: Univ. of California Press, 1959); Charles Hyneman, *The Study of Politics* (Urbana: Univ. of Illinois Press, 1959); Harry S. Kariel, *The Promise of Politics* (Englewood Cliffs, N.J.: Prentice-Hall, 1966); Harold D. Lasswell, *The Future of Political Science* (New York: Atherton Press, 1964); Albert Somit and Joseph Tanenhaus, *American Political Science: A Profile of a Discipline* (New York: Atherton Press, 1964) and *The Development of American Political Science: From Burgess to Behavioralism* (Boston: Allyn and Bacon, 1967); Frank J. Sorauf, *Perspectives on Political Science* (Columbus, Ohio: Merrill, 1966); Glenn Tinder, *The Crisis of Political Imagination* (New York: Scribner's, 1964); Vernon Van Dyke, *Political Science: A Philosophical Analysis* (Stanford: Stanford Univ. Press, 1960); Dwight Waldo, *Political Science in the United States of America* (New York: UNESCO, 1956); René deV. Williamson, *Independence and Involvement: A Christian Reorientation of Political Science* (Baton Rouge: Louisiana State Univ. Press, 1964); and Roland Young, ed.,

The great European sociologists of the recent past gave us major insights into social processes but also showed us the degree to which a penchant for generalization could be combined with accurate social data. Of these scientists we will look at four, in order of their deaths: Durkheim, Weber, Pareto, and Mannheim.

EUROPEAN SOCIOLOGY

Durkheim

Émile Durkheim (1858–1917) led French sociology away from Comte's cosmological dogmatism toward a more solid grounding in empirical fact. He studied, for example— but not a random example—the statistics of suicide and found that an increase in suicides occurred not only in times of depression, as one might expect, but also in times of sudden prosperity. He concluded from this that a rapid change in social norms and a discrepancy between aspirations and the ability to gratify them were more important than external privation or plenty.[2] In this way he brought social theory back to the problem of community, for he found that the suicide-prone individual was, in essence, a communityless individual, one whose identification with a tangible group was defective and who displayed the driftitng and helpless characteristics of a man with ambiguous and shifting norms. This was the *anomic* individual. His condition was *anomie*.

The power of the community-group without which the individual became anomic fascinated Durkheim. He found that nonanomic individuals bear within them a "collective consciousness" (in French, *conscience*) through which the group transmits "collective representations" to its members. These representations include, as one might expect, standards of behavior; but so inclusive did the influence of some groups seem to Durkheim that he held society itself to have created concepts of space and time and all religious beliefs, in each case with the underlying aim of social solidarity. Whether this belief implies a disembodied "group mind" is a moot point in interpreting Durkheim, because he was sometimes given to generous metaphor. Society has within it both ugliness and grandeur but "It is society that has freed us from nature. Is it not then to be expected that we think of it as a mental being higher than ourselves from which our mental powers emanate? This explains why it is that when it demands of us those sacrifices, great or small, that make up our moral life, we bow before its demands with deference."[3]

At any rate, what Durkheim saw most clearly was that under the division of labor and specialization characteristic of modern industry, workers come to lack a sense of performing meaningful work and a sense of belonging to the corporate enterprise. A common purpose is needed to show the relationship between the otherwise disjointed parts. Hence what is taken for granted today, namely that individuals must learn to "adjust" to their groups if they are to avoid anxiety and leaders must pay attention to subordinates' feelings of belonging if the enterprise is to function smoothly, was implicit in the sociology of Durkheim. We have so far accepted these conclusions, indeed, that today

---

Approaches to the Study of Politics (Evanston: Northwestern Univ. Press, 1958).

[2] *Suicide: A Study in Sociology* (1897), trans. by J. A. Spaulding and George Simpson (New York: Free Press, 1951). See also *The Division of Labor in Society*, 2nd ed., trans. by George Simpson (New York: Free Press, 1949). In the latter Durkheim argues that in primitive, kinship-based societies, where the individual's role is not differentiated, there is a strong common conscience and all law tends to be punitive, whereas in the advanced society with a division of labor, the common conscience is weakened and law becomes more cooperative and regulative. Durkheim's use of the terms "mechanical solidarity" to explain the former society and "organic solidarity" to explain the latter may be misleading. See also Harry Alpert, *Émile Durkheim and His Sociology* (New York: Russell and Russell, 1961), and Sebastian De Grazia, *The Political Community, A Study of Anomie* (Chicago: Univ. of Chicago Press, 1948).

[3] *Sociology and Philosophy* (1924), trans. by D. F. Pocock (London: Cohen & West, 1953), p. 73.

their unthinking application is being looked at by fresh and critical eyes. Not only social science is today community-minded.

Weber

Max Weber (1864–1920) is often called the greatest of the twentieth-century sociologists, for no one else tried so hard to combine the rigor of method so much admired today with the rich historical insight and sensitivity to human feelings that have given scholars of the past their standing. Weber's insistence on a hard distinction between "value judgments" and empirical fact is the premise of "value-free science," accepted as axiomatic in most social research today; but mistaken conclusions are often drawn from this by supporters as well as critics. Metaphysically minded critics[4] find nihilism in the implication that, because the choice of values is outside rational method and hence presumably arbitrary, the ordering of life by some kind of hierarchical principles is impossible. Some pragmatists, though hostile to metaphysics, hope to verify values scientifically, at least as "ends in view," and so reject the value-fact dichotomy.

Arnold Brecht has examined this whole question in his ambitious *Political Theory: The Foundations of Twentieth Century Political Thought* (1959). He vigorously asserts that the value-fact dichotomy does not mean and did not mean to Weber the suspension of critical judgment in inquiry pertaining to values nor does it make impossible an operative hierarchy of values. In his article "Die 'Objectivität' in sozialwissenschaftlicher und sozialpolitischer Erkenntnis" (Objectivity in Social-scientific and Socio-political Knowledge, 1904) Weber explicitly says that his position "is certainly not that value judgments are to be withdrawn from scientific discussion in general. . . . Practical action . . . would always reject

such a proposition." Again, "criticism is not to be suspended in the presence of value judgments. The problem is rather what is the meaning and purpose of the scientific criticism of ideals and value judgments."[5] What "value-free" science could do for values was to examine the rationality of *means* to any given posited *end* and to examine the probable consequences of any policy. To this extent Weber's position has something in common with pragmatism. But it is in every case the personal conscience of the acting individual that decides what to do with this knowledge. "An empirical science cannot tell anyone what he *ought* to do, but rather what he *can* do and, under certain circumstances, what he wishes to do."[6]

But what those who would make Weber into a scientific pragmatist forget is that the value-fact dichotomy as a logical proposition was meant not only to protect science from the intrusions of warping values but to protect the realm of personal affirmation from spurious scientific direction. The methodological problem becomes acute only when we take account of the personal affirmations of the individual scholar, for to say that he will stoically do the best he can to keep his own feelings out of the investigation does not answer all the questions in the field of social studies. As revealed in Weber's studies of Chinese culture or in his *Protestant Ethic and the Spirit of Capitalism* (1922), it is necessary to immerse oneself in the ethos of the culture actually to feel the culture. The result is a profound methodological tension.

This methodological tension was reflected in—possibly created by—the extreme psychological tensions Weber felt in himself and, more importantly for our concerns, reflected also in the substance of his descriptive conclusions. Whereas Marx could see ideas as

---

[4] See Leo Strauss, *Natural Right and History* (Chicago: Univ. of Chicago Press, 1953), Ch. 2, and Eric Voegelin, *The New Science of Politics* (Univ. of Chicago Press, 1952), pp. 13–22.

[5] Quoted in Brecht, *Political Theory: The Foundations of Twentieth Century Political Thought* (Princeton: Princeton Univ. Press, 1959), p. 223. See also *Max Weber on the Methodology of the Social Sciences* (1922), trans. by Edward A. Shils and Henry A. Finch (New York: Free Press, 1949). Originally trained in law, Weber was a professor at Berlin, Freiburg, and Heidelberg.

[6] Quoted *ibid.*, p. 225.

mere reflections of social interests and Nietzsche could see ideas as reflections of psychic interests, Weber could see the interdependence, the correspondence, and the tensions between ideas in history and interests in history.[7] The satisfactions and simplifications of single-factor analyses were not to be his.

One of the best known of Weber's projects was the development of an "ideal-type" bureaucratic structure, that is, the distillation of the essence of bureaucracy from the murky vapors of contemporary historical reality—actually, the term "descriptive model" might be closer to our understanding than "ideal type." He worked out various principles (centralization, integration, hierarchy, qualification for office, standardization of forms, etc.), by which casual organization became bureaucratized organization. The one term that would describe the whole process was "rationalization." This in turn was seen as itself the tendency of the whole of modern industrial society.[8] Weber distinguished three types of leaders: the traditional, such as a hereditary monarch; the "charismatic," the leader touched by a divine spark who galvanizes his followers; and the bureaucratic, who control superior organization. The last type, he felt, was coming to dominate more and more in a modern world of big organizations.

Here again Weber's tensions, which may today have their counterpart in popular feeling, are apparent. He admired the efficiency of bureaucratic leadership but felt that this efficiency and orderliness were achieved at the expense of "the disenchantment of the world," a loss of heroic grandeur. "The fate of the classical hero was that he could never overcome contingency or *fortuna;* the special irony of the modern hero is that he struggles in a world where contingency has been routed by bureaucratized procedures and nothing remains for the hero to contend against."[9] In the famous essay "Politics as a Vocation" this conflict manifests itself between the new bureaucratic party official and the politician-leader who is part hero—or would-be hero. And there is internal conflict within the politician who acts on the "ethic of responsibility" while acknowledging an "ethic of ultimate ends." Somewhat like Weber himself, the politician—the real politician, not the nine out of ten who are "windbags"—must be one who can accomplish the almost impossible combination of passionate involvement in the issues of his day (for only this attracts followers) and the cool detachment to see where the real power is (for only this produces success). Such a man will see and appreciate the "ethic of ultimate ends," the call to perfection, even if he cannot live by it:

it is immensely moving when a *mature* man—no matter whether old or young in years—is aware of a responsibility for the consequences of his conduct and really feels such responsibility with heart and soul. He then acts by following an ethic of responsibility and somewhere he reaches the point when he says: "Here I stand; I can do no other." That is something genuinely human and moving. And every one of us who is not spiritually dead must realize the possibility of finding himself at some time in that position. In so far as this is true, an ethic of ultimate ends and an ethic of responsibility are not absolute contrasts but rather supplements, which only in unison can constitute a genuine man—a man who *can* have the "calling for politics."[10]

Like Durkheim, Weber saw the moral

[7] H. H. Gerth and C. Wright Mills, in the Introduction to their edition of *From Max Weber: Essays in Sociology* (London: Routledge & Kegan Paul, 1948), p. 62. The statement is well illustrated in Weber's *Protestant Ethic and the Spirit of Capitalism*, trans. by Talcott Parsons (London: Allen & Unwin, 1930), in which Weber shows how the Calvinists' passion for otherworldly blessedness and their ascetic discipline made possible this-worldly capitalist accumulation and a remarkable degree of materialistic success.

[8] See *The Theory of Social and Economic Organization*, trans. by A. M. Henderson and Talcott Parsons (New York: Oxford Univ. Press, 1947).

[9] Sheldon Wolin, *Politics and Vision* (Boston: Houghton Mifflin, 1960), p. 423.

[10] Gerth and Mills, p. 127. An important American follower of Weber and Mannheim who, like them, tried to combine scientific and moral impulses was C. Wright Mills. See his *The Sociological Imagination* (New York: Oxford Univ. Press, 1959); Irving Horowitz, ed., *Power, Politics, and People* (New York: Ballantine Books, 1963); and the Introduction to his anthology,

element in society as that most worthy of study; but even more than Durkheim did he appreciate the quality of ambiguity and mystery in social morality, a quality, he was aware, that might be destroyed by the very methodology he espoused.

Pareto

No such qualms inhibited Vilfredo Pareto (1848–1923), professor of political economy at the University of Lausanne and one-time teacher of Mussolini. Pareto was so bent upon becoming scientific and detached in his study of society that he fell into the trap of cynicism, holding little sacred but his own views. This post-Machiavelli Machiavellianism had a certain vogue among hard-boiled social scientists of the complacent twenties and frantic thirties. The urge to "see through" our fellows, what Reisman would later call the "inside-dopester" mentality, is no doubt always a factor in social science and Pareto, quite apart from whatever influence he may have had on fascism, exemplified this mentality. He was scornful of natural law, metaphysics, and a priori reasoning in general.[11] But Pareto's own social views got in the way of the pure detachment he no doubt genuinely sought.[12] He was attracted to logical fallacy in the collective thought of the world as a moth is attracted to flame and he pointed out fallacies with such thoroughness that some readers wondered if logical thought was humanly possible. He opposed democracy, humanitarianism, and socialism as naive and futile. But, clearly, social stability was

his implicit good and capitalism was his favorite economic system.

All this is not to say that Pareto's theoretical work was negligible. Although the Pareto vogue has passed, his distinction between "residues," "derivatives," and "derivations" still holds interest. Homans and Curtis illustrate the relationship by means of a triangle. Angle *A* is what inclines men to action—"sentiments," "instincts," and "drives." The words are immaterial but Pareto generally preferred "sentiments." Angle *B* is the action itself. Angle *C* is what men say about what they do. Since what men say influences what sentiments they feel and possibly act upon, the triangle is closed from *C* to *A* as elsewhere; all angles interact on each other. This is social reality as Pareto sees it, a network of interactions against which a search for unilateral causation is futile. The most that the social scientist can hope to do is describe certain relationships in human behavior, what might be called variables and functions.[13]

The uniformities that can be observed, whether of action or speech, Pareto called "residues," that is, the things that have *remained* constant in variable phenomena. (He also lapses at times into a looser usage in which "residues" is almost a synonym for "sentiments"—the *A* of the triangle.) The things men say about what they do—the *C* of the triangle—are "derivatives." Reluctantly, Pareto was forced to recognize that some of the derivatives should also be called residues, for there are uniformities of speech and behavior that can be observed. The rest of the derivatives, which he called "derivations," are what we would call rationalizations, nice words that do not really affect our behavior. This designation applied to almost all historical political theories.

The object of all this was not simply to express in other language the belief that most of what men said and wrote was irrelevant nonsense—though this motive may have been present. It was to display a kind of episte-

---

Images of Man: The Classic Tradition in Sociological Thinking (New York: Braziller, 1960).

[11] His scorn may have been a displacement of some of the hostility Pareto showed toward his idealistic father. The senior Pareto had been exiled from Italy for his support of Mazzini's liberal *Risorgimento* movement.

[12] To help assure this detachment, most of the historical illustrations in Pareto's monumental *Trattato di sociologia* (1916) were drawn from ancient and medieval times, even though their import was often contemporary. The English translation of this work is Arthur Livingston, ed., *The Mind and Society* (New York: Harcourt, Brace & World, 1935).

[13] George Homans and Charles P. Curtis, Jr., *An Introduction to Pareto* (New York: Knopf, 1934), Ch. 4.

mological self-denial, a recognition that the scientific observer must work within the limits of his observation and the student of society cannot go much beyond words and overt actions. The method of residues was one way of canceling out the fortuitous cause at the same time one disregarded the irrelevant utterance. It was a way of getting at what really could be known. Pareto was willing to dismiss much of reality in order to get one part of it in an iron grip. And it must be admitted he did thus manage to conceive of society as a system without the organic or mechanistic metaphors characteristic of most such attempts.

We need not discuss the elaborate extrapolations of Pareto's system—the six classes of residues, the four classes of derivations, or the attempts at graphic representation of society as an equilibrium situation. We may note in passing the "circulation of elites." With a certain fatalism Pareto added to the many theories of inevitable elite rule the view that elites are never permanent but are continually being displaced from below by rising classes. None, however, can disrupt for long the basic social equilibrium and survival is the only utilitarian value they or the system can know.[14]

Mannheim

A far more optimistic yet in one way more profound political sociologist of twen-

tieth-century Europe was Karl Mannheim (1893–1947). Mannheim posed the problem of historical relativism more acutely than any other contemporary social scientist yet, ironically, none struggled with greater determination to escape from its implications. Mannheim's most important work was *Ideology and Utopia,* 1929,[15] the first major statement of his "sociology of knowledge."

After the breakdown of feudalism, Mannheim argued, philosophers, as always, reflected the social situation in which they found themselves. Modern epistemology and psychology approached the individual mind as if it could be separated from group influences. Infected by an individualistic and rationalistic bias, a Descartes or a Locke thought he could approach the truth of the mind free of the superstitions and authoritarian restraints of the past. But, says Mannheim, knowledge is partly a group product that presupposes a community and a "collective unconscious."

Even mathematical knowledge, perhaps the least obviously influenced by group norms, is a function of such norms. But the "irrational foundation of rational knowledge" is most conspicuously demonstrated by political thought:

Politics is conflict and tends increasingly to become a life-and-death struggle. . . .

Political discussion possesses a character fundamentally different from academic discussion. It seeks not only to be in the right but also to demolish the basis of its opponent's social and intellectual existence. Political discussion therefore penetrates more profoundly into the existential foundation of thinking. . . .

In political discussion in modern democracies where ideas were more clearly representative of certain groups, the social and existential determination of thought became easily visible. In principle it was politics which first discov-

---

[14] *Mind and Society,* Vol. 4, pp. 1787–90. Two noted scholars of the inevitable elite-rule persuasion who were contemporaries of Pareto were Gaetano Mosca (1858–1941) and Roberto Michels (1876–1936). See Mosca's *Elementi di scienza politica* (1896), trans. by Hannah D. Kahn as *The Ruling Class,* Arthur Livingston, ed. (New York: McGraw-Hill, 1939). Livingston, the editor of both Pareto and Mosca, claims their ideas were arrived at independently (*Ibid.,* pp. xxxix–xxxix). See also James H. Meisel, *The Myth of the Ruling Class* (Ann Arbor: Univ. of Michigan Press, 1957). Michels's famous "iron law of oligarchy," expounded despite his democratic leanings, is found in *Political Parties: A Sociological Study of the Oligarchical Tendencies of Modern Democracy* (1915), trans. by Eden and Cedar Paul (New York: Free Press, 1949). See also his *First Lectures in Political Sociology* (1927), trans. by Alfred De Grazia (Minneapolis: Univ. of Minnesota Press, 1949).

[15] *Ideology and Utopia,* trans. by Louis Wirth and Edward Shils (New York: Harcourt, Brace & World, 1949). Subsequent quotations are from this edition. The book consists of a translation of *Ideologie und Utopie,* a 1931 article, and a specially written introduction. Mannheim was a professor at Heidelberg, Frankfurt, and, after the Nazis came to power, the London School of Economics.

ered the sociological method in the study of intellectual phenomena. Basically it was in political struggles that for the first time men became aware of the unconscious collective motivations which had always guided the direction of thought.[16]

If, then, all thought is socially conditioned, there is no fixed point in historical existence by reference to which all thought may be judged. We are all prisoners of the age in which we live. Relativism was, of course, not Mannheim's invention. But he pushed its implications a bit further. The older relativism recognized that the content of human thought was relative to the social position of the thinker but took for granted that the structure of thought was constant and could be understood categorically by a permanently true epistemology. Yet, "Actually, epistemology is as intimately enmeshed in the social process as is the totality of our thinking." To differentiate it from the older relativism, Mannheim called his view "relationism."

Relationism signifies merely that all of the elements of meaning in a given situation have reference to one another and derive their significance from this reciprocal interrelationship in a given frame of thought. Such a system of meanings is possible and valid only in a given type of historical existence, to which, for a time, it furnishes appropriate expression. When the social situation changes, the system of norms to which it had previously given birth ceases to be in harmony with it.[17]

The transience of human thought revealed by this position would seem to pose insuperable barriers to significant social reform, not only with reference to obtaining rational guidance of the direction of reform but with reference to the elemental problem of maintaining community morale in the face of cosmic ambiguity. It was to precisely this problem that Mannheim gave the bulk of his energies. The morale problem had

been faced many times before. In every age, Mannheim could easily demonstrate, certain beliefs, suppositions, and myths had been absolutized and used as instruments for leadership, as tools whereby contingent policies were given the sanction of eternal truths. Where these were used to maintain the *status quo*, Mannheim called them "ideologies." Where they were used to change the social system, he called them "utopias." (We need to remember that the vernacular use of "ideology" would include both "ideology" and "utopia" in Mannheim's sense.)

The thorny problem was how to achieve some kind of rational guidance for the social scientist or the would-be leader. How could he avoid being the victim of his own group's ideology, his own false absolutes? Mannheim's first answer to this was to recognize them. The more one is able in retrospect to probe one's own motives and interests "the more it is apparent that this empirical procedure (in the social sciences at least) can be carried on only on the basis of certain meta-empirical, ontological, and metaphysical judgments . . . He who makes no decisions has no questions to raise."

It is not possible to prove the validity of these basic ontological assumptions; but it may be possible to recognize some of them and thereby cast light on differing systems of thought so that they may be seen more clearly for what they are. In this way group, class, and national biases may be slowly stripped away so that the social scientist can determine "which of all the ideas current are really valid in a given situation"—although in a footnote Mannheim admits that "exposure of ideological and utopian elements in thought is effective in destroying only those ideas with which we ourselves are not too intimately identified."

It can be argued that this rather pragmatic "validity" is nothing but old-fashioned rational truth by a different name, now limited more severely than ever to the rare social scientist—could Aristotle have been such? —who is most fortunate in purging himself of bias. The description of such a person, a member of the so-called socially unattached

---

[16] *Ibid.*, pp. 34–35.
[17] *Ibid.*, p. 76. Marx's influence on Mannheim is clear in this passage.

intelligentsia, comes remarkably close to a description of Mannheim himself.

Yet however detached and however intellectual the scholar on whom Mannheim depends, this scholar cannot really lead us out of the dilemma of relationism Mannheim has described. If you are asked whether a painting of a person you have never seen is a good likeness, you have no way of answering. And it matters not how many paintings of him you see. You still cannot answer until you see the person himself. Mannheim's "valid" ideas would seem to be very much like the unseen portrait subject. The "socially unattached intellectual" is only offering one more portrait, a composite of all the rest.[18]

Without trying to summarize Mannheim's provocative discussion of the requirements for a science of politics we can say that, despite what might seem to be the tragic implications of his relationism, he is optimistic rather than pessimistic over the possibilities of such a science. Further, he contends that to the degree that a science of politics is possible politics in the sense of group conflict will disappear and ideological warfare will be replaced by rational "administration," a "purely technical" operation.

Mannheim treats the means to this end of endless means in a number of writings, most notably *Man and Society in an Age of Reconstruction* (1940) and *Freedom, Power, and Democratic Planning* (1950). He argues that democracy and planning are compatible and even necessary, that an open society as far as ultimate ends are concerned is consistent with the rational direction of means. Such rational "nonpolitical" direction would, however, require both increased centralization and a deflection of the "artificial" consumer wants stimulated by the "psychological anarchy of liberal capitalism."[19]

Everything connected with the reorganization of industry and the encouragement and discouragement of investment will take precedence, for the effect on the whole cycle is more important than the satisfaction of individual desires. . . . People will learn that consumer choice is not sacred and the entrepreneur will find that he has more control over his business, if he can be guided in his investments by a central plan.[20]

Mannheim hoped the transition could be accomplished "without much fuss or propaganda."

Whether taking the form of Pareto's cynical conservatism or Mannheim's optimistic reformism, the common tendency of European and much of American sociology has been antiliberal. The concept of the group has gained the ascendancy over the concept of the autonomous individual.

While European sociology was giving political science a new appreciation of group influences in the formation of individual values, an important European philosophical movement was doing its utmost to free the methodology of science, including social science, from the taint of subjective values.

LOGICAL POSITIVISM

The historical roots of positivism go back through Comte and Mill and Hume but the springboard of action in the twentieth century was clearly the so-called Vienna Circle, which grew up under the leadership of Moritz Schlick at the University of Vienna in the early 1920s. The influence of the group was dispersed westward by the migrations of Otto Neurath to England, Rudolph Carnap to the University of Chicago, Felix Kaufmann to the New School for Social Research in New York, and, via Berlin, Hans Reichenbach to the University of California at Los Angeles. Other centers developed around Ludwig Wittgenstein at Cambridge University and A. J. Ayer at Oxford. The terminology changed to "logical

---

[18] I am indebted for the portrait analogy to Gustav Bergmann, *The Metaphysics of Logical Positivism* (London: Longmans, Green, 1954), p. 316.

[19] *Man and Society in an Age of Reconstruction*, trans. by Edward Shils (New York: Harcourt, Brace & World, 1940), p. 352.

[20] *Ibid.*, p. 347.

empiricism," or "neopositivism," or simply "analytic philosophy" but, whatever the labels, few doubt that they designate a major intellectual movement.

Logical positivism represents one of the most consistent attempts to transfer the rigorous methodology of the physical sciences to philosophic inquiry, if not, indeed, to make the two disciplines one. (Schlick, like his predecssor at Vienna, Ernst Mach—jet pilots will know the name if not the man—was trained in physics.) To begin with the negative, logical positivists rejected as hopelessly imprecise the formulations of "speculative" philosophy, the metaphysical questions that have been the chief occupation of philosophers since the classical period: the one and the many, the nature of reality, the problem of evil, and the nature of the true, the beautiful, and the good. These are put aside as pseudoquestions, beyond the realm of meaning. Logical positivists deny not only that "eternal questions" are eternal; they deny that they are questions. In a striking reversal of Plato's distinction between knowledge and opinion, logical positivists hold that answers to these alleged questions can never be more than opinion, for "meaningful propositions," the only basis of knowledge, are those that can be verified by the methods of the natural sciences, that is, experimentation with data derived from direct sensory perception and/or logical inference from those data. Any statement—such as "God is love"—for which there is no possibility of refutation by appeal to specific empirical data is held to have no grounds for confirmation, either. Early members of the Circle held that conclusive scientific verification was the only condition of significance. Ludwig Wittgenstein, whose *Tractatus Logico-Philosophicus* (1922) was a bible for the group, there held—he later recanted—that the complete body of natural science would exhaust the totality of true propositions. Later disciples have softened to the extent of accepting as sufficient a high degree of probability and admitting a few nonscientific statements into their lexicon.

All acknowledged positivists agree with the basic tenet of the *Tractatus* that philosophy is not a subject matter but an activity. Its purpose is not to construct propositions (the scientist does this) or to ascribe value to them (everyone does this) but to clarify them. The analysis of the logical syntax of language, thus, has been one of their central occupations. For the positivist there are two fundamental types of "meaningful statements." One is the empirical, "I see the satellite," and the other is the logical, "two plus two is four." Statements of value, "I like the satellite. The satellite is good," fall into neither of these categories. At one point it was argued that statements of value have no empirical content or logical structure. They are expressions of emotional preference. However much they must live as *men* by valuing, as *philosophers,* the logical positivists felt that they were bound to regard value statements as meaningless—one is tempted to say as valueless. The stringency with which they identified this Weberian distinction between the "positive" fact and values with the distinction between knowledge and nonknowledge is what most distinguishes them from their next of kin, the pragmatists. More recently, analytic philosophers have been breaking down these simple fact-value dichotomies. Finally, logical positivism is marked by the tendency to avoid the question of causation and substitute the concept of function, to speak of correlations and probabilities rather than causes.

The continual reduction of traditional philosophic questions to questions of scientific methodology would seem to have the effect of particularizing inquiry to such an extent that broad-gauge generalizations become impossible. Some critics of positivism have felt that this was the case. Yet, despite this tendency, the drive toward the unity of all scientific thought has been powerful within the logical positivist movement, as shown by the *International Encyclopedia of Unified Science* begun in 1938 under the editorship of Neurath, Carnap, and Charles W. Morris.

To speak of logical-positivist political theory is to speak of a movement that tends to conceive of political theory as generalized political science, as descriptive and hypothetical rather than "normative." This tendency may be seen in the work of three prominent American political scientists—Herbert S. Simon, Harold D. Lasswell, and Robert A. Dahl. Such influence should not be taken as "explaining" them or as characterizing the whole of their work. But when we judge by their willingness to bother with traditional political philosophy, we may possibly be justified in using them here as, respectively, left-wing, middle-of-the-road, and right-wing representatives of the logical positivist influence.

Simon

Herbert Simon (1916–   ), professor of administration at the Carnegie Institute of Technology, is a social scientist often better understood by mathematicians than by colleagues in his own discipline. His introduction to what we might call scientific theorizing was by way of the problems of administrative decision-making[21] but he can hardly be restricted to a designation more narrow than social theorist. Of his essays in *Models of Man* he says, "economists are aware of them chiefly as they impinge upon the theory of the firm, social psychologists and sociologists as they relate to the small group theory, learning theorists as they relate to problem solving, political scientists as they relate to the phenomena of power, and statisticians as they relate to the identification problem."[22] The two basic concerns that unite these apparently diverse threads are, he says, the "mechanism of influence" and the "mechanism of choice." In both cases, he has arrived at a middle ground between the assumptions that man has a high degree of rationality (economics) and that man's behavior is basically a product of emotions (psychology). But the median assumption is it-

[21] See his *Administrative Behavior* (1947), 2nd ed. (New York: Macmillan, 1956), and, with James G. March, *Organizations* (New York: Wiley, 1958).

[22] *Models of Man* (New York: Holt, Rinehart and Winston, 1957), p. VII. Subsequent quotations are from this edition.

self only an assumption and Simon, to his credit, does not claim that his models are more than models. This epistemological self-denial is no doubt a reflection of his acknowledged debt to logical positivism, especially on the matter of causation.

Accepting the Humean critique of causation as necessary connection and wishing to avoid the ontological overtones of traditional views on the subject, Simon nevertheless finds that "working scientists" cannot seem to get along without using the word "cause." His aim is to make the word "operational" by keeping its usage strictly within the logical model, thus implying, as we have seen, nothing of necessity about the empirical world. In other words, he is willing to say, "Sentence *A* stands in a causal relation to sentence *B*," but he is not willing to say, "That which is denoted by sentence *A causes* that which is denoted by sentence *B*." So conceived, "Causality is an asymmetrical relation among certain variables, or subset of variables, in a self-contained structure. There is no necessary connection between the asymmetry of this relation and the asymmetry in time"—although, he goes on to say, it may be useful to assume that "lagged" relations are causal relations.

What does this have to do with politics? Of course, any contribution to the methodology of the social sciences is a contribution to political theory. But the connection is much closer than that. In the first part of *Models of Man*, Simon attempts to relate three questions that, on the face of it, seem wholly unrelated:

(1) How should we define influence, power, and authority, and measure the strength of influence relations? This is a question central to political science.

(2) ". . . in determining the relationship between two variables by the method of least squares, which variable should be taken as independent and which as dependent?" This is a problem in statistics.

(3) If a prediction in the social sciences is published so that the people whose behavior is predicted know about it, is the prediction thereby falsified? This is a long-standing

problem of general social science methodology.

It was about 1950, Simon says, that he began to put these questions together:

influence, power, and authority are all intended as *asymmetrical* relations. When we say that *A* has power over *B*, we do not mean to imply that *B* has power over *A*. The mathematical counterpart to this asymmetrical relation appeared to be the distinction between independent and dependent variable—the independent variable determines the dependent, and not the converse. But in algebra, the distinction between independent and dependent variable is purely conventional—we can always rewrite our equations without altering their content in such a way as to reverse their roles. Thus, if $y = ax$, it is equally true that $x = by$, where $b = 1/a$. Neither way of writing the equation is preferred to the other.

When I had stated the question in this form —as a problem in giving operational meaning to the asymmetry of the relation between independent and dependent variable—it became clear that it was identical with the general problem of defining a *causal relation* between two variables. That is to say, for the assertion, "*A* has power over *B*," we can substitute the assertion, "*A*'s behavior causes *B*'s behavior." If we can define the causal relation, we can define influence, power, or authority, and vice versa.[23]

In other words, Simon is seeking and thinks he has found a method for handling data on power relations at a very high degree of generality, so high, in fact, that the same operation that isolates the independent variable among a collection of abstract integers can isolate the power-holder and, given the right data, measure his power. We can scarcely follow through on the implications of this juxtaposition of the political with the statistical and, indeed, it cannot be said that Simon does; but obviously handling descriptions of power relations at this level not only of generality but of precision would have far-reaching implications for the development of a unified body of scientific social knowledge.

There is still, however, question (3) and its correlates. Power relations cannot be dealt with

like inert algebraic relations because, while abstract symbols *A* and *B* may be perfectly asymmetrical, Mr. Able and Mr. Baker are never in a wholly asymmetrical or unilateral relationship. There is almost always the softening effect of compassion or the hardening effect of fear. There are what Friedrich calls "anticipated reactions" or what others call "feedback," which make the hypothecated asymmetry (or symmetry) of human relations in fact ambiguous. Human beings may, for example, turn honest prophecies into self-fulfilling prophecies by conforming to what is predicted of them. With the help of an elaborate statistical exercise, Simon has claimed to have minimized the descriptive errors resulting from this tendency. He also has some useful suggestions on how political scientists can beat the rule of anticipated reactions by taking advantage of the errors of public officials.

Obviously, what Simon gives us is not the confirmation of substantive hypotheses about politics but the confirmation of statistical methods of analysis that may give us more precise knowledge about politics. That more can be done with the mathematical approach to social phenomena goes without saying. That it can do as much as positivistic admirers of natural science think it can may be another question. "Mathematics," says Simon, "has become the dominant language of the natural sciences not because it is quantitative—a common delusion—but primarily because it permits clear and vigorous reasoning about phenomena too complex to be handled in words. This advantage of mathematics over cruder languages should prove of even greater significance in the social sciences, which deal with phenomena of the greatest complexity, than it has in the natural sciences."[24] Whether the subtleties of English or any other verbal

---

[23] *Ibid.*, p. 5.

[24] Herbert J. Storing has given us a vigorous critique of Simon's methodology in *Essays on the Scientific Study of Politics* (New York: Holt, Rinehart and Winston, 1963), Ch. 2. He is particularly critical of Simon's inexplicit assumptions that "rationality" can be limited to the choice of operational means and that mathematical social science can usefully proceed without examining fundamental assumptions as to the nature of man.

language are as crude as Simon suggests is open to question. And whether his optimism concerning what the social sciences will become is free of the distorting influence of his own infectious enthusiasm for mathematical manipulations seems quite dubious. But, then, without enthusiastic confrontation, would we take seriously even the prospects of a mathematical political theory, as now we must?

Lasswell

Harold D. Lasswell (1902–), professor of law and political science at Yale, stepped into the positivists' circle with *Power and Society: A Framework for Political Inquiry* (1950),[25] a kind of *Tractatus Logico-Philosophicus* for political scientists. The book was written with Abraham Kaplan, a former philosophic colleague of Reichenbach. Lasswell had earlier made his mark as an empirically oriented theorist with his psychoanalytic study, *Psychopathology and Politics* 1930), and the more widely read *Politics: Who Gets What, When, How* (1936), an elite model analysis emphasizing as motive forces of politics the drives of income, safety, and deference. Lasswell is known for his studies of political language and the application of Freudian concepts to politics, especially the judicial decision-making process. Like others influenced by positivism, Lasswell has been attracted to the world of science and the behavioral sciences. It may be more than merely accidental that his presidential address to the American Political Science Association in 1956 was entitled "The Political Science of Science" and called attention to the discipline's neglect of policy problems and opportunities created by scientific change.

Power and Society is a series of defini-

tions and propositions dovetailed together in such a way that an almost self-contained language results. For example: to know what it means to say that authority is "formal power" we must know that *power* is "participation in the making of decisions," a *decision* is "a policy involving severe sanctions," and a *policy* is "a projected program of goal values and practices." We must also know that *formal* is "pertaining to the political formula," the *political formula* is "the part of the political myth describing and prescribing in detail the social structure," the *political myth* is "the pattern of basic political symbols current in a society," and so on. For their purposes it might have been better if Lasswell and Kaplan had used much more esoteric symbols than English words for the subjects of their definitions. When students genuinely try to use this set of definitions as a "framework for political inquiry," they almost always lapse into ordinary English from time to time, so that "decision" or "formula" on one page has a Lasswellian meaning and on another page a more common meaning. The result is often hopeless confusion. Lasswell and Kaplan cannot really be blamed if others misuse their terminology; but even in natural science the most important words are defined by usage and not by pronouncement. Impatience with ambiguity seems to be a characteristic of modern positivism and indeed the very purpose of a precisely defined (and authoritative) lexicon and a logically interrelated set of operational propositions reflects the positivistic tenor of the enterprise.

The positivistic orientation is also evident in the authors' conception of values. Their commitment to "objective" analysis requires a prefatory confession of their own subjective values ("those of the citizen of a society that aspires toward freedom") along with the disclaimer that these values will not affect the book's findings. As between empirical propositions and value judgments, "Only statements of the first kind are explicitly formulated in the present work."[26] Despite the

[25] See also his *World Politics and Personal Insecurity* (New York: McGraw-Hill, 1935), *Power and Personality* (New York: Norton, 1948), and *The Analysis of Political Behavior: An Empirical Approach* (New York: Oxford Univ. Press, 1948). Kaplan's own contribution to social science methodology is the significant book *The Conduct of Inquiry* (San Francisco: Chandler, 1964).

[26] *Power and Society: A Framework for Political Inquiry* (New Haven: Yale Univ. Press, 1950), p. XIII.

fact that this book is in large part concerned with the operation of certain "welfare values" and "deference values" in the political arena, these are viewed from the outside, so to speak; they are viewed as "goal events" whose fulfillment can be checked off by a detached observer. "Value" itself is one of the undefined terms of the lexicon.

Again, as in the case of Simon, what this positivistic endeavor offers is not so much significant knowledge, not so much the fruits of research, but stimulation to research. In natural science, system-building has come after the amassing of a pressing quantity of non–self-evident or even contradictory "facts." In political science, as many critics of this book have pointed out, system-building has seemed to come before the facts. There is no doubt more attraction in being a political Einstein than in being a political Michelson and Morley. Yet it would be unfair to suggest that this criticism lies with particular force against Lasswell. Despite *Power and Society,* he cannot be written off as a nonempirical empiricist. More than many other theorists he has immersed himself in concrete studies within what he calls the "policy sciences," thereby qualifying himself as an empiricist as well as a theorist of empiricism. He has deigned to deal with quite ordinary historical and even impressionistic data.[27] He has encouraged more than one approach to political reality. Positivism can easily become a cult. If Lasswell has been one of the leading cult figures, he has at least kept himself from becoming a cultist.

Dahl

Robert A. Dahl (1915–   ), 1967 president of the American Political Science Association,

is a political scientist at Yale who would no doubt shy away from the designation positivist, and we should not quibble about it. Whereas Simon is not much concerned with thinkers who thought before the days of the chi-square test, whereas Lasswell nods to Plato, Locke, and Rousseau and puts them under the heading of political doctrine, Dahl pays political theorists of the past the honor of analyzing them into a shambles. He is positivistic perhaps only in the sense that the logical analysis of language is his critical weapon and the reconstruction of propositions to make them "operational" and "testable" is his constructive task. Although *Politics, Economics, and Welfare* (1953), written with his economics colleague Charles E. Lindblom, would mark him as a system-builder, *A Preface to Democratic Theory* (1956)[28] is a more modest venture, yet of considerable significance. In that work Dahl subjects the allegedly democratic theories of Madison, Rousseau, and others to meticulous linguistic analysis. The logical implications of words, phrases, and sentences are drawn out, in some cases reduced to nonverbal symbols, and compared with the implications of other words, phrases, and sentences. The result is that the Madisonian or natural-rights view of democracy and the Rousseauistic-majoritarian view of democracy—Dahl calls it populistic—look a bit tattered. Dahl does not belittle their historical significance, emotive import, or richness of language but he pitilessly exposes their defective logic and operational limitations.

After the demolition, Dahl turns to the constructive task of devising a concept of democracy precise enough to permit its meaningful application to a series of discrete,

[27] See his *National Security and Individual Freedom* (New York: McGraw-Hill, 1950). In a detailed critique, Robert Horwitz calls Lasswell a propagandist for "social control through science." The charge is overdramatized but some valid points are scored along the way (Storing, ed., *Essays on the Scientific Study of Politics,* Ch. 4). The whole Storing volume was subject to overheated attack by John Schaar and Sheldon Wolin and overheated defense by the authors in *American Political Science Review,* Vol. 57 (1963), pp. 125–60.

[28] See also Dahl's *Modern Political Analysis* (Englewood Cliffs, N. J.: Prentice-Hall, 1963), and his textbook *Pluralist Democracy in the United States* (Chicago: Rand McNally, 1967). His case study of New Haven, *Who Governs?* (New Haven: Yale Univ. Press, 1961), won the 1962 Woodrow Wilson Award of the American Political Science Association. The shortcomings of a purely descriptive science are criticized by Kariel, with Dahl as an example: "Dahl's approach precludes his identifying what New Haven might have been or what it might yet become" (*The Promise of Politics,* p. 109).

empirical events. The task is not easy and it cannot be said that Dahl altogether succeeds—but he certainly tries. His concept of "polyarchal democracy" is defined by a set of eight criteria with at least hypothetically quantifiable indices. He even provides a suggested classification of polyarchies: "egalitarian polyarchies" are those in which the eight conditions are scaled at values equal to or greater than 0.75; "nonegalitarian polyarchies" fall between 0.50 and 0.75; "oligarchies" between 0.25 and 0.50; and "dictatorships" below 0.25. If all this sounds a bit premature, or even futile, it must be said that Dahl is well aware of the hypothetical nature of what he is doing and tempers every proposition with a commendable awareness of the "real world." In fact, his great virtue is the degree to which he has sought to bridge the gap between traditional historical-political theories and the solid empirical data of hard-headed political researchers. The softening of the partisan positivist temper without loss of logical vigor and operationalism is a welcome contribution of Dahl's writings.

TOWARD A SCIENCE OF LAW

Jurisprudence is a complicated and heavily chronicled subject that has not figured prominently in these pages. Seventy-five years ago it would have been otherwise. Then the prevailing conception of the nature of political theory made it almost synonymous with legal theory. Today not only political theory but legal theory itself is heavily weighted with sociological and psychological terminology. The positivistic emphasis has been felt in law, too. But even as we say this, we must note that the trend is by no means unilateral. A reaction against legal positivism and the relativism it implies began almost as soon as it had reached full tide. The reaction took the form of a return to natural-law thinking, but not always natural law in traditional dress. The lawlessness of totalitarian-

ism accelerated the reaction. "In the secure days of constitutional order during the last century, there was a general inclination to transfer such [higher law] standards, even when recognized, from jurisprudence into ethics or religion. The lawless rule of totalitarian power has made it evident that jurisprudence once again must consider the development of such standards as one of its most essential tasks."[29]

German Positivism

Radbruch

A leader of the relativists was Gustav Radbruch (1878–1949)[30] of Heidelberg. His basic premise was that of the positivists, namely that a system built on value preferences must give up any claim to scientific validity. A science of law required, he felt, the development of a "system of systems" with no attempt to express preferences among them. Radbruch thereupon tried to describe and organize all previous types of legal theories around three presumably impartially chosen categories of value: the individual, human collectivities, and human works or culture. Significantly, the rise of Nazism, under which Radbruch personally suffered, led him to unfortunately uncompleted postwar attempts to overcome some of the limitations of relativism.

Kelsen

Another and better known legal positivist who has tried to purge his theory of all value

[29] Carl J. Friedrich, *The Philosophy of Law in Historical Perspective* (Chicago: Univ. of Chicago Press, 1958), p. 182.
[30] See his *Rechtsphilosophie*, 3rd ed., trans. by Kurt Wilk (Cambridge, Mass.: Harvard Univ. Press, Twentieth Century Legal Philosophy Series, Vol. 2, 1950). See also Anton-Hermann Chroust, "The Philosophy of Law of Gustav Radbruch," *Philosophical Review*, Vol. 53 (1944), pp. 23–45; *The Legal Philosophies of Lask, Radbruch and Dabin*, trans. by Kurt Wilk (Cambridge, Mass.: Harvard Univ. Press, Twentieth Century Legal Philosophy Series, Vol. 4, 1950); and Brecht, pp. 233–36 and 357–61.

judgments is Hans Kelsen (1881–   ),[31] father of the "pure theory of law." The "purity" is found in the system's complete formalism. Kelsen is as uninterested in the content of law as one can be. He is uninterested in speculations about the will behind law. Rather he takes for granted in any given society a basic norm (*Grundnorm*) with coercive sanctions behind it, from which flows everything that can be called law. He proceeds to develop a system of logical correlates built upon such a norm—whatever its specific content may be. In a sense, the whole operation is a tautology. It pretends to do no more than provide a structure that may help one think about law. There is no law but positive law and any state can be a *Rechtsstaat*. But since other organizations exercise coercive power over its members and law is wholly relative to such power, the boundaries of statehood are not altogether clear in Kelsen's system.

Kelsen has been a defender of philosophical relativism in its more extreme form and remains a forthright critic of natural-law doctrines. He argues that, if natural law were in any meaningful sense "self-evident," positive law would be superfluous; and if natural law is open to interpretation, the only interpretation that counts is that approved by the authorities established by positive law. He grants that natural-law doctrines may serve a function in giving people a sense of deep-seated moral justification as they obey laws. In this respect, natural law is a kind of Platonic myth: "That the natural-law doctrine, as it pretends, is able to determine in an objective way what is just, is a lie; but those who consider it useful may make use of it as a useful lie."[32]

Legal Realism

Less philosophically minded but also defenders of a form of legal positivism are the so-called legal realists of American jurisprudence. Their origins go back at least to Professor John Chipman Gray's *Nature and Sources of the Law* (1909) and the earthy naturalism of Justice Oliver Wendell Holmes' miscellaneous essays. A later candidate for the school would be Thurman Arnold, whose slightly sardonic *Symbols of Government* (1935) and *Folklore of Capitalism* (1937) disemboweled a number of sacred cows. Another representative would be Karl N. Llewellyn. His *Bramble Bush* (1930) instructed a whole generation of law students to think of law not as a collection of rules but as what officials—be they judges, clerks, or lawyers—actually do to settle disputes. "Law *is*, to the community, what law *does*."[33]

Frank

A legal realist deeply influenced by the findings of social science was Jerome Frank (1889-1957),[34] who found in Freudian psychology an explanation of the almost universal tendency to deify the law and dignify

[31] See his *General Theory of Law and the State*, trans. by Anders Wedberg (Cambridge, Mass.: Harvard Univ. Press, 1945). A former professor at Vienna, Kelsen has been in the United States since 1940. An important precursor of Kelsen was Stammler of Halle and Berlin, a leading neo-Kantian.

[32] "The Natural-Law Doctrine Before the Tribunal of Science," *Western Political Quarterly*, Vol. 2 (1949), p. 513. See also Kelsen's *What Is Justice?* (Berkeley: Univ. of Cal. Press, 1957).

[33] *The Bramble Bush; On Our Law and Its Study*, 3rd ed. (New York: Oceana Publications, 1960), p. 91. In a foreword to a 1950 edition of the book, Llewellyn chides those who made so much of "the teapot tempest in which 'realism' (which was and still is an effort at more effective legal technology) was mistaken for a philosophy and made the scapegoat for all the sins (real and suppressed) of administrators and autocrats and the ungodly in general" (pp. 9–10). See also Llewellyn, ed., *Jurisprudence: Realism in Theory and Practice* (Chicago: Univ. of Chicago Press, 1962). A critique of legal realism is found in Lon L. Fuller, *The Law in Quest of Itself* (Cambridge, Mass: Harvard Univ. Press, 1940). More sympathetic treatments are in Morris R. Cohen, *Reason and Law* (New York: Free Press, 1950), Chs. 3 and 8, and Edwin N. Garlan, *Legal Realism and Justice* (New York: Columbia Univ. Press, 1941).

[34] See Frank, *Law and the Modern Mind* (Gloucester, Mass.: Peter Smith, 1930); *If Men were Angels* (New York: Harper & Row, 1942); *Courts on Trial; Myth and Reality in American Justice* (Princeton: Princeton Univ. Press, 1949); and Barbara F. Kristein, ed., *A Man's Reach; the Philosophy of Judge Jerome Frank* (New York: Macmillan, 1965). See also Julius Paul, *The Legal Realism of Jerome N. Frank* (The Hague: Nijhoff, 1959).

judges beyond their normal human stature. Frank's aim was to use the resources of social science to demythologize the popular image of the legal system in order that mature, that is, modern, men will accept responsibility for the fact that law is really made and not discovered: ". . . this Blackstonian lie (or myth) serves to shield the courts from popular understanding and criticism by making their work a mystery; and, in a democracy, no part of government should be mysterious."[35]

For Frank, fact-finding is the basis of justice. Yet American courts, he thought, were not well equipped to get the facts. The trouble with relying only on "the facts," however, is that a rulelessness can develop that encourages inconsistency and can even verge on the arbitrary when a line of cases is compared. Frank came to realize this: "From 'rule-skepticism' Frank moved on to 'fact-skepticism' which allowed him to salvage all the legalistic values without having to abandon his war against the traditional court system."[36]

[35] Frank, "A Sketch of an Influence," in Paul Sayre, ed., Interpretations of Modern Legal Philosophy, Essays in Honor of Roscoe Pound (New York: Oxford Univ. Press, 1947), p. 233. Against these implied and explicit attacks on natural law, Catholic neo-Thomism maintained a variegated yet solid front. See Thomas E. Davitt, The Nature of Law (St. Louis: Herder, 1951); Giorgio Del Vecchio, Justice (Edinburgh: The University Press, 1952); Jacques Maritain, The Rights of Man and Natural Law, trans. by Doris C. Anson (New York: Scribner's, 1943); Heinrich Rommen, The Natural Law, trans. by Thomas Hanley (St. Louis: Herder, 1947); and Yves R. Simon, The Tradition of Natural Law: A Philosopher's Reflections, Vukan Kuic, ed. (New York: Fordham Univ. Press, 1965). Other important Catholic legal writers are Victor Cathrein, Francois Geny, and Jacques Leclerq. Other antipositivist writers sought an ethical basis for law without relying on traditional natural-law concepts. The Dutchman Hugo Krabbe found it in an instinctive sense of right in the community; the Frenchman Léon Duguit found it in solidarité.

[36] Judith Shklar, Legalism (Cambridge, Mass.: Harvard Univ. Press, 1964), p. 97. Miss Shklar goes on to argue that the passion for scientific expertise represented by Frank is, as a legal standard, as "ideological" as was natural law before it. The counterattack on legal positivism has come not only from the Thomists but from non-Catholic Christian theists like Eric Voegelin and

Pound

A more moderate position is exemplified in the United States by Roscoe Pound (1870–1964), the great Harvard law dean and founder of the "sociological" theory of law.[37] The essence of his position is that law is not, as it was for the nineteenth century, a set of deductions; it is, as Pound said, "social engineering." Law should be conceived always in light of the social conditions within which it is expected to operate. Pound criticized the way private litigation operating under an unrealistic but protective cloak of abstract individual rights was used to settle social issues of major importance to the community. Pound was the enemy of pharisaical artificiality, Germanic hair-splitting, and nostalgic devotion to natural-law doctrines. Above all, he took the social sciences seriously.

In one chapter of *Social Control Through Law* (1942) Pound sketches the changes in the conceptions of law characteristic of the twentieth century; the list reads like a statement of Pound's own tenets. This is not prejudicial reporting; it is a testament to his own influence. He mentions, for example, a

John Hallowell and from classical natural-law scholars coming out of a Jewish background like Leo Strauss and Harry Jaffa. For two scholarly debates in which, as usual, each side is brilliant but the issue is not squarely joined, see Felix Oppenheim, "The Natural Law Thesis: Affirmation or Denial?" Jaffa, "Comment on Oppenheim"; and Oppenheim, "Non-Cognitivist Rebuttal," American Political Science Review, Vol. 51 (1957), pp. 41–66; and Kelsen, "The Natural Law Doctrine Before the Tribunal of Science" and Edgar Bodenheimer, "The Natural Law Doctrine Before the Tribunal of Science: a Reply to Hans Kelsen," Western Political Quarterly, Vols. 2 and 3 (1949 and 1950), pp. 481–513 and 335–63, respectively.

[37] Sociological jurisprudence is obviously not without many antecedents, especially in the theories of Rudolf von Ihering and Ludwig Gumplowicz. Of Pound's many works see Contemporary Juristic Theory (Claremont, Calif.: Claremont Colleges, 1940); Social Control Through Law (New Haven: Yale Univ. Press, 1942); Justice According to Law (New Haven: Yale Univ. Press, 1951); and An Introduction to the Philosophy of Law (1924), rev. ed. (New Haven: Yale Univ. Press, 1954). Perhaps the classic example of Pound's attempt to relate legal abstraction to hard social realities was his article "Liberty of Contract," Yale Law Journal, Vol. 18 (1909), pp. 454–87.

pragmatic concern for function, legal action aiming at the satisfaction of concrete human wants rather than serving an abstract freedom of will. He speaks of a recognition of the problem of value as both integral to the judicial process (in contrast to the "pure theory of law") and wider than the judicial process (in contrast to the judicial "realist"). It is, he said, "a problem of all the social sciences":

we have to note the movement for teamwork with the other social sciences; the study of law as part of a whole process of social control. This is an essential point in the twentieth-century sociological jurisprudence. Compare it with the characteristic noncooperation of the social sciences in the nineteenth century. This ignoring by each of the social sciences of each of the others was by no means wholly due to the exigencies of university organization and academic courtesy, requiring each scholar to keep off his neighbor's premises. It was in the very spirit of the last century—every man for himself, every subject for itself. It was in the spirit of the atomistic conception of humanity as an aggregate of individuals engaged, with a minimum of organization, in a competitive acquisitive struggle for existence.[38]

Pound once proposed that courts should be fully staffed with social scientists to compile the background data necessary for sound judicial decisions—a technique followed on his own initiative by Justice Brandeis.

In his later years Pound criticized some of those who have carried the sociological principle of law too far. The Freudian analysis of judicial motives identified with Frank is not, in Pound's view, a fruitful course. A proper concern for the law involves finding standards that can restrain and nullify personal idiosyncrasy rather than magnify it. The purpose of law is distorted if it is treated only as subjective preference. While judges have access to no absolute standards, they have an obligation to serve standards outside themselves. But Pound, as a pragmatist, was perhaps most weak on this very question of values, deferring at various times to "harmony," "consensus," and "social

needs" without offering any higher criterion by which the harmony and consensus and fulfilled social need of a group of opium-smokers is distinguished from that of Plato's Academy. One of Pound's concluding admonitions to the courts represents a typical pragmatic statement of value, or evasion of value: ". . . the courts must . . . go on finding out by experience and developing by reason the modes of adjusting relations and ordering conduct which will give the most effect to the whole scheme of interests with the least friction and the least waste."[39]

Law and Analytic Philosophy

In recent years the philosophy of linguistic analysis has had an impact on law as well as in other areas. The work of H. L. A. Hart[40] stands out as a leading effort to clarify the meanings in use of words like *law, morality, justice,* and *rights.* In jurisprudence as in philosophy, the work of clarification is here taken to be the fundamental and self-justifying task. Hart treats laws as the given rules of a game, hence free of moral connotations, even though he is able to "elucidate" —a favorite concept of his—a minimum content to natural law by taking the impulse to survive as the key to what is natural. Survival itself thus becomes a game requiring rules to sustain it. Hart's effort to keep law and morals apart seems not in fact wholly neutral but is probably born of the negative desire to discredit those who wish to improve the morals of their fellows by legislation. One of the curious results of this

---

[38] *Social Control Through Law,* pp. 124–25.

[39] *Social Control,* p. 134. See also *Introduction to the Philosophy of Law,* pp. 45–47.

[40] See H. L. A. Hart, "Definition and Theory in Jurisprudence," *Law Quarterly Review,* Vol. 70 (1954), pp. 38–49; "The Separation of Law and Morals," *Harvard Law Review,* Vol. 71 (1958), pp. 594–600; "Legal Responsibility and Excuses," in Sidney Hook, ed., *Determinism and Freedom in the Age of Modern Science* (New York: New York Univ. Press, 1958); *The Concept of Law* (London: Oxford Univ. Press, 1961); *Law, Liberty, and Morality* (Stanford: Stanford Univ. Press, 1963); and "The Ascription of Rights and Responsibilities," in Anthony Flew, ed., *Logic and Language,* First Series (Garden City, N. Y.: Doubleday, Anchor, 1965).

method is that, though Hart begins with the actual usages of legal terms, his logical asceticism leads him, as it did Kelsen, into purely hypothetical exercises—*if* the legal system is taken to mean such and such, *then* it is correct to say "*X* has a right."[41] We have a kind of clarity but it is sometimes difficult to find our way back to the real world from Hart's logical land of "if."

BEHAVIORALISM

Movement away from both the alleged moralistic quality of earlier political studies and the hypothetical quality of analytical jurisprudence seems, at least initially, to characterize behavioral approaches to politics. A behavioralist acknowledges that classical political theory deals with the behavior of man but he will argue that "counter to the behavioral persuasion, it is predominantly prescriptive rather than descriptive."[42] What behavioral studies describe is not the legal and institutional structures that seemed important to an earlier generation but the way human participants within those structures vote, act, speak, associate, communicate, and what "roles" they play. Behavioral studies tend to be interdisciplinary because they can usefully combine the techniques of psychologists and sociologists as well as the residual techniques of political scientists.[43]

Charles Merriam of the University of Chicago was a pioneer in attempting some of these syntheses in the 1920s. The proliferation and refinement of survey research studies since the early days of public opinion polling in the late 1930s has been a crucial factor in the behavioral movement, for they have provided much of the data being analysed. A "traditionalist" will consult newspapers, books, and documents, talk to people, and then write up an account of, say, how a particular governor has influenced his party. The behavioralist will most likely try to get a balanced sample of respondents in the governor's party and weigh their responses by generally accepted criteria of validity and reliability in order to demonstrate a correlation between certain abstract patterns of behavior, such as, for example, propensity toward reformism and position in a hierarchy. The traditionalist is closer to the narrative historian, sensitive to the unique and the dramatic. The behavioralist is closer to the biological taxonomist, sensitive to regularities and uniformities. The distinction is close to what the psychologist Wundt called in the nineteenth century the "ideographic" and the "nomothetic," that is, the capturing of a fleeting moment in time and the postulation of general and presumably timeless patterns or laws.

The scientific pretensions of behavioralism have been such that by 1961 Dahl was

[41] See Jerome Hall, "Analytical Philosophy and Jurisprudence," *Ethics*, Vol. 77 (1966), pp. 14–28. Two who have been influenced by analytic philosophy but who grant more validity to certain moral symbols than does Hart are Margaret Macdonald (see "Natural Rights" in Peter Laslett, ed., *Philosophy, Politics, and Society* [New York: Macmillan, 1956], pp. 35–55) and John Rawls (see "Justice as Fairness," in Laslett and W. G. Runciman, eds., *Philosophy, Politics, and Society*, Second Series [Oxford: Blackwell, 1962], pp. 132–57, and "Two Concepts of Rules," *Philosophical Review*, Vol. 64 [1955], pp. 3–32).

[42] Heinz Eulau, *The Behavioral Persuasion in Politics* (New York: Random House, 1963), p. 7.

[43] Discussions of behavioralism and examples of its methods will be found in James C. Charlesworth, ed., *The Limits of Behavioralism in Political Science*, a sym-

posium (Philadelphia: The American Academy of Political and Social Science, 1962); James C. Davies, *Human Nature in Politics* (New York: Wiley, 1963); Heinz Eulau, Samuel Eldersveld, and Morris Janowitz, eds., *Political Behavior: A Reader in Theory and Research* (New York: Free Press, 1956); Austin Ranney, ed., *Essays on the Behavioral Study of Politics* (Urbana: Univ. of Illinois Press, 1962); and S. Sidney Ulmer, ed., *Introductory Readings in Political Behavior* (Chicago: Rand McNally, 1961). Good examples of special studies employing behavioral techniques would be Edward C. Banfield and James Q. Wilson, *City Politics* (Cambridge, Mass.: Harvard Univ. Press, 1963); Donald Matthews, *U.S. Senators and Their World* (Chapel Hill: Univ. of North Carolina Press, 1960); Lucian Pye, *Politics, Personality, and Nation-Building* (New Haven: Yale Univ. Press, 1962); and J. David Singer, *Human Behavior and International Politics* (Chicago: Rand McNally, 1965). See also the journals *Behavioral Science* and *The American Behavioral Scientist*.

able to say—probably prematurely—that the struggle over the propriety of the behavioral emphasis in American political science was over and that behavioralism had won.[44] In discussing Simon, Lasswell, and Dahl above, we were, of course, discussing behavioralism as well as positivism. In pointing to positivism we are highlighting assumptions about how meaningful knowledge is validated; in pointing to behavioralism we are highlighting assumptions about the way the social sciences should study their human subjects. The two are separable but obviously related. Various quantitative studies involving demographic data, voting statistics, the content analysis of documents and speeches, or even the voting records of judges and congressmen may not have much to do with psychological categories yet may still be referred to by many as "behavioral studies," suggesting that what is at stake is not so much a subject as a methodology. That, no doubt, is why we are discussing the topic here.

Behavioral data, whether collected through interviews or through the distillations of statistical manipulations, come onto the stage of political theory when their meaning and import become subject to speculation. When that happens, large, integrative terms like "action" (Parsons), "decision" (Simon), "function" (Merton), or "system" (Easton) are employed,[45] and the discussion, ostensibly technical, soon becomes entangled with prescientific assumptions about the nature of the reality being explained. Behaviorists see this,[46] although they disagree sharply among

themselves as to the optimum level of abstraction for theoretical potency. Their aim is to be not only empirical—"raw empiricism" is in disfavor these days—but also explanatory; and explanation seems to require a system.

TOWARD SYSTEM AND BEYOND

The twentieth century is said to be a century in which architectonic political theory is impossible. Life is too fragmented, work is too specialized, the old verities have disappeared. Our chapter on twentieth-century political thought seems to confirm this view. Yet we are not without a good many system-builders. That they call themselves social scientists rather than philosophers may have significance beyond their own criteria of significance.

Two Systems Theorists

Basing his work on a general theory of action, Talcott Parsons (1902–   ) has for some time been the leading system-builder in the sociological fraternity.[47] According to those who have mastered the system, Parsons' statement of it has moved from a focus on action conceived through a rather narrow behavioralist orientation to an emphasis on "macro-functionalism," in which the equi-

[44] "The Behavioral Approach," *American Political Science Review*, Vol. 55 (1961), pp. 763–72. Grave doubts about the victory will be found in the Storing and Crick volumes mentioned above. See also Andrew Hacker, "Mathematics and Political Science," in James C. Charlesworth, ed., *Mathematics and the Social Sciences* (Philadelphia: American Academy of Political and Social Science, 1963), pp. 58–76.

[45] See Robert K. Merton, *Social Theory and Social Structure* (New York: Free Press, 1949) and Gabriel A. Almond, "A Functional Approach to Comparative Politics," in Almond and James S. Coleman, eds., *The Politics of Developing Areas* (Princeton: Princeton Univ. Press, 1960). See references cited above for Simon and below for Parsons and Easton.

[46] "Once one approaches problems analytically rather

than concretely, whether as a behavioralist or institutionalist, the interdisciplinary orientation makes for generic rather than special explanations. A generic explanation is undoubtedly preferable to a special one" [Eulau, *Behavioral Persuasion,* p. 24]. What is generic may lead back into the past. For an interesting attempt to juxtapose traditional classics of political thought with present-day political analyses, see William T. Bluhm, *Theories of the Political System* (Englewood Cliffs, N. J.: Prentice-Hall, 1965).

[47] See his *Structure of Social Action* (New York: McGraw-Hill, 1937), and *The Social System* (New York: Free Press, 1951). See also *The Alpha Kappa Deltan,* Vol. 29, No. 1 (Winter, 1959), a whole issue devoted to Parsons' work. With Edward Shils Parsons edited *Toward a General Theory of Action* (Cambridge, Mass.: Harvard Univ. Press, 1951).

librium pattern of stable groups is the center of attention. The latter has provided a used and therefore useful framework for what has sometimes been criticized as a rather static analysis of stabilizing cultural norms. The system has been less useful in dealing with the generation of groups and group conflict. Those outside the sociological guild have most often accused Parsons of laboring the obvious with fancy words. Parsons, in effect, replies that the obvious has been neglected too long already. For our purposes it is important to note that from the beginning Parsons, due no doubt to the Weberian influence upon him, has subsumed political phenomena within his analytical system. And he has given special attention to a model of the two-party system in the United States.[48] To the extent that he and other generalists are successful, political sociology and political science will become indistinguishable, which perhaps they have been in essence all along.

One of the best known systematizers in current political science is Chicago's David Easton (1917-   ). In *The Political System* (1953)[49] Easton assaults not only raw empiricism—"hyperfactualism," he called it—but the "historicism" of such widely respected works as Sabine's *History of Political Theory* (1937), which becomes, in Easton's view, little more than the history of ideology presented noncommittally. While Easton accepts the fundamental difference between factual and value propositions, he rejects the idea of a wholly value-free social science. He calls instead for an explicit and thorough exposition of value premises as a

prerequisite for any systematic study. This should not inhibit the possibility of the truly general theory political science needs. He speaks of the possibility rather than the actuality, for most of what has passed for theory in the recent past he regards as moralizing and low-level descriptive propositions. A beginning on the kind of theory Easton calls for in *The Political System* is provided in *A Systems Analysis of Political Life* (1965), in which he aims "to explore in detail what may be called the life processes of a political system."[50] Curiously, "life" and "life processes" are biological terms yet the metaphorical basis of Easton's theory is electronic. The computer is not only the means whereby political data may be organized but the model by which political society may be known. Political influence is an "input," policy is an "output," and response to policy is "feedback." If we plug in at random to a discussion of "the systematic feedback loop" we can read:

Through the interlocking chain of feedback loops, all of the participating members of any one loop may be coupled, if only loosely, with many other members in the system. To point this up, I have deliberately selected the participants in the various feedback diads so that an unbroken line could be drawn through the six different actors who make up the six pairs in the six different loops. If we look at each loop as a link in a continuous chain—which they indeed form pictorially *and literally* [our italics]—we can appreciate that the interaction around any one feedback loop has the potential, if it is strong enough, to pass its influence down the chain to other units in the system.[51]

But what does it mean to say that the chain

---

[48] See his " 'Voting' and the Equilibrium of the American Political System," in Eugene Burdick and Arthur Brodbeck, eds., *Continuities of Social Research*, Vol. 3, *Studies of Voting Behavior* (New York: Free Press, 1958).

[49] *The Political System* (New York: Knopf, 1953). Dahl has chided Easton for the labored attempt of *The Political System* to provide an adequate definition of political science. "It is," he says, "an almost medieval search for essences." Do physicists, he asks, spend much time and energy arguing over "What is physics?" ("The Science of Politics: New and Old," *World Politics*, Vol. 7 [1955], pp. 479–89).

[50] *A Systems Analysis of Political Life* (New York: Wiley, 1965), p. VII. Easton has also provided a "structure of concepts" in *A Framework for Political Analysis* (Englewood Cliffs, N.J.: Prentice-Hall, 1965) and has edited *Varieties of Political Theory* (Englewood Cliffs, N.J.: Prentice-Hall, 1966). Empirical political theory is certainly not limited to behavioral or systems approaches. Writing from a traditional perspective, Carl J. Friedrich subtitles his major study, *Man and His Government, An Empirical Theory of Politics* (New York: McGraw-Hill, 1963). Pp. 24–27 form a useful critique of some systems theorists.

[51] *Ibid.*, p. 376.

is both pictorial and literal? It is surely not literal in reference to what, say, a black-power organizer may do to a big-city mayor. Is it then literal in reference to what a figurative computer would do?

Easton declares that his system is not yet ready for microscopic data—which means, presumably, data about specific human beings:

At this preliminary stage in a theory of political systems, when we are still trying to get our general bearings, a detailed analysis of this kind cannot and need not be undertaken. . . . for purposes of macroanalysis we do not need to push any more deeply. . . . It is as though we were initially reconciling ourselves to using a telescope rather than a microscope because we are not yet sufficiently confident of the units and processes that we want to lay open to detailed analysis.[52]

This is a very strange analogy. We do not yet know what to put under our microscopes; but we will know if we spend more time looking at stars through our telescopes. The very inaptness of the analogy may, however, reveal a truth to us. It suggests—whether or not this is Easton's intention—that in cognition wholeness precedes particularity, that there must be some coherent entity by which to comprehend a set of particulars. In Pepper's language, we cannot assemble any data, that touchstone of empirical research, without first having some "danda."[53] In Polanyi's personalistic epistemology, we cannot understand the purpose of a watch merely by taking it apart but

must learn of its purpose by other means.[54] Perhaps the same may be said of a political system.

System and Metaphor

System-builders in the social sciences more than in the natural sciences build their systems on analogies and metaphors. Aristotle was biological. Hobbes was physicalistic. Bentham was mechanistic. Easton is electronic. Karl Deutsch is neurological.[55] The metaphors are products of a particular historical experience and are therefore presumably limited by that historical experience. Yet the impulse toward universality in science is such that the scientist, natural or social, seeks for more and more general hypotheses, expressable in more and more neutral and nonmetaphorical language, which means in practice mathematical language. A dilemma results: the more general the hypotheses the less descriptive and the more hypothetical they become. The more hypothetical they become the less empirical they are. One can try to escape the dilemma by postulating a deterministic system so that everything that happens in actuality is as-

---

[52] *Ibid.*, pp. 376–77.

[53] *Data* is evidence refined through multiplicative corroboration—by repetitive tests and by observations of a similar kind made by a series of observers. *Danda* is evidence refined through structural corroboration, by measuring conformity to a preexisting construct. Both may involve observation but data-seekers will strive for repeatability with a given type of observation, whereas danda-seekers will strive for a coherent pattern amid diverse observations. The former is a more social, the latter a more individualized pathway toward reality. The failure to make some such distinction has spawned endless confusion in the social sciences. See Stephen Pepper, *World Hypotheses* (Berkeley: Univ. of Cal. Press, 1961).

[54] Michael Polanyi, *The Study of Man* (Chicago: Univ. of Chicago Press, 1963), p. 49. See also his *Personal Knowledge* (Chicago: Univ. of Chicago Press, 1958).

[55] Karl W. Deutsch, *The Nerves of Government* (New York: Free Press, 1966). The eclecticism of Deutsch's models of communication and control is attractive. For Deutsch the integration of individual neurological systems is of a piece with the integration of subnational, national, and international political units. His terminology—cybernetics, communication models, and decision systems—is sufficiently contemporary to command scientific attention yet his thought is sufficiently subtle to accommodate older problems—spirit, evil, sin, and grace. His reach is vast, though his claims are modest, perhaps because, like too few of his fellow systems theorists, he is sensitive to the finiteness of historical experience. See Glenn Tinder, "The Necessity of Historicism," *American Political Science Review*, Vol. 55 (1961), pp. 560–65. See Deutsch's paper "Recent Trends in Research Methods in Political Science" and the comment thereon in James C. Charlesworth, ed., *A Design for Political Science: Scope, Objectives, and Methods* (Philadelphia: American Academy of Political and Social Science, 1966), pp. 149–237.

sumed to be an aspect of the causal pattern postulated by the theory. But the presumptuousness of such a course does not sit well with modest men, so they tend to substitute less pretentious game-theory models for causal models or to mitigate the deterministic quality of the causal model by inserting stochastic stipulations, that is, by setting up a range of probabilities within which "free" choice may be assumed.[56] The most ardent game theorists will grant that, while politics has many similarities with certain kinds of games, it is not exactly the same as, nor is its description exhausted by identification with, any particular game.

Game theories, communication models, or structural-functional analyses can be suggestive of reality without being determinative of reality—but so can works of art and artists are supposed to be different creatures from scientists. But perhaps artists and scientists are not as far apart as we often think. Thomas Kuhn, in *The Structure of Scientific Revolutions* (1962), shows us that, when Renaissance painters were concerned with perfecting the techniques of linear perspective, or of transforming three-dimensional vision onto a two-dimensional surface, they thought of themselves as scientists. When perspective ceased to be an interesting problem to them, they stopped being scientists and began calling themselves artists. The

problem of perspective seemed scientific because it was amenable to progressive solution by measurable steps. As important, perhaps, as other more obvious marks of scientific endeavor is the sense of forward motion within historical time. Scientific paradigms provide the structure within which researchers can work and feel they are "making progress." When unusually creative men come up with new paradigms that give promise of greater forward movement, old paradigms can lose their grip on the imagination with remarkable rapidity. Copernicus destroyed but did not replace the earlier view of terrestrial motion; the same could be said for Newton on gravity, Lavoisier on the property of metals, and Einstein on space and time. This is what Kuhn calls the incommensurability of scientific paradigms.

That the sense of forward motion is important to the sense of scientific accomplishment is evident from a reading of political-science-journal articles that are replete with phrases like "our exploration into this new area," "The scientific study of judicial decision-making has only begun to," "the frontiers of political research," and "More research will be needed if." The mood of discovery is genuine and should not be made light of. This impelling future-orientation is harmful only when it becomes parochial and the incommensurability of (social) scientific paradigms is forgotten amid imperialistic enthusiasms. Easton's enthusiasm, for example, leads him to computerize history itself. Under the heading "Rules for the retrieval of stored experiences," he refers to "a social memory bank" as a "potential resource for the authorities":

Members could not possibly recall the whole of history transmitted to each generation, even if it were desirable or necessary. Retrieval is always selective. What a person recalls will hinge on those rules governing the ways in which he scans his memory, the criteria of appropriateness used to make selections from the information retrieved, and the rules regulating the way he goes about synthesizing and reorganizing the knowledge recalled for immediate use. . . . The rules themselves constitute part of the

---

[56] See Anatol Rapoport, "The Use of Theory in the Study of Politics," in Edward H. Beuhrig, ed., *Essays in Political Science* (Bloomington: Indiana Univ. Press, 1966), pp. 3–36. See also David Braybrooke, *A Strategy of Decision* (New York: Free Press, 1963); Rapoport, *Fights, Games, and Debates* (Ann Arbor: Univ. of Michigan Press, 1960); and Mulford Q. Sibley, "The Limits of Behavioralism," in Charlesworth, ed., *The Limits of Behavioralism*, pp. 68–93. Sibley is criticizing the "if . . . then" quality of some behavioral political studies in terms similar to the criticism of Hart's jurisprudence aired above. Building on Aristotle's disparagement of "mere theory" as unreal in its abstraction, Jaffa has criticized the causal and descriptive theories of modern social science. In Jaffa's terminology, what is of value in the present volume should be called not political theory but political philosophy, for philosophy, in the classical sense of love of wisdom, begins not with abstractions but with practice (See Harry V. Jaffa, "The Case Against Political Theory," *Journal of Politics*, Vol. 22 [1960], pp. 259–75).

available resources necessary for handling feed-back response.[57]

In more literal English the gist of these words might be: "Habit affects memory and people remember from history what is use-ful for them to remember." The longer statement is, curiously, both more scientific and more metaphorical than the shorter—curious because it is an attribute of meta-phor that it can be taken in more than one way. In this case, we are not quite sure whether we are reading about a computer-like way of dealing with history or with a history that is computerlike. This is not to suggest that we can do without either meta-phor or political science but to suggest only that neither is final truth or the sole means

[57] *A Systems Analysis*, p. 458.

to truth and that ambiguity may sometimes be a friend as well as an enemy of truth. "Empirical" theory, "normative" theory, nar-rative history, and all kinds of artistic crea-tions stand between us and the truth, reveal-ing as through a window some things that lie beyond but blocking out other things.

Those of us who study political theory in a historical way should feel neither threat-ened by nor superior to the scientific enthu-siasms of an ahistorical political science. Our constructs are grounded on metaphors, too. We ought rather to accept empirical politi-cal science for what it can contribute to our understanding of the complex human prob-lems of the twentieth century without relin-quishing our duty to see it in its historical context, for only in that way can we gain the perspective necessary to illumine both its accomplishments and its limitations.

28

CONCLUSION:
THEORY AND IDEOLOGY

The problem of concluding a history of political theory is similar to that of introducing it. Before one has entered into the dialogue that makes up that history, little can be said; and afterward little need be said. Why conclude at all, then? One concludes out of a decent respect for all that has not been said and all that might have been said. One concludes, in other words, in order not to leave a false impression of conclusiveness.

If an elaborate defense of the best political theory would, at this point, be gratuitous, a defense of political theory itself as a worthy enterprise might be in order. In Chapter 1 we suggested that systematic reflection on politics emerged in the West out of a special historical-mythical context. We there promised for this chapter a defense of theory against ideology. The implication was that theory aims at the truth and ideology aims at victory over human opponents. Political victory is fairly determinate; one either wins or loses. But the truth of a political theory is elusive, personal, and infinitely complex. It may be destroyed by an overrigid formulation. It may be missed by not "getting inside" the theorist in question. Even after considerable effort, we are never quite sure we understand a theorist who looked upon a world that is not ours. How much less are we able to summarize his kernel of truth in an easily digestible, preservative-coated capsule? Second-rate political thinkers are apt to rant, preach, and mumble in order to score points in a debate. The first-rate thinkers are engaged in a dialogue[1] in which opposing ideas are absorbed and transformed instead of beaten down or evaded. Debates can be summarized fairly easily by simple score-keeping but dialogues are not easy to summarize. Too much of their character resides in the flavor, the subtle shading, the play of idea upon idea.

The term "theory," we have said once or twice, may include every sort of abstraction from loose opinion to a tight scientific hypothesis. Political ideology is certainly a form of theory and so is political philosophy, which can mean what Plato and Aristotle did or the love of political wisdom expressed by less articulate thinkers. Let us not bog down at this late stage in a massive lexocographical sandpit. All the preceding chapters

---

[1] From the Greek *dia logos,* "through words"; hence, not merely battling *with* words but clarifying one's point *through* words.

should have supported the claim made here, namely that all political theorists are not ideologues even though some ideologues may be political theorists.

There is a sense, no doubt, in which ideology is only the other fellow's beliefs; but this too easily cynical view is an inhibitor rather than a stimulus to fruitful analysis. To be sure, we see the other fellow's ideologies—his rationalizations, pat answers, and crutchlike dogmas—more readily than we can see our own. But that bare perception neither explains nor justifies ideology in either of us. There has been much talk recently about ideological counteroffensives against the communist threat, doing a better job of selling America abroad, and the like. Sometimes this sort of enterprise, which no doubt has its own quite legitimate justification, is confused with rational political theorizing. It is important that it not be. Whether ideologies as such can account for the rise and fall of nations is doubtful. Ideologies as justifications for mass behavior are obviously tremendously important to the morale of individuals in large groups—more important to the less emotionally stable, no doubt. But the content of a particular ideology is probably less important than its availability. Consistency may be important to an ideology, but consistency as an internal factor rather than as a harmonic response to a changing external world. The ideologically zealous opponents of increased federal intervention in local public education do not seem bothered by the intervention of Congressional investigating committees in local public education. The ideologically zealous advocates of proletarian democracy do not seem bothered by one-party rule within their own labor unions. The enemy is an aggressor. We attack in the name of freedom. The ideology is available for use against opponents but it is not, merely for the sake of consistency, used against allies. What is democracy to one group is tyranny to another group. An imaginative leader will find adequate verbal symbols almost anywhere to give his followers the verbal equipment necessary to rationalize their support of him. Given the choice of a better ideology or a better leader, a nation is well advised to choose the latter, for good leadership implies the proper use and nonuse of ideology, whereas a good ideology—whatever that may mean—does not necessarily imply good leadership.

But even granting for the moment that a better ideology might be necessary for national survival, we must recognize that this would in no way invalidate the distinction between ideology and theory, for, if by our definition a political ideology aims first and foremost at political victory and if a nation is victorious in some contest thanks to an ideology, once victory has been achieved the ideology is dead. By doing its appointed job it has killed itself. First-rate political theory has value precisely because it outlives the crises that may have generated it. Victories may be and often are won in pursuit of an illusion. But in the long run neither personal nor collective life can go on unless there exists some hold on reality strong enough to survive the shock of disillusion. Political ideologies dominate the stage; but enduring political theories are with the actors and theatergoers as they walk out into the chill night air.

Some say that the condition of free inquiry and free expression, which enables political theorists to practice their trade openly, is itself a product of ideology, in this case the ideology of the Western liberal tradition. Therefore, it is biting the hand that feeds him for a theorist to attack this ideology. The Western liberal tradition has indeed permitted and even encouraged the open pursuit of political theory. But we should not forget that political theory in the disguise of history, fables, children's stories, and advice to the monarch has been produced under all sorts of repressive conditions. As theory, it is no less valid because of its disguise; there is, in fact, a certain esoteric quality to all original theorizing that the Western liberal tradition has sometimes failed to appreciate. But, in any case, a clear distinction must be drawn between liberalism as a tradition and liberalism as an ideology. A tradition includes all sorts of customary behavior patterns not reducible to the structured intellectual formulas of an ideology. We can rise above ideologies in a way that we cannot rise above traditions. If an ideology is a deliberately prefabricated set of answers whose effect is to close off inquiry, it is difficult to call the tradition of free inquiry an ideology. There are certainly ideologies that include free inquiry as one of their positive symbols but the authentic practice of free inquiry tends to be corrosive of ideological cohesion, since it generates embarrassing questions asked in unlikely places at unlikely times.

A lack of ideological cohesion is not necessarily the equivalent of anarchy. People who have developed the ability to live with a variety of conflicting ideologies are able, as it is often put, to agree to disagree. This ability, which would seem to be essential to both the representative and the libertarian aspects of Western democracy, implies a degree of consensus about social goals and a certain trust in the reasonableness of others. But it would be a mistake to call such consensus and such trust ideological. The trust is prerequisite to and more important than the consensus. It is the cement of the social fabric. Trust grows out of an experience of honest relationships. What meaning could there be to "common social goals" if we could not trust as honest those things told us by parents, friends, teachers, authors of books, newspapers, and political leaders? Part of the horror of a totalitarian regime is that no one can trust anyone else. The network of honest reports is broken down. A credibility gap widens beyond the official tolerance level and more and more harsh measures are taken to extinguish it. More or less spontaneous personal confidence is dissolved and has to be replaced by an implacable, impersonal ideology—the "logic" of an idea bent and twisted into an all-purpose guide to everything from personal relations to the purpose of history.

Citizens are less likely to succumb to frantic appeals for political uniformity, however, if they understand the degree of unity involved in their merely being citizens of a common *res publica* with a tradition of its own. This is why totalitarian movements try to undermine a sense of tradition and historical continuity and to encourage an irrational dependence upon the achievement of a glorious plan for the future. A regime impelled to claim omniscience in seeing the good and foreseeing the future may win support but it courts eventual disorder. Ordinary people with ordinary skepticism are dubious of the moral and intellectual pretenses of such regimes. Ordinary people tend to seek a more enduring source of meaning and morality than a transient political order can provide. They turn to tradition or religious faith or both. Political ideologies sometimes try to make use of tradition by rewriting history and often seek the status of religious faiths. But neither the past nor the stirrings of divinity are, one hopes, controllable by the men who manufacture ideologies. We must wish them failure in their attempt to transform the human community into the political community and the political community into their private cult.

The proper role of the political theorist is not to concoct an ideology that can substitute for lost trust after other ideologies have helped destroy it. His role is not even to create trust through philosophy. Trust is a relationship of personal confidence between persons seen or unseen. It is a willingness to concede unproven qualities. It is a capacity to act beyond the point at which intellectual assurance guarantees the results of action. It is, if you will, the capacity to act on faith. Theories and philosophies and theologies rarely instill this capacity in large numbers of people, since theories and philosophies and theologies—and, yes, ideologies—are the very intellectual assurances beyond which trustful action occurs. But theories can clarify the meaning of what men have done and this enriched knowledge of past action can influence future action. The political theorist has, in a way, the same responsibility as that of newspapers: to inform the public honestly. His immediate public is smaller, however, and he informs it not of the transient facts but of the more enduring meanings behind them. He is obliged to penetrate the illusions he can recognize and to disclose the reality he can underestand. If power has no reality to him but the public good does—or vice versa—that is what he must honestly report. Good theories, it is our thesis, are honest reports. Bad theories (ideologies) are dishonest reports.

Granting these distinctions, we can see that the more widespread the habit of honest reporting the more likely is theory to be encouraged and ideology to be discouraged. But to call for collective honesty is to call for something at once complex and simple. How many individuals can live without self-deception and the deception of others? To tell nothing but the truth is difficult enough but to tell the whole truth is probably impossible. The desire to tell people what they want to hear often springs from a laudable compassion but leads to false impressions. For each role that we play—son, father, husband, executive, churchman, socializer, leader, or follower—a different standard of honesty tends to apply. And many are the occasions when a fragment of the truth, honest in itself, betrays the larger truth of which it is a part.

If honesty is this great a challenge to the well-integrated individual, how much greater a challenge is it to a whole society? In our present society, half-truths and untruths scream at us and plead with us unendingly in commercial advertising, political advertising, religious advertising, educational advertising, and various other forms of distortion. Most people accept all this quite blandly, the naive because they think it part of the natural environment, the sophisticated because they know each age has its own form of untruth.

And yet simple honesty is not an illusion. There are moments of truth when it breaks through even in totalitarian societies steeped in ideological pretense. A worker accosts a lavishly dressed member of the Supreme Soviet in Red Square and taunts him for his nonproletarian clothes. A young girl being feted in Moscow for winning a prize is handed a prepared statement to read over the state radio and refuses because the statement is not true. In our country, an agency head says what everyone knows is true even when it offends his "clients" and their Congressional allies. A Congressman overcomes the temptation to win votes with a flamboyant speech on a delicate international situation on which he does not yet have adequate information. A newsman admits his bias. A voter admits he is voting for the party rather than the man.

There is no assured salvation in countless such acts of individual honesty—honesty can be cruel and agitational, too—but it is by virtue of them that reality is known and the world of illusion is dissipated. Sometimes we wonder if political theory does as much. We look back on the manifest illusions about quantifiable units of pleasure and pain in Bentham and think his function must have been other than to dispel illusion. But in so doing we forget the seriousness and pungency of his critique of obscurity and flabbiness in eighteenth-century legal thinking. We look at the obscurities in Hegel and say wistfully that a lot of nonsense would have been spared the world had Hegel not inspired so many disciples. But in so doing we forget that he saw process where none had been seen before. Even the good is less than perfect. All theories unintentionally build up illusions that must be torn apart by the next generation. Like thought itself, political theory is a never ending process.

Yet a further complication arises. Is "honest report" what we have any right to expect from a political theorist? How can any political theorist give an honest report *on* an entire body politic *to* an entire body politic? "Body politic" is itself a metaphor, meant to encompass what no single man can experience. The historic purposes of bodies politic, we suggested in Chapter 1, are impregnated with myth. Is the evocation of these myth-shrouded purposes properly equated with reportage or does such evocation properly belong to another enterprise than political theory?

The scientific mentality of the modern age has affected us all to such a degree that we are apt to cope with past thought, including past political thought, by making it propositional even when not originally conceived or expressed in propositional form. The memorable political theorists were not quite myth-makers, for myths are not, strictly speaking, made. But they were surely inheritors and progenitors of myth. Concerned tacitly or explicitly with the grounds of authority, they sought to find the Word amid words. They articulated a sense of authority that was meant to be exemplary, as befits man the historical creature, or was meant to be promissory, as befits man the speech-making creature. For all their diversity, there is a common thread of response to the need for embodied authority in, for example, the figures of Plato's philosopher-king, Machiavelli's prince, Hobbes's sovereign, and Rousseau's legislator.

What we see in a literary tradition as the search for a hero-ruler we can see in contemporary practical politics as the search for a flawless leader. Every democratic election and many elections that are not so democratic illustrate the parallel—how else could the election experience be felt as a subjectively significant ritual even when no effective choice is available? Historical political theory can evoke a sense of these authoritative imperatives even when they are not stated as propositions reducible to a logical system. Therefore both the poetic-mythic and the propositional are included under the term "honest report." The mythic masquerading as the propositional is not included, for that is deceptive, that puts us in jeopardy of being enslaved rather than served by words. That turns honest myth into dishonest ideology.

By whatever name, there will be political theory as long as people live outside caves and as long as there are men with the ability and courage to think for themselves. The degree to which the fruits of their best thought will permeate the body politic depends upon a variety of factors. Many forces in our present world will continue to inhibit this permeation. The increasing complexity of the subject matter of politics places a great strain on the institutions of popular consultation. Defective theories of democracy, often transformed into ideologies, do not help. The democratic politician frequently exaggerates the degree to which he must be a crowd-pleaser. But politicians may be more honest about their role—at least when talking among themselves—than are many average citizens, who, confused by the view that they-the-people are supposed to know all about running a government, try to reassure themselves and impress others by mouthing secondhand political slogans as if they were scientific dogma. The more unsure one is of his own beliefs or of whether they are really his own, the more likely he is to insist that everyone else agree with him. Excessive confidence in mass wisdom can actually induce a falling away from that degree of political excellence attainable under more realistic assumptions.

Rousseau's poignant goal that "every citizen should speak his opinion entirely from himself" is still a valid democratic goal. It is certainly a compelling goal in today's age of identity crises, participation explosions, and new student restlessness. But an opinion is more genuine if it expresses an honest but limited competence than if it pretends to omnicompetence. This statement is as applicable to the opinions of experts who manage the routine of public affairs as it is to those of the citizens who set the general direction of political life. It is especially hard to speak one's opinions entirely from oneself in an age of insistent electronic communication, when news is fast moving, information is overcondensed, and standardized opinions, neatly packaged, emanate from highly centralized agencies of transmission. The continuing internationalization of politics will no doubt complicate the task of achieving collective honesty. Nationalist pride will garble facts with emotion and the high stakes of nuclear war or peace may be used as an end to justify deceptive means. Some Americans, unable to carry the weight of starving and rebellious foreigners on their well-padded shoulders, will eagerly accept dishonestly simple answers to excruciating problems. They will also accept the scapegoats who invariably accompany the too simple answer.

Meanwhile, the painful search for political reality will go on and some solitary searchers will continue to ask why rather than how. Some future Socrates will care more for truth than safety. Some future Plato will have a vision of political perfection. Some future Hegel will put it all in a system. These will be the political theorists, and to them, as to their predecessors, we shall owe such knowledge as we have of the latent body politic to which we all are bound.

SELECTED READINGS

Chapter 1 **INTRODUCTION**

BARKER, ERNEST. *Principles of Social and Political Theory.* London: Oxford Univ. Press (Galaxy Books), 1961.

BENN, S. J., AND R. S. PETERS. *Principles of Political Thought.* New York: Free Press, 1959.

BOWLE, JOHN. *Western Political Thought; An Historical Introduction from the Origins to Rousseau.* New York: Barnes & Noble (University Paperbacks), 1961.

EBENSTEIN, WILLIAM, ed. *Great Political Thinkers.* 3rd ed. New York: Holt, Rinehart and Winston, 1960. Selections from leading political theorists with prefatory statements. Good bibliography, pp. 869–974.

ELIADE, MIRCEA. *Myths, Dreams and Mysteries; The Encounter Between Contemporary Faiths and Archaic Realities.* New York: Harper & Row, 1960.

D'ENTREVES, ALEXANDER PASSERIN. *The Notion of the State: An Introduction to Political Theory.* New York: Oxford Univ. Press, 1967.

SABINE, GEORGE H. *A History of Political Theory.* 3rd ed. New York: Holt, Rinehart and Winston, 1961.

STRAUSS, LEO. *What Is Political Philosophy?* New York: Free Press, 1960.

———, AND JOSEPH CROPSEY, eds. *History of Political Philosophy.* Chicago: Rand McNally, 1964.

VEREKER, CHARLES. *The Development of Political Theory.* New York: Harper & Row (Colophon Books), 1965.

VOEGELIN, ERIC. *Order and History.* Vol. 1, *Israel and Revelation.* Baton Rouge: Louisiana State Univ. Press, 1956.

WOLIN, SHELDON S. *Politics and Vision; Continuity and Innovation in Western Political Thought.* Boston: Little, Brown, 1960.

Chapter 2 **PLATO**

Works by Plato

Collected Dialogues. Ed. by Edith Hamilton and Huntington Cairns. New York: Pantheon, 1961. The only one-volume edition in English.

Dialogues. Tr. by Benjamin Jowett. 4th ed. London: Oxford Univ. Press, 1953. 4 vols.

Euthyphro, Apology and Crito, and the Death Scene from Phaedo. Tr. by F. J. Church. 2nd rev. ed. New York: Liberal Arts Press, 1956.

Gorgias. Tr. by W. Hamilton. Baltimore: Penguin Books, 1960.

The Laws. Tr. by A. E. Taylor. London: Dent (Everyman's), 1960.

Parmenides, Theaitetos, Sophist, Statesman. Tr. by John Warrington. London: Dent (Everyman's), 1961.

The Republic. Tr. by F. M. Cornford. New York: Oxford Univ. Press, 1958.

The Republic. In Greek with Eng. tr. by Paul Shorey. Cambridge, Mass.: Harvard Univ. Press (Loeb Classical Library), 1953, 1956. 2 vols.

Statesman. Tr. by J. B. Skemp. New York: Liberal Arts Press, 1957.

Secondary Works

BARKER, ERNEST. *Greek Political Theory; Plato and His Predecessors.* New York: Barnes & Noble (University Paperbacks), 1960.

BOSANQUET, BERNARD. *A Companion to Plato's Republic.* New York: Macmillan, 1895.

CROSSMAN, R. H. S. *Plato Today.* Rev. ed. New York: Oxford Univ. Press, 1959.

FOSTER, MICHAEL B. *The Political Philosophies of Plato and Hegel.* Oxford: Clarendon Press, 1935.

GOULDNER, ALVIN W. *Enter Plato; Classical Greece and the Origins of Social Theory.* New York: Basic Books, 1965.

GRENE, DAVID. *Greek Political Theory; The Image of Man in Thucydides and Plato.* Chicago: Univ. of Chicago Press (Phoenix Books), 1965.

GRUBE, G. M. A. *Plato's Thought.* Boston: Beacon Press, 1958.

NETTLESHIP, RICHARD LEWIS. *Lectures on the Republic of Plato.* 2nd ed. London: Macmillan, 1901.

POPPER, KARL R. *The Open Society and Its Enemies.* Vol. 1, *The Spell of Plato.* 3rd ed. rev. London: Routledge & Kegan Paul, 1957.

TAYLOR, A. E. *Plato, The Man and His Work.* New York: World (Meridian Books), 1956.

——. *Socrates.* Garden City, N.Y.: Doubleday (Anchor Books), 1960.

THORSON, THOMAS L., ed. *Plato: Totalitarian or Democrat.* Englewood Cliffs, N.J.: Prentice-Hall (Spectrum Books), 1963.

VOEGELIN, ERIC. *Order and History.* Vol. 3, *Plato and Aristotle.* Baton Rouge: Louisiana State Univ. Press, 1957.

WILD, JOHN D. *Plato's Theory of Man; An Introduction to the Realistic Philosophy of Culture.* Cambridge, Mass.: Harvard Univ. Press, 1946.

Chapter 3 ARISTOTLE

Works by Aristotle

The Ethics of Aristotle. Tr. by J. A. K. Thomson. Baltimore: Penguin Books, 1958.

The Nicomachean Ethics. Tr. by D. P. Chase. New York: Dutton (Everyman's Library), 1915.

The Politics of Aristotle. Ed. and tr. by William L. Newman. Oxford: Clarendon Press, 1887–1902. 4 vols. Vol. 1 is Newman's introduction.

Politics and the Athenian Constitution. Tr. by John Warrington. New York: Dutton (Everyman's Library), 1961.

The Politics of Aristotle. Tr. by Ernest Barker. New York: Oxford Univ. Press, 1958.

The Works of Aristotle Translated into English. Ed. by W. D. Ross. Oxford: Clarendon Press, 1908–31. 11 vols.

Secondary Works

BARKER, ERNEST. *The Political Thought of Plato and Aristotle.* New York: Dover, 1959.

JAEGER, WERNER. *Aristotle.* 2nd ed. Tr. by Richard Robinson. New York: Oxford Univ. Press, 1962.

KAGEN, DONALD. *The Great Dialogue: A History of Greek Political Thought from Homer to Polybius.* New York: Free Press, 1964.

RANDALL, JOHN HERMAN, JR. *Aristotle.* New York: Columbia Univ. Press, 1962.

ROSS, W. D. *Aristotle.* 2nd ed. New York: World (Meridian Books), 1960.

TAYLOR, A. E. *Aristotle.* Rev. ed. New York: Dover, 1956.

WHEELWRIGHT, PHILIP. *Aristotle.* New York: Odyssey Press, 1951.

Chapter 4 THE STOICS AND ROME

Primary Works

AURELIUS ANTONINUS, MARCUS. *Communings with Himself.* Tr. by C. R. Haines. New York: Putnam's (Loeb Classical Library), 1916.

——. *Meditations* (with Epictetus, *Enchiridion*). Tr. by George Long. Chicago: Regnery (Gateway Editions), 1956.

CICERO, MARCUS TULLIUS. *De officiis.* With Eng. tr. by Walter Miller. Cambridge, Mass.: Harvard Univ. Press (Loeb Classical Library), 1951.

——. *De republica; De legibus.* With Eng. tr. by C. W. Keyes. New York: Putnam's (Loeb Classical Library), 1928.

——. *On the Commonwealth.* Tr. by George H. Sabine and Stanley B. Smith. New York: Liberal Arts Press, 1959.

EPICTETUS. *The Discourses and Fragments.* Tr. by W. A. Oldfather. New York: Putnam's (Loeb Classical Library), 1926, 1928. 2 vols. Vol. 2 reprinted by Harvard Univ. Press, 1952.

GAIUS. *The Institutes of Gaius.* Tr. by Francis de-Zulcuta. Oxford: Clarendon Press, 1946, 1953. 2 vols. Vol. 2 is commentary.

POLYBIUS. *The Histories of Polybius.* Tr. by Evelyn Shuckburgh. Bloomington: Univ. of Indiana Press, 1962. 2 vols.

Secondary Works

ARNOLD, EDWARD V. *Roman Stoicism.* London: Cambridge Univ. Press, 1911.

CARLYLE, R. W., AND A. J. CARLYLE. *A History of Medieval Political Theory in the West.* 2nd ed. 6 vols., Vol. 1. New York: Barnes & Noble, 1927. Part 1 is on the Stoics.

COCHRANE, CHARLES N. *Christianity and Classical Culture.* Rev. ed. New York: Oxford Univ. Press (Galaxy Books), 1957.

FRITZ, KURT VON. *The Theory of the Mixed Constitution in Antiquity: A Critical Analysis of Polybius' Political Ideas.* New York: Columbia Univ. Press, 1954.

HICKS, ROBERT D. *Stoic and Epicurean.* New York: Russell & Russell, 1962.

MURRAY, GILBERT. *Stoic, Christian and Humanist.* London: Allen & Unwin, 1940.

RICHARDS, GEORGE C. *Cicero, A Study.* Boston: Houghton Mifflin, 1935.

WALBANK, F. W. *A Historical Commentary on Polybius.* Oxford: Clarendon Press, 1957.

ZELLER, EDUARD. *The Stoics, Epicureans and Sceptics.* Tr. by Oswald J. Reichel. New and rev. ed. New York: Russell & Russell, 1962.

Chapter 5 AUGUSTINE

Works by Augustine

An Augustine Synthesis. Ed. by Erich Przywara. New York: Sheed & Ward, 1936; Harper & Row (Torchbooks), 1958.

Basic Writings of Saint Augustine. Ed. by Whitney J. Oates. New York: Random House, 1948. 2 vols.

City of God. Tr. by Marcus Dods. New York: Random House (Modern Library), 1950.

The City of God. Tr. by John Healey (1610). New York: Dutton (Everyman's Library), 1945.

Confessions. Tr. by Rex Warner. New York: New American Library (Mentor Books), 1963.

Confessions and Enchiridion. Ed. by Albert C. Outler. (Library of Christian Classics, Vol. 7). Philadelphia: Westminster Press, 1955.

Earlier Writings. Ed. and tr. by J. H. S. Burleigh. (Library of Christian Classics, Vol. 6). Philadelphia: Westminster Press, 1953.

Later Works. Ed. and tr. by John Burnaby. (Library of Christian Classics, Vol. 8). Philadelphia: Westminster Press, 1955.

Political Writings of St. Augustine. Ed. by Henry Paolucci. Chicago: Regnery (Gateway Editions), 1962.

Works. Ed. by Marcus Dods. Edinburgh: T. & T. Clark, 1872–1934. 8 vols.

Secondary Works

ANDRESON, CARL, ed. *Bibliographia Augustiniana.* Darmstadt, Germany: Wissenschaftliche Buchgesellschaft, 1962.

BATTENHOUSE, ROY, ed. *A Companion to St. Augustine.* New York: Oxford Univ. Press, 1955.

BROOKS, EDGAR H. *The City of God and the Politics of Crisis.* London: Oxford Univ. Press, 1960.

COMBES, GUSTAVE. *La Doctrine politique de Saint Augustin.* Paris: Librairie Plon, 1927.

CULLMANN, OSCAR. *The State in the New Testament.* New York: Scribner's, 1956.

D'ARCY, M. C., ed. *Saint Augustine.* New York: World (Meridian Books), 1957. A symposium.

DEANE, HERBERT A. *The Political and Social Ideas of Saint Augustine.* New York: Columbia Univ. Press, 1963.

FIGGIS, JOHN NEVILLE. *The Political Aspects of S. Augustine's City of God.* London: Longmans, Green, 1921.

GILSON, ÉTIENNE. *The Christian Philosophy of St. Augustine.* Tr. by L. E. M. Lynch. New York: Random House, 1960.

POPE, HUGH. *St. Augustine of Hippo.* London: Longmans, Green, 1954.

PORTALIÉ, EUGENE. *A Guide to the Thought of Saint Augustine.* Tr. by Ralph J. Bastian. Chicago: Regnery, 1960.

VERSFELD, MARTHINUS. *A Guide to the City of God.* New York: Sheed & Ward, 1958.

Chapter 6 AQUINAS

Works by Aquinas

On Kingship to the King of Cyprus. Tr. by Gerald B. Phelan. New ed., rev. by I. T. Eschmann. Toronto: Pontifical Institute of Medieval Studies, 1949. (1938 ed. titled *On the Governance of Rulers.*)

Philosophical Texts. Ed. and tr. by Thomas Gilby. New York: Oxford Univ. Press (Galaxy Books), 1960.

The Political Ideas of St. Thomas Aquinas. Ed. by Dino Bigongiari. New York: Hafner, 1953.

Selected Political Writings. Tr. by J. G. Dawson. Ed. by A. P. d'Entreves. Oxford: Blackwell & Mott, 1948.

Summa contra Gentiles. Tr. by English Dominican Fathers. London: Burns & Oates, 1928–29. 5 vols.

Summa Theologica. Tr. by English Dominican Fathers. Amer. ed. New York: Benziger, 1947–49. 3 vols.

Treatise on Law. Tr. by English Dominican Fathers. Chicago: Regnery (Gateway Editions), n.d.

Secondary Works

BRENNAN, ROBERT E., ed. *Essays in Thomism.* New York: Sheed & Ward, 1942.

CHESTERTON, G. K. *St. Thomas Aquinas.* Garden City, N.Y.: Doubleday (Image Books), 1956.

COPLESTON, FREDERICK C. *Aquinas.* Baltimore: Penguin Books (Pelican Books), 1955.

D'ARCY, MARTIN. *St. Thomas Aquinas.* Glen Rock, N.J.: Newman Press, 1955.

FARRELL, WALTER. *A Companion to the Summa.* New York: Sheed & Ward, 1939–42. 4 vols.

GILBY, THOMAS. *The Political Thought of Thomas Aquinas.* Chicago: Univ. of Chicago Press, 1958.

————. *Principality and Polity; Aquinas and the Rise of State Theory in the West.* London: Longmans, Green, 1958.

GILSON, ÉTIENNE. *The Christian Philosophy of Saint Thomas Aquinas.* Tr. by L. K. Shook. New York: Random House, 1956.

JAFFA, HARRY V. *Thomism and Aristotelianism; A Study of the Commentary by Thomas Aquinas on the Nicomachean Ethics.* Chicago: Univ. of Chicago Press, 1952.

MARITAIN, JACQUES. *St. Thomas Aquinas.* New York: World (Meridian Books), 1958.

MIHALICH, JOSEPH C. *Existentialism and Thomism.* New York: Philosophical Library, 1960.

SERTILLANGES, ANTONIN G. *Saint Thomas Aquinas and His Work.* Tr. by Godfrey Anstruther. London: Blackfriars, 1957.

Chapter 7 SOME MEDIEVAL LEGACIES

General

CARLYLE, R. W., AND A. J. CARLYLE. *A History of Medieval Political Theory in the West.* New York: Barnes & Noble, 1953. 6 vols.

COPLESTON, FREDERICK C. *Medieval Philosophy.* New York: Harper & Row (Torchbooks), 1961.

DUNNING, WILLIAM A. *A History of Political Theories: Ancient and Medieval.* New York: Macmillan, 1936.

D'ENTREVES, ALEXANDER PASSERIN. *The Medieval Contribution to Political Thought.* London: Oxford Univ. Press, 1939.

FIGGIS, JOHN NEVILLE. *The Divine Right of Kings.* 2nd ed. New York: Harper & Row (Torchbooks), 1965.

GIERKE, OTTO. *Political Theories of the Middle Age.* Tr. by F. W. Maitland. Boston: Beacon Press, 1958.

GILSON, ÉTIENNE. *A History of Christian Philosophy in the Middle Ages.* New York: Random House, 1955.

HEARNSHAW, F. J. C., ed. *The Social and Political Ideas of Some Great Medieval Thinkers.* London: Harrap, 1923.

JENKS, EDWARD. *Law and Politics in the Middle Ages.* New York: Holt, Rinehart and Winston, 1932.

KANTOROWICZ, ERNST H. *The King's Two Bodies; A Study in Medieval Political Theology.* Princeton, N.J.: Princeton Univ. Press, 1957.

KERN, FRITZ. *Kingship and Law in the Middle Ages.* Tr. by S. B. Chrimes. Oxford: Blackwell & Mott, 1939.

LERNER, RALPH, AND MUHSIN MAHDI, eds. *Medieval Political Philosophy: A Sourcebook.* New York: Free Press, 1963.

LEWIS, EWART K., ed. *Medieval Political Ideas.* London: Routledge & Kegan Paul, 1954. 2 vols.

McILWAIN, CHARLES H. *The Growth of Political Thought in the West.* New York: Macmillan, 1932, chs. 5 and 6.

MORRALL, JOHN B. *Political Thought in Medieval Times.* Rev. ed. New York: Harper & Row (Torchbooks), 1962.

RIESENBERG, PETER N. *The Inalienability of Sovereignty in Medieval Political Thought.* New York: Columbia Univ. Press, 1956.

ROSENTHAL, ERWIN I. J. *Political Thought in Medieval Islam.* London: Cambridge Univ. Press, 1958.

TIERNEY, BRIAN. *The Crisis of Church and State, 1050–1300.* Englewood Cliffs, N.J.: Prentice-Hall (Spectrum Books), 1964. With selected documents.

ULLMAN, WALTER. *History of Political Thought: The Middle Ages.* Baltimore: Penguin Books (Pelican Books), 1965.

————. *Medieval Papalism; The Political Theories of the Medieval Canonists.* London: Methuen, 1949.

WILKS, MICHAEL J. *The Problem of Sovereignty in the Later Middle Ages.* London: Cambridge Univ. Press, 1963.

John of Salisbury

JOHN OF SALISBURY. *Early Letters.* Vol. 1, *Letters.*
Ed. by W. J. Millor and H. E. Butler. Rev. by
C. N. L. Brooke. London: Nelson, 1955.
——. *Policraticus.* Ed. by C. C. J. Webb. Ox-
ford: Clarendon Press, 1909. 2 vols.
——. *The Statesman's Book of John of Salisbury.*
Tr. by John Dickinson. New York: Knopf,
1927.
LIEBESCHUTZ, HANS. *Medieval Humanism in the
Life and Writings of John of Salisbury.* Lon-
don: Univ. of London Press (Warburg Insti-
tute), 1950.
WEBB, CLEMENT C. J. *John of Salisbury.* London:
Methuen, 1932.

Dante

DANTE ALIGHIERI. *The Divine Comedy.* Italian
with Eng. tr. by Geoffrey L. Bickersteth. Cam-
bridge, Mass.: Harvard Univ. Press, 1965.
——. *De Monarchia.* Tr. by Henry Aurelia. Bos-
ton: Houghton Mifflin, 1904.
——. *On World Government.* Tr. by Herbert W.
Schneider. 2nd rev. ed. New York: Liberal Arts
Press, 1957.
DAVIS, CHARLES T. *Dante and the Idea of Rome.*
London: Oxford Univ. Press, 1957.
D'ENTREVES, ALEXANDER PASSERIN. *Dante as a Po-
litical Thinker.* Oxford: Clarendon Press, 1952.
GILSON, ÉTIENNE. *Dante and Philosophy.* Tr. by
David Moore. New York: Harper & Row
(Torchbooks), 1963.
LENKEITH, NANCY. *Dante and the Legend of Rome.*
London: Univ. of London Press (Warburg In-
stitute), 1952.
ROLBIECKI, JOHN J. *The Political Philosophy of
Dante Alighieri.* Washington, D.C.: Catholic
Univ. of America Press, 1921.

Marsilio of Padua

ALLEN, J. W. "Marsilio of Padua and Medieval Sec-
ularism." In F. J. C. Hearnshaw, ed., *The So-
cial and Political Ideas of Some Great Medieval
Thinkers.* London: Harrap, 1923, ch. 7.
EMERTON, EPHRAIM. *The Defensor Pacis of Marsilio
of Padua: A Critical Study.* Gloucester, Mass.:
Peter Smith, 1951.
D'ENTREVES, ALEXANDER PASSERIN. *The Medieval
Contribution to Political Thought.* London:
Oxford Univ. Press, ch. 2.
MARSILIUS OF PADUA. *The Defender of Peace.* Ed.
and tr. by Alan Gewirth. New York: Columbia
Univ. Press, 1951. 2 vols. Vol 1 is commen-
tary.

PREVITÉ-ORTON, C. W. *Marsilius of Padua.* London:
Milford, 1935.

Nicholas of Cusa

BETT, HENRY. *Nicholas of Cusa.* London: Methuen,
1932.
MORRALL, JOHN B. *Gerson and the Great Schism.*
Manchester, Eng.: Manchester Univ. Press,
1960.
NICOLAI DE CUSA. *De Concordantia Catholica.* Ed.
by Gerhard Kallen. Hamburg: Meiner, 1964–
65. 2 vols.
——. *Unity and Reform: Selected Writings of
Nicholas de Cusa.* Ed. by John P. Dolan.
Notre Dame, Ind.: Univ. of Notre Dame Press,
1962.
SIGMUND, PAUL. *Nicholas of Cusa and Medieval
Political Thought.* Cambridge, Mass.: Harvard
Univ. Press, 1963.
TIERNEY, BRIAN. *Foundations of the Conciliar The-
ory.* New York: Cambridge Univ. Press, 1955.
WATANABE, MORIMICHI. *The Political Ideas of Nich-
olas of Cusa.* Geneva: Libraire Droz, 1963.

Chapter 8 MACHIAVELLI

Works by Machiavelli

Chief Works and Others. Ed. and tr. by Allan H.
Gilbert. Durham, N.C.: Duke Univ. Press,
1965. 3 vols.
The Discourses. Tr. by Leslie J. Walker. New
Haven, Conn.: Yale Univ. Press, 1950. 2 vols.
*The Historical, Political and Diplomatic Writings
of Niccolo Machiavelli.* Tr. by Christian E. Det-
mold. Boston: Houghton Mifflin, 1882–91. 4
vols.
History of Florence and of the Affairs of Italy.
Intro. by Felix Gilbert. New York: Harper &
Row (Torchbooks), 1960.
The Prince and The Discourses. Tr. by Luigi Ricci
and Christian Detmold. New York: Random
House (Modern Library), 1940.

Secondary Works

BUTTERFIELD, HERBERT. *The Statecraft of Machiavelli.* New York: Macmillan (Collier Books),
1962.
CHABOD, FREDERICO. *Machiavelli and the Renaissance.* Tr. by David Moore. Cambridge, Mass.:
Harvard Univ. Press, 1958.
GILBERT, ALLAN H. *Machiavelli's Prince and Its
Forerunners.* Durham, N.C.: Duke Univ. Press,
1938.

Gilbert, Felix. *Machiavelli and Guicciardini; Politics and History in Sixteenth-Century Florence.* Princeton, N.J.: Princeton Univ. Press, 1965.

Guicciardini, Francesco. *Maxims and Reflections of a Renaissance Statesman.* Tr. by Mario Domandi. New York: Harper & Row (Torchbooks), 1965.

Hale, John Rigby. *Machiavelli and Renaissance Italy.* New York: Macmillan, 1960.

Meinecke, Friedrich. *Machiavellism; The Doctrine of Raison D'Etat and Its Place in Modern History.* Tr. by Douglas Scott. London: Routledge & Kegan Paul, 1957.

Ridolfi, Roberto. *The Life of Niccolo Machiavelli.* Tr. by Cecil Grayson. Chicago: Univ. of Chicago Press, 1963.

Strauss, Leo. *Thoughts on Machiavelli.* New York: Free Press, 1958.

Whitfield, John H. *Machiavelli.* Oxford: Blackwell & Mott, 1947.

Chapter 9 **THE REFORMATION**

General

Allen, J. W. *Political Thought in the Sixteenth Century.* Rev. ed. New York: Barnes & Noble, 1957.

Ames, Russell A. *Citizen Thomas More and His Utopia.* Princeton, N.J.: Princeton Univ. Press, 1949.

Bainton, Roland H. *The Reformation of the Sixteenth Century.* Boston: Beacon Press, 1952.

Church, William Farr. *Constitutional Thought in Sixteenth-Century France.* Cambridge, Mass.: Harvard Univ. Press, 1941.

Daly, Lowrie John. *The Political Theory of John Wyclif.* (Jesuit Study, No. 17.) Chicago: Loyola Univ. Press, 1962.

Dodge, Guy H. *The Political Theory of the Huguenots of the Dispersion.* New York: Columbia Univ. Press, 1947.

Dunning, William A. *A History of Political Theory from Luther to Montesquieu.* New York: Macmillan, 1905.

Erasmus, Desiderius. *The Education of a Christian Prince.* Tr. by Lester K. Born. New York: Columbia Univ. Press, 1936.

Hamilton, Bernice. *Political Thought in Sixteenth-Century Spain.* Oxford: Clarendon Press, 1963.

Harbison, E. Harris. *The Age of Reformation.* Ithaca, N.Y.: Cornell Univ. Press, 1955.

Kautsky, Karl. *Thomas More and His Utopia.* New York: Russell & Russell, 1959.

More, Thomas. *Utopia.* Tr. by H. S. V. Ogden. New York: Appleton-Century-Crofts, 1949.

Mosse, George L. *The Holy Pretence; A Study in Christianity and Reason of State from William Perkins to John Winthrop.* Oxford: Blackwell & Mott, 1957.

Murray, Robert H. *The Political Consequences of the Reformation.* London: Benn, 1926.

Reynolds, E. E. *St. Thomas More.* New York: Kenedy, 1953.

Smith, Preserved. *Erasmus.* New York: Harper & Row, 1923.

Tawney, R. H. *Religion and the Rise of Capitalism.* New York: New American Library (Mentor Books), 1958.

Troeltsch, Ernst. *The Social Teaching of the Christian Churches.* Tr. by Olive Wyon. New York: Macmillan, 1950. 2 vols.

Vindiciae contra tyrannos. Tr. by H. J. Laski. London: Bell, 1924.

Weber, Max. *The Protestant Ethic and the Spirit of Capitalism.* Tr. by Talcott Parsons. New York: Scribner's, 1950.

Luther

Bainton, Roland H. *Here I Stand: A Life of Martin Luther.* New York: New American Library (Mentor Books), 1955.

Cranz, Ferdinand Edmund. *An Essay on the Development of Luther's Thought on Justice, Law and Society.* Cambridge, Mass.: Harvard Univ. Press, 1959.

Erikson, Erik H. *Young Man Luther.* New York: Norton, 1958.

Forell, George. *Faith Active in Love: An Interpretation of Principles Underlying Luther's Social Ethics.* New York: American Peoples Press, 1954.

Luther, Martin. *Reformation Writings.* Tr. by Bertram Lee Wolf. London: Lutterworth Press, 1952, 1956. 2 vols.

———. *Selections from His Writings.* Ed. by John Dillenberger. Garden City, N.Y.: Doubleday (Anchor Books), 1961.

———. *Works.* Ed. by Jaroslav Pelikan and Helmut T. Lehman. St. Louis, Mo.: Concordia; Philadelphia: Muhlenberg Press. 1955 et sec. 55 vols.

Mueller, William A. *Church and State in Luther and Calvin.* Nashville, Tenn.: Abingdon, 1954.

Ritter, Gerhard. *Luther, His Life and Work.* Tr. by John Riches. New York: Harper & Row, 1963.

SCHWEIBERT, ERNEST G. *Luther and His Times.* St. Louis, Mo.: Concordia, 1950.

WARING, LUTHER H. *The Political Theories of Martin Luther.* New York: Putnam's, 1910.

Calvin

CHENEVIERE, MARC-EDOUARD. *La Pensée politique de Calvin.* Geneva: Éditions Labor, 1937.

CALVIN, JOHN. *Institutes of the Christian Religion.* Ed. by J. T. McNeill. Tr. by F. L. Battles. (Library of Christian Classics, Vols. 20, 21.) Philadelphia: Westminster Press, 1960. 2 vols.

———. *Tracts Relating to the Reformation.* Tr. by H. Beveridge. Grand Rapids, Mich.: Eerdmans, 1957. 3 vols.

HARKNESS, GEORGIA. *John Calvin: The Man and His Ethics.* Nashville, Tenn.: Abingdon (Apex Books), 1958.

MACKINNON, JAMES. *Calvin and the Reformation.* London: Longmans, Green, 1936.

MCNEILL, JOHN T. *The History and Character of Calvinism.* New York: Oxford Univ. Press, 1954.

MOSSE, GEORGE L. *Calvinism, Authoritarian or Democratic?* New York: Holt, Rinehart and Winston, 1957.

Bodin

BODIN, JEAN. *Method for the Easy Comprehension of History* (1566). Tr. by Beatrice Reynolds. New York: Columbia Univ. Press, 1945.

———. *Oeuvres philosophiques.* Tr. by Pierre Mesnard. Paris: Presses Universitaires de France, 1951, 1952. 2 vols.

———. *The Six Bookes of a Commonweale* (Eng. tr. of 1606). Ed. by Kenneth D. McRae. Cambridge, Mass.: Harvard Univ. Press, 1962.

———. *Six Bookes of the Commonwealth.* Abridged ed. Tr. by M. J. Tooley. (Blackwell's Political Texts.) New York: Macmillan, 1955.

FRANKLIN, JULIAN H. *Jean Bodin and the Sixteenth-Century Revolution in the Methodology of Law and History.* New York: Columbia Univ. Press, 1963.

REYNOLDS, BEATRICE. *Proponents of Limited Monarchy in Sixteenth-Century France: Francis Hotman and Jean Bodin.* New York: Columbia Univ. Press, 1931.

Hooker

DAVIES, E. T. *The Political Ideas of Richard Hooker.* London: Society for Promoting Christian Knowledge, 1946.

HOOKER, RICHARD. *Works.* Ed. by John Keble. 7th ed. Oxford: Clarendon Press, 1888. 3 vols.

———. *Hooker's Ecclesiastical Polity, Book VIII.* Intro. by R. Houk. New York: Columbia Univ. Press, 1931.

———. *Of the Laws of Ecclesiastical Polity.* New York: Dutton (Everyman's Library), 1907. 2 vols.

MORRIS, CHRISTOPHER. *Political Thought in England, Tyndale to Hooker.* London: Oxford Univ. Press, 1953, ch. 9.

MUNZ, PETER. *The Place of Hooker in the History of Thought.* London: Routledge & Kegan Paul, 1952.

SHIRLEY, F. J. *Richard Hooker and Contemporary Political Ideas.* London: Society for Promoting Christian Knowledge, 1949.

Chapter 10 THE SEVENTEENTH CENTURY

General

BOULENGER, JACQUES. *The Seventeenth Century.* (The National History of France, No. 3.) New York: Putnam's, 1920.

CARRÉ, MAYRICK. *Phases of Thought in England.* Oxford: Clarendon Press, 1949.

CLARK, G. N. *The Seventeenth Century.* New York: Oxford Univ. Press (Galaxy Books), 1961. An intellectual survey of Europe.

GOOCH, G. P. *Political Thought in England from Bacon to Halifax.* London: Butterworth, 1914.

STANKIEWICZ, W. J. *Politics and Religion in Seventeenth-Century France.* Berkeley: Univ. of California Press, 1960.

WILLEY, BASIL. *The Seventeenth Century Background; Studies in the Thought of the Age in Relation to Poetry and Religion.* New York: Columbia Univ. Press, 1934; Garden City, N.Y.: Doubleday (Anchor Books), 1953.

The Political Obligation of Subjects

ALLEN, J. W. *English Political Thought, 1603–1644.* London: Methuen, 1938.

BACON, FRANCIS. *Essays or Counsels Civil and Moral.* London: Dent (Everyman), 1906. A reprint of the fifth and last edition written by Bacon and published in 1625. The first edition was published in 1597.

FIGGIS, JOHN NEVILLE. *The Theory of the Divine Right of Kings.* 2nd ed. New York: Harper & Row (Torchbooks), 1960.

FILMER, ROBERT. *Patriarcha and Other Political Works.* Ed. by Peter Laslett. Oxford: Blackwell & Mott, 1949.

GROTIUS, HUGO. *De juri belli et pacis.* London: Cambridge Univ. Press, 1853. 3 vols. Latin text of 1625 with tr. by William Whewell. The *Prolegomena* is published by Liberal Arts Press, 1957.

JAMES I. *The Political Works of James I.* Ed. by Charles H. McIlwain. Cambridge, Mass.: Harvard Univ. Press, 1918.

KNIGHT, W. S. M. *The Life and Work of Hugo Grotius.* London: Sweet & Maxwell, 1925.

KRIEGER, LEONARD. *The Politics of Discretion: Pufendorf and the Acceptance of Natural Law.* Chicago: Univ. of Chicago Press, 1965.

PUFENDORF, SAMUEL. *De officio hominis et civis* (1673). (Carnegie Classics in International Law.) New York: Oxford Univ. Press, 1921. 2 vols. Vol. 2 tr. by F. G. Moore.

———. *De jure naturae et gentium* (1688). (Carnegie Classics in International Law.) Oxford: Clarendon Press, 1934. 2 vols. Vol. 2 tr. by C. H. Oldfather and W. A. Oldfather.

SPINOZA, BENEDICT DE. *Writings on Political Philosophy.* Ed. by A. G. A. Balz. New York: Appleton-Century-Crofts, 1937. Contains the *Tractatus politicus* of 1677 in full in the R. H. M. Elwes tr. of 1883.

———. *The Political Works.* Ed. and tr. by A. G. Wernham. Oxford: Clarendon Press, 1958. Contains the *Tractatus politicus* in full and the *Tractatus theologico politicus* (1670) in part.

SYKES, NORMAN. "Bossuet." In F. J. C. Hearnshaw, ed. *The Social and Political Ideas of Some Great French Thinkers of the Age of Reason.* London: Harrap, 1930, ch. 2.

VREELAND, HAMILTON. *Hugo Grotius.* New York: Oxford Univ. Press, 1917.

Restraints upon Rulers: Constitutionalism

ALTHUSIUS, JOHANNES. *Politica methodica digesta.* Ed. by Carl J. Friedrich. Cambridge, Mass.: Harvard Univ. Press, 1932.

———. *The Politics of Johannes Althusius.* Abridged ed. Tr. by Frederick S. Carney. Boston: Beacon Press, 1964.

BARKER, ARTHUR. *Milton and the Puritan Dilemma, 1641–1660.* Toronto: Univ. of Toronto Press, 1942.

BOWEN, CATHERINE DRINKER. *The Lion and the Throne; The Life and Time of Sir Edward Coke.* Boston: Little, Brown, 1956.

COKE, EDWARD. *The First Part of the Institutes of the Laws of England.* Ed. by Francis Hargrove and Charles Butler. London: Clarke, 1832.

CROMWELL, OLIVER. *The Writings and Speeches of Oliver Cromwell.* Ed. by Wilbur C. Abbott. Cambridge, Mass.: Harvard Univ. Press, 1937–47. 4 vols.

GARDINER, SAMUEL RAWSON, ed. *The Constitutional Documents of the Puritan Revolution.* Oxford: Clarendon Press, 1889.

GERBRANDY, P. S. *National and International Stability; Althusius, Grotius, Van Vollenhoven.* London: Oxford Univ. Press, 1944.

GOOCH, G. P. *English Democratic Ideas in the Seventeenth Century.* 2nd ed. New York: Harper & Row (Torchbooks), 1960.

MILLER, PERRY. *The New England Mind; The Seventeenth Century.* New York: Macmillan, 1939.

MILTON, JOHN. *Areopagitica.* New York: Dutton (Everyman's Library), 1927.

PERRY, RALPH BARTON. *Puritanism and Democracy.* New York: Vanguard, 1944.

WILLIAMS, ROGER. *Works.* Providence, R.I.: Narragansett Club, 1866. 6 vols. The standard edition.

———. *Roger Williams; His Contribution to the American Tradition.* Indianapolis, Ind.: Bobbs-Merrill, 1953.

WOODHOUSE, A. S. P., ed. *Puritanism and Liberty; Being the Army Debates (1647–1649) from the Clarke Manuscripts.* 2nd ed. Chicago: Univ. of Chicago Press, 1951.

ZAGORIN, PEREZ. *A History of Political Thought in the English Revolution.* London: Routledge & Kegan Paul, 1954.

The Ground of Political Authority: Populism

BLITZER, CHARLES. *An Immortal Commonwealth: The Political Thought of James Harrington.* New Haven: Yale Univ. Press, 1960.

FRANK, JOSEPH. *The Levellers; A History of the Writings of Three Seventeenth-Century Social Democrats: John Lilburne, Richard Overton, William Walwyn.* Cambridge, Mass.: Harvard Univ. Press, 1955.

GIBB, M. A. *John Lilburne the Leveller; A Christian Democrat.* London: Drummond, 1947.

HALLER, WILLIAM. *Liberty and Reformation in the Puritan Revolution.* New York: Columbia Univ. Press, 1955.

———, ed. *Tracts on Liberty in the Puritan Revolution, 1638–1647.* New York: Columbia Univ. Press, 1934. 3 vols.

———, AND GODFREY DAVIES, eds. *The Leveller Tracts, 1647–1653.* New York: Columbia Univ. Press, 1944.

HARRINGTON, JAMES. *Political Writings; Representative Selections.* Ed. by Charles Blitzer. New York: Liberal Arts, 1955.

HARRISON, WILFRED. *Conflict and Compromise; A History of British Political Thought, 1593–1900.* New York: Free Press, 1965.

JONES, RUFUS M. *Mysticism and Democracy in the English Commonwealth.* Cambridge, Mass.: Harvard Univ. Press, 1932.

ROBERTSON, D. B. *The Religious Foundations of Leveller Democracy.* New York: Columbia Univ. Press, 1951.

WINSTANLEY, GERRARD. *Works.* Ed. by George H. Sabine. Ithaca, N.Y.: Cornell Univ. Press, 1941.

WOLFE, DON M. *The Leveller Manifestoes of the Puritan Revolution.* Camden, N.J.: Nelson, 1944.

Natural Law, Reason of State, and Comparative Politics

D'ENTREVES, ALEXANDER PASSERIN. *Natural Law.* New York: Hillary House, 1952.

GIERKE, OTTO. *Natural Law and the Theory of Society, 1500–1800.* London: Cambridge Univ. Press, 1934. 2 vols.; 1 vol. ed., 1950; Boston: Beacon Press, 1957.

HALIFAX, LORD (George Savile). *The Complete Works of George Savile, First Marquess of Halifax.* Ed. by Walter Raleigh. Oxford: Clarendon Press, 1912.

Chapter 11 HOBBES

Works by Hobbes

The English Works of Thomas Hobbes. Ed. by William Molesworth. London: Bohn, 1839–45, 11 vols.

Behemoth, or the Long Parliament. Ed. by F. Tonnies. London: Simpkin Marshall, 1889.

De cive, or The Citizen. Ed. by Sterling P. Lamprecht. New York: Appleton-Century-Crofts, 1949.

The Elements of Law, Natural and Politic. Ed. by F. Tonnies. London: Simpkin Marshall, 1889.

Leviathan. Ed. by A. D. Lindsay. New York: Dutton (Everyman's Library), 1950.

Leviathan. Ed. by Michael Oakeshott. Oxford: Blackwell & Mott, 1946.

Selections. Ed. by Frederick J. E. Woodbridge. New York: Scribner's, 1930.

Secondary Works

BOWLE, JOHN. *Hobbes and His Critics; A Study in Seventeenth-Century Constitutionalism.* London: Cape, 1951.

BROWN, KEITH C., ed. *Hobbes Studies.* Cambridge, Mass.: Harvard Univ. Press, 1965.

GOLDSMITH, M. M. *Hobbes's Science of Politics.* New York: Columbia Univ. Press, 1966.

HOOD, F. C. *The Divine Politics of Thomas Hobbes: An Interpretation of Leviathan.* Oxford: Clarendon Press, 1964.

JESSOP, THOMAS EDMUND. *Thomas Hobbes.* London: Longmans, Green, 1960.

LAIRD, JOHN. *Hobbes.* London: Oxford Univ. Press, 1934.

MACPHERSON, C. B. *The Political Theory of Possessive Individualism: Hobbes to Locke.* New York: Oxford Univ. Press, 1962.

PETERS, RICHARD. *Hobbes.* Harmondsworth, Eng.: Penguin Books, 1956.

STEPHEN, LESLIE. *Hobbes.* New York: Macmillan, 1904.

STRAUSS, LEO. *The Political Philosophy of Hobbes.* Tr. by Elsa M. Sinclair. Chicago: Univ. of Chicago Press (Phoenix Books), 1963.

WARRENDER, J. HOWARD. *The Political Philosophy of Hobbes; His Theory of Obligation.* Oxford: Clarendon Press, 1957.

WATKINS, J. W. N. *Hobbes's System of Ideas: A Study in the Political Significance of Philosophical Theories.* London: Hutchinson, 1965.

Chapter 12 LOCKE

Works by Locke

The Correspondence of John Locke and Edward Clarke. Ed. by Benjamin Rand. London: Oxford Univ. Press, 1927.

An Essay Concerning Human Understanding (1690). Ed. by Alexander Campbell Fraser. Oxford: Clarendon Press, 1894. 2 vols. A convenient abridged ed. is Russell Kirk, ed., Chicago: Regnery (Gateway Editions), 1956.

Essays on the Law of Nature (c. 1670's). Ed. by Wolfgang von Leyden. Oxford: Clarendon Press, 1954. Latin with Eng. tr.

A Letter Concerning Toleration (1685). Ed. by J. W. Gough. Oxford: Blackwell & Mott, 1947. See also entry below under *Two Treatises.*

The Reasonableness of Christianity (1695). Ed. by I. T. Ramsey. (Library of Modern Religious Thought.) Stanford, Cal.: Stanford Univ. Press, 1958.

Two Tracts on Government. Ed. and tr. by Philip Abrams. New York: Cambridge Univ. Press, 1967. Two early tracts on civil power and religion.

Two Treatises of Government. Intro. and Apparatus Criticus by Peter Laslett. London: Cambridge Univ. Press, 1960. The definitive edition, incorporating for the first time Locke's final revisions. See also Thomas I. Cook, ed. New York: Hafner, 1947; *A Treatise of Civil Government and A Letter Concerning Toleration.* Ed. by Charles L. Sherman. New York: Appleton-Century-Crofts, 1937; and *Of Civil Government.* Chicago: Regnery (Gateway Editions), 1955.

The Works of John Locke. London: Tegg, 1823. 10 vols.

Secondary Works

AARON, R. I. *John Locke.* 2nd ed. New York: Oxford Univ. Press, 1955.

COX, RICHARD H. *Locke on War and Peace.* New York: Oxford Univ. Press, 1960.

CRANSTON, MAURICE. *John Locke; A Biography.* New York: Macmillan, 1957.

CZAJKOWSKI, C. J. *The Theory of Private Property in Locke's Political Philosophy.* Notre Dame, Ind.: Univ. of Notre Dame Press, 1941.

FOX-BOURNE, H. R. *The Life of John Locke.* London: King & Jarrett, 1876. 2 vols.

GOUGH, JOHN W. *John Locke's Political Philosophy; Eight Studies.* Oxford: Clarendon Press, 1950.

LAMPRECHT, STERLING P. *The Moral and Political Philosophy of John Locke.* (Archives of Philosophy, No. 1.) New York: Columbia Univ. Press, 1918.

LASLETT, PETER. Intro. to his ed. of Robert Filmer's *Patriarcha.* Oxford: Blackwell & Mott, 1949.

O'CONNOR, D. J. *John Locke.* Baltimore: Penguin Books, 1952.

POLIN, RAYMOND. *La Politique morale de John Locke.* Paris: Presses Universitaires de France, 1960.

VAUGHN, C. E. *Studies in the History of Political Philosophy Before and After Rousseau.* Manchester, Eng.: Univ. of Manchester Press, 1925. 2 vols. Vol. 1, pp. 130–204.

YOLTON, JOHN Y. *John Locke and the Way of Ideas.* London: Oxford Univ. Press, 1956. Excellent bibliography.

Chapter 13 THE EIGHTEENTH CENTURY

The Enlightenment

BECKER, CARL L. *The Heavenly City of the Eighteenth-Century Philosophers.* New Haven, Conn.: Yale Univ. Press, 1932.

CASSIRER, ERNST. *The Philosophy of the Enlightenment.* Tr. by F. C. A. Koelln and J. P. Pettegrove. Boston: Beacon Press, 1955.

COBBAN, ALFRED. *In Search of Humanity: The Role of the Enlightenment in Modern History.* New York: Braziller, 1960.

DE TOCQUEVILLE, ALEXIS. *The Old Regime and the French Revolution* (1856). Tr. by Stuart Gilbert. Garden City, N.Y.: Doubleday (Anchor Books), 1955.

FLEISHER, DAVID. *William Godwin: A Study in Liberalism.* London: Allen & Unwin, 1951.

FRANKEL, CHARLES. *The Faith of Reason; The Idea of Progress in the French Enlightenment.* New York: Columbia Univ. Press, 1948.

GAY, PETER. *The Enlightenment: An Interpretation.* New York: Knopf, 1966. The bibliographic essay, pp. 423–555, is a tour de force.

———. *Voltaire's Politics; The Poet as Realist.* Princeton, N.J.: Princeton Univ. Press, 1959.

GODWIN, WILLIAM. *An Enquiry Concerning Political Justice.* Ed. by F. E. L. Priestly. 3rd ed. Toronto: Univ. of Toronto, 1946. 2 vols.

HAZARD, PAUL. *European Thought in the Eighteenth Century; From Montesquieu to Lessing.* Tr. by J. Lewis May. New Haven, Conn.: Yale Univ. Press, 1954.

HEARNSHAW, F. J. C., ed. *Social and Political Ideas of Representative Thinkers of the Revolutionary Age.* New York: Barnes & Noble, 1950.

———, ed. *Social and Political Ideas of Some Great French Thinkers of the Age of Reason.* New York: Barnes & Noble, 1950.

KANT, IMMANUEL. *Metaphysical Elements of Justice.* Ed. by John Ladd. New York: Liberal Arts Press, 1963.

KEGAN PAUL, C. *William Godwin.* London: King & Jarrett, 1876. 2 vols.

KETTLER, DAVID. *The Social and Political Thought of Adam Ferguson.* Columbus: Ohio State Univ. Press, 1965.

LASKI, HAROLD J. *The Rise of European Liberalism.* London: Allen & Unwin, 1936.

———. *Political Thought in England; Locke to Bentham.* London: Oxford Univ. Press (Home University Library), 1920.

MARTIN, KINGSLEY. *The Rise of French Liberal Thought; A Study of Political Ideas from Bayle to Condorcet.* Ed. by J. P. Mayer. New York: New York Univ. Press, 1954.

ROBBINS, CAROLINE. *The Eighteenth-Century Commonwealthman.* Cambridge, Mass.: Harvard Univ. Press, 1959.

ROCKWOOD, RAYMOND O., ed. *Carl Becker's Heavenly City Revisited.* Ithaca, N.Y.: Cornell Univ. Press, 1958.

ROWE, CONSTANCE. *Voltaire and the State.* New York: Columbia Univ. Press, 1955.

STEPHEN, LESLIE. *History of English Thought in the Eighteenth Century.* 3rd ed. New York: Harcourt, Brace & World (Harbinger Books), 1962. 2 vols.

VOLTAIRE. *Oeuvres Complètes.* Ed. by Louis Moland. Paris: Garnier, 1883–85. 52 vols.

———. *Philosophical Dictionary.* Sel. and ed. by H. I. Woolf. New York: Knopf, 1938.

———. *Selections.* Ed. by George R. Havens. New York: Century, 1925.

VYVERBERG, HENRY. *Historical Pessimism in the French Enlightenment.* Cambridge, Mass.: Harvard Univ. Press, 1958.

WILLEY, BASIL. *The Eighteenth-Century Background; Studies on the Idea of Nature in the Thought of the Period.* London: Chatto & Windus, 1940.

Economics and Politics

BEER, MAX. *An Inquiry into Physiocracy.* New York: Macmillan, 1940.

CROPSEY, JOSEPH. *Polity and Economy; An Interpretation of the Principles of Adam Smith.* The Hague: Nijhoff, 1957.

GINZBERG, ELI. *The House of Adam Smith.* New York: Columbia Univ. Press, 1934.

HEILBRONER, ROBERT L. *The Worldly Philosophers.* New York: Simon and Schuster, 1953, chs. 1–4.

HIGGS, HENRY. *The Physiocrats.* New York: Macmillan, 1897.

POLANYI, KARL. *The Great Transformation.* Boston: Beacon Press, 1957.

SCHUMPETER, JOSEPH A. *A History of Economic Analysis.* New York: Oxford Univ. Press, 1954, Part 2.

SMITH, ADAM. *Adam Smith's Moral and Political Philosophy.* Ed. by Herbert W. Schneider. New York: Hafner, 1948.

———. *An Inquiry into the Nature and Causes of the Wealth of Nations.* Ed. by E. B. Bax. London: Bell, 1896. 2 vols.

History and Politics

ADAMS, H. P. *The Life and Writings of Giambattista Vico.* London: Allen & Unwin, 1935.

BOLINGBROKE, LORD (HENRY ST. JOHN). *A Dissertation on Parties.* 10th ed. London: Davies and Cadell, 1775 (orig. ed., 1734).

———. *The Idea of a Patriot King* (1738). Ed. by Sydney W. Jackman. New York: Liberal Arts Press, 1965.

———. *Letters on the Study and Use of History.* 2nd ed. London: Cadell, 1770 (orig. ed., 1735).

CAPONIGRI, A. R. *Time and Idea; The Theory of History in Giambattista Vico.* Chicago: Regnery, 1953.

CONDORCET, MARQUIS DE (MARIE JEAN ANTOINE NICHOLAS DE CARITAT). *Outlines of an Historical View of the Progress of the Human Mind.* Philadelphia: Carey, Rice, Orwood, Bache, and Fellows, 1796.

CROCE, BENEDETTO. *The Philosophy of Giambattista Vico.* Tr. by R. G. Collingwood. New York: Macmillan, 1913.

PETRIE, CHARLES. *Bolingbroke.* London: Collins, 1937. A critical biography.

SCHAPIRO, J. SALWYN. *Condorcet and the Rise of Liberalism.* New York: Harcourt, Brace & World, 1934.

VICO, GIAMBATTISTA. *The New Science.* Tr. by Thomas G. Bergin and Max H. Fisch. Ithaca, N.Y.: Cornell Univ. Press, 1948. From 3rd ed. of 1744.

Law and Constitutionalism

ADAMS, JOHN. "A Defense of the Constitution." In *Works.* Ed. by Charles Francis Adams. Boston: Little, Brown, 1851. Vol. 6.

BECKER, CARL. *The Declaration of Independence: A Study in the History of Political Ideas.* New York: Random House (Vintage Books), 1957.

BLACKSTONE, WILLIAM. *Commentaries on the Laws of England.* Ed. by William G. Hammond. 8th ed. San Francisco: Whitney, 1890. Also Oxford: Clarendon Press, 1765–69. 4 vols.

BOORSTIN, DANIEL J. *The Mysterious Science of the Law; An Essay on Blackstone's Commentaries.* Boston: Beacon Press, 1958.

FARRAND, MAX, ed. *The Records of the Federal Convention of 1787.* New Haven, Conn.: Yale Univ. Press, 1911. 2 vols.

The Federalist. New York: Random House (Modern Library), 1937.

FRIEDRICH, CARL J. *The Philosophy of Law in Historical Perspective.* Chicago: Univ. of Chicago Press, 1958.

GOUGH, JOHN. *Fundamental Law in English Constitutional History.* Oxford: Clarendon Press, 1955.

HANDLER, EDWARD. *America and Europe in the Political Thought of John Adams.* Cambridge, Mass.: Harvard Univ. Press, 1964.

HARTZ, LOUIS. *The Liberal Tradition in America.* New York: Harcourt, Brace & World (Harvest Books), 1955.

LOCKMILLER, DAVID A. *Sir William Blackstone.* Chapel Hill: Univ. of North Carolina Press, 1938.

OTIS, JAMES. *Rights of British Colonies Asserted and Proved.* London: Williams, 1766.

WHITE, ANDREW DICKSON. *Seven Great Statesmen in the Warfare of Humanity with Unreason.* New York: Century, 1912. Ch. 3 is on Thomasius.

WILSON, JAMES. *Works.* Ed. by J. D. Andrews. Chicago: Callaghan, 1896. 2 vols.

Theory of Revolution

ACTON, LORD (JOHN E. E. D. ACTON). *Lectures on the French Revolution.* London: Macmillan, 1910.

BEST, M. A. *Thomas Paine; Prophet and Martyr of Democracy.* New York: Harcourt, Brace & World, 1927.

BRINTON, CRANE. *The Anatomy of Revolution.* New York: Norton, 1938.

CONWAY, M. C. *The Life of Thomas Paine.* New York: Putnam's, 1892. 2 vols.

JEFFERSON, THOMAS. *Life and Selected Writings.* Ed. by Adrienne Koch and William Peden. New York: Random House (Modern Library), 1944.

———. *Political Writings.* Ed. by Edward Dumbauld. New York: Liberal Arts Press, 1955.

PAINE, THOMAS. *The Complete Writings.* Ed. by Philip Foner. New York: Citadel Press, 1945. 2 vols.

TALMON, J. L. *The Origins of Totalitarian Democracy.* New York: Praeger, 1960.

WICKWAR, W. HARDY. *Baron d'Holbach: A Prelude to the French Revolution.* London: Allen & Unwin, 1935.

Chapter 14 MONTESQUIEU

Works by Montesquieu

Cahiers, 1716–1755. Ed. by Bernard Grasset. Paris: Grasset, 1941.

Considerations on the Causes of the Grandeur and the Decadence of the Romans. Tr. by Jehu Baker. New York: Appleton-Century-Crofts, 1894.

Oeuvres complètes. Ed. by Edouard Laboulaye. Paris: Garnier, 1875–79. 7 vols.

Persian and Chinese Letters. Tr. by John Davidson. New York: Dunne, 1901.

The Spirit of the Laws. Ed. by Franz Neumann. Tr. by Thomas Nugent. New York: Hafner, 1949. Many other editions.

Secondary Works

CABEEN, DAVID C. *Montesquieu Bibliography.* New York: New York Public Library, 1947. An extended and excellent annotated bibliography.

COURTNEY, CECIL PATRICK. *Montesquieu and Burke.* Oxford: Blackwell & Mott, 1963.

DEDIEU, JOSEPH. *Montesquieu; L'Homme et l'oeuvre* (1913). Paris: Boivin, 1943.

DURKHEIM, ÉMILE. *Montesquieu et Rousseau; Precurseurs de la sociologie.* Intro. by George Davy. Paris: Rivière, 1953. (Written 1892 and 1918.)

FAGUET, ÉMILE. *La Politique comparée de Montesquieu, Rousseau, et Voltaire.* Paris: Société d'Imprimerie et de Librairie, 1902.

GRANT, A. J. "Montesquieu." In F. J. C. Hearnshaw, ed., *The Social and Political Ideas of Some Great French Thinkers in the Age of Reason.* London: Harrap, 1930.

HOLMES, OLIVER WENDELL. "Montesquieu." In *Collected Legal Papers.* New York: Appleton-Century-Crofts, 1921.

LEVIN, LAWRENCE MEYER. *The Political Doctrine of Montesquieu's Esprit des Lois; Its Classical Background.* New York: The Institute of French Studies, 1936.

SHACKLETON, ROBERT. *Montesquieu: A Critical Biography.* London: Oxford Univ. Press, 1961.

STARK, W. *Montesquieu: Pioneer of the Sociology of Knowledge.* Toronto: Univ. of Toronto Press, 1961.

TEBERT, COURTNEY. *Montesquieu.* Oxford: Clarendon Press, 1904.

VAUGHN, C. E. *Studies in the History of Political Philosophy Before and After Rousseau.* Manchester, Eng.: Univ. of Manchester Press, 1939. 2 vols. Vol. 1, pp. 253–302.

Chapter 15 ROUSSEAU

Works by Rousseau

The Confessions. Tr. by Edmund Wilson. New York: Knopf, 1923. 2 vols. Many other editions.

Émile. Tr. by Barbara Foxley. New York: Dutton (Everyman's Library), 1948.

The First and Second Discourses. Ed. by Roger D. Masters and Judith R. Masters. New York: St. Martin's Press, 1964.

Oeuvres complètes. Paris: Hachette, 1886–1911. 13 vols.

The Political Writings of Jean-Jacques Rousseau. Ed. by C. E. Vaughn. New York: Wiley, 1962 (orig. ed., 1915). 2 vols. Note Vaughn's introduction.

Rousseau; Political Writings. Tr. by Frederick W. Watkins. London: Nelson, 1953.

The Social Contract and Discourses. Tr. by G. D. H. Cole. New York: Dutton (Everyman's Library), 1950. Note Cole's introduction.

The Social Contract. Ed. by Charles Frankel. New York: Hafner, 1947. An eighteenth-century translation revised by Frankel.

Secondary Works

BABBITT, IRVING. *Rousseau and Romanticism.* Boston: Houghton Mifflin, 1919; New York: World (Meridian Books), 1955.

BROOME, J. H. *Rousseau; A Study of His Thought.* London: Arnold, 1963.

CASSIRER, ERNST. *The Question of Jean-Jacques Rousseau.* Trans., ed., and intro. by Peter Gay. New York: Columbia Univ. Press, 1954.

——. *Rousseau, Kant, and Goethe.* Princeton, N.J.: Princeton Univ. Press, 1945.

CHAPMAN, JOHN W. *Rousseau—Totalitarian or Liberal?* New York: Columbia Univ. Press, 1956.

COBBAN, ALFRED. *Rousseau and the Modern State.* Hamden, Conn.: Shoe String Press (Archon Books), 1961.

DERATHÉ, ROBERT. *Jean-Jacques Rousseau et la science politique de son temps.* Paris: Presses Universitaires de France, 1950.

——. *Le Rationalisme de Jean-Jacques Rousseau.* Paris: Presses Universitaires de France, 1948.

GREEN, F. C. *Jean-Jacques Rousseau; A Critical Study of His Life and Writings.* London: Cambridge Univ. Press, 1955.

GRIMSLEY, RONALD. *Jean-Jacques Rousseau; A Study of Self-Awareness.* Cardiff, Wales: Univ. of Wales Press, 1961.

HENDEL, CHARLES W. *Jean-Jacques Rousseau, Moralist.* London: Oxford Univ. Press, 1934. 2 vols.

HØFFDING, HARALD. *Jean-Jacques Rousseau and His Philosophy.* Tr. by William Richards and Leo Saidla. New Haven, Conn.: Yale Univ. Press, 1930.

MCDONALD, JOAN. *Rousseau and the French Revolution, 1762–1791.* London: Athlone Press, 1965.

MORLEY, JOHN. *Rousseau.* London: Macmillan, 1905. 2 vols.

OSBORNE, ANNIE M. *Rousseau and Burke.* London: Oxford Univ. Press, 1940.

SCHINZ, ALBERT. *La Pensée de Jean-Jacques Rousseau.* Northampton, Mass.: Smith College, 1929.

STAROBINSKI, JEAN. *Jean-Jacques Rousseau: La Transparence et l'obstacle.* Paris: Librairie Plon, 1957.

WRIGHT, ERNEST HUNTER. *The Meaning of Rousseau.* London: Oxford Univ. Press, 1929.

Chapter 16 HUME

Works by Hume

David Hume's Political Essays. Ed. by Charles W. Hendel. New York: Liberal Arts Press, 1953. From the 1777 edition of *Essays, Moral and Political.*

Dialogues Concerning Natural Religion. Ed. by Norman Kemp Smith. 2nd ed. London: Nelson, 1947.

An Enquiry Concerning Human Understanding. Ed. by L. A. Selby-Bigge. Oxford: Clarendon Press, 1894. From the 1777 edition.

Essays and Treatises on Several Subjects. Edinburgh: Bell and Bradfate, 1800. 2 vols. Vol. 1 is *Essays, Moral, Political, and Literary.* Vol. 2 contains, among other works, *An Enquiry Concerning the Principles of Morals* and *The Natural History of Religion.*

The History of England from the Invasion of Julius Caesar to the Revolution of 1688. London: Cadell and Davies, 1802 (orig. ed., 1754–62). 8 vols.

The History of England from the Revolution to the Death of George II. Ed. by T. G. Smollett. London: Cadell and Baldwin, 1804. 5 vols.

Hume; Theory of Politics. Ed. by Frederick Watkins. Austin: Univ. of Texas, 1953. Note Watkins' introduction.

Moral and Political Philosophy. Ed. by Henry Aiken. New York: Hafner, 1948.

Treatise of Human Nature. Ed. by L. A. Selby-Bigge. Oxford: Clarendon Press, 1896.

Secondary Works

BONGIE, LAURENCE L. *David Hume: Prophet of the Counter-Revolution.* Oxford: Clarendon Press, 1965.

BRYSON, GLADYS. *Man and Society; The Scottish Inquiry of the Eighteenth Century.* Princeton, N.J.: Princeton Univ. Press, 1945.

HUXLEY, THOMAS. *Hume.* London: Macmillan, 1881.

KYDD, RACHEL M. *Reason and Conduct in Hume's Treatise.* London: Oxford Univ. Press, 1946.

LAING, B. M. *David Hume.* London: Benn, 1932.

LAIRD, JOHN. *Hume's Philosophy of Human Nature.* London: Methuen, 1932.

LETWIN, SHIRLEY R. *The Pursuit of Certainty: David Hume, Jeremy Bentham, John Stuart Mill, Beatrice Webb.* London: Cambridge Univ. Press, 1965.

MOSSNER, ERNEST C. *The Life of David Hume.* Austin: Univ. of Texas, 1954.

ROSS, WILLIAM G. *Human Nature and Utility in Hume's Social Philosophy.* Berea, Ky.: published by the author, 1942.

SMITH, NORMAN KEMP. *The Philosophy of David Hume.* London: Macmillan, 1941.

STEWART, JOHN B. *The Moral and Political Philosophy of David Hume.* New York: Columbia Univ. Press, 1963.

Chapter *17* BURKE

Works by Burke

Appeal from the New to the Old Whigs. Ed. by John M. Robson. New York: Liberal Arts Press, 1962.

Burke's Politics. Ed. by Ross Hoffman and S. J. Levack. New York: Knopf, 1949.

The Philosophy of Edmund Burke; A Selection from His Speeches and Writings. Ed. by L. I. Bredvold and R. G. Ross. Ann Arbor: Univ. of Michigan Press, 1961.

Reflections on the Revolution in France. Ed. by Russell Kirk. Chicago: Regnery, 1955.

Selected Writings of Edmund Burke. Ed. by Walter J. Bate. New York: Random House (Modern Library), 1960. *Appeal from the New to the Old Whigs* is a conspicuous omission from this collection.

Selected Writings and Speeches. Ed. by Peter J. Stanlis. Garden City, N.Y.: Doubleday (Anchor Books), 1963.

The Writings and Speeches of Edmund Burke. Boston: Little, Brown, 1901. 12 vols.

Secondary Works

CANAVAN, FRANCIS. *The Political Reason of Edmund Burke.* Durham, N.C.: Duke Univ. Press, 1960.

COBBAN, ALFRED. *Edmund Burke and the Revolt Against the Eighteenth Century.* New York: Macmillan, 1929.

COPELAND, THOMAS W. *Edmund Burke; Six Essays.* London: Cape, 1950.

HARRIS, RONALD W. *Political Ideas, 1760–1772.* London: Gollancz, 1963.

KIRK, RUSSELL. *The Conservative Mind; From Burke to Santayana.* Chicago: Regnery, 1953.

LASKI, HAROLD J. *Political Thought in England; Locke to Bentham.* London: Hutchinson, 1937, ch. 6.

MACCUNN, JOHN. *The Political Philosophy of Burke.* London: Longmans, Green, 1913.

MANSFIELD, HARVEY C., JR. *Statesmanship and Party Government; A Study of Burke and Bolingbroke.* Chicago: Univ. of Chicago Press, 1965.

MURRAY, ROBERT H. *Edmund Burke; A Biography.* Oxford, Clarendon Press, 1931.

PARKIN, CHARLES. *The Moral Basis of Burke's Political Thought; An Essay.* London: Cambridge Univ. Press, 1956.

STANLIS, PETER J. *Edmund Burke and the Natural Law.* Ann Arbor: Univ. of Michigan Press, 1958.

Chapter *18* THE NINETEENTH CENTURY

General

BARKER, ERNEST. *Political Thought in England, 1848–1914.* 2nd ed. London: Oxford Univ. Press (Home University Library), 1928.

BOWLE, JOHN. *Politics and Opinion in the Nineteenth Century.* New York: Oxford Univ. Press (Galaxy Books), 1964. See bibliography, pp. 500–02.

BRINTON, CRANE. *English Political Thought in the Nineteenth Century.* Cambridge, Mass.: Harvard Univ. Press, 1933.

FAGUET, ÉMILE. *Politiques et moralistes du dix-neuvième siècle.* Paris: Boivin, 1899. 3 vols.

HEARNSHAW, F. J. C., ed. *Essays in the Social and Political Ideas of the Age of Reaction and Reconstruction.* London: Harrap, 1932.

———, ed. *Social and Political Ideas of the Victorian Age.* London: Harrap, 1933.

KRIEGER, LEONARD. *The German Idea of Freedom.* Boston: Beacon Press, 1957. See bibliography, pp. 529–33.

LÖWITH, KARL. *From Hegel to Nietzsche.* Tr. by David E. Green. New York: Holt, Rinehart and Winston, 1964.

MAYER, J. P. *Political Thought in France from Sieyès to Sorel.* London: Faber & Faber, 1948.

MURRAY, R. H., ed. *Studies in English Social and Political Thinkers of the Nineteenth Century.* Heffer, 1929. 2 vols. Vol. 1 contains selections from Malthus, Bentham, James Mill, John Stuart Mill, Owen, Coleridge, Disraeli, Carlyle, Cobden, and Kingsley. Vol. 2 contains selections from Spencer, Maine, Ruskin, Arnold, Seeley, Bagehot, Green, Bryce, Maitland, and assorted socialists.

REISS, H. S., ed. *The Political Thought of the German Romantics, 1793–1815.* Oxford: Blackwell & Mott, 1955. Selections from Fichte, Novalis, Müller, Schleiermacher, Savigny.

RUGGIERO, GUIDO DE. *A History of European Liberalism.* Tr. by R. G. Collingwood. London: Oxford Univ. Press, 1927; Boston: Beacon Press, 1959. See bibliography.

SCHAPIRO, J. SALWYN. *Liberalism and the Challenge of Fascism; Social Forces in England and France, 1815–1870.* New York: McGraw-Hill, 1949. See bibliography, pp. 405–13.

SOLTAU, ROGER. *French Political Thought in the Nineteenth Century.* New Haven, Conn.: Yale Univ. Press, 1931.

English Utilitarianism [See also the bibliography for Chapter 19, "Bentham."]

AUSCHUTZ, R. P. *The Philosophy of John Stuart Mill.* Oxford: Clarendon Press, 1953.

AUSTIN, JOHN. *Austinian Theory of Law.* Ed. by W. Jethro Brown. London: Murray, 1906.

———. *The Province of Jurisprudence Determined; and, The Uses of the Study of Jurisprudence.* Ed. by H. L. A. Hart. London: Weidenfeld & Nicolson, 1954.

BRITTON, KARL. *John Stuart Mill.* Harmondsworth, Eng.: Penguin Books, 1953.

BULLOCK, ALAN, AND MAURICE SHOCK. *The Liberal Tradition: Fox to Keynes.* London: Oxford Univ. Press (Galaxy Books), 1967.

COWLING, MAURICE. *Mill and Liberalism.* New York: Cambridge Univ. Press, 1964.

HAMBURGER, JOSEPH. *Intellectuals in Politics: John Stuart Mill and the Philosophical Radicals.* New Haven, Conn.: Yale Univ. Press, 1965.

MILL, JAMES. *Essays on Government, Jurisprudence, Liberty of the Press, and Law of Nations.* Ed. by Philip Wheelwright. (Doran Series.) Garden City, N.Y.: Doubleday, Doran, 1935. Bound with works by Bentham and John Stuart Mill.

MILL, JOHN STUART. *Disquisitions and Discussions.* London: Longmans, Green, 1859–75. 4 vols.

———. *Essays on Politics and Culture.* Garden City, N.Y.: Doubleday, 1963.

———. *A Selection of His Works.* Ed. by John M. Robson. New York: St. Martin's Press, 1966.

———. *A System of Logic.* 8th ed. London: Longmans, Green, 1925, Book 6.

———. *Utilitarianism, Liberty, and Representative Government.* New York, Dutton (Everyman's Library), 1951. Many other editions.

Continental Liberalism

BASTID, PAUL. *Benjamin Constant et sa doctrine.* Paris: Colin, 1966. 2 vols.

CONSTANT, BENJAMIN. *Principes de politique,* in *Oeuvres.* Ed. by Alfred Roulin. Paris: Gallimard, 1957, pp. 1099–1249.

DE TOCQUEVILLE, ALEXIS. *Democracy in America.* Ed. by H. S. Commager. Tr. by Henry Reeve. London: Oxford Univ. Press, 1946. Many other editions.

———. *The Old Regime and the French Revolution.* Tr. by Stuart Gilbert. Garden City, N.Y.: Doubleday (Anchor Books), 1955. From 4th French ed. (1858).

GUIZOT, FRANÇOIS. *Democracy in France.* New York: Appleton-Century-Crofts, 1849.

HERR, RICHARD. *Tocqueville and the Old Regime.* Princeton, N.J.: Princeton Univ. Press, 1962.

LIVELY, JACK. *The Social and Political Thought of Alexis de Tocqueville.* London: Oxford Univ. Press, 1962.

MAZZINI, JOSEPH. *The Duties of Man and Other Essays.* New York: Dutton (Everyman's Library), 1929.

ROYER-COLLARD, PIERRE PAUL. *Les Fragments philosophiques.* Intro. by André Schimberg. Paris: Alcan, 1913.

SCHERMERHORN, ELIZABETH W. *Benjamin Constant.* London: Heinemann, 1924.

TALMON, J. L. *Political Messianism: The Romantic Phase.* New York: Praeger, 1961.

VON TREITSCHKE, HENRICH. *Politics.* Tr. by Blanche Dugdale and T. de Bille. New York: Macmillan, 1916. 2 vols.

Social Darwinism

BAGEHOT, WALTER. *Physics and Politics.* New York: Appleton-Century-Crofts, 1873.

DEWEY, JOHN. *The Influence of Darwin on Philosophy.* New York: Holt, Rinehart and Winston, 1910.

HOBHOUSE, LEONARD. *Social Evolution and Political Theory.* New York: Columbia Univ. Press, 1911.

HOFSTADTER, RICHARD. *Social Darwinism in American Thought.* Philadelphia: Univ. of Pennsylvania Press, 1944; Boston: Beacon, 1955. See bibliography.

RITCHIE, DAVID G. *Darwinism and Politics.* London: Sonnenschein, 1889.

RUMNEY, JUDAH. *Herbert Spencer's Sociology*. London: Williams and Norgate, 1934.

SPENCER, HERBERT. *First Principles*. New York: Appleton-Century-Crofts, 1864.

———. *The Man Versus the State*. Caldwell, Ida.: Caxton, 1940.

———. *Social Statics*. New York: Appleton-Century-Crofts, 1864.

STARR, HARRIS. *William Graham Sumner*. New York: Holt, Rinehart and Winston, 1925.

SUMNER, WILLIAM GRAHAM. *The Challenge of Facts and Other Essays*. New Haven, Conn.: Yale Univ. Press, 1914.

———. *Essays*. Ed. by A. G. Keller and M. R. Davie. New Haven, Conn.: Yale Univ. Press, 1934. 2 vols.

Conservatism [See also the bibliography for Chapter 20, "Hegel."]

BERLIN, ISAIAH. *The Hedgehog and the Fox; An Essay on Tolstoy's View of History*. New York: Simon and Schuster, 1953. Relates De Maistre to Stendahl and Tolstoy.

CAIRD, EDWARD. *The Social Philosophy and Religion of Comte*. London: Macmillan, 1885.

COMTE, AUGUSTE. *A General View of Positivism* (1848). Tr. by J. H. Bridges. Stanford, Cal.: Academic Reprints, n. d.

DE BONALD, LOUIS. *Legislation primitive*. 5th ed. Paris: Le Clere, 1857.

DEMAISTRE, JOSEPH. *The Works of Joseph deMaistre*. Ed. by Jack Lively. New York: Macmillan, 1965.

———. *On God and Society*. Tr. by Elisha Greifer. Chicago: Regnery (Gateway Editions), 1959.

FICHTE, JOHANN G. *Addresses to the German Nation*. Tr. by R. F. Jones and G. F. Turnbull. LaSalle, Ill.: Open Court, 1922.

GIANTURCO, ELIO. *Joseph de Maistre and Giambattista Vico*. Washington, D.C.: published by the author, 1937.

LASKI, HAROLD J. *Authority in the Modern State*. New Haven, Conn.: Yale Univ. Press, 1919, ch. 1.

MILL, JOHN STUART. *Auguste Comte and Positivism*. 3rd ed. London: Turner, 1882.

British Idealism

BOSANQUET, BERNARD. *Philosophical Theory of the State*. 4th ed. London: Macmillan, 1923.

BRADLEY, F. H. *Ethical Studies; Selected Studies*. Intro. by Ralph Ross. New York: Liberal Arts Press, 1951 (orig. ed., 1876).

GREEN, THOMAS HILL. *Lectures on the Principles of Political Obligation* (1879). Intro. by A. D. Lindsay. London: Longmans, Green, 1941.

———. *The Political Theory of T. H. Green*. Ed. by John R. Rodman. New York: Appleton-Century-Crofts, 1964.

HOBHOUSE, LEONARD. *The Metaphysical Theory of the State*. London: Allen & Unwin, 1918.

RICHTER, MELVIN. *The Politics of Conscience: T. H. Green and His Age*. Cambridge, Mass.: Harvard Univ. Press, 1964.

RITCHIE, DAVID G. *Natural Rights*. London: Allen & Unwin, 1894.

Elitism

CARLYLE, THOMAS. *Critical and Miscellaneous Essays*. 2nd ed. New York: Appleton-Century-Crofts, 1871.

———. *Heroes, Hero-Worship, and the Heroic in History*. New York: Burt, n. d. (orig. ed., 1841).

CASSIRER, ERNST. *The Myth of the State*. New Haven, Conn.: Yale Univ. Press, 1946, 1960. Ch. 15 is on Carlyle.

CHAMBERLAIN, HOUSTON STEWART. *The Foundations of the Nineteenth Century*. Tr. by John Lees. London: Lane, 1911. 2 vols.

DE GOBINEAU, ARTHUR. *The Inequality of Human Races*. Tr. by Adrian Collins. New York: Putnam's, 1915.

LIPPINCOTT, BENJAMIN E. *Victorian Critics of Democracy*. Minneapolis: Univ. of Minnesota Press, 1938. On Carlyle, Ruskin, Arnold, Stephen, Maine, and Lecky.

ROE, FREDERICK WILLIAM. *The Social Philosophy of Carlyle and Ruskin*. New York: Harcourt, Brace & World, 1921.

RUSKIN, JOHN. *The Seven Lamps of Architecture, Sesame and Lilies, Unto This Last*. Sterling ed. Boston: Estes, n. d.

Socialism and Anarchism [See also the bibliographies for Chapter 21, "Marx," and Chapter 24, "Lenin."]

AURICH, PAUL. *The Russian Anarchists*. Princeton, N.J.: Princeton Univ. Press, 1967.

BAKUNIN, MICHAEL. *Marxism, Freedom, and the State*. Tr. and ed. by K. J. Kenafick. London: Freedom, 1950.

———. *The Political Philosophy of Bakunin*. Ed. by G. P. Maxinoff. New York: Free Press, 1964.

BELLAMY, EDWARD. *Looking Backward* (1887). Memorial ed. Boston: Houghton Mifflin, 1898. Many other editions.

BERNERI, MARIE LOUISE. *Journey Through Utopia.* London: Routledge & Kegan Paul, 1950. See bibliography, pp. 320–29.

BRISBANE, ALBERT. *The Social Destiny of Man.* Philadelphia: Stollmeyer, 1840. By Fourier's chief American disciple.

BROGAN, DENIS W. *Proud'hon.* London: Hamilton, 1934.

BUBER, MARTIN. *Paths in Utopia.* Tr. by R. F. C. Hull. Boston: Beacon Press, 1960.

CARR, E. H. *Michael Bakunin.* London: Macmillan, 1937.

COLE, G. D. H. *A History of Socialist Thought.* London: Macmillan, 1953–60. 5 vols. A monumental work covering the period from 1789 to 1939. See the bibliographies in each volume.

———. *Robert Owen.* London: Benn, 1925.

COLE, MARGARET. *The Story of Fabian Socialism.* Stanford, Cal.: Stanford Univ. Press, 1962.

FOURIER, CHARLES. *Selections from the Works of Fourier.* Tr. by Julia Franklin. London: Swan, Sonnenschein, 1901.

GEORGE, HENRY. *Progress and Poverty* (1881). New York: Vanguard, 1929.

JAURÈS, JEAN, ed. *Histoire socialiste, 1789–1900.* Paris: Rouff, 1901–08. 4 vols.

KROPOTKIN, PETER. *Mutual Aid.* Rev. ed. London: Heinemann, 1904.

LLOYD, HENRY DEMAREST. *Wealth Against Commonwealth.* New York: Harper & Row, 1894.

MANUEL, FRANK E. *The New World of Henri Saint-Simon.* Cambridge, Mass.: Harvard Univ. Press, 1956.

———. *The Prophets of Paris: Turgot, Condorcet, Saint-Simon, Fourier, and Comte.* New York: Harper & Row (Torchbooks), 1965.

OWEN, ROBERT. *Book of the New Moral World.* London: Wilson, 1836.

———. *A New View of Society and Other Writings* (1813). New York: Dutton (Everyman's Library), 1927.

PROUDHON, PIERRE JOSEPH. *What Is Property?* Tr. by Benjamin R. Tucker. New York: Humboldt, 1876.

SAINT-SIMON, COMTE DE (CLAUDE DE ROUVROY). *Social Organization, The Science of Man, and Other Writings.* Ed. and tr. by Felix Markham. New York: Harper & Row (Torchbooks), 1966.

SCHAPIRO, J. SALWYN, ed. *Movements of Social Dissent in Modern Europe.* Princeton, N.J.: Van Nostrand (Anvil Books), 1962.

WILSON, EDMUND. *To the Finland Station; A Study on the Writing and Acting of History.* Garden City, N.Y.: Doubleday (Anchor Books), 1959, Part 2, chs. 1–4.

WOODCOCK, GEORGE. *Pierre-Joseph Proud'hon.* London: Routledge & Kegan Paul, 1956.

Chapter 19 BENTHAM

Works by Bentham

A Fragment on Government. Ed. by F. C. Montague. Oxford: Clarendon Press, 1891.

A Fragment on Government and Introduction to the Principles of Morals and Legislation. Ed. by Wilfred Harrison. Oxford: Blackwell & Mott, 1948.

Handbook of Political Fallacies. Ed. by Harold A. Larrabee. New York: Harper & Row (Torchbooks), 1962.

Introduction to the Principles of Morals and Legislation. Oxford: Clarendon Press, 1879. New ed., 1907.

Introduction to the Principles of Morals and Legislation. Ed. by Lawrence J. Lafleur. New York: Hafner, 1948.

Theory of Legislation. Ed. by C. K. Ogden. London: Routledge & Kegan Paul, 1950.

The Works of Jeremy Bentham. Ed. by John Bowring. Edinburgh: Tait, 1838–42. 22 vols.

Secondary Works

ALBEE, ERNEST. *A History of English Utilitarianism.* London: Swan, Sonnenschein, 1900.

BAUMGART, DAVID. *Bentham and the Ethics of Today.* Princeton, N.J.: Princeton Univ. Press, 1952.

DAVIDSON, WILLIAM L. *Political Thought in England; The Utilitarians from Bentham to J. S. Mill.* New York: Oxford Univ. Press, 1950.

EVERETT, CHARLES W. *The Education of Jeremy Bentham.* New York: Columbia Univ. Press, 1931.

HALÉVY, ELIE. *The Growth of Philosophic Radicalism.* Tr. by Mary Morris. Boston: Beacon Press, 1955. See bibliography, pp. 522–46.

KEETON, G. W., AND GEORGE SCHWARZENBERGER, eds. *Jeremy Bentham and the Law.* London: Stevens, 1948.

LEAVIS, F. R., ed. *Mill on Bentham and Coleridge.* London: Chatto & Windus, 1950.

MACK, MARY P. *Jeremy Bentham: An Odyssey of Ideas.* New York: Columbia Univ. Press, 1963.

OGDEN, C. K. *Bentham's Theory of Fictions.* New York: Harcourt, Brace & World, 1932.

PLAMENATZ, JOHN. *The English Utilitarians.* London: Oxford Univ. Press, 1949.

STEPHEN, LESLIE. *The English Utilitarians.* London: Duckworth, 1900. 3 vols. Vol. 1 is on Bentham.

Chapter 20 HEGEL

Works by Hegel

Early Theological Writings. Tr. by T. M. Knox. Chicago: Univ. of Chicago Press, 1948. Reprinted as *On Christianity.* New York: Harper & Row (Torchbooks), 1961. In the latter see Richard Kroner's introduction, pp. 1–66.

Hegel's Political Writings. Tr. by T. M. Knox. Intro. by Z. Pelczynski. London: Oxford Univ. Press, 1964.

Phenomenology of Mind. Tr. by J. B. Baillie. 2nd ed. rev. London: Allen & Unwin, 1961.

The Philosophy of Hegel. Ed. by Carl J. Friedrich. New York: Random House (Modern Library), 1954.

Philosophy of History. Tr. by J. Sibree. London: Bell, 1905; New York: Dover, 1955.

Philosophy of Right. Tr. by T. M. Knox. Oxford: Clarendon Press, 1942; Corrected eds., 1945, 1949, 1953.

Reason in History. Tr. by R. S. Hartman. New York: Liberal Arts Press, 1953. Contains introduction to *Philosophy of History.*

Sämtliche Werke. Vols. 1–27. ed. by G. Lasson. Vols. 28–30 ed. by J. Hoffmeister. Vols. 1–26, Leipzig, 1923–32; Vol. 27, Hamburg, n.d.; Vols. 28–30, Hamburg, 1952–58. All published by Meiner. A critical edition, the best of several collected works. 35 vols. projected.

Selections. Ed. by J. Loewenberg. Rev. ed. New York: Wiley, 1944.

Secondary Works

CAIRD, EDWARD. *Hegel.* Edinburgh: Blackwood, 1883.

CROCE, BENEDETTO. *What Is Living and What Is Dead in Hegel's Philosophy?* Tr. by D. Ainslie. London: Macmillan, 1915 (orig. Italian ed., 1906).

FINDLAY, JOHN N. *Hegel: A Re-examination.* New York: Macmillan (Collier Books), 1962.

FOSTER, MICHAEL B. *The Political Philosophies of Plato and Hegel.* Oxford: Clarendon Press, 1935.

KAUFMANN, WALTER. *Hegel: A Reinterpretation.* Garden City, N.Y.: Doubleday (Anchor Books), 1966.

LOEWENBERG, JACOB. *Hegel's Phenomenology: Dialogues on the Life of the Mind.* LaSalle, Ill.: Open Court, 1965.

MARCUSE, HERBERT. *Reason and Revolution; Hegel and the Rise of Social Theory.* Boston: Beacon Press, 1960.

MURE, G. R. G. *An Introduction to Hegel.* Oxford: Clarendon Press, 1940.

REYBURN, HUGH A. *The Ethical Theory of Hegel; A Study of the Philosophy of Right.* Oxford: Clarendon Press, 1921.

ROSENZWEIG, FRANZ. *Hegel und der Staat.* Munich: Oldenbourg, 1920. 2 vols.

STACE, W. T. *The Philosophy of Hegel.* New York: Dover, 1955.

TRAVIS, D. C., ed. *A Hegel Symposium.* Austin: Univ. of Texas Press, 1962.

WEIL, ERIC. *Hegel et l'état.* Paris: Vrin, 1950.

Chapter 21 MARX

Primary Works

ENGELS, FRIEDRICH. *Herr Eugen Dühring's Revolution in Science [Anti-Dühring]* (1877–78). London: Lawrence & Wishart, 1894. Three chapters of *Anti-Dühring* were published separately as *Socialism, Utopian and Scientific* in 1880 and subsequently. See Edward Aveling's tr. Chicago: Kerr, 1902.

——. *The Origin of the Family, Private Property, and the State* (1884). Tr. by Ernest Untermann. Chicago: Kerr, 1902.

Handbook of Marxism. Ed. by Emile Burns. New York: Random House, 1935.

MARX, KARL. *Capital* (1867–94). Tr. by Samuel Moore and Edward Aveling. Chicago: Kerr, 1904–09. 3 vols.

——. *The Civil War in France* (1871). Intro. by Friedrich Engels. New York: International Publishers, 1933.

——. *A Critique of the Gotha Program* (1891). Ed. by C. P. Dutt. New York: International Publishers, 1933.

——. *Critique of Political Economy* (1859). Tr. by N. I. Stone. Chicago: Kerr, 1904. From the 2nd German ed.

——. *Early Writings.* Ed. and tr. by T. B. Bottomore. New York: McGraw-Hill, 1964.

——. *The Poverty of Philosophy* (1847). Tr. by H. Quelch. Chicago: Kerr, 1920.

————, AND FRIEDRICH ENGELS. *Basic Writings on Politics and Philosophy.* Ed. by Lewis S. Feuer. Garden City, N.Y.: Doubleday (Anchor Books), 1959.

————. *The Communist Manifesto.* Tr. by Eden Paul and Cedar Paul. New York: International Publishers, 1930.

————. *The Communist Manifesto, with Selections from the Eighteenth Brumaire of Louis Napoleon.* Ed. by Samuel Beer. New York: Appleton-Century-Crofts, 1955. There are countless editions of the Manifesto.

————. *Selected Works of Marx and Engels.* Ed. by C. P. Dutt. New York: International Publishers, 1936. 2 vols.

Marx on Economics. Ed. by Robert Freedman. New York: Harcourt, Brace & World (Harvest Books), 1961.

Writings of the Young Marx on Philosophy and Society. Ed. and tr. by Loyd D. Easton and Kurt H. Guddat. Garden City, N.Y.: Doubleday (Anchor Books), 1967.

Secondary Works

BERLIN, ISAIAH. *Karl Marx; His Life and Environment.* 2nd ed. New York: Oxford Univ. Press, 1948 (Galaxy Books, 1959). See bibliography.

BÖHM VON BAWERK, E. *Karl Marx and the Close of His System.* Ed. by Paul M. Sweezy. New York: Kelley, 1949.

BOBER, M. M. *Karl Marx's Interpretation of History.* Rev. ed. Cambridge, Mass.: Harvard Univ. Press, 1948.

CARR, E. H. *Karl Marx; A Study in Fanaticism.* London: Dent, 1935.

CROCE, BENEDETTO. *Historical Materialism and the Economics of Karl Marx.* Tr. by C. M. Meredith. London: Allen & Unwin, 1922.

FROMM, ERICH. *Marx's Concept of Man.* New York: Ungar, 1961.

HOOK, SIDNEY. *From Hegel to Marx.* Ann Arbor: Univ. of Michigan Press, 1962.

HUNT, R. N. CAREW. *The Theory and Practice of Communism.* 5th ed. New York: Macmillan, 1957.

KAUTSKY, KARL. *The Economic Doctrines of Karl Marx.* London: Black, 1925.

LICHTHEIM, GEORGE. *Marxism; An Historical and Critical Study.* New York: Praeger, 1964.

LINDSAY, A. D. *Karl Marx's Capital: An Introductory Essay.* 2nd ed. London: Oxford Univ. Press, 1947 (orig. ed., 1925).

MAYO, HENRY B. *Introduction to Marxist Theory.* New York: Oxford Univ. Press, 1960. Note Mayo's excellent bibliography, pp. 310–25.

MEYER, ALFRED G. *Marxism.* Cambridge, Mass.: Harvard Univ. Press, 1954.

SCHUMPETER, JOSEPH A. *Capitalism, Socialism, Democracy.* 3rd ed. New York: Harper & Row, 1950, Part 2.

TUCKER, ROBERT M. *Philosophy and Myth in Karl Marx.* London: Cambridge Univ. Press, 1961.

WILSON, EDMUND. *To the Finland Station; A Study in the Writing and Acting of History.* New York: Harcourt, Brace & World, 1940; Garden City, N.Y.: Doubleday (Anchor Books), 1959.

WOLFE, BERTRAM D. *Marxism: One Hundred Years in the Life of a Doctrine.* New York: Dial Press, 1965.

Chapter 22 NIETZSCHE

See Herbert Reichert and Karl Schlechta, eds., *International Nietzsche Bibliography.* Chapel Hill: Univ. of North Carolina Press, 1960.

Works by Nietzsche

Beyond Good and Evil. Tr. by Helen Zimmern. New York: Boni and Liveright, 1917; tr. by Marianne Cowan. Chicago: Regnery, 1955.

The Birth of Tragedy; and The Genealogy of Morals. Tr. by Francis Golffing. Garden City, N.Y.: Doubleday (Anchor Books), 1956.

Complete Works. Tr. by Oscar Levy. New York: Macmillan, 1924. 18 vols.

The Genealogy of Morals; A Polemic. Tr. by Horace B. Samuel. New York: Macmillan, 1924.

The Joyful Wisdom. Tr. by Thomas Common. 2nd ed. London: Foulis, 1918.

The Philosophy of Nietzsche. New York: Random House (Modern Library), 1937.

The Portable Nietzsche. Ed. by W. Kaufmann. New York: Viking Press, 1954.

Thus Spake Zarathustra. Tr. by Thomas Common. New York: Macmillan, 1911; New York: Random House (Modern Library), n. d.

The Use and Abuse of History. Tr. by Adrian Collins. New York: Liberal Arts Press, 1949.

Werke. Leipzig: Naumann, 1899–1904. 15 vols.

The Will to Power. Tr. by Anthony M. Ludovici. Edinburgh: Foulis, 1910.

Secondary Works

BRINTON, CRANE. *Nietzsche.* Cambridge, Mass.: Harvard Univ. Press, 1941.

DANTO, ARTHUR C. *Nietzsche as a Philosopher.* New York: Macmillan, 1965.

JASPERS, KARL. *Nietzsche: An Introduction to the Understanding of His Philosophical Activity.* Tr. by C. F. Wallraff and F. J. Schmitz. Tucson: Univ. of Arizona Press, 1965.

KAUFMANN, WALTER A. *Nietzsche; Philosopher, Psychologist, Anti-Christ.* Princeton, N.J.: Princeton Univ. Press, 1950. See bibliography, pp. 383–95.

LEA, FRANK A. *The Tragic Philosopher; A Study of Friedrich Nietzsche.* New York: Philosophical Library, 1957.

MENCKEN, H. L. *The Philosophy of Friedrich Nietzsche.* 3rd ed. Boston: Luce, 1913.

MORE, PAUL ELMER. *Nietzsche.* Boston: Houghton Mifflin, 1912.

MORGAN, GEORGE ALLEN, JR. *What Nietzsche Means.* New York: Harper & Row, 1965.

REYBURN, HUGH A. *Nietzsche; The Story of a Human Philosopher.* London: Macmillan, 1948.

Chapter 23 THE TWENTIETH CENTURY

The multiplicity of books and the uncertainty of criteria of importance make this selection even more arbitrary than the selections for other chapters. For more extended bibliographies see Christian Bay, *The Structure of Freedom* (Stanford, Cal.: Stanford Univ. Press, 1958), pp. 391–408; Arnold Brecht, *Political Theory* (Princeton, N.J.: Princeton Univ. Press, 1959), pp. 499–574; Albert R. Chandler, ed., *The Clash of Political Ideals,* 3rd ed. (New York: Appleton-Century-Crofts, 1957), pp. 334–74; Henry S. Kariel, *In Search of Authority: Twentieth-Century Political Thought* (New York: Free Press, 1964), *passim;* William Kornhauser, *The Politics of Mass Society* (New York: Free Press, 1959), pp. 239–47; and J. Roland Pennock, *Liberal Democracy* (New York: Holt, Rinehart and Winston, 1950), pp. 373–94.

Totalitarianism

ARENDT, HANNAH. *The Origins of Totalitarianism.* New York: Harcourt, Brace & World, 1951; rev. and exp. ed., New York: World (Meridian Books), 1958.

CARSTEIN, F. L. *The Rise of Fascism.* Berkeley: Univ. of California Press, 1967.

EBENSTEIN, WILLIAM. *Totalitarianism: New Perspectives.* New York: Holt, Rinehart and Winston, 1962.

FRIEDRICH, CARL J., ed. *Totalitarianism.* Cambridge, Mass.: Harvard Univ. Press, 1954.

——, AND ZBIGNIEW BRZEZINSKI. *Totalitarian Dictatorship and Autocracy.* Cambridge, Mass.: Harvard Univ. Press, 1956.

GENTILE, GIOVANNI. *The Genesis and Structure of Society.* Tr. by H. S. Harris. Urbana: Univ. of Illinois Press, 1960.

HARRIS, H. S. *The Social Philosophy of Giovanni Gentile.* Urbana: Univ. of Illinois Press, 1960.

HITLER, ADOLF. *Mein Kampf.* Tr. by Ralph Manheim. Boston: Houghton Mifflin, 1943.

HOFFER, ERIC. *The True Believer.* New York: Harper & Row, 1951.

MILOCZ, CESLAW. *The Captive Mind.* Tr. by Jane Zielonko. New York: Knopf (Vintage Books), 1953.

MUSSOLINI, BENITO. *The Political and Social Doctrine of Fascism.* Tr. by Jane Soames. London: Hogarth, 1933.

ROCCO, ALFREDO. "The Political Doctrine of Fascism." Tr. by D. Bigongiari in *International Conciliation Bulletin No. 223.* New York: Carnegie Endowment for International Peace, 1926.

SCHNEIDER, HERBERT W. *Making the Fascist State.* New York: Oxford Univ. Press, 1928.

SOREL, GEORGES. *Reflections on Violence.* Tr. by T. E. Hulme and J. Roth. New York: Free Press, 1950.

WEBER, EUGEN J. *Varieties of Fascism.* Princeton, N.J.: Van Nostrand (Anvil Books), 1964.

Liberalism-Conservatism [For Socialism, see the bibliography for Chapter 24, "Lenin."]

AUERBACH, MORTON. *The Conservative Illusion.* New York: Columbia Univ. Press, 1959.

BAY, CHRISTIAN. *The Structure of Freedom.* New York: Atheneum, 1965.

BERLIN, ISAIAH. *Two Concepts of Liberty.* Oxford: Clarendon Press, 1958.

CRANSTON, MAURICE. *Freedom; A New Analysis.* 2nd ed. London: Longmans, Green, 1954.

FRANKEL, CHARLES. *The Democratic Prospect.* New York: Harper & Row, 1962.

FRIEDMAN, MILTON. *Capitalism and Freedom.* Chicago: Univ. of Chicago Press (Phoenix Books), 1962.

GALBRAITH, JOHN KENNETH. *The Affluent Society.* Boston: Houghton Mifflin, 1958.

——. *American Capitalism.* Rev. ed. Boston: Houghton Mifflin, 1956.

——. *The New Industrial State.* Boston: Houghton Mifflin, 1967.

——. *Studies in Philosophy, Politics and Economics.* Chicago: Univ. of Chicago Press, 1967.

KENDALL, WILLMOORE. *The Conservative Affirmation.* Chicago: Regnery, 1963.

KEYNES, JOHN MAYNARD. *The Economic Consequences of the Peace.* New York: Harcourt, Brace & World, 1920.

——. *The General Theory of Employment, Interest, and Money.* London: Macmillan, 1936; New York: Harcourt, Brace & World, 1936.

LASKI, HAROLD J. *A Grammar of Politics.* London: Allen & Unwin, 1925.

——. *Liberty in the Modern State.* New York: Harper & Row, 1930.

——. *The State in Theory and Practice.* New York: Viking Press, 1935.

LIPPMANN, WALTER. *Essays in the Public Philosophy.* New York: New American Library (Mentor Books), 1957.

——. *The Essential Lippmann.* Ed. by Clinton Rossiter and James Lare. New York: Random House (Vintage Books), 1965.

——. *An Inquiry into the Principles of the Good Society.* Boston: Little, Brown, 1937.

——. *Public Opinion.* New York: Harcourt, Brace & World, 1922; Baltimore: Penguin Books, 1946.

McGOVERN, WILLIAM M., AND DAVID S. COLLIER. *Radicals and Conservatives.* Chicago: Regnery, 1957.

MEYER, FRANK S., ed. *What Is Conservatism?* New York: Holt, Rinehart and Winston, 1964.

MINOGUE, KENNETH. *The Liberal Mind.* London: Methuen, 1963.

OAKESHOTT, MICHAEL. *Rationalism in Politics.* New York: Basic Books, 1962.

ORTEGA Y GASSET, JOSÉ. *The Revolt of the Masses.* New York: Nelson, 1932.

RUSSELL, BERTRAND. *Authority and the Individual.* New York: Simon and Schuster, 1945.

VON HAYEK, FRIEDRICH A. *The Constitution of Liberty.* Chicago: Univ. of Chicago Press, 1960.

Freudianism

BIRNBACH, MARTIN. *Neo-Freudian Social Philosophy.* Stanford, Cal.: Stanford Univ. Press, 1961.

BROWN, NORMAN. *Life Against Death; The Psychoanalytic Meaning of History.* New York: Random House (Vintage Books), 1961.

FREUD, SIGMUND. *Civilization and Its Discontents* (1930). Tr. by Joan Rivière. London: Hogarth, 1939, 1951.

——. *Civilization, War, and Death.* Ed. by John Rickman. London: Hogarth, 1939. Consists of three essays written in 1915, 1929, 1933.

——. *The Future of an Illusion.* Tr. by W. D. Robson-Scott. London: Hogarth, 1928; Garden City, N.Y.: Doubleday (Anchor Books), 1957.

FROMM, ERICH. *Escape from Freedom.* New York: Holt, Rinehart and Winston, 1941.

——. *The Sane Society.* New York: Holt, Rinehart and Winston, 1955.

HORNEY, KAREN. *The Neurotic Personality of Our Time.* New York: Norton, 1937.

JOHNSON, THOMAS. *Freud and Political Thought.* New York: Citadel Press, 1965.

JUNG, CARL G. *Modern Man in Search of a Soul.* London: Kegan Paul, Trench, Trübner, 1933.

MARCUSE, HERBERT. *Eros and Civilization.* New York: Random House (Vintage Books), 1962.

NELSON, BENJAMIN, ed. *Freud and the Twentieth Century.* New York: World (Meridian Books), 1957.

PROGOFF, IRA. *Jung's Psychology and Its Social Meaning.* New York: Grove Press, 1957.

RIEFF, PHILIP. *Freud: The Mind of the Moralist.* Garden City, N.Y.: Doubleday (Anchor Books), 1961.

SCHAAR, JOHN H. *Escape from Authority; The Perspectives of Erich Fromm.* New York: Basic Books, 1961.

Existentialism

ARENDT, HANNAH. *Between Past and Future; Six Exercises in Political Thought.* New York: Viking Press, 1961.

——. *The Human Condition.* Chicago: Univ. of Chicago Press, 1958.

——. *On Revolution.* New York: Viking Press, 1963.

BARRETT, WILLIAM. *Irrational Man.* Garden City, N.Y.: Doubleday (Anchor Books), 1962.

CAMUS, ALBERT. *The Myth of Sisyphus and Other Essays.* Tr. by Justin O'Brien. New York: Knopf, 1955.

——. *The Rebel.* Tr. by Anthony Bower. London: Hamilton, 1953; New York: Random House (Vintage Books), 1959.

——. *Resistance, Rebellion, and Death.* Tr. by Justin O'Brien. New York: Knopf, 1961.

CRANSTON, MAURICE. *Jean-Paul Sartre.* New York: Grove Press, 1962.

CRUICKSHANK, JOHN. *Albert Camus and the Literature of Revolt.* New York: Oxford Univ. Press (Galaxy Books), 1960.

DESAN, WILFRED. *The Marxism of Jean-Paul Sartre.* Garden City, N.Y.: Doubleday, 1965.

DOUGLAS, KENNETH. *A Critical Bibliography of Existentialism (The Paris School).* Yale French Studies, Special Monograph No. 1, 1950.

GREENE, NORMAN N. *Jean-Paul Sartre, The Existentialist Ethic.* Ann Arbor: Univ. of Michigan Press, 1960.

GRENE, MARJORIE. *Introduction to Existentialism.* Chicago: Univ. of Chicago Press (Phoenix Books), 1959.

HEINEMANN, FREDERICK. *Existentialism and the Modern Predicament.* 2nd ed. New York: Harper & Row (Torchbooks), 1958.

JASPERS, KARL. *The Future of Mankind.* Tr. by E. B. Ashton. Chicago: Univ. of Chicago Press, 1961.

————. *Man in the Modern Age.* Tr. by Eden Paul and Cedar Paul. Garden City, N.Y.: Doubleday (Anchor Books), 1957 (orig. German ed., 1931).

SARTRE, JEAN-PAUL. *Théorie des ensembles pratiques.* Vol. 1, *Critique de la raison dialectique.* Paris: Gallimard, 1960.

————. *Existentialism and Humanism.* Tr. by Philip Mairet. London: Methuen, 1948.

————. *Literary and Philosophical Essays.* Tr. by Annette Michelson. New York: Criterion Books, 1955.

————. *Search for a Method.* Tr. by Hazel Barnes. New York: Knopf, 1963.

WILLHOITE, FRED H., JR. *Beyond Nihilism: Albert Camus's Contribution to Political Thought.* Baton Rouge: Louisiana State Univ. Press. To be published in 1968.

Chapter 24 LENIN

Useful bibliographies may be found in Henry B. Mayo, *Introduction to Marxist Theory* (New York: Oxford Univ. Press, 1960), pp. 310–25; and Harry Overstreet and Bonaro Overstreet, *What We Must Know about Communism* (New York: Norton, 1958), pp. 314–24. See also works listed below by Daniels, Haimson, Hammond, and Meyer.

Works by Lenin

Collected Works. New York: International Publishers, 1927–42. Vols. 4, 13, 18–20, 21 only are translated (badly) into English.

Essentials of Lenin. London: Lawrence & Wishart, 1947. 2 vols.

Marx-Engels-Marxism. 3rd Eng. ed. Moscow: Foreign Language Publishing House, 1947. Includes excerpts from "State and Revolution," "What Is to Be Done?" and most of the major tracts.

Selected Works. New York: International Publishers, 1935–43. 12 vols.

Selected Works. Moscow: Foreign Language Publishing House, 1946. 2 vols.

Sochineniya (Works). 5th ed. Moscow: Marx-Engels-Lenin Institute, 1958–65. 55 vols. Many of the various Lenin tracts have been published separately in English by International Publishers, New York.

The Suppressed Testament of Lenin; The Complete Original Text with Two Explanatory Articles by L. Trotsky. New York: Pioneer, 1935. Lenin's famous criticism of Stalin, not published in the Soviet Union until 1956.

Secondary Works

APTHEKER, HERBERT, ed. *Marxism and Alienation: A Symposium.* New York: Humanities Press, 1965.

BARON, SAMUEL H. *Plekhanov, The Father of Russian Marxism.* Stanford, Cal.: Stanford Univ. Press, 1963.

BUKHARIN, NIKOLAI I. *Historical Materialism.* New York: International Publishers, 1925. Author's tr. from 3rd Russian ed.

CARR, EDWARD H. *The Bolshevik Revolution, 1917–1923.* New York: Macmillan, 1954. 3 vols.

CHEN, YUNG PING. *Chinese Political Thought: Mao Tse-tung and Liu Shao-chi.* The Hague: Nijhoff, 1966.

DANIELS, ROBERT V. *The Conscience of the Revolution; Communist Opposition in Soviet Russia.* Cambridge, Mass.: Harvard Univ. Press, 1960.

FISCHER, LOUIS. *The Life of Lenin.* New York: Harper & Row, 1964.

HAIMSON, LEOPOLD H. *The Russian Marxists and the Origins of Bolshevism.* Cambridge, Mass.: Harvard Univ. Press, 1955. See bibliography, pp. 235–40.

HAMMOND, THOMAS TAYLOR. *Lenin on Trade Unions and Revolution, 1893–1917.* New York: Columbia Univ. Press, 1957. See bibliography, pp. 130–50.

HILLQUIT, MORRIS. *From Marx to Lenin.* New York: Hanford, 1921.

History of the Communist Party of the Soviet Union (Bolsheviks): Short Course. New York: International Publishers, 1939. The so-called Stalin history.

KAUTSKY, KARL. *The Economic Doctrines of Karl Marx.* Tr. by H. J. Stenning. London: Black, 1925.

——. *Terrorism and Communism; A Contribution to the Natural History of Revolution.* Tr. by W. H. Kerridge. London: Allen & Unwin, 1920.

MAO TSE-TUNG. *Mao Tse-tung: An Anthology of His Writings.* Ed. by Anne Freemantle. New York: New American Library (Mentor Books), 1962.

MEYER, ALFRED G. *Leninism.* Cambridge, Mass.: Harvard Univ. Press, 1957. See bibliography, pp. 295–98.

PLAMENATZ, JOHN. *German Marxism and Russian Communism.* New York: Harper & Row (Torchbooks), 1965.

PLEKHANOV, GEORGI. *The Development of the Monist View of History* (1895). Tr. by Andrew Rothstein. Moscow: Foreign Language Publishing House, 1956.

POSSONY, STEFAN T. *Lenin: The Compulsory Revolutionary.* Chicago: Regnery, 1963.

SCHRAM, STUART A. *The Political Thought of Mao Tse-tung.* New York: Praeger, 1963.

STALIN, JOSEPH. *Problems of Leninism.* 11th ed. Moscow: Foreign Language Publishing House, 1941. Moscow-published works by Stalin tend to be unreliable.

TREADGOLD, D. W. *Lenin and His Rivals.* New York: Praeger, 1955.

TROTSKY, LEON. *Lenin.* Author's trans. New York: Minton, Balch, 1925.

——. *My Life; An Attempt at an Autobiography.* New York: Scribner's, 1931.

——. *The Permanent Revolution.* Tr. by Max Schachtman. New York: Pioneer, 1931.

ULAM, ADAM B. *The Unfinished Revolution.* New York: Random House, 1960.

WILSON, EDMUND. *To the Finland Station; A Study in the Writing and Acting of History.* Garden City, N.Y.: Doubleday (Anchor Books), 1959.

WOLFE, BERTRAM D. *Three Who Made a Revolution.* Boston: Beacon Press, 1956.

Chapter 25 DEWEY

Works by Dewey

Democracy and Education. New York: Macmillan, 1916.

Ethics, with James H. Tufts. Rev. ed. New York: Holt, Rinehart and Winston, 1932.

Experience and Nature. LaSalle, Ill.: Open Court, 1925.

Freedom and Culture. New York: Putnam's, 1939.

German Philosophy and Politics. New York: Holt, Rinehart and Winston, 1915; Boston: Beacon Press, 1945.

Human Nature and Conduct. New York: Holt, Rinehart and Winston, 1922; New York: Random House (Modern Library), 1930.

The Influence of Darwin on Philosophy. New York: Holt, Rinehart and Winston, 1910.

Intelligence in the Modern World. Ed. by Joseph Ratner. New York: Random House (Modern Library), 1939.

John Dewey and Arthur F. Bentley: A Philosophical Correspondence, 1932–1951. Ed. by Sidney Ratner and Jules Altman. New Brunswick, N.J.: Rutgers Univ. Press, 1964.

Liberalism and Social Action. New York: Putnam's, 1935.

The Public and Its Problems. New York: Holt, Rinehart and Winston, 1927; Chicago: Regnery (Gateway Editions), 1946; Denver, Colo.: Swallow, 1957.

The Quest for Certainty. New York: Minton, Balch, 1930.

Reconstruction in Philosophy. New York: Holt, Rinehart and Winston, 1920; enl. ed. Boston: Beacon Press, 1949.

School and Society. Rev. ed. Chicago: Univ. of Chicago Press, 1915.

Secondary Works

EDMAN, IRWIN. *John Dewey; His Contribution to the American Tradition.* Indianapolis, Ind.: Bobbs-Merrill, 1955.

Essays in Honor of John Dewey on the Occasion of His Seventieth Birthday. New York: Holt, Rinehart and Winston, 1929.

FELDMAN, W. T. *The Philosophy of John Dewey.* Baltimore: Johns Hopkins Press, 1934.

GEIGER, GEORGE R. *John Dewey in Perspective.* London: Oxford Univ. Press, 1958.

HOOK, SIDNEY. *John Dewey; An Intellectual Portrait.* New York: Day, 1939.

——, ed. *John Dewey; Philosopher of Science and Freedom.* New York: Dial Press, 1950.

JOHNSON, A. H., ed. *The Wit and Wisdom of John Dewey.* Boston: Beacon Press, 1949.

LAMONT, CORLISS, ed. *Dialogue on Dewey.* New York: Horizon Press, 1959.

LEANDER, FOLKE. *The Philosophy of John Dewey.* Göteborg, Sweden: Elanders, 1939.

MOORE, EDWARD C. *American Pragmatism; Peirce, James, and Dewey.* New York: Columbia Univ. Press, 1961.

RATNER, SIDNEY, ed. *The Philosopher of the Common Man.* New York: Putnam's, 1940.

SCHILPP, PAUL, ed. *The Philosophy of John Dewey.* Evanston, Ill.: Northwestern Univ. Press, 1939.

"Symposium on John Dewey," *Journal of the History of Ideas,* Vol. 20 (1959), pp. 515–76.

WHITE, MORTON G. *The Origin of Dewey's Instrumentalism.* New York: Columbia Univ. Press, 1943.

Chapter 26 NIEBUHR

For a complete bibliography of the writings of Reinhold Niebuhr see Harry R. Davis and Robert C. Good, eds., *Reinhold Niebuhr on Politics* (New York: Scribner's, 1960), p. 359. For a listing of Niebuhr's writings to 1956 see Kegley and Bretall, *Reinhold Niebuhr* (listed below), pp. 455–78. Issues of *Christianity and Crisis* from the early 1940's on provide a record of Niebuhr's political commentary.

Works by Niebuhr

The Children of Light and the Children of Darkness. New York: Scribner's, 1944.

Christian Realism and Political Problems. New York: Scribner's, 1953.

Christianity and Power Politics. New York: Scribner's, 1940.

Faith and History. New York: Scribner's, 1949.

An Interpretation of Christian Ethics. New York: Harper & Row, 1935.

The Irony of American History. New York: Scribner's, 1952.

Man's Nature and His Communities. New York: Scribner's, 1965.

Moral Man and Immoral Society. New York: Scribner's, 1932.

The Nature and Destiny of Man. New York: Scribner's, 1941. 2 vols.

Pious and Secular America. New York: Scribner's, 1958.

Reflections on the End of an Era. New York: Scribner's, 1934.

Secondary Works

BENNETT, JOHN C. *Christians and the State.* New York: Scribner's, 1958.

BINGHAM, JUNE. *The Courage to Change; An Introduction to the Life and Thought of Reinhold Niebuhr.* New York: Scribner's, 1961.

CARTER, PAUL A. *The Decline and Revival of the Social Gospel; Social and Political Liberalism in American Protestant Churches, 1920–1940.*

Ithaca, N.Y.: Cornell Univ. Press, 1954. See bibliography, pp. 251–60.

GILL, THEODORE. *Recent Protestant Political Theory.* London: Hunt, Barnard, 1953.

HARLAND, GORDON. *The Thought of Reinhold Niebuhr.* New York: Oxford Univ. Press, 1960.

HOFMAN, HANS. *The Theology of Reinhold Niebuhr.* New York: Scribner's, 1956.

HUTCHISON, JOHN A., ed. *Christian Faith and Social Action.* New York: Scribner's, 1953.

KEGLEY, CHARLES W., AND ROBERT W. BRETALL, eds. *Reinhold Niebuhr; His Religious, Social, and Political Thought.* New York: Macmillan, 1956.

MARITAIN, JACQUES. *Man and the State.* Chicago: Univ. of Chicago Press, 1951.

MEYER, DONALD. *The Protestant Search for Political Realism, 1919–1941.* Berkeley: Univ. of California Press, 1960.

ODEGARD, HOLTAN P. *Sin and Science; Reinhold Niebuhr as Political Theologian.* Yellow Springs, Ohio: Antioch Press, 1956. See bibliography, pp. 221–34.

SCHNEIDER, HERBERT W. *Religion in Twentieth-Century America.* Cambridge, Mass.: Harvard Univ. Press, 1952.

TILLICH, PAUL. *Love, Power, and Justice.* New York: Oxford Univ. Press, 1954.

WHITE, MORTON G. *Social Thought in America; The Revolt Against Formalism.* Rev. ed. Boston: Beacon Press, 1958. Epilogue contains a critique of Niebuhr.

Chapter 27 POLITICAL THEORY AND THE SCIENCE OF POLITICS

CHARLESWORTH, JAMES C. *Contemporary Political Analysis.* New York: Free Press, 1967.

COWLING, MAURICE. *The Nature and Limits of Political Science.* New York: Cambridge Univ. Press, 1963.

EASTON, DAVID, ed. *Varieties of Political Theory.* Englewood Cliffs, N.J.: Prentice-Hall, 1966.

FRIEDRICH, CARL J. *Man and His Government; An Empirical Theory of Politics.* New York: McGraw-Hill, 1963.

FROHOCK, FRED M. *The Nature of Political Inquiry.* Homewood, Ill.: Dorsey, 1967.

RUNCIMAN, W. G. *Social Science and Political Theory.* London: Cambridge Univ. Press, 1963.

INDEX

Works discussed in depth are indexed under their titles. All other works are indexed under authors and are grouped alphabetically at the end of the author entries. Pages on which the chief discussion of a topic appears are printed in bold type.